MW01241477

KNIGHTS OF HUMAN RIGHTS, LADIES OF LASTING DEMOCRACY

Handbook Manifesto of the Educated
Global Solidarity Movement
Against Uneducated Global 'Creeping Totalitarianism' Now
Accelerating

WILLIAM BAPTISTE

Human Rights and Freedoms Forever!

THE INTELLECTUAL HONESTY CHALLENGE

HUMAN RIGHTS EDUCATION FOR LASTING FREE DEMOCRACY

Visit William Baptiste's websites at
WilliamBaptisteHumanRightsAndFreedomsForever.com
WilliamBaptiste.com

This handbook for the new *Global Solidarity Movement* (which flies the Flag of Democracy in Chapter 2) draws from the author's much longer books in the HUMAN RIGHTS EDUCATION FOR LASTING FREE DEMOCRACY Series, *DEMOCRACY 101* and *PRO-LIFE EQUALS PRO-DEMOCRACY*, and from the author's upcoming books *KILLING HUMANS IS WRONG* and *THINKING REVOLUTION: THE INTELLECTUAL HONESTY CHALLENGE.* The longer books are recommended reading for the reader to gain a more in-depth *HUMAN RIGHTS EDUCATION FOR LASTING FREE DEMOCRACY* to pass on to their children and grandchildren for a *free, safe future.*

Those readers who wish to become Knights of Human Rights and Ladies of Lasting Democracy, or Volunteer Democracy Leaders, are encouraged to host Lasting Democracy Study Nights in your town/city/area/online, thoughtfully reading and discussing together and then **spreading this Human Rights Education until there are enough educated voters to end the threat of uneducated politicians.**

Support Human Rights and Democratic Freedoms for All Humans that Last for Centuries on their Firm Foundations!
Donations for Democracy can be made on the above website or email
donate@WilliamBaptisteHumanRightsAndFreedomsForever.com
Copyright © 2021 William Baptiste.

WILLIAM BAPTISTE
Human Rights and Freedoms Forever!
THE INTELLECTUAL HONESTY CHALLENGE

Knights of Human Rights, Ladies of Lasting Democracy
Unedited 1st Emergency Edition/Advance Reader Copy, First Printing
Printed in the United States of America
ISBN: 9798704438809

DEDICATION

To my soon-coming first grandchild

I wrote this book so you, and everyone else's grandchildren, have the best chance of growing up with uncompromised democratic freedoms in countries which recognize Equal Human Rights for All Humans without any bigoted exceptions

"Politics sets the parameters of how you live your life; what choices you have or do not have; how free or not free you are in your country. So, it is silly to not be involved in politics. Every citizen where democracy still exists should at least be minimally engaged in politics by making *educated* votes that ensure their country at least maintains the foundations of Human Rights and freedoms, and so does not eventually become a totalitarian State due to voter ignorance of and a lack of voter vigilance for *The Foundational Principles of Human Rights and Democracy* . . .

. . . *DEMOCRACY 101* (like *Human Rights and Freedoms Forever!* which published it) is utterly non-partisan, and does not care which party governs as long as democracy's foundations are intact, and so is not inclined to vilify any particular party of "Left" or "Right" in any country but simply calls ALL political parties worldwide (and bureaucrats, judges and journalists and "Big Tech" billionaires and personnel who now wield such massive influence) **to get back to their democracy's historical and logical *foundations* if they have forgotten them and strayed** . . .

. . . Remember that in democratic governments "of the people, by the people, for the people," citizens *govern themselves, through their elected representatives.* This means the responsibility of governing well ultimately rests with each citizen voter. And they cannot possibly govern themselves well and democratically, through intelligently elected representatives who govern well and avoid totalitarianism, if neither the citizen voters nor their elected representatives even know *The Foundational Principles of Human Rights and Democracy,* nor are even held constitutionally accountable to uphold them . . .

—WILLIAM BAPTISTE, *DEMOCRACY 101*

SHORT CONTENTS

TABLE OF CONTENTS OVERVIEW   ix

INTRODUCTION: HUMAN RIGHTS AND FREEDOMS ARE INHERENT, EQUAL, INALIENABLE AND NON-PARTISAN   1

CHAPTER 1: FACTS   65

CHAPTER 2: PRINCIPLES   109

CHAPTER 3: PHILOSOPHY   145

CHAPTER 4: STRATEGY   201

CHAPTER 5: FOUNDATIONS   213

CHAPTER 6: HUMAN RESPONSIBILITIES COME WITH YOUR HUMAN RIGHTS   227

CHAPTER 7: THE THINKING REVOLUTION AND THE INTELLECTUAL HONESTY CHALLENGE   237

ABOUT THE AUTHOR OF THIS HUMAN RIGHTS EDUCATION FOR LASTING FREE DEMOCRACY   247

YOU CAN HELP FREE DEMOCRACY LAST FOREVER!   257

TABLE OF CONTENTS OVERVIEW

INTRODUCTION: HUMAN RIGHTS AND FREEDOMS ARE INHERENT, EQUAL, INALIENABLE AND NON-PARTISAN   **1**
The Warning of a Non-Partisan Human Rights Scholar Whose Ethnic Group Was Victim of One of History's Biggest Bigoted Genocides:

Today's Good Citizens Must Determine to Be Like the Good Poles (Who Helped Overturn Brutal Soviet Extremist Left-Wing Totalitarianism by *Standing Up Together in Solidarity* for Traditional Western Values as the Necessary Guide of Public Policy) and Not Like the Good Germans (Who Lost their Democracy to Nazi Extremist Right-Wing Totalitarianism by Letting Themselves Be *Intimidated into Silence* and Separation by Those Who Did Not Hold the Traditional Western Values Which Include and Support *The Foundational Principles of Human Rights and Democracy*).

The Traditional Western Values Including and Supporting *The Foundational Principles of Human Rights and Democracy* (Such as *Equal Human Preciousness* and *Free Speech*) Which the *Global Solidarity Movement* Stands together in *Solidarity* for as the Continued Guide of Public Policy, so that Free Democracy Can Last for Centuries on its Historical and Logical *Foundations,* are *Non-Partisan*, and Were Magnificently Expressed in the 1948 *Universal Declaration of Human Rights.* Healthy Democracies have a "Progressive Left" and "Conservative Right" in Fruitful Balance, Both Committed to Democratic Foundations and Neither Exhibiting Signs of Political Extremism, "Left" or "Right."

CHAPTER 1: FACTS   **65**
Science, Logic, and the TOP 6 FACTS of Human Rights History that Prove Pro-Life Equals Pro-Democracy and Pro-Choice Equals Pro-Totalitarianism

Legally Recognized and Protected Human Rights Began with the 4th Century Criminalization of Abortion because Human Life was Then First Recognized as *Precious Not Cheap*; Human-Killing by Abortion was First Legalized by the Genocidal Extremist Left-Wing Totalitarian Soviet Marxists in 1920; and Next by the Genocidal Extremist Right-Wing Totalitarian Nazi Fascists in 1934

CHAPTER 2: PRINCIPLES   **109**
The Foundational Principles of Human Rights and Democracy;
The Core Principles of Lasting Democracy;
The Pledge of Allegiance to Democracy;
The Necessity to Constitutionally Enshrine *Equal Human Rights for All Humans* to Ensure Lasting Democracy.

Announcing the Flag of Democracy and the *Global Solidarity Movement* for Traditional Western Values in Public Policy to Ensure Human Rights and Freedoms Last Forever on their Firm Traditional, Historical, Logical Foundations (Including Philosophical *Realism* Which Grounds Science Instead of *Relativism* Which Grounds *Politically Extremist Legal Human-Killing* Marxism, Nazism, and All Current Threats to Free Society – Notably Legal Human-Killing by Abortion Which Was First Legalized by Genocidal Relativist Marxists and Nazis).

CHAPTER 3: PHILOSOPHY   **145**
Lasting Human Rights and Democratic Freedoms (and Science Itself) Can Only Be Built Upon a Consistent Underlying Philosophical Worldview of Philosophical

Realism; All Current Threats to Human Rights and Free Democracy (and to Science Itself) Come from Undue Influence of Philosophical *Relativism*.

Understanding the History of Ideas (Philosophy) Helps One to Understand that Today's Destabilizing Political Polarization Over Several Issues Including the Abortion Debate (The Human Rights for All Humans Debate) is Rooted in a Bifurcation in Western Thought Going Back to the 17th Century – a Bifurcation Fundamentally Separating Radically *Skeptical, Relativistic* (Including Nazi, Marxist-Communist-Socialist, *Extremist*) Thinkers from *Realist, Scientific* and Logical Thinkers.

Meaning Everyone Should Self-Reflect and (Consciously) Identify Their (Usually Unconscious) Underlying Philosophical Worldview (at Base Predominantly either *Skeptical and Relativistic* or *Realist and Scientific*) So They Can Make an Intelligent Decision Whether or Not They Want to Keep It in the Light of the Key Facts of Science, Logic, Human Rights History (and the History of Ideas). CITIZENS AND POLITICIANS HAVING A THOUGHTFUL, CONSCIOUS WORLDVIEW IS PART OF THE THINKING REVOLUTION NECESSARY TO ENSURE LASTING FREE DEMOCRACY Based on *Education*, Rather Than Citizens and Politicians (and Judges and Journalists and "Big Tech" Billionaires and Personnel) with Thoughtless *Ideology* Tearing Down Democracy's Realistic, Scientific, and Pro-Life Foundations in Ignorance.

(Ideologues Witlessly Destroying Democracy with Their Uneducated Pro-Choice Legal-Human-Killing Ideology Witlessly Following 1920 Marxist Soviet Legal Abortion Precedent;

and/or with their Neo-Marxist Identity Politics with its "Cancel Culture" Censoring ("Cancelling") Those Who Disagree with Them, *even Hard Scientists and Medical Experts* Who Naturally Disagree with the Unscientific Absurdities of *Relativists Not Realists*;

and/or with their Radically Skeptical Postmodernist Ideology that Denies Objective Facts and Science, Developed by Marxists to Protect Marxism from Facts).

Otherwise Put: Current Society and Politics are Divided by Two Incompatible Underlying Philosophical Worldviews: (Scientific) Realism Versus (Skeptical) Relativism.

REALISM GAVE THE WORLD: Science, Logic, Technology, and the ("Pro-Life") *Foundational Principles of Human Rights and Democracy*.

(SKEPTICAL) RELATIVISM GAVE THE WORLD: Solipsism Which Denies One Can Certainly Know Anything Outside One's Own Mind Even Exists;

Nihilism and Absurdism Claiming Human Life is Meaningless;

Relativism Denying Objective Facts Exist and Moral Relativism Denying Any Moral Absolutes Like *Killing Humans Is Wrong*;

Marxism (Communism-Socialism) Which Has Killed Over 94 Million Born Humans So Far, as Well as Marxists Being the First to Legalize ("Pro-Choice") Human-Killing Abortion Which Legally Eradicates *the Inherent Human Right to Live*;

Radically Skeptical Postmodernism Denying All Objective Facts (Developed by Marxists to Protect Marxism from the Overwhelming Facts that *Relativistic* Marxism Does Not Work in the *Real* World, as Attested by Over 94 Million Born Humans Plus Preborn Humans Killed in Numerous Attempts to Implement the Seductive but *Unrealistic* Marxist Egalitarian Utopia);

Neo-Marxist "Identity Politics" (and its "Cancel Culture" Censorship of Those Who Disagree with Them); "Identity Politics" Which Encourages Hatred Between Groups Given Marxist Labels of "Oppressed" and "Privileged" to Create the Political Instability Needed for a Marxist Takeover – Hence Self-Described Marxists are Leading the Current (Starting 2020) Riots and Car-Burnings in the U.S. –

– and Hence Pro-Choice Neo-Marxist Identity Politics Ideologues Worldwide are Enthusiastically Using the Coronavirus Pandemic as an Excuse to Attempt a Global "Great Reset" on Marxist Principles. Being *Relativists* who Deny or Doubt There Even are Any Objective Facts, Their *Subjective Opinions* are Unaffected by the *Objective Facts* Proving Marxism in Practice *Consistently* Devolves into Oppressive Totalitarian Governments Killing Millions, the First Ten Million Killed by Marxism Being of the Author's Ethnic Group. Hence the Author's Warning That What the World Needs Instead of a Marxist "Great Reset" is a "Democratic Reboot" that Explicitly "Reloads *The Foundational Principles of Human Rights and Democracy* Identified in This Book from the Academic Disciplines of History, Science, and Logic (and Reloads the Philosophical *Realism,* Opposed to *Relativism,* Which Grounds Science, Logic, and Technology).

CHAPTER 4: STRATEGY   201
The WINNING STRATEGY for the 'Culture of Life' (and Philosophical Realism) to WIN the 'Cultural War' with 'The Culture of Death' (and Philosophical Relativism) to Save Humanity Forever from Bigotry and 'Creeping Totalitarianism' Now Accelerating

CHAPTER 5: FOUNDATIONS   213
Honestly Acknowledging the Foundations of Western Civilization's Freedom: The Common Creed of Christianity Includes and Supports *The Foundational Principles of Human Rights and Democracy* (Principles Which Since the 4th Century Became Embedded into Traditional Western Values - The Neglect of Which Leads Naturally to Today's Accelerating Loss of Freedom to Totalitarianism)

CHAPTER 6: HUMAN RESPONSIBILITIES COME WITH YOUR HUMAN RIGHTS
     227
A Non-Partisan Appeal to All Voters and to All with Even More Influence (Especially Billionaires, Media Moguls, Journalists and "Big Tech" Who Control News and Information; Especially Politicians, Political Parties, Civil Servants, Judges, Police and Military Who Control or Enforce Laws and Public Policy):
STOP Neglecting or Avoiding Your Human Responsibilities to Recognize and Protect Human Rights in All Other Humans, and START Standing Up Together in *Solidarity* for *Equal Human Rights for All Humans Without Exception*; and
START Standing Against Uneducated 'Creeping Totalitarianism,' *So That Everyone in the World has a Free Future* (including this author's first grandchild soon to be born).
Get and Spread a Solid HUMAN RIGHTS EDUCATION FOR LASTING FREE DEMOCRACY.
STOP Being (or Being Pawns of) Ideologues *Without a Clue* What are *The Foundational Principles of Human Rights and Democracy*, Because They Lack the *Human Rights Education* Culled from the Disciplines of History, Philosophy, Science and Logic in this Book Series.
START Spreading this HUMAN RIGHTS EDUCATION FOR LASTING FREE DEMOCRACY Until Each Country has More *Educated* Voters (and More *Educated* Politicians, Judges, Billionaires, Journalists etc.) than *Uneducated* Voters (and *Uneducated* "Big Tech" Media Moguls, Police, Civil Servants and Political Parties, etc.) Tearing Down Worldwide Human Freedom and Trampling Human Rights *in Their Ignorance.*

Those Who Refuse this Non-Partisan Appeal to Good Sense and to *Education over Ideology* Must Take the Below INTELLECTUAL HONESTY CHALLENGE or Else They Just Prove Their Lack of Intelligence or Their Lack of Honesty (for All to See).

CHAPTER 7: THE THINKING REVOLUTION AND THE INTELLECTUAL HONESTY CHALLENGE   237

"Abortion is the touchstone issue for determining the health and longevity of any democracy, because wherever human-killing abortion is legal, there is no legally recognized Inherent, Equal, Inalienable Human Right to Live, and therefore no basis for lasting Free Democracy."
– William Baptiste (né Boyko, One of Most Common Ukrainian Surnames), Representative of (only) the First Ten Million Murdered Victims of Marxism in the Holodomor Genocide in Marxist Soviet Ukraine, Committed by the Very First Marxist, Socialist State, which was the Very First Modern State to Legalize Human-Killing Abortion

---

The Intellectual Honesty Challenge in Brief: Everyone is uneducated in something before they have opportunity to be educated. It is no shame to admit that one simply did not previously have the necessary Human Rights Education to choose an intelligent and intellectually honest position on the Human Rights for All Humans Debate (the Abortion Debate). No Pro-Choice Legal Abortion supporter (politician or voter or journalist or Big Tech Media outlet) ever chose that position *after* knowing the established facts of History, Science and Logic and Philosophy collected in the author's *Pro-Life Equals Pro-Democracy* and summarized in this *handbook Manifesto*, which means every Pro-Choice Abortion supporter holds a position based on *ignorance* and *lack of knowledge*, which lack of *Human Rights Education* will be corrected by this book. This powerful collection of facts demands a thoughtful and intellectually honest response. *The Intellectual Honesty Challenge* posits that there is no such intelligent response which allows for legal abortion to continue. Anyone currently "Pro-Choice" who disagrees is hereby *challenged* to mount an intelligent and intellectually honest response to this book's conclusions based on facts to see if they can intelligently and honestly "justify" remaining Pro-Choice in light of all the facts, or else concede to this book's conclusions and change their position, as intellectual honesty demands, if they cannot.

This means that:

any politician or political party or police or civil servant or judge or court (which control or enforce public policies and laws), and any billionaires, media moguls, journalists and "Big Tech" employees (which control news and information) –

any of these (or any regular voters) that claim today's democracies can somehow sustain Free Democracy and Human Rights long-term while remaining Pro-Choice(-to-Kill-Humans), in violation of The Foundational Principles of Human Rights and Democracy and the Core Principles of Lasting Democracy identified from Human Rights History, Science, Logic, and the History of Philosophy in this book (and already declared in essence in the United Nations' 1948 Universal Declaration of Human Rights) –

any of these are proven incompetent/unintelligent or dishonest/evil by the powerful collection of undisputed facts in this author's HUMAN RIGHTS EDUCATION FOR LASTING FREE DEMOCRACY book series including this handbook. If they disagree with this statement, they are hereby *challenged* to mount an intelligent and intellectually honest response to this book's conclusions based on facts to see if they can intelligently and honestly explain *just how* they think they know a better way to sustain Human Rights and democratic freedoms long-term than by implementing and maintaining *The Foundational Principles of Human Rights and Democracy* and the *Core Principles of Lasting Democracy* clarified in this book – or else concede to this book's conclusions and change their position from "Pro-Choice" to "Pro-Life," as intellectual honesty demands, if they cannot. For politicians (or judges or "Big Tech" billionaires and media moguls) to remain Pro-Choice and not take *The Intellectual Honesty Challenge* is to fail it; is tantamount to admitting that one has no intelligent nor intellectually honest justification for remaining Pro-Choice; and therefore, tantamount to admitting one is a danger to Human Rights and freedoms everywhere because of uneducated bigotry that does not recognize democracy-grounding *Equal Human Rights for All Humans.*

Note that major political parties being "officially" Pro-Choice and/or "purging" their parties of Pro-Lifers is a very recent trend, and a very totalitarian trend, following the totalitarian example of the politically Extremist Left Soviet (Marxist) Communist Party and the politically Extremist Right German (Fascist) Nazi Party which were the first two political parties to legalize human-killing by abortion (the Nazi Party being first to also legalize human-killing by euthanasia). So, it should not be too hard for now-Pro-Choice politicians and political parties to abandon this fairly recent trend of being "officially" Pro-Choice and/or "purging" their parties of Pro-Lifers, *for the sake of lasting rights and freedom for every human.* **This book provides a brief window of opportunity for currently Pro-Choice politicians and parties (and the "Big Tech" billionaires and media moguls who control the news/information politicians set policy by) to "save face"** by simply admitting they previously did not have the necessary Human Rights Education to choose an intelligent and intellectually honest position on the Human Rights for All Humans Debate (the Abortion Debate). This book provides a brief window of opportunity for influential leaders of government, tech, media and industry to simply admit they previously did not have the necessary Human Rights Education (including not having the necessary familiarity with the most pertinent facts of History, Philosophy, Science, and Logic) which they needed in order to know that they should avoid Relativism/ Marxism/ Socialism (which first legalized human-killing by abortion – and then by genocide). They have a brief window of opportunity only to admit that they certainly should not support any current ideas about a "Great Reset" of the globe according to the Relativist, Marxist, Socialist thinking which is in fact behind many of History's greatest atrocities (and remember that Relativism is likewise behind all the Nazi Fascist atrocities on the other extreme of the political spectrum from Marxism/Socialism).

All who consider themselves "Pro-Choice" must realize that from now on, the numbers of Human-Rights-educated citizen voters (and clients of "Big Tech") will just grow and grow, and the longer it takes a currently Pro-Choice politician or political party (or "Big Tech" company or mainstream media channel) to abandon their Pro-Choice stance (and to abandon the Relativist/Marxist/Socialist ideologies which led Socialists to be the very first to legalize human-killing by abortion – and then by genocide) – the more incompetent/ unintelligent or dishonest/ evil (rather than simply uninformed) they will prove themselves to be – for all the voters (and clients) to see. Voters can hasten the restoration of *The Foundational Principles of Human Rights and Democracy*, which should be constitutionally enshrined in their country, by learning and sharing this HUMAN RIGHTS EDUCATION FOR LASTING FREE DEMOCRACY with other voters, so they no longer cast uneducated votes for uneducated politicians (and parties) who have *not a clue* what Democracy is built on nor how to maintain it. Voters should share this HUMAN RIGHTS EDUCATION FOR LASTING FREE DEMOCRACY with their elected representative and political leaders and high court judges, so they learn how to be good, Human-Rights-educated leaders of a LASTING democracy secure on Democracy's historic and logical (and "Pro-Life") *foundations.* Because *Pro-Life equals Pro-Democracy and Pro-Choice equals Pro-Totalitarianism.*

"You can resolve to live your life with integrity. Let your credo be this: Let the lie come into the world, let it even triumph. But not through me."
— Aleksandr Solzhenitsyn

"I add this caveat for Pro-Choice politicians and voters: Stop the lie. Before you read this, you already knew that preborn humans are humans. You already knew that abortion kills humans. You already knew that killing humans is wrong. So all you have to do is stop lying."
– William Baptiste (Whose Ethnic Group Suffered World History's Biggest Genocide at the Hands of the World's First Socialist State, Which was the First State to Legalize Abortion)

"The simple step of a courageous individual is not to take part in the lie. One word of truth outweighs the world."
— Aleksandr Solzhenitsyn

"What good fortune for governments that the people do not think."
– Adolf Hitler
(Whose Genocidal Nazi Party Government was the First Government, Other Than the Genocidal Marxist Soviet Communist Party Government, to Legalize Abortion)

ABOUT THE AUTHOR OF THIS HUMAN RIGHTS EDUCATION FOR LASTING FREE DEMOCRACY   **247**

YOU CAN HELP FREE DEMOCRACY LAST FOREVER!   **257**

INTRODUCTION: HUMAN RIGHTS AND FREEDOMS ARE INHERENT, EQUAL, INALIENABLE AND NON-PARTISAN

The Warning of a Non-Partisan Human Rights Scholar Whose Ethnic Group Was Victim of One of History's Biggest Bigoted Genocides:

Today's Good Citizens Must Determine to Be Like the Good Poles, Who Helped Overturn Brutal Soviet Extremist Left-Wing (Marxist) Totalitarianism by *Standing Up Together in Solidarity for Traditional Western Values as the Necessary Guide of Public Policy*; and Not Like the Good Germans Who Lost their Democracy to Nazi Extremist Right-Wing (Fascist) Totalitarianism by Letting Themselves Be Intimidated into Silence and Separation by Those Who Did Not Hold the Traditional Western Values Which Include and Support *The Foundational Principles of Human Rights and Democracy*).

The Traditional Western Values Including and Upholding The Foundational Principles of Human Rights and Democracy (Such as Equal Human Preciousness and Free Speech) Which the Global Solidarity Movement Stands together in Solidarity for as the Continued Guide of Public Policy, So that Free Democracy Can Last for Centuries on its Historical and Logical Foundations, are Non-Partisan, and Were Magnificently Expressed in the 1948 Universal Declaration of Human Rights. Healthy Democracies have a "Progressive Left" and "Conservative Right" in Fruitful Balance, Both Committed to Democratic Foundations and Neither Exhibiting Signs of Political Extremism, "Left" or "Right."

"There can be no acceptable future without an honest analysis of the past."
— *Aleksandr Solzhenitsyn*

"In actual fact our Russian experience [of totalitarianism] ... is vitally important for the West, because by some chance of history we have trodden the same path seventy or eighty years before the West. And now it is with a strange sensation that we look at what is happening to you; many social phenomena that happened in Russia before its collapse are being repeated. Our experience of life is of vital importance to the West, but I am not convinced that you are capable of assimilating it without having gone through it to the end yourselves..."
— *Aleksandr Solzhenitsyn*

[Note on this unedited 1st Emergency Edition/Advance Reader Copy: If this book is occasionally disjointed with updates and revisions and rougher sections, it is because the author cannot think and write as fast as thousands of influential totalitarian-oriented ideologue politicians and civil servants and judges and journalists and "Big Tech" personnel worldwide (who have no idea just what are Free Democracy's historical and logical and philosophical foundations identified in this book) can (purposefully or unwittingly) undermine human freedom because of their *lack of knowledge.* However, hopefully the very defects of this book can help readers consciously enter into the flow of *Living History* and get a sense of the present *urgent* need for this book to help restore the forgotten *foundations* of all Human Rights and democratic freedoms. *Past* Living History naturally resulted in the *Present Moment* of Living History, and what we do (or do not do) in the Present will naturally form the shape of *Future* Living History – including whether that future is oppressive and totalitarian or free and democratic.

Intro: Human Rights & Freedoms Are Non-Partisan

In this Present Moment of Living History, it is difficult to keep up with all the current accelerating threats to worldwide human freedom, especially during the 2020 Coronavirus Pandemic now ongoing into 2021, which has provided so much global instability that it is every ideologue's dream – the best opportunity ever to "Reset" the whole world according to their unrealistic and dangerous *ideology instead of education*. This author, as a member of the ethnic group murdered in the millions by the first national government to embrace the underlying philosophy and ideology that motivates much (though not all) of today's 'Creeping Totalitarianism' now accelerating during the Pandemic, is duty-bound to the dead, honor-bound towards the millions murdered by the same ideology, to speak out a grave warning to the West, and to make an urgent call to get back to the Free World's *foundations* which have been far too long neglected.

"To destroy a people, you must first sever their roots."
— *Aleksandr Solzhenitsyn*

The warning was already given by the very wise Nobel Prize-winning intellectual Aleksandr Solzhenitsyn *but not heeded* – apparently because the nascent "Cancel Culture" hell-bent on disconnecting the world today from the lessons of Living History *years ago quietly "cancelled" Solzhenitsyn and his warning* so effectively that most young university students I talk to *have never even heard of him or his hugely historically important book The Gulag Archipelago which sold 35 million copies, was translated into 30 languages and helped peacefully end the Cold War that threatened humanity with nuclear annihilation* (*Time* declared it "Best Non-Fiction Book of the Twentieth Century"). Today the "Cancel Culture" extremist ideologues (who usually know so little Human Rights History themselves that they absurdly call their opponents "extremists") continue to do their best to make sure nobody knows the facts of Past Living History that are most pertinent to *lasting* Human Rights and freedoms, so that, in a world cut off from its history, and cut off from the lessons of the past, ideologues can attempt to rebuild (or "Reset") the world according to their dangerous and literally *unrealistic* ideologies (rooted in philosophical *Relativism* that is opposed to the philosophical *Realism* which is the root of Science, Logic, Technology, Common Sense, and which is the philosophical framework within which developed *The Foundational Principles of Human Rights and Democracy* identified in this handbook – see CHAPTER 3: PHILOSOPHY). Amidst all the ideological and political threats to human life and freedom which were accelerating even *before* the Coronavirus Pandemic sped things up, this handbook is written to ensure that the world's citizens know (and to make sure no extremist ideologues "cancel") the facts of History, Science, Logic, and Philosophy which are most pertinent to *lasting* human freedom for every inherently, equally, inalienably *precious* human being.]

In 1930s Germany and in today's West, no matter how high the evidence piles up, most people keep themselves in *denial* about just how badly their democracy is failing under political parties in power which no longer recognize the underlying *Foundational Principles of Human Rights and Democracy* identified from the disciplines of History, Science, Logic and Philosophy in this book. Understandably. Who wants the hassle of looking reality in the face when it is unpleasant? Especially when acknowledging the problem obligates one to work towards a solution, and the problem, once acknowledged, at first seems overwhelming, with no solution immediately in sight. **Thankfully, this book will go back centuries to get to the bottom of the problems undermining Free Democracy today, identify the underlying problems and their development clearly, and in the end this book will furnish historically proven strategy for solving the problems.** So that for centuries to come the electorate of voting citizens in Western democracies *will know better than to elect politicians and political parties who do not know nor uphold the historically implicit Foundational Principles of Human Rights and Democracy now explicitly elaborated in this book* (and the other books of this author's HUMAN RIGHTS EDUCATION FOR LASTING FREE DEMOCRACY book series). In fact, in the future (thanks to this book series clearly identifying them) the underlying principles upon which Free Democracy is built will be so firmly constitutionally enshrined by democracies that want to remain democracies – and taught to the citizens of free democracies so they may guard them with their votes – that politicians will either know better than to violate democratic foundations, or they will be held constitutionally accountable to them even if they forgot.

But because they did not know any better, in 1930s Germany, Germans *through democratic processes not held accountable to democratic foundations* put Adolf Hitler and his Nazi Party into power. And then they, ostrich-like, "stuck their heads in the sand" and *denied* the growing evidence that their free democracy was slowly becoming a totalitarian State. Germany never had a military coup. Even the formal end of democracy in Germany came from another *vote* (to give the elected Nazi Party and Hitler "emergency powers" do deal with an apparent Communist threat). During this whole process the good Germans' *denial* of the problem and its seriousness made them miss all the opportunities they had to *stop* the momentum of bigoted Nazi evil that *denied equal Human Rights to all humans* before it got completely out of control in their country (and spilled into other countries). In the early days of Nazi Germany, when the democratically elected Nazi government introduced bigoted new laws that violated the *equal human preciousness without exception* that Modern Democracy assumes, such as laws forbidding ethnically Jewish German citizens to own bicycles or gramophones (early record players), the good Germans had *opportunities* to stand up *together* in *Solidarity* against such unjust laws. Had they stood up *together in Solidarity* for Traditional Western Values which imply *equal Human Rights for all humans* and told their democratically elected Nazi Party government that they would not put up with such foolish (and bigoted) nonsense, treating some humans in their country radically differently, as somehow less than human, the Nazis, whose legitimacy as the government initially depended upon keeping the trappings of democracy, would have been greatly hampered in their evil designs. If the good people stood up *together* in *Solidarity* against bigoted stupidity the Nazis likely could never have gotten near so far as they did, in the end murdering millions of people all while the good Germans kept themselves in *denial* of growing evidence just how bad things were; kept to themselves hoping they themselves would just be left alone; and they put up with everything from their government which did not believe any more in principles implicit in Traditional Western Values like *equal human preciousness without exception which governments are obligated to protect*; principles which had transformed the previously brutal ancient Western world starting in the 4th Century; principles which gradually but logically over the centuries had grown up into Human Rights, International Law, and Modern Democracy.

Before the 4th Century, "popular entertainment," the "TV" of the day, was public torture and murder in the Roman arenas (and you thought hockey in arenas was violent!). The government was frequently the biggest threat to human life and freedom. Before the 4th Century, governments were judged by their civic accomplishments, often built on the backs of slaves – and one third of the population were slaves. Starting in the 4th Century, Western governments came to be judged instead by *how they treated the humans they governed*, because of the 4th Century introduction into Western governments of the implicit form of what are explicitly clarified in this book as The *Foundational Principles of Human Rights and* Democracy. There was still governmental tyranny and legal slavery in the West after the 4th Century, but much less; and after the 4th Century, governments were remembered and judged harshly for the tyranny and totalitarianism which before the 4th Century had been *normal*.

But because they did not know the historical and logical sources of Western freedom, instead of standing up *together* in *Solidarity* for Traditional Western Values as the continued guide of public policy in their Western nation; instead of reminding their Nazi-Party-controlled government that since the 4th Century, Western governments had been *obligated* to *protect* all their human citizens and no longer arbitrarily hold the power of life and death over them, instead with each new government violation of democracy and human equality the good Germans just vainly hoped "surely it can't get any worse than this." The good Germans found out, in unprecedented millions of precious humans killed, just how bad it can get *when good people do not stand up together in Solidarity for their good, Traditional Western Values as the continued guide of public policy.* If the good people do not stop bigoted and stupid evil from politicians, it will not get stopped. Because,

---

"The only thing necessary for the triumph of evil is for good men to do nothing."
"When bad men combine, the good must associate; else they will fall, one by one, an unpitied sacrifice in a contemptible struggle."
– Edmund Burke

Edmund Burke's above quotes were proven true in the negative example of Nazi Germany, where the good Germans did not associate together but allowed themselves to remain separately intimidated into silence in the face of bigoted evil perpetrated by a political party in power which denied the Traditional Western principle of *equal human preciousness* which in modern terms implies *Equal Human Rights for All Humans.* Burke was proven right when each good German separately doing nothing separately fell one by one into uselessness and allowed murderous evil to flourish and triumph in Germany. But thankfully, Burke's words were also proven true in the positive example where the good *did* associate as Burke said they must; *did* stand up *together* in *Solidarity* against even the totalitarian Marxist, Communist government of Soviet Bloc Poland, the Polish *Solidarity* movement guided by Traditional Western Values, and seeking for Traditional Western Values to once again have their proper place as the guide of public policy in their country. Undermining brutal hardline Marxism in the Soviet Bloc. And in about a decade, the totalitarian Cold War Soviet

Bloc was no more, collapsing from within without any war or bloodshed, crumbling under the weight of its thick web of lies.

Today in the West, the good Canadians, the good Americans and the good Europeans and Australians and so on, must determine in their hearts that they want to be like the good Poles, and not like the good Germans. They must be alert and on guard for their good, Traditional Western Values which include and support *The Foundational Principles of Human Rights and Democracy* clearly identified from the disciplines of History, Science, Logic and Philosophy in this book. They must resist the temptation to stay *comfortably in denial* about how their free democracies are unravelling because of their lack of vigilance.

Because in 2021, alert citizen voters the world over are aware that in the last year (and more) there have been unprecedented compromises to Free Democracy globally. And a debacle in the U.S., as predicted by the sagacious Nobel Prize-winning historian of Soviet Marxist totalitarianism Aleksandr Solzhenitsyn, who lived 18 years in the U.S. after being exiled from Soviet Russia. The world's foremost expert on Soviet totalitarianism warned us this was coming (though he lamented, "I am not convinced that you are capable of assimilating [the warning] without having gone through it to the end yourselves . . ."). Now, *unprecedentedly politically polarized sides accuse each other of threatening Democracy* while neither side has a deep knowledge of the key facts of Human Rights History nor of the underlying principles and philosophy which make Modern Democracy possible. Which is why for decades neither side when in power have been maintaining the foundations of Free Democracy for future generations, so more totalitarian laws and policies keep being passed in the West (particularly in this author's country). THIS HANDBOOK HELPS TO UNDERSTAND THE DEEP ROOT SOURCES OF ALL THE TROUBLE AND PROVIDES HISTORICALLY PROVEN WINNING STRATEGY TO END IT! First by clearly identifying explicitly from the disciplines of History, Science, Logic and Philosophy the implicit origins of all Human Rights and democratic freedoms. Identifying just what are *The Foundational Principles of Human Rights and Democracy* implicitly laid in the 4th Century, gradually but logically growing up to yield Human Rights, International Law and Modern Democracy. Then by identifying the counter-development of bad philosophy since the 17th Century which unhinged Western Philosophy from the *Realism* which grounds Science, Logic, Technology, Human Rights and Free Democracy – revealing that those who today wittingly or unwittingly threaten Democracy usually do not even have a good grip on Science nor on Reality! This book also details ten *Core Principles of Lasting Democracy* which today's countries need to implement if they want to remain free democracies long-term. Democracy is sure to fail, if neither the voters nor their elected representatives (or their political parties) even know *The Foundational Principles of Human Rights and Democracy*.

Today, the citizens of the Western World can no longer afford to remain in *denial of growing totalitarian trends* as did the good Germans in Hitler's day. Back when in America, "land of the free," the majority for a false peace of mind (just like today!) kept themselves *in denial* of the growing totalitarian realities poising to snuff out democratic freedoms and Human Rights worldwide.

Back then, beloved children's author and cartoonist Dr. Seuss (real name: Theodor Seuss Geisel) was a political cartoonist in America when Adolf Hitler and his National Socialist German Worker's Party (the Nazi Party for short) rose to power in

Germany. The clever and sharp-witted future Dr. Seuss was no denier. But seeing it prevalent in his fellow Americans, he drew an insightful political cartoon about widespread American *denial of the present danger* dated April 29, 1941 – several months before America in December 1941 would be forcibly dragged into World War II after losing a substantial portion of its Pacific fleet in the Pearl Harbor sneak attack by Hitler's Japanese allies. With the caption, "We Always Were Suckers for Ridiculous Hats …," the cartoon depicts a line of people lining up to trade their current hat for a new one distributed under a big sign reading

GET YOUR
OSTRICH BONNET HERE
RELIEVES
HITLER HEADACHE
"FORGET THE TERRIBLE
NEWS YOU'VE READ.
YOUR MIND'S AT EASE
IN AN OSTRICH HEAD!"

The "Ostrich Bonnet" hat, looking exactly like ostrich-type animals in Dr. Seuss' children's books, entirely covers the citizens' heads, with a long ostrich neck sticking up with an ostrich head on top. A long line of citizens who have already received their "Ostrich Bonnets" are bent over, with their ostrich heads buried in the sand just like the proverbial ostrich with its head in the sand, foolishly "avoiding" danger by pretending it does not exist!

Dr. Seuss' image of denial and *pretending the danger to Free Democracy for everyone does not exist* applies today to everyone who is not consciously aware of the fact that Human Rights and democratic freedoms in the West are today more seriously in jeopardy than they have been since the Cold War ended. In danger from totalitarian and Human-Rights-denying ideologies *against free speech* which are now so entrenched in the West that this author had to give a eulogy at the funeral for an elderly, peaceful and loving *Equal Human Rights for All Humans* advocate born the year of the *Universal Declaration of Human Rights* (1948), who died from heart problems surely exacerbated by the stress of awaiting unjust trial after being arrested twice in my nation's capital. Arrested twice just around the corner from the Parliament Buildings of our very unhealthy democracy, arrested just for being a "known" *Equal Human Rights for All Humans* advocate holding signs reading "FREEDOM OF EXPRESSION AND RELIGION. NO CENSORSHIP" and "GOD SAVE OUR CHARTER RIGHTS." Arrested just for this peaceful protest of new anti-democratic laws taking away his *freedom of speech* to (where it is most pertinent to do so) express (specifically) what are identified from Human Rights History, Science and Logic in this book as *The Foundational Principles of Human Rights and Democracy*! This author and Human Rights scholar would be arrested and imprisoned or heavily fined under this current law passed in the regional legislature in *only three weeks* (October 4-25, 2017) just for saying peacefully, "killing humans is wrong, because Human Rights are for all humans," precisely where it is most pertinent to defend *Equal Human Rights for All Humans.*

Yes, this law would specifically censor and imprison me for saying that. Yes, in my country, you can be arrested for peaceful Human Rights advocacy just like you can in totalitarian States. But bad philosophy growing in influence since the 17th Century,

7

and anti-democratic, totalitarian-oriented ideologies built on this bad philosophy, are now so entrenched in my country (and the rest of the West – as Aleksandr Solzhenitsyn warned us) that media barely covered it and there was no public outcry about the outrageous travesty of new laws targeting peaceful *Equal Human Rights for All Humans* advocates and making peaceful Human Rights advocacy a crime; nor any ire over the outrage of a 70-year-old man dying before trial after being arrested twice merely for holding signs peacefully advocating for *freedom of speech on behalf of Human Rights* which had specifically been restricted by new totalitarian government laws which would never exist in a healthy democracy. Instead of *outrage* against this assault on Democracy itself (and its foundations in *Equal Human Rights for All Humans*) by the regional government, other regional governments equally as clueless about *The Foundational Principles of Human Rights and Democracy* since have *copied* this totalitarian law. Yet another regional government passed a very similar totalitarian law against normal democratic freedoms of speech, expression, assembly, conscience and religion in *only eight days* (March 2-10, 2020). So how much less freedom might we have *next week,* since we now know from experience that supposedly democratic governments entirely ignorant of *The Foundational Principles of Human Rights and Democracy* are capable of introducing totalitarian bills and passing them into law in only eight days?

Yes, those who are alert and awake and intellectually honest – and who refuse to let their minds sink unthinkingly into the constant, 24/7 distractions and entertainments which technology now tempts us with to keep us unaware – knows that Human Rights and Free Democracy are in deep trouble in the West in 2021. Particularly aware are those familiar with Nobel Prize-winning author and fiercely honest intellectual Aleksandr Solzhenitsyn's repeated warnings, after suffering decades under Soviet Marxist totalitarianism then living 18 years in the U.S., that **the same insidious (and philosophically *Relativist*) ideology (contrary to the philosophically *Realist* foundations of Science) which destroyed his native Russia (and made *Soviet* Russia commit one of history's biggest genocides upon this author's ethnic group) was taking the West to *the same oppressive totalitarian ends*, just more slowly and by a different route.** Solzhenitsyn's prediction is now knocking at our door at the end of 2020 and the beginning of 2021, especially in America.

America's Past (But No Longer) Bi-Partisan Support of The Foundational Principles of Human Rights and Democracy

For good or for ill, America still leads world trends. This non-partisan, non-American author and Human Rights scholar notes that in the past, both major U.S. parties used to implicitly assume *The Foundational Principles of Human Rights and Democracy* which are embedded in Traditional Western Values. And so, representatives of both major U.S. parties have in the past made huge strides in protecting *Equal Human Rights for All Humans* – Republican President Abraham Lincoln, on the "conservative Right," whose 1863 *Emancipation Proclamation* helped free the Black human slaves, and Democrat First Lady Eleanor Roosevelt (widow of FDR), on the "progressive Left," who led the formation of the 1948 United Nations'

Universal Declaration of Human Rights which declared that Human Rights are for all humans:

"without distinction of any kind," because "recognition of the inherent dignity and of the equal and inalienable rights of all members of the human family is the foundation of freedom, justice and peace in the world."
– from Article 2 and from the Preamble of the Universal Declaration of Human Rights

---

Eleanor's husband, Democrat President Franklin Delano Roosevelt (FDR), insightfully noted

---

"Democracy cannot succeed unless those who express their choice are prepared to choose wisely. The real safeguard of Democracy, therefore, is education."
—U.S. President Franklin Delano Roosevelt

President Roosevelt's sentiment here is stated more precisely in this book in CORE PRINCIPLE OF LASTING DEMOCRACY #5: HUMAN RIGHTS EDUCATION which states

---

"Lasting Democracy requires that all citizens as part of their basic education as citizens of a Free Democracy be taught and know The Foundational Principles of Human Rights and Democracy which all Human Rights and democratic freedoms are historically and logically built on and cannot last without… Uneducated ignorance of the foundations of Free Democracy guarantees its eventual failure."

At the time Roosevelt was President, most of those underlying principles which this author's HUMAN RIGHTS EDUCATION FOR LASTING FREE DEMOCRACY book series (including this short handbook) identifies as *The Foundational Principles of Human Rights and Democracy* (plus ten *Core Principles of Lasting Democracy*) were still more or less passed on from generation to generation more or less implicitly within Traditional Western Values. Even though a counter-development in Western Philosophy (traced back to the 17th Century in CHAPTER 3: PHILOSOPHY) had already led to the totalitarian, politically Extremist Right Nazi Fascism FDR fought in World War II; and had already led to the totalitarian, politically Extremist Left Soviet Marxism which FDR's successors would fight in the Cold War. Unfortunately, American and Western education and culture in FDR's time had already started to be influenced by the same underlying philosophical errors which ultimately birthed totalitarian Fascism on the extreme political Right and totalitarian Marxism on the extreme political Left. So, eventually American and Western governments stopped using Traditional Western Values (within which *The Foundational Principles of Human Rights and Democracy* were implicitly embedded) as the guide for public political policies and laws. Meaning these vital foundational principles of Free Democracy for decades now have no longer been consistently passed down in our Western democracies (which explains why this author can be arrested and jailed under current laws in several regions of my country just for peacefully saying "killing humans is wrong" precisely where it is most pertinent to stand up for *Equal Human Rights for All Humans*).

Yet still, since *The Foundational Principles of Human Rights and Democracy* are utterly non-partisan, this non-partisan author can below quote both (another) Democrat and a Republican past U.S. President in support of the solid HUMAN RIGHTS EDUCATION FOR LASTING FREE DEMOCRACY culled from History, Science, Logic and Philosophy in this book:

"Every child must be encouraged to get as much education as he has the ability to take. We want this not only for his sake - but for the future of our nation's sake. Nothing matters more to the future of our country: not our military preparedness - for armed might is worthless if we lack the brainpower to build world peace; not our productive economy - for we cannot sustain growth without trained manpower; not our democratic system of government - for freedom is fragile if citizens are ignorant."
— *Lyndon B. Johnson (U.S. Democrat President)*

"Freedom is never more than one generation away from extinction. We didn't pass it to our children in the bloodstream. It must be fought for, protected, and handed on for them to do the same."
– *Ronald Reagan (U.S. Republican President)*

Of course, any country that wants its free democracy to last long-term must keep its elected politicians and its judges and its unelected bureaucrats/civil servants and police *accountable* to democratic foundations and *teach* these foundations to its citizen voters (and especially to citizens who end up working in influential fields like journalism/media, and "Big Tech" which is now inextricably intertwined with mainstream media). **But our modern democracies have utterly failed on both counts.** So, there is widespread ignorance of those facts of Human Rights History, Science, Logic, and the History of Ideas (Philosophy) collected in this author's HUMAN RIGHTS EDUCATION FOR LASTING FREE DEMOCRACY book series (including this handbook). Widespread ignorance of the facts which are most pertinent to the historic development and current maintenance of the West's Human Rights and democratic freedoms (and even of Science itself!) — which has led to politicians and judges and government bureaucrats and civil servants *uneducated in democratic* *foundations.* Who are now regularly passing laws and policies and making court judgements against normal democratic freedoms of speech, expression, assembly, conscience and religion (which are enforced by police likewise entirely ignorant of Free Democracy's foundations). In my country, people can even be arrested for speaking *established and verifiable scientific facts* which are not supportive of current unscientific government ideologies (absurd and inhuman ideologies rooted in philosophical *Relativism* which denies the philosophical *Realism* which grounds Science and Common Sense, as discussed in CHAPTER 3: PHILOSOPHY).

This widespread ignorance of democratic foundations has also led to uneducated but influential media moguls and "Big Tech" personnel who are regularly encouraging the dismantling of Free Speech and other normal democratic freedoms, if only *because they do not know any better.* That is, if they are not actually deliberately promoting an ultimately anti-democratic and totalitarian-oriented, politically extremist ideology such as Right-wing Fascist Neo-Nazism or Left-wing Marxism (Communism/ Socialism; or Marxism's common new form of Neo-Marxist "Identity Politics" with its "Cancel Culture"), then just in their uneducated ignorance of *The Foundational Principles of Human Rights and Democracy* they are still unwittingly dismantling free democracy from its foundations without any idea what they are doing. Indeed, it is often unclear whether many of today's politicians and journalists/news media (the latter now intertwined with "Big Tech" and social media) are merely incompetent or actually evil. But either way, whether by evil ideological design or by mere uninformed ignorance, many of today's governments and much of mainstream media have certainly been actively undermining democratic foundations for a long time now – just as the brilliantly insightful proven prognosticator Aleksandr Solzhenitsyn observed, and predicted would worsen as it has. With a recent huge increase in "Big Tech" and mainstream media censoring pertinent facts; censoring much highly qualified scientific medical testimony concerning the Coronavirus Pandemic; and censoring opinions supportive of Traditional Western Values and the lasting Free Democracy which depends on them. At the turn of 2021 the gradual dismantling of Free Democracy has suddenly accelerated in ways that surprised even this author, despite researching, reflecting, and writing since 2015 on the phenomenon of decades of slowly 'creeping' totalitarianism now maturing its rotten fruit in the West – and poisoning the well out of which we drink.

The failure of Western societies to know, teach, and hold politicians, judges, journalists, police (and civil servants and "Big Tech") accountable to Western Civilization's foundational principles undergirding Human Rights and Free Democracy (and Science itself) is why 'creeping totalitarianism' has been slowly growing in Western democracies since even before the 1960s, when Western societies, having forgotten the facts of the long but logical development of modern Human Rights and Modern Democracy (and even of Modern Science itself!), started actively rejecting Traditional Western Values including *The Foundational Principles of Human Rights and Democracy* identified from History, Science, and Logic herein, and no longer used them as the guidelines for public policy in Western nations. Western societies since then have even abandoned the underlying philosophical worldview of (Aristotelian and Scholastic) *Realism* (which underlies all Science, Logic, Technology, and which was the *Realistic* philosophical framework in which Human Rights and Free Democracy were built) for *Relativism* (which opposes Realism and which underlies Fascism, Marxism, and all political extremism). It is imperative that citizens of Western countries learn and spread to others knowledge of the foundations of their freedom. Which is why this handbook exists.

Understanding Politics: The Greek Root of Policy, Politics, Politicians and Police

[Adapted from the author's book *DEMOCRACY 101*]

It is important to an educated understanding of government to know the Greek root and history of certain political terms. The original organized State government was the government of the city, or City-State, the Greek word for city being *polis*. Thus, from this Greek root word *polis* or city, we get the words **policy; politics; politicians; and police**. *Politics* is the action of the *politicians* setting the *policies* by which the *polis*/city/State will be governed, and these *policies* (many made into formal laws) are enforced by *police*. Still today most police forces are hired by the local *polis*/city government, though this level of local city government is now known as the *municipal* government which operates within the jurisdiction of a larger *regional* government of a province or state etc. which operates within the jurisdiction of a federal or national government which is now the highest level of government in a sovereign State or country. These higher levels of government also often hire police forces to enforce the policies adopted into law by the State, such as the Canadian Mounties (Royal Canadian Mounted Police/RCMP) or the American FBI (Federal Bureau of Investigations), which are national level police forces (the Mounties also functioning as provincial police in the younger Western Canadian provinces where they were first formed).

It is entirely appropriate that we sometimes call a totalitarian State that is oppressive to human life and/or freedom a "Police State." This is because it is the *political* norm for the *police* to enforce the *policies/laws* of the State government (originally the *polis* or City-State) which is run by the *politicians, whether those politicians and their policies are totalitarian or democratic*. Note that even the ancient Greeks had only "democracy experiments" by the standards of modern democracy. Only upper-class, aristocratic / land-owning Athenian men could vote, and people could own slaves, because there was no principle of *human equality* nor of *Human Rights* (both are essential to Modern Democracy as we know it); and the Greek Draco, the first legislator of "democratic" Athens, made such harsh laws – including the death penalty for most criminal offenses – that to this day the word *Draconian* is used to describe harsh or oppressive laws, strictly enforced, as in totalitarian States.

This reveals an important point: The only reason we in the West have come into the habit of thinking that "the government has our best interests in mind" and "the police are our friends" or that "the government/police are here to help" or "the government/police are here to protect and serve the citizens" is because for many centuries in the West our State governments were guided in their policy-making by Traditional Western (Judeo-Christian) Pro-Life Family Values including the *Foundational Principles of Human Rights and Democracy* identified from History, Science, Logic and Philosophy in this book. Traditional principles which say the government is *obligated* to protect (and ultimately serve) *every human without exception as equally precious.* Thus, the *policies* (some made into formal laws) made by the governing *politicians* to guide the State, which the *police* are responsible to the State government to *enforce*, have for a very long time in the West tended to be Human Rights and Democracy-supporting policies and laws. *But this is no longer the case since democracy-grounding Traditional Western Values have been abandoned by the West as its "guiding principles."* Which is why this author ended up giving a eulogy at the funeral of an elderly man arrested twice for peacefully promoting Free Speech in support of *Equal Human Rights for All Humans.* Which is why people in this author's country can be arrested for speaking verifiable scientific facts which do not agree with newfangled unscientific ideologies promoted by political parties now officially opposed to *The Foundational Principles of Human Rights and Democracy.* Which is why, during the extra (and global) instability of the Coronavirus Pandemic, totalitarian-oriented political parties in power, which were *already* passing totalitarian-oriented laws largely along Marxist lines, are using the Pandemic as an excuse to promote their party's anti-democratic values and ideology at an accelerated rate. Like in Marxist States, for several months now entirely banning all public religious services where this author lives, using the Pandemic as an excuse, while hypocritically allowing hundreds at a time to gather for secular activities in crowded malls, museums, "fun centers" and restaurants smaller than many worship houses. **The "enormous number" of Western Marxist-influenced who Solzhenitsyn warned us about are even enthusiastically proposing the global Pandemic as a wonderful opportunity for a global "Great Reset" along Marxist lines (Marx always intended his ideas to dominate the globe), when what the world really needs is a "Democracy Reboot." Reloading into the "active memory" of Western countries the forgotten *Foundational Principles of Human Rights and Democracy*, and ten *Core Principles of Lasting Democracy*, and the philosophical *Realism* which grounds Science – all clearly identified in this handbook.**

The mere force of habit of many centuries have for decades so far kept Western citizens used to trusting their governments (and police) to protect and serve their precious humanity, and has generally kept Western politicians from actually oppressing their citizens or telling them what to believe and do (and from using *police* to *enforce* the government's will on the governed people). But unfortunately, without any solid grounding in the Traditional Western *Foundational Principles of Human Rights and Democracy* for decades now, Western governments are now naturally more and more acting like totalitarian States, by now starting to tell citizens what to believe and do and speak (or not speak) – creating tribunals against free speech and legalizing the killing of more and more humans (in this author's country, as in all countries which legalized euthanasia, the list of which humans can be legally killed by euthanasia or "assisted suicide" just keeps getting longer and longer. For the elderly, euthanasia-killing is promoted and expanded instead of *palliative care* which today is so advanced it can effectively manage pain in the dying without violating the ancient non-killing doctors' Hippocratic Oath. Note that the Nazis who did not believe *killing humans is wrong* were the first political party to legalize euthanasia). And they are even starting to arrest Christians and other Pro-Life Human Rights Advocates with Traditional Western Values merely for expressing their democracy-grounding beliefs that *killing humans is wrong* because *Human Rights are for all humans.* It is so significant it cannot be repeated too much: *this author can be arrested and imprisoned for peaceful Human Rights advocacy under current laws in various provinces of his country,* while the ruling political party has been purging from its ranks anyone "old school" enough to still believe in what this book identifies from the disciplines of History, Science, Logic, and Philosophy as *The Foundational Principles of Human Rights and Democracy.*

CHAPTER 3: PHILOSOPHY really digs deep to get to the bottom of these increasing affronts to Free Democracy, tracing them all the way back to a 17th Century philosophical error from 1641. For now just remember that Fascist Nazism on the Extremist Right of the political spectrum was inspired in part by the German Relativist Atheist philosopher Friedrich Nietzsche, a Moral Relativist who advocated that the exceptional or elite should make their own "master morality" instead of following what he called the "slave morality" of Traditional Judaism and Christianity — Biblical Judeo-Christianity which provided Western Civilization with its guiding principles for public policy like democracy-grounding *equal human preciousness without exception which governments are obligated* (to something *higher* than the government) *to protect.* Remember that Marxism, Communism, and Socialism all refer to the same thing – the sophisticated and seductively beautiful but literally *unrealistic*, philosophically *Relativist not Realist* political and economic philosophy (on the Extremist Left) of Nietzsche's fellow German Relativist Atheist philosopher Karl Marx. Marx himself mocked as "castles in the air" all pre-Marxist forms of socialism which were less violent than Marx proposed was necessary to set up a Socialist State; and no Socialism since has been without the strong influence of Marx and his sophisticated and tantalizingly good-sounding (though unrealistic) ideas – including today's commonly-practiced Neo-Marxist *Identity Politics.* **Marx's seductive system sets up Socialist States aiming for the ultimate Communist egalitarian utopia where everyone is equal, nobody owns anything and everyone is happy, as the highly centralized State (micro)manages all resources and (in theory) distributes them equitably. But, built on the philosophical assumptions of (Skeptical)** *Relativism* **instead of (Scientific)** *Realism*, **Marxism in the** *Real World* **has consistently proven wholly incapable of ever being successfully implemented, the best and most concerted efforts to implement Marxism/ Communism/ Socialism on the State level resulting in over 94 million deaths in the 20th Century alone**[1] – the first ten million Marxist murders (of many more tens of millions to follow) being of this author's ethnic heritage group in the *Holodomor* ("Murder by Starvation") Genocide in Soviet Ukraine.

But facts like this matter little to those who have been "ideologically lobotomized" by the supremely bad underlying (and usually unconscious) philosophical worldview of *Skeptical Relativism,* on which Marxism/ Communism/ Socialism is built, which in its purest form results in *Solipsism* – the deranged belief that nothing outside one's own mind can even be certainly known to exist. As discussed at length in CHAPTER 3: PHILOSOPHY, since deep down, Skeptical and Relativist *subjectivists* are not certain anything at all *objectively* exists beyond their own minds, today's Marxists and Neo-Marxist Identity Politics ideologues and other Relativists with *ideology instead of education* **never let** *facts* **get in the way of their** *subjective* **opinions about how public political policy should be run. No matter what Science testifies and no matter how many are harmed** (does this sound familiar in your country, dear reader? Especially during the Coronavirus Pandemic?).

---

[1] As calculated in *The Black Book of Communism: Crimes, Terror, Repression*, the 1997 large scholarly tome written by several European academics.

"Communism is breathing down the neck of all moderate forms of socialism, which are unstable."— Aleksandr Solzhenitsyn

---

Note that one of the many fatal flaws of Marxism related to this is that Marxist thinking cannot tolerate any free-thinking variety of opinion as is normal in free societies. So much so that millions of dedicated Marxists, along with millions of others, were sent to the dehumanizing and deadly Soviet *Gulag* prison system just for being *not quite like-minded enough* with their Marxist superiors (for the same reason, current Neo-Marxist-influenced political parties just at the beginning of the totalitarian spiral are already likewise ideologically "purging" their parties of those with democracy-grounding Traditional Western Values, to keep their witlessly totalitarian-oriented parties "ideologically pure" and uniform. Specifically rooting out of their parties anyone old-fashioned enough to still believe in *The Foundational Principles of Human Rights and Democracy*).

Solzhenitsyn himself, conceived just months after what the Soviets officially called the Great October Socialist Revolution of 1917 (otherwise known as bloody "Red October," firmly establishing Relativist Atheist Marxist Socialists into political power for the first time) had been schooled to be one of these dedicated Marxist Socialists. Solzhenitsyn was himself a good captain in the Soviet Red Army; a good Marxist; when he was sent to the Gulag for 11 years for not entirely agreeing with his Marxist superiors (remember, Socialist States cannot handle normal free-thinking variety. And neither can today's Socialist-inclined political parties which keep becoming more and more ideologically uniform and intolerant of *The Foundational Principles of Human Rights and Democracy* revealed from History, Science, Logic and Philosophy in this handbook). In the Gulag, Solzhenitsyn woke up from the literally *unrealistic –* based on philosophical *(Skeptical) Relativism* not *(Scientific) Realism* – Socialist dreamworld. As formerly Socialist British journalist Malcolm Muggeridge woke up from the literally *unrealistic* Socialist dreamworld when he enthusiastically went to the Union of Soviet Socialist Republics (USSR), excited to see the world's first Socialist State in action, and there witnessed first-hand the *Holodomor* Genocide of this author's Ukrainian ethnic group (this Ukrainian Canadian author has had the privilege of camping with Muggeridge's descendants – a little touch of *Living History!*).

Honest Muggeridge tried to expose the *Holodomor* ("Murder by Starvation") Genocide while it was happening. But he was discredited and fired for trying to tell the truth about the world's first Socialist State. Discredited and fired by the same *Western* Marxist-influenced mainstream media which Solzhenitsyn (who died only in 2008) later testified was *still* very much Marxist-influenced, and taking the West more slowly *towards the same totalitarian fate as the Soviet Union*. So no-one should be surprised if they find that Western mainstream media today is hiding some extremely pertinent facts testified to by literally tens of thousands of medical professionals and medical scientists (more on this below) which would lead honest politicians to very different government responses to the Coronavirus Pandemic than those policies which have so far been forthcoming — including many unnecessary policies which *both* ignore considerable medical science testimony *and* directly support the Marxist "Great Reset" piggy-backing on the Coronavirus Pandemic, which is no longer even hidden by Neo-Marxist ideologues. The "Great Reset" has now been on the cover of

15

Time in a special issue which partnered with the World Economic Forum, the primary body (other than Communist China) still spouting the utterly unrealistic lie of pure Marxism/ Communism, "let us Socialists control everything and eventually nobody will own anything but everyone will be happy." That's right, the same lie under which over 94 million people were killed in the 20th Century. Starting with ten million of my ethnic group – which is why I insist all who are still foolish (or intellectually dishonest) enough to want to try to make Marxism miraculously work somehow must first consider THE CHALLENGE OF THE MILLIONS MURDERED (excerpts below) and must take THE INTELLECTUAL HONESTY CHALLENGE in this book (Chapter 7), and see if they are still foolish and dishonest enough to remain Marxists or Neo-Marxists, Communists or Socialists (or Pro-Choicers, witlessly following the Soviet Marxist precedent of legal human-killing by abortion, first legalized in Soviet Socialist Russia not long before also legalizing the genocide mass-murder of my ethnic group).

"The clock of communism has stopped striking. But its concrete building has not yet come crashing down. For that reason ... we must try to save ourselves from being crushed by its rubble."
— *Aleksandr Solzhenitsyn*

In the meantime, no matter how many have died in every single attempt to implement Marxism/ Communism/ Socialism at the State level, they still want to do a global Marxist "Great Reset" so the whole world can experience Marxism in practice! No wonder Solzhenitsyn pointed out that if Marxist Communism was "a dead dog" in the former Soviet Bloc countries, it was still "a living lion" in the West. The still-dangerous "rubble" of the Cold War Soviet Marxist Communist Bloc, which Solzhenitsyn (who died just in 2008) repeatedly warned us is still a major threat to Western freedom, includes radically Skeptical and Relativist Postmodernist Philosophy which denies there are any objective facts — invented by Western Marxists like Jacques Derrida in Western universities to protect Marxism from the *objective facts* (like 94 million killed under Marxist policies in the 20th Century) which overwhelmingly prove *Relativist* Marxism just cannot work in the *Real* World. Solzhenitsyn noted that such Relativism results in "impaired thinking ability." Which is *why* dedicated Marxists and Socialists have never *learned* from the overwhelming evidence that Marxist ideals are too *unrealistic* to ever work in the *Real* World. Yes, an intellectual impairment rooted in bad and literally *anti-realistic, anti-scientific* philosophy, discussed at length in Chapter 3, is behind "the Great Reset" — and behind the more needlessly oppressive "Coronavirus Measures" which are currently setting the world up for the Marxist "Great Reset."

The dangerous "rubble" of Marxist Communism still threatening the West includes Neo-Marxist Identity Politics, today deeply entrenched in many major political parties worldwide, which exactly like classic Marxism over-simplistically and unrealistically reinterprets all history as toxic, adversarial "class struggle" between those given Marxist labels of "oppressed" and "privileged," specifically fomenting resentment and hatred between groups in order to produce enough political instability to support a Marxist takeover (this is precisely why the self-described Marxists who run the BLM organization still have cars burning and rioting and looting going on in the U. S.). **Marxism thrives on chaos and is diametrically opposed to democracy-grounding** *mutual respect and cooperation for the Common Good* **based on the** *equal human preciousness without exception* **embedded in the Traditional Western (Judeo-Christian; and philosophically** *Realist*) **Values which Relativist Atheist Marx rejected.** Marxism thrives on chaos, which is why so many Marxists/ Socialists/ Neo-Marxist Identity Politics ideologues are giddy with excitement about the Coronavirus Pandemic as their great opportunity to "Reset" the world on their Marxist principles. Which is why they were talking about a global "new normal" *right from the beginning of the Pandemic*, without any intention of ever letting the world return to normal. So of course, the dangerous "rubble" of Communism Solzhenitsyn spoke of above most recently includes the now publicly proposed, Marxism-inspired "Great Reset," dishonestly misusing the current Coronavirus Pandemic as an excuse to advance government overreach for ultimately Marxist purposes. But Marx from the beginning intended his unrealistic Marxist political and economic system to so dominate the entire globe.

How to Recognize Counterfeits and Not Be Fooled

But, while the serious threats to lasting freedom posed by all Relativist and all Marxist thinking deserves some attention and explication, this author learned years ago the fruitful analogy that to identify counterfeit money, bankers do not spend much time examining and studying counterfeit money. Rather, they spend much time examining and studying and becoming intimately familiar with real money — and then they can easily identify fake, counterfeit money simply because it does not match the Real Thing. This author hopes this handbook (and the longer books in the HUMAN RIGHTS EDUCATION FOR LASTING FREE DEMOCRACY series) will make readers so intimately familiar with *The Foundational Principles of Human Rights and Democracy* and the *Core Principles of Lasting Democracy* and the underlying philosophical worldview of philosophical *Realism* on which Science itself, as well as Human Rights and freedoms were historically and logically built — that readers will become capable of easily recognizing and identifying bad philosophy; and easily recognizing counterfeit political principles (such as Marxist or Fascist, *extremist* principles) which cannot possibly sustain Free Democracy like the Real Thing can.

This is important, especially because the end of 2020 and the beginning of 2021 saw a massive acceleration of global 'Creeping Totalitarianism' worldwide (as alert and aware citizens of the world already well know. The ones not in denial nor constantly distracted from noticing what is most important by 24/7 entertainment technologies which just encourage the natural temptation to bury one's head in the sand and pretend the danger does not exist, like in Dr. Seuss's wartime political cartoon described above). The kind of politicians and political parties (and Western media) which were *already* manifesting Solzhenitsyn's prediction that "an enormous number" of Western Marxist-influenced ideologues were (through Marxist-influenced education and media) taking the West inexorably towards the same ultimate oppressive totalitarian fate which Soviet Russia suffered, are, again, *no longer even hiding their intentions* to misuse the global instability of the global Coronavirus Pandemic to try to implement a global "Great Reset" of the world on Marxist principles (when, again, what the world actually needs is a "Democracy

Reboot" reloading *The Foundational Principles of Human Rights and Democracy* clearly and explicitly identified and articulated in this book series).

There is much more this author could write about multiple major assaults on Free Democracy worldwide coming to light from November 2020 to January 2021, but in March 2021 when this book is submitted for publication, it is too recent and there is no time to research and organize it properly. Even this Introduction is first-draft! But I trust that this unedited "Emergency 1st Edition" handbook's presentation of the real, genuine *Foundational Principles of Human Rights and Democracy*, and of ten eminently sensible *Core Principles of Lasting Democracy* (Chapter 2), and of the *Realist not Relativist* philosophical worldview that undergirds them (and undergirds Science itself – Chapter 3), will make the reader intimately familiar enough with the Real Thing that you, the reader will be able to easily identify and reject *counterfeit and dangerous* political ideologies and bad philosophy presented to you in the current political policies and laws (and media) in your country – policies regarding the Coronavirus Pandemic or anything else.

This author (though I cannot rule this out) is not inclined to believe in one vast and intricately ordered conspiracy to end Free Democracy. I do not have the resources to definitively identify, prove and expose one anyway, so I find it not fruitful to pursue such things. Instead, because the counterfeit is easily seen for what it is once considered next to the Real Thing, my first emphasis in this HUMAN RIGHTS EDUCATION FOR LASTING FREE DEMOCRACY book series is to simply articulate clearly and display for all to see the real historical, scientific, logical, philosophical foundations of Western Civilization's Free Democracy. Because, as a scholar and educator, sometime professor who believes that *education is the answer to problems rooted in ignorance*, I notice that those (usually philosophically *Relativist not Realist*, Pro-Choice Neo-Marxist Identity Politics "Cancel Culture" ideologues, whether politicians, voters, journalists or "Big Tech" billionaires and employees) who are doing so much to dismantle Free Democracy (wittingly or unwittingly) simply *do not know* most of the key facts of Human Rights History, Science, Logic, and the History of Philosophy collected in this book and the rest of the author's HUMAN RIGHTS EDUCATION FOR LASTING FREE DEMOCRACY book series (facts which for the most part are well-known, at least to scholars in the relevant fields, easily verifiable and even "textbook" facts of History, Science, Logic and Philosophy).

Thus, this author takes the approach that to end current 'creeping' totalitarianism now accelerating (and to end most of whatever hidden conspiracies there may be), we only need to *educate* as many citizen voters as possible (and especially educate as many politicians, judges, civil servants, media and "Big Tech" people, who are wittingly or unwittingly doing most of the damage, as possible) in these key facts they did not know. Educate them in *Realism* (the foundation of Science) versus *Relativism* (which is radically skeptical and anti-scientific, and which underlies all political extremism, Left-wing or Right-wing); educate them in *The Foundational Principles of Human Rights and Democracy*, and the ten sensible *Core Principles of Lasting Democracy* identified in this book (and book series). This author believes that just like the Abolitionists educated *first themselves,* and then everyone else they could, in democracy-grounding *equal human preciousness* and *how legal slavery compromised it*, until there were too many *educated* people for slavery to sustain itself, so widespread *education* replacing (Relativist, Pro-Choice, Neo-Marxist) *ideology* will be enough to solve most of the current threats to Free Democracy. Because **this author** believes that however confused they may be due to bad philosophy and bad ideology, *most people who live in the Free West actually like living in the Free West.* The Free West which, as Professor Jordan Peterson has pointed out, (whatever genuine improvements can yet be made) today is demonstrably the most free, caring, and materially affluent society in world history – except for the recent totalitarian laws which motivated this book, laws passed by ungrateful (usually Pro-Choice) Neo-Marxist Identity Politics ideologue politicians **who Solzhenitsyn pointed out in 1983 have been taught by Marxist-influenced professors to hate their own free society.** Their bad ideology meaning that their (usually Marxist-influenced) attempts to "improve" Western Society are wrong-headed and just make things worse, just like every attempt to implement the Marxist ideal (but utterly *unrealistic*) "classless egalitarian utopia where nobody owns anything and everyone is happy" has always failed *murderously* miserably, because Relativists and Marxists lack sufficient contact with scientifically verifiable *reality* and its real constraints. Solzhenitsyn comments below on the irony that those oppressed by totalitarian Marxist ideology (like those in the Polish *Solidarity* Movement in Soviet Bloc Poland) managed to free themselves (first in spirit, eventually in body too), while those in the Free West somehow managed to become discontent with Western freedom and foolishly look to the Marxist/ Socialist ideal which, as Solzhenitsyn testified in a 1983 speech,[2] for all its seductive egalitarian beauty, in *reality* only ever brings "the equality of destitute slaves."

"how is it that people who have been crushed by the sheer weight of slavery and cast to the bottom of the pit can nevertheless find strength to rise up and free themselves, first in spirit and then in body; while those who soar unhampered over the peaks of freedom suddenly appear to lose the taste for freedom, lose the will to defend it, and, hopelessly confused and lost, almost begin to crave slavery. Or again: why is it that societies which have been benumbed for half a century by lies they have been forced to swallow find within themselves a certain lucidity of heart and soul which enables them to see things in their true perspective and to perceive the real meaning of events; whereas societies with access to every kind of information suddenly plunge into lethargy, into a kind of mass blindness, a kind of voluntary self-deception."
– Aleksandr Solzhenitsyn

This author proposes the HUMAN RIGHTS EDUCATION FOR LASTING FREE DEMOCRACY in this book series as a huge part of the answer to creeping totalitarianism now accelerating, **because this author thinks most in the Free West including its Neo-Marxist ideologues actually like Western freedom and affluence and will abandon Marxist principles once *educated* in the real *source* of everything they do like about living in the West, a source which any form of Relativism or Marxism ultimately opposes and tears down.** Many Pro-Choice (legal human-killing, therefore fundamentally *extremist*) Neo-Marxist Leftists generally present themselves as more *ignorant* (or perhaps "wilfully unintelligent" via "ideological lobotomy") than actually *evil*, and I do not believe most are up to the

---

[2] While accepting one of his numerous international awards, awards which include the Nobel Prize.

full-blown Marxist violence that would be necessary for them to truly establish and sustain their Marxist ideological stupidity long-term as the Socialist Soviet Union did – the USSR itself falling quickly and bloodlessly in the end, its 70 years of Marxist Relativist ideology having already spent all its violent force.

So far, the Neo-Marxist Identity Politics crowd is mostly using the standard "fallback" Marxist Socialist tactics for when you *cannot* (at least not yet) violently overthrow the present government and use military force to impose Marxism on all citizens (which was Marx's recommended method for setting up a Socialist State). The Marxist fallback strategies include *emotional manipulation* through simplistically and unrealistically reinterpreting all history in terms of adversarial "class struggle" between those given Marxist labels of "oppressed" and "privileged," Marxists (and Neo-Marxists) always taking the side of those they have labelled "oppressed" in order to garner *sympathy* for their cause; then showing never-ending "manufactured outrage" at past injustices (no matter how long past) and painting themselves as the "compassionate" people (today they say "social justice warriors") trying to right all the wrongs. However far back they have to dig up old wrongs to have resentment over, which Marxists deliberately fan into the flames of current hatred, deliberately fomenting discord between groups in the hopes of causing enough political instability to provide the opportunity for a Marxist takeover. As philosophical Relativists, the actual facts of the case do not matter, as long as they can generate enough chaos to manipulate people into voting for them or otherwise letting them take over and impose order according to Marxist principles. Facts are fluid and ultimately unimportant to Relativists, which is why the BLM organization, which is the epitome of Neo-Marxist Identity Politics and run by *self-described Marxists*, amidst all the burning cars, rioting and looting they have stimulated in the U.S. (because "oppressed" people find "justice" by smashing storefronts and taking things not theirs?), has also resulted in blatant stupidity like tearing down statues of Abraham Lincoln, who freed the Black slaves! "Sympathy" riots in the U.K. tore down statues of Winston Churchill, who successfully fought and beat the Nazi bigots! But who cares about such niggling details, their "evil" White skin means they represent the (Marxist-labeled) "White privileged" culture which must be torn down (even though modern International Law, Human Rights and Free Democracy all developed in Europe, where the natives happen to have White Skin. But Identity Politics "Cancel Culture" ideologues are bigots who cannot get past the hated White skin color. It does not matter to them that Shakespeare's writing so brilliantly captures the essence of *common human nature* that centuries later Japanese film-makers have done movies based on Shakespeare's plays. Nope! To them Shakespeare is just another "Old White Man" to be "cancelled" from school curricula). Neo-Marxist Identity Politics is brainlessly relativistic and so toxically adversarial and bigoted it *inhibits any possibility of fruitful political collaboration based on mutual respect and for the Common Good.* The term "Identity Politics" was first coined in 1978 but did not become common until much later. But Solzhenitsyn described it in 1983:

"Atheist teachers in the West are bringing up a younger generation in a spirit of hatred of their own society... [they say] why should one refrain from burning hatred, whatever its basis—race, class, or ideology? Such hatred is in fact corroding many hearts today.

This eager fanning of the flames of hatred is becoming the mark of today's free world.
Indeed, the broader the personal freedoms are, the higher the level of prosperity or even of
abundance—the more vehement, paradoxically, does this blind hatred become...
This deliberately nurtured hatred then spreads to all that is alive, to life itself...
— Aleksandr Solzhenitsyn

Living in the affluent and free West is not enough for Identity Politics ideologues who still want to tear it down, claiming they want to rebuild it better (now they want to "Reset" it) on their Neo-Marxist, Socialist principles. But Solzhenitsyn showed with statistics, facts and figures that all the "Tsarist oppression" which the Marxist Socialists said justified *resentment* of the aristocratic "privileged class," *resentment* which the Marxists fanned into the flames of enough boiling *hatred* to bloodily overthrow the Tsar and the "privileged" aristocracy and "bourgeoisie" in the Russian Revolution (including the "Great October Socialist Revolution" which put Relativist Socialists in sole political power for the first time), was greatly *exaggerated* into such violently hateful resentment, and (more importantly) all the "Tsarist oppression" together was *not one ten thousandth* of the violent oppression which the Marxists then inflicted upon all the people of Russia and the whole Socialist Soviet Union in the vain pursuit of their seductive but flawed and unrealistic Marxist Atheist Socialist "dream egalitarian society."

All because Marxism preaches a philosophically *unrealistic* egalitarian dreamworld which puts the State before individuals even though theoretically "serving" all "the people" *together*. Meaning in practice that free-thinking *individuals* who do not *fully* share the Marxist ideology cannot be tolerated in a Marxist system. So, countless individuals have to be crushed – often politically imprisoned or murdered – for "the good of the State." And even people who thought they were good Marxists (like Solzhenitsyn, a captain in the Soviet Red Army before he found himself suddenly in the gulag) frequently find themselves "purged" because even as Marxists their ideology was not "pure" enough for a Marxist State to function. Ultimately because Marxism is so seriously flawed it can never function as advertised. Thus, in practice every Marxist State has quickly devolved from an initially exhilarating seductive utopian egalitarian ideal into daily oppressive – and often genocidal – totalitarian States. Remember the first, great genocide by Marxist Socialists (described below) killed many millions of my ethnic group, which is why I am compelled to warn the West with this handbook. And remember that now in 2021 only the latest of many Marxist Socialist genocides since is going on in Marxist Communist China, as it has recently also been stamping out the vestiges of freedom in the formerly British territory of Hong Kong. While the Pro-Choice Neo-Marxist Identity Politics Left major political parties in my country (and my national leader who openly admires Communist China) similarly "purge" or "cancel" all the Pro-Life *Equal Human Rights for All Humans* advocates from their parties (the national leader made it very clear starting in 2015 that *Equal Human Rights for All Humans* advocates are *not welcome* in his currently ruling party); and the Marxist-influenced mainstream media Solzhenitsyn warned us about pressures the major non-(or not yet)-extremist parties (including the only regional Liberal Party which is still relatively near political center and not yet Pro-Choice *legal human-killing extremist*) to likewise kick out of the government any vocal members with a following who actually stand up for Traditional Western Values which include and support the (fundamentally "Pro-Life") *Foundational Principles of Human Rights and Democracy.* And the spineless non-extremist parties typically cave in to Marxist-influenced media pressure and eject from their parties precisely their members most competent to make Free Democracy last because they actually believe in and have courage to stand for Free Democracy's foundations described in detail in this HUMAN RIGHTS EDUCATION FOR LASTING FREE DEMOCRACY book series.

So, This Human Rights scholar and logician here boldly posits that indeed the counterfeit stands out as fake when it is considered next to the Real Thing. Real, free and prosperous countries (however imperfect thanks to their imperfect humanity) are historically and logically built on the principles identified in CHAPTER 2: PRINCIPLES and built on the underlying philosophical worldview identified in CHAPTER 3: PHILOSOPHY. THE INTELLECTUAL HONESTY CHALLENGE in Chapter 7 is for those who insist on rejecting the foundations of Human Rights and Free Democracy identified in this book series (and for all those politicians too spineless to stand up for them when they are assaulted). Even whole countries now built on (philosophically *Relativist not Realist*) Marxist / Communist / Socialist principles are hereby challenged to seriously identify the principles on which they have built their society, and compare them to the Real Thing in this book, the principles that naturally and logically tend to bring freedom and prosperity to a nation. *Without killing any humans*, who are without exception recognized as having *inherent, equal, inalienable* Human Rights, as already proclaimed in the 1948 United Nations *Universal Declaration of Human Rights*, a crucial document which has been endlessly violated by the Marxist-influenced, Pro-Choicers and by other political extremist ideologues including many *among our current Western leaders and in today's UN.*

Whether we have up until now been alert and knowledgeable enough to recognize this or not, the global political situation in 2021 is *urgent.* This author hopes that the real-time urgency of this book to restore lost democratic foundations before we suffer the full totalitarian ends the very wise Aleksandr Solzhenitsyn long warned us the West was heading into, will draw the reader into a conscious sense of *Living History*, which as a teacher/ professor I have always sought to instill in my students. The *past* events (and philosophies) of Living History have brought us to the *present moment* of Living History, and what we do (or do not do) in this *current* moment will determine *future* Living History – will determine whether that future is free and democratic or totalitarian and oppressive. YOUR actions (or inactions) in the present will shape that. This author has done the best I can, within my limitations (including poor health limitations since a bad accident in 2018 with ongoing complications and debilitating headaches which are finally starting to lift in 2021), to make sure YOU the reader have access to the best, most pertinent information from *past* Living History to make the wisest choices in the *present moment* of Living History, in order to bring about a *future* Living History where our children and grandchildren live free, with uncompromised and *effectively* constitutionally protected *Equal Human Rights for All Humans.* My own first grandchild is about to be born in 2021, and so the urgent need for political sanity and stability to be restored amid the current Neo-Marxist ideological misuse of the Coronavirus Pandemic is (most personally) pressing hard upon me.

The Genocide Missed My Family; So, I Am Obligated to Speak for The Dead Who Cannot Speak, to Warn my Country's Leaders and All Worldwide Leaders Who Like Them Witlessly Follow the Same Ideologies as the Genocidal Murderers

---

"If you are willing to say that murder and genocide in many cultures over many decades is wrong, then Marxism is wrong."
– Professor Jordan B. Peterson

I am likely only alive today because my (*Boyko*) family moved from Ukraine to Canada in 1908, a mere nine years before the 1917 "Great October Socialist Revolution," as the Soviet Marxists officially called it, put into political power for the first time philosophically *Relativist not Realist*, religiously *Atheist*, and politically *Marxist* Socialists. Socialists who by 1922 (and by military conquest) reorganized Soviet Russia into the Union of Soviet Socialist Republics (USSR), including Soviet Ukraine. Socialists who in 1932-33, in order to help establish the world's first Socialist State, murdered an estimated 7-10 million Ukrainians (mostly Eastern Rite Christian farmers like me who were not enthusiastic about Atheist Marxism and Socialism. Yes, like millions of *Holodomor* victims sacrificed on the altar of Relativist, Socialist ideology which considers their (unrealistic) stated ends justify *any* means (even atrocities), I live on a farm; I have Ukrainian blood; and I go to a Ukrainian, Eastern Rite Christian Church). So, as a representative of (*only* the *first*) ten *million* human victims of Marxist, Socialist ideology (of *over 94 million* victims in the 20th Century alone, in several Socialist countries) – Marxist ideology which is built upon and contains within it many of the (literally *anti-Realistic*, literally *anti-Scientific*) philosophical errors described in CHAPTER 3: PHILOSOPHY like *Skepticism* and *Relativism* – I am compelled, as much as any Jewish human cognizant of the *responsibility* to ensure nothing like the *Holocaust* Genocide of six million Jews *ever happens again*, to *warn* Western democracies of the extreme danger they are *right now* in from the same bad, Relativist and Marxist philosophy and inherently totalitarian and oppressive, extremist ideology which much of the West has already been deceived by – again, as Aleksandr Solzhenitsyn, the Nobel Prize-winning author and historian of Soviet (Relativist) Marxism, who lived 18 years in the U.S., *already tried to warn the West, but the West did not listen to him.*

"In actual fact our Russian experience [of totalitarianism]... is vitally important for the West, because by some chance of history we have trodden the same path seventy or eighty years before the West. And now it is with a strange sensation that we look at what is happening to you; many social phenomena that happened in Russia before its collapse are being repeated. Our experience of life is of vital importance to the West, but I am not convinced that you are capable of assimilating it without having gone through it to the end yourselves..."

It is perhaps understandable why Marxist ideology in various forms (including today's Identity Politics) is still so popular. Marxism presents as its end goal a Marxist egalitarian utopia, where everyone is equal, no-one owns anything, and everyone is happy, as the highly centralized State (in theory) equitably redistributes all resources, "from each, according to his ability, to each, according to his need." Marxism from the very beginning planned to be a *global* political and economic system dominating the entire world, and today's globalists supportive of the currently proposed "Great Reset" along Marxist lines see the Coronavirus Pandemic as a *great opportunity* to "reset" the world according to Marxist principles. Thus globalists are still promoting videos like one (on a webpage which starts with the words "Global Agenda") which starts with the phrase of pure Marxism, "you will own nothing, and you'll be happy."[3] But the biggest problem with Marxism has never been as much with its stated end goals, however simplistic and unrealistic they may be, but with the fact that Marxists are philosophical *Relativists not Realists* who therefore do not have a sufficient grasp of *Reality* to work within realistic constraints. One of those constraints is the *normal free-thinking variety of thought and opinion* of any free country – Freedom of Thought which by practical necessity *must be squelched* wherever any serious attempt to implement Marxist principles is made. Hence, so many millions even of good Marxists (like Solzhenitsyn had been) who were sent to the Gulag prison camps just for *not being quite like-minded enough* with their Marxist superiors. Again, Marxism in practice cannot tolerate free-thinking variety – which is why it is so disturbing that today's political parties which now propose originally Marxist principles (and originally Marxist practices, like legal human-killing by abortion, first legalized in Marxist Soviet Russia in 1920) are today purging their parties of anyone who does not "tow the party line" in these areas – and specifically getting rid of those who still hold the herein-identified *Foundational Principles of Human Rights and Democracy* in our Western governments.

To further demonstrate the insane level of ideological commitment to Marxism and Socialism (and the bad, *Relativist not Realist* philosophy underlying them) *regardless of the facts* which is sadly typical of those blinded by the seductively beautiful but hopelessly flawed Marxist utopian egalitarian vision, the following discussion is adapted from this author's short work *The Challenge of the Millions Murdered:*

Timothy Snyder, the Levin Professor of History at Yale University, in his internationally best-selling book *Bloodlands: Europe Between Hitler and Stalin*, gives this harrowing description of the *Holodomor* ("Murder by Starvation") man-made hunger in Soviet Ukraine produced by the Union of Soviet Socialist Republics in service of their Atheist Socialist dream:

---

[3] 8 predictions for the world in 2030 | World Economic Forum (weforum.org), accessed January 17, 2021.

"Survival was a moral as well as a physical struggle. A woman doctor wrote to a friend in June 1933 that she had not yet become a cannibal, but was "not sure that I shall not be one by the time my letter reaches you." The good people died first. Those who refused to steal or to prostitute themselves [with Soviet soldiers] died. Those who gave food to others died. Those who refused to eat corpses died. Those who refused to kill their fellow man died. Parents who resisted cannibalism died before their children did."

To the Relativist/ Atheist/ Marxist/ Communist/ Socialist ideologue mindset, all this massive human suffering and death of people of this author's Ukrainian ethnic background was worth it because it supported the Soviet Socialist ideal, the Marxist utopian vision. In his 1937 book *Word from Nowhere*, Fred Erwin Beal, editor of the American Communist newspaper *Tempo*, testified that while working as a propaganda official in the Ukrainian city of Kharkiv,

"In 1933, I had occasion to call on Gregorii Petrovsky, the [titular] President of the Ukrainian Soviet Republic, in his office in Kharkiv . . . 'Comrade Petrovsky,' I said, "the men in our factory are saying millions of peasants are dying. They say that five million people have died this year, and they hold it up to us [propaganda officials] as a challenge and mockery [to the Soviet Socialist System as not working]. What are we going to tell them?' 'Tell them nothing,' answered President Petrovsky. 'What they say is true. We know that millions are dying. That is unfortunate, but the glorious future of the Soviet Union will justify that."

The Atheist Extremist Left Marxist Soviet Socialist ideologues, freed from all Traditional Western, Judeo-Christian ideas like *equal human preciousness without exception which governments are obligated to protect*, were able to legalize human-killing abortion for the first time since brutal ancient pagan Rome; and able to legalize and implement the *Holodomor* Genocide; and able to support the Marxist Socialist totalitarian government which implemented all this human-killing (tens of millions more murders long after the *Holodomor;* such as those in the Soviet *Gulag* prison system described in detail by Nobel Prize-winning historian of Soviet Marxism Aleksandr Solzhenitsyn); all for the sake of their Socialist dream following Marx's vision (using the violence Marx sanctioned as necessary). Ukraine's independent spirit – a very Christian spirit ever since the 988 AD mass baptisms in rivers – did not share the Atheist Marxist vision. So, the spirit of the freedom-loving Ukrainian (Eastern Rite) Christians, particularly successful peasant farmers known as *kulaks* (mostly belonging to the Eastern Orthodox Church – Moscow or Constantinople Patriarchate – or to the Eastern, Ukrainian Greek Catholic Church to which this author belongs[4]), had to be broken for their Atheist Socialist ideology to prevail.

---

[4] This author is a member of the largest underground church of the 20th Century, which officially did not exist under oppressive Marxist Soviet Communism, yet 5 million Ukrainian Greek Catholic Christians emerged from the underground when the Soviet Bloc "Iron Curtain" was finally lifted.

In the service of that breaking, on August 7, 1932, Soviet Communist Leader Josef Stalin signed the "Decree on the Protection of the Property of State Enterprises, Collective Farms and Cooperatives, and on the Consolidation of Public (Socialist) Property." To deal with "stealing of collective farm property." Sounds reasonable, does it not? What this actually meant was the Atheist Soviet Communist/ Socialist State took and "consolidated" the homes and farms of the (mostly Christian) people and executed them if they tried to use or "steal" any of the "State property" which had been theirs, *including the food they needed to live.* This law became known as the "Law of Five Grain Stalks" because under this law the starving Ukrainians would be shot and killed just for "stealing" a handful of fallen wheat grain ("State property") in an attempt to feed themselves. The Union of Soviet Socialist Republics in 1933 made money selling 1.7 million tons of grain confiscated at gunpoint from Ukraine in 1933, while 28,000 Ukrainians per day were dying of starvation at the height of the *Holodomor* Genocide. Much of the grain was sold to Nazi Germany, which in 1933 had just opened Dachau, the first Nazi Concentration (Death) Camp.

Note the typical dishonesty of the "ideologically lobotomized" who have lost respect for human life so far as to *legalize human-killing* by abortion like the genocidal Soviets (in 1920) and the genocidal Nazis (in 1934) were the first to do. Such legal human-killing ideologues are never honest about what they are doing when they name their laws. Like Stalin's 1932 law sounded reasonable but really meant genocide, so the 2017 law (copied in other provinces in 2018 and 2020) under which this Human Rights scholar and author can still be arrested and imprisoned *sounds reasonable* but really means *totalitarian suppression of Free Speech on behalf of Equal Human Rights for All Humans.* The officially Pro-Choice political party in power, showing their common ideology with the Soviet Marxist government which first legalized human-killing by abortion, called this law "The Safe Access to Abortion Services Act" – as if there was some need to ensure "safety" of people entering the National Capital's abortion clinic, even though most Pro-Life protesters (especially polite Canadians) are there precisely because they are Human Rights Advocates who *value all human lives equally* and are not a threat to anyone. The provincial government could not supply a single clear example of anyone being harassed at the clinic so as to justify their draconian thought-police law. So draconian that local police in my nation's capital told local Pro-Life *Equal Human Rights for All Humans* advocates to not even *look* at the abortion clinic within the large (under the law up to 150 meters/500 feet) "no-free-speech-on-behalf-of-Human-Rights bubble zone" or else "known Pro-Lifers" would be arrested, because the police would take *looking* at the abortion clinic as *staring* at the abortion clinic; and the police would take *staring* at the abortion clinic as showing the "disapproval of abortion" which is now *illegal* to show in any manner under this totalitarian thought-police law. As a Ukrainian Canadian whose family escaped the *Holodomor* Genocide, perpetrated by the first modern State to legalize human-killing abortion, by leaving Ukraine for Canada early enough, I am now deeply embarrassed to say that now you can be arrested *just for looking the wrong way* in my supposed democracy's capital city, if you are "known" to be a Pro-Life *Equal Human Rights for All Humans* advocate who actually believes in *The Foundational Principles of Human Rights and Democracy* like *equal human*

There were surely many more than 5 million underground Christians in oppressive Marxist Communist China in the 20th Century (and today), but from many hundreds of different Christian sects or denominations – not so many as 5 million from one particular underground Christian Church, as in Marxist Soviet Ukraine.

preciousness without exception. This anti-democratic law was introduced into the provincial legislature and passed into law in *only three weeks,* October 4-25, 2017 (the very month this author published the short run "Emergency Edition/Advance Reader Copy" printing of my first book *DEMOCRACY 101: A Voter's and Politician's Manual for Lasting Democracy* – proving how pertinent and vitally necessary that book was (and is) to current Western society! But the current speed record for passing new totalitarian bills into law is for one that mostly copied this law in another Canadian province, introduced and passed in *only eight days,* March 2-10, 2020).

THE LIMITS OF FREEDOM: Behind the "Boundary" signs in these photos taken by the author in a national capital city (and in an increasing number of provinces in this country), you can be arrested and jailed for *any* kind of peaceful Pro-Life *Equal Human Rights for All Humans* Advocacy, even for saying "killing humans is wrong because Human Rights are for all humans;" even for informing people of established medical, scientific facts about abortion; even for just being a "known" Pro-Life Human Rights advocate "staring" or "looking" at an abortion-providing facility (including pharmacies that give "abortion pills"). Pro-Lifers can be arrested literally for "looking the wrong way." Police warned local Pro-Lifers *not to even look at* the capital's abortion clinic because just "staring" will be taken by police as a sign of the "disapproval of abortion" that it is now *illegal* to show under totalitarian thought-police laws passed by officially Pro-Choice political parties in power, laws which restrict normal democratic freedoms of assembly, speech, expression, conscience and religion within up-to-500 foot (150 meter) radius "no-free-speech-bubble-zones."

Within half an hour of this totalitarian bill being passed into law on October 25, 2017, the legal human-killing abortion clinic called the police, who came immediately and dispersed all the silently praying Christians on about Day 30 of a "40 Days for Life" peaceful silent prayer vigil across the street from the abortion clinic – the police informing the peaceful and silent Pro-Life *Equal Human Rights for All Humans* advocates that they no longer had the normal democratic freedoms of speech, expression, assembly, conscience and religion which would allow them to peacefully and silently pray for legal recognition of *Equal Human Rights for All Humans* across the street from where humans were being legally killed, following the 1920 Soviet totalitarian Extremist Left and 1934 Nazi totalitarian Extremist Right precedents (legal human-killing is, of course, *extremist* from any angle, "Left" or "Right"). This author received a phone call from the local 40 Days for Life organizer in the capital right after this, telling me that the rest of the 40 Days for Life was cancelled. Cancelled, including my own Ukrainian Greek Catholic Church's upcoming scheduled day to send a few church members every hour to peacefully, silently pray for *Equal Human Rights for All Humans* with the 40 Days for Life. Cancelled due to *fear of police arrest* for exercising *normal* democratic freedoms peacefully in support of *The Foundational Principles of Human Rights and Democracy* which of course include *equal human preciousness* and *Equal Human Rights for All Humans.*

The provincial government in this jurisdiction of 14 million people had provided no clear example of anyone ever being harassed while going into the national capital's abortion clinic (nor any other clinic), even though this was their excuse for passing such a draconian and totalitarian law. Though actually, of course, nothing even if they found it could ever justify this law, since normal laws and by-laws already cover any *hypothetical* case where a Pro-Life *Human Rights for All Humans* advocate got unruly. An investigation asking for all police reports of all incidents at the Ottawa Morgentaler Clinic over the years revealed that indeed the clinic's claims of harassment or violence by Pro-Lifers around the abortion clinic were exaggerated or entirely fabricated and for years there were no injuries nor charges resulting. The first person charged under this law (who himself had been spit on and even pushed into traffic by Pro-Choicers) did not even technically break it by daring to express anything against abortion; the elderly man did not even *look* at the abortion clinic, as the police had instructed, but was arrested and charged twice anyway just for being a "known Pro-Lifer" carrying signs promoting Free Speech! This author personally delivered a eulogy at his funeral, as he died while awaiting unjust trial after his two arrests just for being a "known Pro-Lifer" daring to advocate for Free Speech in the newly legislated "No-Free-Speech-on-Behalf-of-Human-Rights Bubble Zones." The police thus sent the message to Pro-Life Human Rights Advocates province-wide, "SHUT UP, and don't even SHOW UP, because we are willing to arrest 'known Pro-Lifers' whether or not they actually break the law." No surprise here. Any country that is so out-of-touch with Free Democracy's foundations that they would pass such a law, cannot be reasonably expected to only arrest people who actually break laws! Everything about this law, which has no place in a Free Democracy in any case, is **the totalitarian *politics of intimidation,* pure and simple**. Intimidation (and in the USA, Pro-Choice "antifa" violence against high profile Pro-Lifers) made necessary by the fact that Pro-Choicers who really want to keep their legal abortion "right-to-kill-humans" simply cannot win an honest, rational, scientific, logical argument based on facts, as overwhelmingly proved in this book (especially in CHAPTER 1: FACTS). But nothing is more inherently *violent* than their Pro-Choice position which accepts the legal dismemberment, decapitation, and disembowelment of a living, growing, healthy human baby in a typical abortion, so it is not surprising that when facts give them no justification for legal abortion, they resort to *violence* or intimidation (or intimidating legislation) to keep abortion legal and accessible.

"Abortion is not a 3rd option [to parenthood or adoption] because [unlike parenthood or adoption] it dismembers, decapitates, and disembowels a baby."
– Stephanie Gray
"Violence does not and cannot flourish by itself; it is inevitably intertwined with lying." —
Aleksandr Solzhenitsyn
"Let us not forget that violence does not live alone and is not capable of living alone: it is necessarily interwoven with falsehood. Between them lies the most intimate, the deepest of natural bonds. Violence finds its only refuge in falsehood, falsehood its only support in

violence. Any man who has once acclaimed violence as his method must inexorably choose falsehood as his principle."
— Aleksandr Solzhenitsyn

"Violence does not necessarily take people by the throat and strangle them. Usually it demands no more than an ultimate allegiance from its subjects. They are required merely to become accomplices in its lies."
— Aleksandr Solzhenitsyn

Returning to the *Holodomor* Genocide which was the result of the same kind of Relativist and Marxist thinking as my country's new abortion-supporting laws against Free Speech: Even though Solzhenitsyn's mother was Ukrainian (he observed "Ukraine and Russia are merged in my blood, in my heart, and in my thoughts"), his focus rather than on ethnic genocide was on how the Atheist Marxist Soviet Communist/ Socialist regime committed continual atrocities on all it governed (not just the Ukrainians), including his beloved Russia; but he still commented on the *Holodomor* in 1975:

"they died on the very edge of Europe. And Europe didn't even notice it. The world didn't even notice it—6 million people!"

And it was *Western* Marxists (whose students are still with us today, including many of our professors and politicians) who allowed it to happen! Again, as Solzhenitsyn noted:

"The communist regime in the East could stand and grow due to the enthusiastic support from an enormous number of Western intellectuals who felt a [Marxist; Atheist; Socialist] kinship and refused to see communism's crimes. When they no longer could do so, they tried to justify them."
— Aleksandr Solzhenitsyn

Thus, the British journalists who tried to expose the *Holodomor* Genocide in Ukraine when it was actually happening in the 1930s (Malcolm Muggeridge and Gareth Jones) were silenced (and discredited and fired) by *Western* media policies of not saying anything negative about the great Soviet Socialist experiment which that "enormous number" of Western Atheists and Socialists *wanted* to succeed, and they always pointed to the Soviet Union as justification for their Atheist and Marxist and Socialist ideals. The Western Atheists and Socialists were intellectually dishonest enough to actually *refuse to hear the truth of Soviet atrocities* – and to give the Pulitzer Prize to the New York Times Moscow correspondent (Walter Duranty) who helped the Soviets publicly deny the genocide. Even though the British-born Duranty actually knew, and privately admitted in the British Embassy, that millions were dying in Soviet Ukraine. **Horrifically, it was Duranty, in the context of justifying Soviet Marxist leader Josef Stalin's atrocities in service of setting up the world's first Socialist State, mostly hidden atrocities which included the *Holodomor* Genocide, who coined the phrase, "you can't make an omelet without breaking some eggs." This Ukrainian Canadian author invites the reader to imagine, next time you hear that common phrase, ten million unique and exquisitely decorated traditional Ukrainian Easter Eggs, representing ten million unique and exquisite Ukrainian human beings, smashed to bits in service of practically establishing the "omelet" of the Marxist Atheistic political ideology of Socialism.** In Marxist ideology, the "glorious future" end of the seductively promised but ill-conceived and unrealistic classless Communist Utopia always justifies *any* means in vain attempt to usher in the unrealistic utopia – any means including the most horrifying atrocities and genocides, as proven by Marxist ideologues again and again and again in the USSR/Soviet Bloc countries, China, Cambodia, Vietnam, North Korea and so on. Together killing more than 94 million people in the 20th Century alone (according to the 1997 scholarly tome by multiple scholars, *The Black Book of Communism: Crimes, Terror, Repression*).

To this day the legacy of Western Marxists in universities (and the media) as Solzhenitsyn warned us, has included making sure that the Right-Wing Extremist Nazi atrocities are far more well known in the West than the much larger-scale atrocities over many more decades committed by Marxists in more countries. The over 94 million deaths in the 20th Century alone due to Marxist policies are well-documented, but Marxist Socialist atrocities, unlike the Nazi Fascist atrocities, are rarely talked about or depicted in movies. This author once read an article reporting a study, the headline declaring something like "Today's young people do not know history — and they love Socialism." A more obvious and logical connection between two things could not be stated. Both are the work of the "enormous number" of Western Marxist Socialists in education and media who Solzhenitsyn warned us decades ago were taking the West to the totalitarian ends now knocking on our door.

The overall numbers of Marxist Socialist State murders are far higher than the abominable Nazi Fascist State murders. This below Solzhenitsyn quote describing part of the assigned work of his fellow prisoners in the Soviet Marxist *Gulag* prison camp system sardonically captures perhaps the only significant difference between the Extremist Left Marxist/ Communist/ Socialist ideology which is still embraced by the Pro-Choice legal human-killing Left in the West, and the Extremist Right Nazi (German for National Socialist) ideology which is universally despised for killing millions of Jewish humans in the gas chambers of the Nazi concentration camps:

"The corpses were hauled away on sledges or on carts, depending on the time of the year. Sometimes, for convenience, they used one box for six corpses, and if there were no boxes,

then they tied the hands and legs with cords so they didn't flop about. After this they piled them up like logs and covered them with bast matting. If there was an ammonal available, a special brigade of gravediggers would dynamite pits for them. Otherwise they had to dig the graves, always common graves, in the ground: either big ones for a large number or shallow ones for four at a time. (In the springtime, a stink used to waft into the camp from shallower graves, and they would then send last-leggers to deepen them). On the other hand, no one can accuse us of gas chambers."
— Aleksandr Solzhenitsyn

Marxism/Socialism has killed more precious humans than anything else, but nevertheless:

"Modern society is hypnotized by socialism. It is prevented by socialism from seeing the mortal danger it is in. And one of the greatest dangers of all is that you have lost all sense of danger, you cannot even see where it's coming from as it moves swiftly towards you."
— Aleksandr Solzhenitsyn

The "enormous number" of Western Marxist-influenced intellectuals Solzhenitsyn speaks of have done their job of insidiously preparing the West for a Marxist takeover (and Marxist "Great Reset") well, making sure that the words "Marxist" and "Socialist" do not elicit the same visceral repulsion as the words "Nazi" or "Fascist" – even though Marxist Socialists have killed far more millions of people over more time in more countries than the reprehensible Fascist Nazis ever did. Thus, it is up to honest intellectuals like this author to *warn* the West, in this non-partisan (but anti-extremist) book series highlighting democratic foundations, where the Marxist and Neo-Marxist ideology it blithely accepts is taking the West. This author hereby warns the West as a representative of (only) the first ten million murdered victims of Marxism, of my ethnic heritage; representing ten million shattered unique exquisite Ukrainian human "Easter eggs" smashed to bits just because "you can't make an omelet (a Socialist State) without breaking a few eggs" – as the devilish New York Times Moscow correspondent Walter Duranty, who publicly denied in print but privately admitted the *Holodomor* Genocide – was the first to say (and the Marxist-influenced Western media Solzhenitsyn warned us about rewarded Duranty with the Pulitzer Prize for his journalistic work in the Soviet Union).

Solzhenitsyn again sardonically noted,

"Hitler was a mere disciple, but he had all the luck: his murder camps have made him famous, whereas no one has any interest in ours at all." — Aleksandr Solzhenitsyn

Western Marxists and Communists and Socialists in Western universities and mainstream media have seen to that. It is only very recently, thanks in part to the de-classification of old Soviet secret documents, that the full truth of the *Holodomor* Genocide in the world's first Socialist State is starting to become more well-known. Forty nations (including the post-Soviet Russian Federation, plus the United Nations) have formally acknowledged the *Holodomor* killing millions of this author's fellow Ukrainians in 1932-33. Most use the figure of 7-10 million killed estimate which was used in the United Nations' 2003 Joint Statement on the *Holodomor* signed by twenty-five countries, though outside estimates range from 3.5-12 million killed (though whenever you have to estimate the dead in millions, the precise number should not affect the horror of the genocide). Most acknowledge that the deaths were a specific, targeted genocide of the Ukrainian ethnic group, which is difficult to credibly deny when one considers the many other "Russification" policies within the Soviet Union. Long after the *Holodomor* ("Murder by Starvation" or "Death Famine") the Soviets still tried to stamp out distinct Ukrainian language and culture (this author's cultural heritage), even to the point of rounding up and shooting thousands of *bandurists* – largely street musicians who played the distinctly Ukrainian stringed instrument the *bandura*. Russia is one of the few nations which acknowledges the *Holodomor's* many millions of deaths without calling it a genocide, probably trying to avoid guilty feelings, which they need not do. This Ukrainian Canadian author bears no ill will towards Russian people for the *Holodomor* Genocide, always calling it a *Soviet* or *Marxist* crime against humanity, never a Russian crime, in the same way this author blames the Nazi Party for the *Holocaust* Genocide, and not the German people as a whole. Both Russia and Germany were violated and oppressed by inhuman *ideologies* (both undergirded by Skeptic Atheist Relativist philosophy, as detailed in CHAPTER 3: PHILOSOPHY) which led to these (legal) Soviet and Nazi genocides (and led to legal human-killing by abortion in both countries). The ideologues perpetrating each genocide also oppressed many ethnic Russians or Germans.

Similarly, in the Cold War which threatened the entire world with nuclear annihilation for decades, the enemy of human life and freedom was never the Russians. It was the seriously flawed and ultimately inhuman and totalitarian (and philosophically *Relativist not Realist*) Marxist *ideology* which had fooled the Russians (which had even fooled them into being the first country to legalize human-killing abortion that legally eradicates *The Inherent Human Right to Live*). And this ideology was already in the West too, already fooling Westerners, who later willingly took on legal human-killing abortion without even having been militarily conquered by the totalitarian States (Soviet Russia and Nazi Germany) which first legalized abortion only because they did not believe that *killing humans is wrong*. Westerners have been ideologically conquered from within instead, now *willingly* taking on the *politically extremist*, legal human-killing abortion and euthanasia which the Nazis (the first, extremist political party to legalize *both* forms of human-killing) *would have forcefully imposed upon the West if the Nazis had won World War II.* Westerners already ideologically conquered by *extremist thinking* have willingly taken on extremist legal human-killing abortion and euthanasia which the Nazis were condemned for in 1948 at the Nuremberg War Crimes Trials as yet another Nazi "crime against humanity." The same year that specifically in response to Nazi doctors thus betraying the most ancient and sacred non-killing standards of the Medical Profession, the Declaration of Geneva reiterated the ancient doctors' non-killing Hippocratic Oath in the newly-worded Doctors' Promise "I will maintain the utmost respect for human life, *from the time of conception.*" The same year the newly-formed United Nations produced the

Universal Declaration of Human Rights specifically to prevent future "barbaric acts" as those done in Nazi Germany, *including legal human-killing abortion and euthanasia.* This is why THE THINKING REVOLUTION announced by this author first in the book *Pro-Life Equals Pro-Democracy* is so important to lasting Human Rights and Democratic Freedoms: every human must be on guard against *ideology* instead of *education* that makes *evil* seem *good.*

"To do evil a human being must first of all believe that what he's doing is good…"
"Ideology – that is what gives evildoing its long-sought justification and gives the evildoer the necessary steadfastness and determination. That is the social theory which helps to make his acts seem good instead of bad in his own and others' eyes....
Thanks to ideology the twentieth century was fated to experience evildoing calculated on a scale in the millions."
— Aleksandr Solzhenitsyn

Fortunately, the long-hidden truth about the *Holodomor* Genocide of this author's ethnic group, committed by the world's first Socialist State, and the vital lessons it has for today's West that is still "hypnotized" by Socialism as Solzhenitsyn observed, is starting to come out, and even to at last be depicted in movies (though still not near as often as Nazi evil is shown). The 2017 film *Bitter Harvest* is a Ukrainian love story of childhood sweethearts, partially set against the backdrop of the *Holodomor* Genocide. You can now see Welsh journalist Gareth Jones' true story in the 2020 movie *Mr. Jones.* People should see this movie to help get this reality into their heads: *Like Aleksandr Solzhenitsyn, the Nobel Prize-winning premier historian of Soviet Marxism who lived 18 years in the U.S. testified, Western mainstream media has been Marxist-influenced and hiding/controlling information for Marxist purposes – at least since the 1930s Western media cover-up of the Soviet Marxist Holodomor Genocide of this author's ethnic group.* People should see this movie, especially all who have already forever lost their small family businesses, or who are otherwise still now suffering under unnecessarily oppressive Coronavirus Pandemic lockdowns and other restrictions set by Pro-Choice, Neo-Marxist Identity Politics governments enthusiastically using the Pandemic as an excuse to attempt to implement a global Marxist "Great Reset," *all while the mainstream media Solzhenitsyn long warned us was Marxist-influenced is keeping mind-numbing Coronavirus alarmism and panic unscientifically high by unscientifically treating mere "positive PCR tests" without symptoms as if they were active Covid-19 infections; and by hiding ("cancelling," censoring) the extremely pertinent scientific testimony* of over 55,680 (and counting) medical professionals, including over 13,790 (and counting) *infectious disease epidemiologists* and other *medical scientists* who have signed the Great Barrington Declaration (https://gbdeclaration.org) that (drafted by expert infectious disease epidemiologists and public health scientists from prestigious Harvard, Oxford, and Stanford universities) testifies that lockdowns do far more medical harm than good, and that *life can go back to normal except for "Focused Protection" for the minority actually vulnerable to the novel Coronavirus.* Just as *Western* mainstream media for Marxist purposes hid all the facts of the *Holodomor* Genocide while it was happening, pretending no such genocidal forced starvation of millions existed, and discredited and punished the honest journalists who tried to tell the truth of the matter

(Discrediting and firing honest *Holodomor* whistle-blowers like Malcolm Muggeridge and Gareth Jones, before Jones was eventually murdered), so today the Western mainstream media, still Marxist-influenced as Solzhenitsyn repeatedly testified, similarly pretends the Great Barrington Declaration just does not exist; or tries to discredit and dismiss[5] it when it (rarely) acknowledges its existence at all. And, in further support of the Marxist "Great Reset" piggybacking on the Coronavirus Pandemic, "Big Tech" (now intertwined with mainstream media as primary arms of Neo-Marxist "Cancel Culture" censorship) has been censoring, erasing and "cancelling" much video medical science expert testimony and even cancelling and removing from YouTube entire smaller news channel services which actually report on pertinent medical science concerning the Coronavirus Pandemic which *does not support ongoing lockdowns which serve the Marxist Socialist "Great Reset."*

It serves a Marxist, Communist, Socialist State well to eliminate small businesses by the thousands and make previously financially independent people financially dependent upon the State. Which the Coronavirus Pandemic lockdowns have been excellent at doing. While the governments implementing these ongoing lockdowns are ignoring not only the testimony of tens of thousands of medical professionals and medical scientists that lockdowns do not help prevent the spread of the novel Coronavirus (and do more medical harm than good), but these governments are even ignoring the publicly available Coronavirus statistics from all the world's countries since the beginning of the Pandemic, which demonstrate that in fact countries and states with very strict "Coronavirus Measures" including strict lockdowns and mask mandates had about the same spread of Coronavirus cases and about the same Coronavirus death rate as countries and states with mild Coronavirus Measures and no lockdowns. Meaning, as great as lockdowns are for preparing for a global Marxist "Great Reset," and for damaging the world economy enough to make countries desperate enough to try a global Marxist "Great Reset," there is no medical nor mathematical/ statistical justification for continued economy-destroying lockdowns – much less any justification for the total ban on all public religious worship using the Pandemic as an excuse, in the jurisdiction in which this author lives with over 5 million others. It is very much like I already live in a typical Marxist, Atheist Communist State, because during the Coronavirus Pandemic now ongoing into 2021 I (with over 5 million others) for months now since November 19, 2020 am allowed by the government to be near hundreds of others at a time for unlimited hours for

---

[5] In a blatantly dishonest example of non-expert Marxist-influenced mainstream media trying to discredit exceptionally significant and numerous expert medical science testimonies against oppressive "Coronavirus" lockdowns and mask mandates which ideologue journalists have done their best to hide – like they hid the *Holodomor* genocide – some dishonest journalists misused the Great Barrington Declaration's online signature form to themselves add a (mere) handful of fake signatures, and then other dishonest ideologue journalists reported that the Great Barrington Declaration was fake! But the 13,796 medical scientists (as of mid-March 2021) who have signed the Declaration (the most important category of signatories) are followed up, approved, and vetted, with the university or medical institute they work for published, so anything put up by the dishonest to discredit the Declaration is removed soon enough. The great Barrington Declaration organization itself has posted this in its Q and A on their website: Q: Are all the online signatures real? A: No. Some pranksters added fake signatures such as Dr. Johnny Bananas, Prof. Spon'Ge'Bob SQ.UarePants, Dr. Neal Ferguson, Prof. Ware Thamask, and Dr. Person Fakename. In a strange twist, one journalist bragged on Twitter about adding fake names, after which other journalists criticized the Declaration for having fake signatures. Anyhow, the fake signatures are less than 1% of the total, and most have been removed from the count tracker.

many secular activities (going to crowded malls; museums; "fun centers" and restaurants much smaller than many worship houses), while public religious worship services are entirely banned, in a clearly bigoted against religion double standard for Coronavirus restrictions. Exactly as one would expect from an Atheist Marxist-influenced government. Of course, not all jurisdictions imposing lockdowns are presently run by Neo-Marxist Identity Politics political parties and governors/premiers etc. who want the Marxist "Great Reset." *But they are all highly pressured into imposing (proven medically useless) lockdowns and mask mandates anyway* by the (non-expert) Western mainstream media's continuous extreme "Coronavirus alarmism" which unscientifically treats mere "positive PCR tests" (frequently accompanied by no symptoms) as if they were active cases of Covid-19. And which – just like Western Media pretended the *Holodomor* Genocide did not exist – pretends that there just is no Great Barrington Declaration (http://gbdeclaration.org) in which vast numbers of medical professionals with exceptional medical and scientific qualifications and credibility together declare:

"As infectious disease epidemiologists and public health scientists we have grave concerns about the damaging physical and mental health impacts of the prevailing COVID-19 policies, and recommend an approach we call Focused Protection…"
– First paragraph of The Great Barrington Declaration

The Great Barrington Declaration was drafted October 2020 by the most pertinent medical specialists from world-class prestigious universities, and signed (as of mid-March 2021) by 13,796 (and counting) medical scientists and 41,890 (and counting) doctors and other medical practitioners (hundreds more qualified medical professionals keep adding their signatures each month). The medical scientist signatures are followed up and vetted, publishing the details of which university or medical institute each of these medical scientist signatories works for. So, no *healthy* democracies would ever do what is being done in today's very *unhealthy* democracies – governments egged on by statistically and scientifically unjustified media *alarmism* making needlessly oppressive policies which support a Marxist "Great Reset" *while ignoring* the Great Barrington Declaration and mostly *pretending this substantial movement of medical professionals does not even exist and therefore never addressing it.* In *healthy* democracies this large consensus of highly qualified medical specialists would be very seriously considered before any healthy democracy would dare be so drastic as to impose "Coronavirus Measures" that restrict normal democratic freedoms and civil liberties and do so much damage to the world economy. In *healthy* democracies, if a government were to decide on a policy *against* this considerable medical consensus of medical scientists and doctors, they would be duty-bound to *explain* just *why* they disregarded this considerable medical testimony and did not follow its recommendations. At the very least, medical testimony both for and against drastic lockdown measures would be carefully listened to and thoughtfully weighed (in consideration of the publicly available statistics on the Pandemic so far – which definitely favor the position against continuing lockdowns!) before any healthy democratic government would impose drastic and economy-destroying restrictions on normal freedoms. Only totalitarian-oriented, compromised democracies (and media) would ever do what is being done – *pretending that all qualified medical voices against their preferred policies just do not exist, and never even addressing them.*

But, as this author's HUMAN RIGHTS EDUCATION FOR LASTING FREE DEMOCRACY book series demonstrates, today's democracies are the farthest thing from healthy; long before the Coronavirus Pandemic, today's democracies were *already* teetering on the edge of totalitarianism (since 2017 I already could be arrested and jailed just for saying "killing humans is wrong"). Long before the Pandemic it was already painfully obvious (to the Human-Rights-educated and intellectually honest) that many Western political parties were (wittingly or witlessly) totalitarian-oriented and completely untrustworthy to lead in the global instability of any future conflict or pandemic that gave them an *excuse* for government over-reach nullifying normal democratic freedoms which they were *already legislating away* anyways.

As discussed in more detail in Chapter 3, philosophical *Relativists not Realists* (including Neo-Marxists and Pro-Choicers) have only a dubious grip on *Reality* or *Science.* To them there are no *objective* facts but everything is ultimately *subjective* and therefore *relative.* To them, lying comes easy, since to a subjectivist Relativist, anything ultimately only *is* what they subjectively *say* it is or *accept* it is, and they need not back up their subjective opinions with facts because they ultimately do not believe in facts. This insane (literally *divorced from reality*) underlying (usually unconscious) philosophical worldview of Relativism (versus Realism) explains some of the more bizarre and distressing things we now read in mainstream media and hear from government officials, who have simply labelled as "misinformation about the Coronavirus" any *facts* about the Great Barrington Declaration or about any of the many other large groupings of medical professionals and medical scientists against the oppressive lockdowns and other current "Coronavirus Measures." To a Relativist not Realist, *any medical science – even from world-class, top medical scientists from top universities – even from tens of thousands of doctors and medical scientists in agreement* – can simply be labelled "misinformation about the Coronavirus" and therefore dismissed handily, just because these *facts* get in the way of their preferred oppressive policies which support a Marxist "Great Reset" by destroying the world economy and making previously financially independent people dependent upon the government to (micro)manage everything – like in Marxist, Communist, Socialist totalitarian States. The mainstream media which Solzhenitsyn warned us was Marxist-influenced, and which has obviously been so at least since the Western mainstream media covered up and hid all the facts about the *Holodomor* and later Marxist atrocities in the Socialist Soviet Union (and gave the Pulitzer Prize to the journalist who most covered up the genocide), *is ready and willing to ignore or bury, discredit or dismiss any facts against their preferred narrative* about the Coronavirus Pandemic or anything else. Everyone should become aware of this little-known reality commented on by the Nobel Prize-winning author and preeminent historian of Soviet Marxism, expert in such matters:

"Such as it is, the press has become the greatest power within the Western World, more powerful than the legislature, the executive and judiciary. One would like to ask; by whom has it been elected and to whom is it responsible?"

This is why some Canadians think of the mainstream media as "the Media Party" – which often bullies even the closer-to-center political parties into doing whatever the extremist Media Party wants it to (notably kicking out of their parties any members who are actually bold in speaking up for the "Pro-Life" *Foundational Principles of Human Rights and Democracy*), and these non-extremist parties lack the courage to stand against the Media Party which backs the Pro-Choice (legal human-killing extremist) Neo-Marxist Identity Politics parties. Hopefully this HUMAN RIGHTS EDUCATION FOR LASTING FREE DEMOCRACY book series will at last give such spineless parties the knowledge and courage they need to finally stand up boldly against the Relativist, Marxist ideological takeover of our democracy. And hopefully, many of those in the now "officially Pro-Choice" and Neo-Marxist parties will be intellectually honest enough to *learn* from this book series that they have been on the wrong path. *All* of these politicians need to understand that *once Solzhenitsyn was out of the oppressive Soviet Union and in the "Free West," living in the U.S. for 18 years, he noticed and pointed out that the West was headed, if more slowly, in the same direction as the Marxist Soviet Union (towards totalitarianism), only by a different route.* Solzhenitsyn even noticed and pointed out *how* the censorship of news and ideas which was essential to totalitarian Soviet Socialism and Communism just found a new, more subtle, patient and insidious expression in the West:

"Without any censorship, in the West fashionable trends of thought and ideas are carefully separated from those which are not fashionable; nothing is forbidden, but what is not fashionable will hardly ever find its way into periodicals or books or be heard in colleges. Legally your researchers are free, but they are conditioned by the fashion of the day."
— Aleksandr Solzhenitsyn

Nobody in the West today can afford to remain unaware of this little-known reality because as it was "not fashionable" for Marxist-influenced Western mainstream media to report any facts about genocide and atrocities in the Marxist Socialist Soviet Union, so it is now "not fashionable" for Western mainstream media to report on anything that disagrees with currently prevailing oppressive "Coronavirus Measures" like lockdowns and mask mandates and so on *that support the Marxist "Great Reset"* which is a publicly stated goal of the World Economic Forum featured in *Time* magazine and (openly or secretly) supported by many, many world leaders who have been infected with Relativist, Marxist thinking that, as this book series shows, is *antithetical to lasting Free Democracy, and even antithetical to (Realist not Relativist) Science itself.*

The Relativist and Marxist-influenced have *ideology instead of education*; deep down in their subconscious, they have no use for facts, since deep down, Relativists do not believe in *objective* reality but instead desire to *shape* reality to match their *subjective* opinion of what reality "should" be. So, Relativist and Marxist-influenced mainstream media and governments simply ignore or dismiss or minimize all those facts that would lead intellectually honest policy-makers to a very different Coronavirus Pandemic response than the oppressive, economy-destroying one which is prevailing. They simply label as "misinformation about the Coronavirus" any facts, and *even logical conclusions drawn from publicly available statistics,* which *disagree with currently prevailing oppressive "Coronavirus Measures" like lockdowns and mask mandates, which support their preferred Marxist Socialist "Great Reset."* Again, they simply label as "misinformation about the Coronavirus" any voices *even from world-class, top medical scientists from top universities – even from tens of thousands of doctors and medical scientists in agreement –* that disagree with their Relativist, Marxist-tainted choice to impose unnecessarily oppressive "Coronavirus Measures" like lockdowns which do so much to assist an eventual Marxist "Great Reset" and ideological conquest of the globe, in final fulfillment of Marx's always-global intention of Marxist ideas dominating the whole world. The "Free West" is now teetering on the brink of losing all pretense of Free Democracy because it failed to take Solzhenitsyn's warnings seriously:

"To coexist with communism on the same planet is impossible. Either it will spread, cancer-like, to destroy mankind, or else mankind will have to rid itself of communism (and even then face lengthy treatment for secondary tumors)."
— Aleksandr Solzhenitsyn

Aleksandr Solzhenitsyn's "cancer" metaphor here is very personal, for he had cancer, and used his experience to write his novel *Cancer Ward.* After the fall of Soviet Communism and the end of the Cold War against it, as Solzhenitsyn predicted, we in the West are still needing much "lengthy treatment" for the "secondary tumors" of Marxist Communist Socialist influence. Marxist influence such as legal abortion and Neo-Marxist Identity Politics with its "Political Correctness" and "Cancel Culture" – and now, the Socialist "Great Reset."

"To reject this inhuman Communist ideology is simply to be a human being. Such a rejection is more than a political act. It is a protest of our souls against those who would have us forget the concepts of good and evil."

"Communism is breathing down the neck of all moderate forms of socialism, which are unstable."

"Socialism of any type leads to a total destruction of the human spirit." — Aleksandr Solzhenitsyn

---

I stated above that I do not subscribe to any particular "conspiracy theory." There is no need to, of course, since in general terms it is well known Karl Marx from the beginning intended his Marxist Communist Socialist political and economic system to be *global*, and good Marxists ever since have always openly and/or secretly worked towards this goal just because they are good Marxists. Marx (and Engels)' key book *The Communist Manifesto* itself is quite clear that global domination is the ultimate goal of Marxists. So, no-one should be surprised if the Marxist-influenced are actively, whether openly or secretly, undermining free democracies – it would be surprising if they were not!

"It is astonishing that Communism has been writing about itself in the most open way, in black and white, for 125 years, and even more openly, more candidly in the beginning. The Communist Manifesto, for instance, which everyone knows by name and which almost no one takes the trouble to read, contains even more terrible things than what has actually been done. It is perfectly amazing. The whole world can read, everyone is literate, yet somehow no one wants to understand. Humanity acts as if it does not understand what Communism is, as if it does not want to understand, is not capable of understanding."
– Aleksandr Solzhenitsyn

[In The Communist Manifesto, Marx (writing with his friend Engels) quotes an objection to Marxism that:]
"Communism abolishes eternal truths, it abolishes all religion, and all morality, instead of constituting them on a new basis; it therefore acts in contradiction to all past historical experience."
[In his answer to this objection Marx admits:]
"The Communist revolution is the most radical rupture with traditional property relations; no wonder that its development involved the most radical rupture with traditional ideas."
[Marx and Engels here admit that their
Marxist ideology is the most radical, it wipes the most of the past away, ... which they foolishly claim is necessary because they have radically reinterpreted all history according to their radical ideology (Today's Neo-Marxist "Identity Politics" with its "Political Correctness" and "Cancel Culture" merely continues Marx's simplistic and unrealistic reinterpretation of all history in terms of adversarial "class struggle" between those given Marxist labels of "oppressed" and "privileged"). Marx shows contempt not only for traditional property relations but also for traditional family relations, which he mocks as much as do many of today's totalitarian-oriented Neo-Marxists. Note that all the many current Neo-Marxist trends, habits and specific movements - most recently BLM and its wave of iconoclastic terrorism, which reduce contact with history - all serve to strengthen Atheist Relativist Marxism. After Marx describes in detail why violence is necessary to initiate Marxism, and mocks all pre-Marxist Socialists who wanted to establish a Socialist State without violence, Marx ended his Communist Manifesto with this explicit declaration of the violence inherent in Marxism:]

---

*"The Communists disdain to conceal their views and aims.
They openly declare that their ends can be attained only by
the forcible overthrow of all existing social conditions.
Let the ruling classes tremble at a Communistic revolution."*
– Karl Marx & Friedrich Engels, The Communist Manifesto

---

*"The clock of communism has stopped striking. But its concrete building has not yet come
crashing down. For that reason ... we must try to save ourselves from being crushed by its
rubble."*
— Aleksandr Solzhenitsyn

The global domination of Marxist ideas was always the ultimate goal of Marx and all good Marxists. And today, no-one has to *speculate* or "theorize" a specific current Marxist conspiracy to take over the world any more because the global Marxist Socialist "Great Reset" is now *publicly* proclaimed as the goal of many of our witless ideologue Western politicians, schooled by the "enormous number" of Western Marxist intellectuals Solzhenitsyn warned us about, with their unscientific and "impaired thinking ability" because of the anti-scientific Relativism underlying Marxism, who have not a clue where Western freedom comes from because they sadly have never been exposed to this book series' HUMAN RIGHTS EDUCATION FOR LASTING FREE DEMOCRACY containing and clearly laying out the key facts of History, Science, Logic and Philosophy which are most pertinent to lasting Human Rights and freedoms for every human on this planet. **This author charitably assumes that the majority of today's Marxist-influenced ideologue politicians in my country, in America and around the globe will be (or will suddenly realize they need to be)** *intellectually honest enough* **to receive and learn this vital Human Rights** *education* **to replace their** *ideology* **– the same ideology behind the genocide mass murder of millions of my ethnic group, as described above.** And if that *challenge of the millions murdered* is not enough to make some of today's Pro-Choice Neo-Marxist Identity Politics ideologues actually start to THINK honestly, intelligently and logically enough to abandon their *ideology* for *education* and abandon their uneducated enthusiasm for a Marxist global "Great Reset," this author hereby gives THE INTELLECTUAL HONESTY CHALLENGE in Chapter 7 to those foolish and dishonest politicians (and political parties). I await your written responses in evidence that you have started at last to THINK. Your unthinking, vacuous ideology has now been exposed and you can no longer get away with just playing dumb and doing whatever you want in public policy. From now on you must justify your public policy in terms of *(Scientific) Realism not (Skeptical) Relativism* and in terms of *The Foundational Principles of Human Rights and Democracy* – which are just going to become more and more well-known from now on, leaving you less and less room to hide your dishonesty and lack of critical intelligence.

This author spends little time or attention considering particular "conspiracy theories" (some of which are far more credible, even likely, than others, with at least some good evidence pointing to a need for concern and further investigation where possible). But I do not spend much time on them because even if some of them are true, I am not in any position to prove them definitively; **but as a Human Rights scholar I am in a position to prove definitively from Human Rights History, Science, Logic and the History of Philosophy that the ideologies motivating such things are toxic to lasting Human Rights and democratic freedoms for everyone;** and thus I expect all but the most unintelligent or evil (surely a minority) will *stop* pursuing ultimately anti-realistic, anti-scientific, anti-democratic and anti-human ideologies such as any form of Relativism and Marxism (and stop originally Marxist practices which deny *Equal Human Rights for All Humans*, like human-killing abortion), once exposed to the "most pertinent facts" which they did not previously know. I do honestly believe that for many, vacuous Marxism/ Socialism has merely "filled in the gap" of their *lack of concrete knowledge.* I honestly believe that mere *widespread ignorance* of the *most pertinent to Lasting Free Democracy* facts of History, Science, Logic and Philosophy collected in this book series is enough to account for all the totalitarian-oriented laws and policies that I have been observing (especially in my country) since 2015, without postulating any *necessarily* conscious conspiracy (though I cannot rule these out). I suspect mere *ignorance* leading to *incompetence* to govern a *lasting* democracy motivates many of the Western politicians and parties which have been passing all the totalitarian-oriented laws and policies, at least among the more intellectually honest of them who are not actually "ideologically lobotomized" into "wilful unintelligence," blinded by intellectually dishonest, anti-scientific, relativistic and politically extremist ideologies such as Neo-Nazism, Marxism or Neo-Marxist Identity Politics and its "Cancel Culture."

So, there is little need to look for and directly address any consciously-implemented conspiracies against Western freedom – even though there must at least be some – because it is enough to identify, as this book series does, the *underlying principles* most conducive to lasting freedom and Human Rights; and the *underlying principles* most destructive of them. I do honestly hope that merely by in this book series clearly identifying and laying out all these little known "most pertinent" facts, the majority of those who now are (wittingly or unwittingly) working to dismantle Western Free Democracy and Human Rights worldwide will be intellectually honest enough to *learn better* and stop doing that!

"The truth is like a lion. You do not need to defend it. Unleash it, and it defends itself" – Saint Augustine of Hippo

---

The HUMAN RIGHTS EDUCATION FOR LASTING FREE DEMOCRACY book series (including this handbook) unleashes the truth, the *genuine article* of just what brings freedom and prosperity to any nation (and identifies what naturally destroys a free nation). Solzhenitsyn concurs that "one word of truth outweighs the whole world." His 35-million-copies-selling book *The Gulag Archipelago* has already torpedoed the ship of Marxism/ Communism/ Socialism, by revealing the ideological evil and ultimate violence inherent in all forms of (Relativist) Marxism. The Soviet Union, the world's first Socialist State, was built on such a vacuous philosophical and ideological foundation, and only subsisted at all because of a web of lies which Solzhenitsyn exposed (which is why all the Marxist-influenced Western professors early on worked to erase or "cancel" Solzhenitsyn's memory as well as they could, and most young "university-educated" people I ask now have *never heard* of Nobel Prize-winning Solzhenitsyn who did so much to bring down the totalitarian Socialist Soviet Union which committed only the *first* of many genocides in Marxist Socialist countries, against my ethnic group).

Western mainstream media for Marxist purposes undisputedly hid and discredited real news of the *Holodomor* ("Murder by Starvation") of my ethnic group in Soviet Ukraine. Aleksandr Solzhenitsyn (who died only in 2008) as an unparalleled expert in such matters undisputedly testified Western mainstream media (and education) was *still* Marxist influenced by "an enormous number of Western intellectuals who felt a kinship and refused to see communism's crimes. When they could no longer do so, they tried to justify them." Solzhenitsyn testified as a premier expert in Soviet Marxist Socialism that Western media (and education) were Marxist-influenced and were slowly taking the West to totalitarian ends, though lamenting that he was not sure the West would heed his warning (so far it has not. That is why I can be arrested and jailed in my extremely unhealthy "democracy" for peaceful Human Rights advocacy or for speaking verified scientific facts that disagree with government ideologies or even just for "looking the wrong way" in large "no-free-speech-bubble-zones").

So, ever since successfully covering up the *Holodomor* Genocide and successfully discrediting those who tried to tell the truth about such Marxist Communist Socialist atrocities; ever since successfully ensuring that the words "Marxist," "Communist" and "Socialist" do not evoke the same negative visceral response in Westerners as the words "Nazi" and "Fascist" rightly do, even though Marxist, Communist, Socialist ideologues killed far more people in more countries than the Nazis ever had opportunity to do, *Western mainstream media has seen to it that those who notice and try to point out possible evidence of anti-democratic conspiracies which is at least worth looking into further is mocked and ridiculed as non-credible.* So much so that by today the very term "conspiracy theory" in most people's minds immediately evokes the *assumption* that anyone *suggesting* there *might* be a conspiracy to assault or end Western freedom and set up anti-democratic ideology is a non-credible crackpot *whose concerns should be summarily dismissed.* While some conspiracy theories are indeed not very credible, it is most certainly going too far the other way to assume that *there could never possibly be any kind of conspiracy against or undermining Western democracies.*

It is well said that "the price of freedom is eternal vigilance." But we have been conditioned by the Marxist-influenced mainstream media Solzhenitsyn warned us about *to not be vigilant for Free Democracy at all*; conditioned to *automatically dismiss any evidence or suggestion* of any kind of anti-democratic conspiracy, *as if* it was just impossible that breaches in the security of our free Western way of life could ever happen. *Leaving the Marxist-influenced with a free hand* to undermine Western freedom as they have with their vacuous, anti-scientific and philosophically Relativist not Realist *ideology instead of education.* The long-term insidious sowing of Relativist philosophy and the Marxist ideology built on it (and the adoption of originally Marxist human-killing practices like abortion, first legalized by the same Soviets and Nazis who also legalized genocides) has resulted in the bizarre facts that this author can be arrested and jailed for peacefully saying "killing humans is wrong" where it is most pertinent. And this author had to give a eulogy at the funeral of an elderly man who died while awaiting trial after being arrested twice just for being a "known" *Equal Human Rights for All Humans* advocate peacefully carrying signs promoting Free Speech — and there was no outcry about this travesty, because so many people (even otherwise good people) can no longer even tell the difference between totalitarianism and democracy.

Since this book calls attention to the overwhelming evidence that ideologues who simply *do not know most of the key facts in this book* and so form their politics from *vacuous ideology* instead of *solid education* are in both smaller and greater ways undermining Free Democracy worldwide; and since this book identifies Marxism (also known as Communism or Socialism) as one of the greater threats (as is the philosophical Relativism underlying both Marxism and Fascism), chances are good that the Western Marxist-influenced mainstream media which dishonestly hid the *Holodomor* genocide of my ethnic group, in order to dishonestly distract from and dismiss this evidence, might dishonestly accuse me of another term they have developed to distract attention away from real evidence of Marxist-type totalitarian subversion of a free State: *McCarthyism*. This term has come to be misused as another quick way to dishonestly dismiss evidence of genuine conspiracies against Western Free Democracy.

In the Cold War 1950s, U.S. Senator Joe McCarthy went on a rampage trying to root Soviet Communist spies and collaborators out of the U.S. government. But the vitriolic McCarthy was much more aggressive than sensible or thoughtful in this crusade, viciously accusing people on little evidence. Since then the general consensus on all sides has been that McCarthy was rash; and in the end he undermined any legitimate anti-Communist action by the United States. Since the declassification of old Soviet-era documents and recordings, there has been some vindication of the reality of the Soviet Communist Marxist threat which Senator McCarthy was trying to root out of the U.S. government, even though he went about it the wrong way; there were indeed more Soviet Communist spies and collaborators in the U.S. than many had previously thought — though only 9 of the 159 blacklisted people on McCarthy's lists have proven to have substantive Soviet Communist ties (many others were likely U.S. security threats, but for different reasons).

Reagan Administration Secretary of Education William Bennett wrote in his 2007 book *America: The Last Best Hope*:

"The cause of anti-communism, which united millions of Americans and which gained the support of Democrats, Republicans and independents, was undermined by Sen. Joe McCarthy ... McCarthy addressed a real problem: disloyal elements within the U.S. government. But his approach to this real problem was to cause untold grief to the country he claimed to love ... Worst of all, McCarthy besmirched the honorable cause of anti-communism. He discredited legitimate efforts to counter Soviet subversion of American institutions."

And ever since McCarthy's foolish, prejudiced and partisan, overzealous search for Communist traitors, the Marxist-influenced Western mainstream media which had *already* successfully hid or discredited real news of Marxist Soviet Socialist atrocities *before and during McCarthy's time* (including but not limited to covering up the genocide mass murder of millions of my ethnic group), *have likewise hidden or discredited real news* that points to negative Marxist influence in the West, but to cover their tracks they cry "McCarthyism" or "[assumed crackpot] conspiracy theorist" whenever anyone sensibly calls attention to things which do not add up that have been motivated by their subversive Socialist Marxist ideology that has been steadily growing in influence in the West since before McCarthy's time. As Aleksandr Solzhenitsyn himself (as a premier expert in Soviet Marxism living in the U.S. 18 years) repeatedly testified, and he is the very opposite of a "non-credible, crackpot conspiracy theorist." Solzhenitsyn himself expressed his concern that "I am not convinced that you are capable of assimilating [the warning] without having gone through it to the end yourselves." And in fact, he was so correct about Western education and media being Marxist-influenced and taking the West slowly towards the same totalitarian fate of the Soviet Union, that it turns out one of the first things successfully "cancelled" by Neo-Marxist Identity Politics "Cancel Culture" in the West was Solzhenitsyn himself, and his book *The Gulag Archipelago* which revealed the ugly, atrocious truth about the world's first Socialist State, and how the totalitarianism and endless atrocities of the Soviet Marxists was no aberration but the natural result of the serious flaws in Relativist, Marxist, Socialist principles and thinking (which has also been proved by every Marxist, Socialist State since also quickly descending into the same oppressive totalitarianism). Again, this author has been surprised to find that so many supposedly university-educated young adults today *have never even heard of Aleksandr Solzhenitsyn nor The Gulag Archipelago* – even though the book sold 35 million copies and was translated into 30 languages, and is of immense historical significance for the role it played in bringing down the Cold War Marxist Soviet Bloc by revealing the web of lies which allowed it to exist at all.

Solzhenitsyn very credibly warned the West that "an enormous number" of Relativist, Marxist/ Communist / Socialist-influenced ideologues was taking the West to the same totalitarian ends as every other State built on Relativist and Marxist thinking — and so the ideologues he correctly pointed out were influencing Western education and mainstream media *cancelled him first*, so young people would never hear his warning, and would be totally sucked in by Socialist thinking as they are today. This long ago quiet "cancelling" of Solzhenitsyn is why my fellow Canadian intellectual for Free Speech, Dr. Jordan Peterson, whose deep thoughtfulness and rigorous intellectual honesty causes those who lack these qualities to hate him passionately, has done a great service to the West by re-igniting interest in Solzhenitsyn and his book *The Gulag Archipelago*, calling it "the most important book of the 20th Century" (*Time* had previously deemed it "Best Non-Fiction Book of the Twentieth Century"). Peterson even provided a new forward to the 50th Anniversary Edition of the book. My own book *Pro-Life Equals Pro-Democracy* in this HUMAN RIGHTS EDUCATION FOR LASTING FREE DEMOCRACY series is now subtitled *A Sequel to Aleksandr Solzhenitsyn's The Gulag Archipelago*, mainly because it follows up on what that "enormous number" of Western Marxist-influenced thinkers Solzhenitsyn warned us about, who never went anywhere else, have wrought here in the West since *Gulag* was published (also because it is written with Solzhenitsyn's intellectual passion for speaking truth against falsehood, was written under the duress of the totalitarianism it opposes, and is likewise of great length — though only half the length of the unabridged version of *The Gulag Archipelago*).

In any case, William Bennett's insight above is correct that there were legitimate reasons for America to remain active and bi-partisan in the cause of anti-Communism, in order to preserve America's democratic integrity, but Senator McCarthy's bad approach spoiled things. Yet the simple fact is, McCarthy was not even looking for the danger in the right place. He was (rashly and with shameless partisan political opportunism) looking for traitors trying to sell out the U.S. to its Marxist, Cold War enemy, the Union of Soviet Socialist Republics run by an anti-democratic Marxist one-party system (the Communist Party).

But the most grave Marxist, Communist-Socialist danger to the U.S. was not so much those traitors involved in active political subversion to a foreign power (who did exist). The most grave danger was Americans (especially influential American intellectuals — Solzhenitsyn said "an enormous number" of them) who had no intention of betraying the U.S. to the foreign Socialist State of the Soviet Union, but who were intellectually dishonest and blinded to facts by the same bad Relativist philosophy as the Soviet Communists; who like them were ideologically committed to Marxism, to Socialism, *not realizing how ultimately destructive Socialism is to Free Democracy*. The greatest Marxist threat to America was the intellectual dishonesty and Relativist *lack of grip on reality* which is inherent to Marxist/ Communist/ Socialist thought. Which is why even during McCarthy's time, neither those Americans who liked Socialism nor those who did not *had any idea that the world's first Socialist State had committed atrocities like the Holodomor Genocide of this author's ethnic heritage group.* Those many Socialist/ Communist sympathizers did not know the full (and inherent) evil of Marxism *because the Marxist-influenced mainstream media in the West had already covered up the genocide and deliberately hid all facts about Soviet Marxist atrocities in the world's first Socialist State.*

"The communist regime in the East could stand and grow due to the enthusiastic support from an enormous number of Western intellectuals who felt a [Marxist; Atheist; Socialist] kinship and refused to see communism's crimes. When they no longer could do so, they tried to justify them."
— *Aleksandr Solzhenitsyn*

At time of writing, a few U.S. States have recently repealed mask-wearing mandates and/or ended lockdowns, as recommended by the vast numbers of medical scientists and doctors and other medical professionals who have so far signed the Great Barrington Declaration (and/or joined many other groups of medical professionals against the lockdowns and other needlessly oppressive "Coronavirus" policies). The publicly available statistics of course also justify states taking these kinds of steps that *ignore the endless Coronavirus alarmism* of the mainstream media which "cancelled" and erased knowledge of the *Holodomor* Genocide and other Socialist atrocities, and now in support of the Marxist Socialist "Great Reset" have done their best to "cancel" and erase knowledge of many tens of thousands of medical professionals and (at time of writing 13,796) medical scientists who in the Great

45

Barrington Declaration heartily affirm life can go back to normal except for reasonable "Focused Protection" for the minority actually vulnerable to the novel Coronavirus. Even if a return to normal life and a healthy economy is not so good for the Marxist "Great Reset" which depends on the desperation of a devastated world economy (that lockdowns bring!) to manipulate the whole world into trying Marx's unrealistic system this time globally (while they hope everyone will forget the over 94 million killed under Marxist policies in the 20th Century alone. The first ten million killed, of my ethnic group, compel me to make sure everyone remembers. Hence, I wrote this book series).

The month of this handbook's submission for publication "Big Tech" such as Google/YouTube still seems determined to go down in history as "CensorTube" by aiding and abetting the killing of Free Speech (even of experts) and the killing of Free Democracy, all for the sake of a global Marxist "Great Reset" attempt using the Coronavirus as an excuse. Earlier this month, yet another group of medical doctors and medical scientists, this one from my country, posted yet another video stating their collective expert medical opinions against Coronavirus alarmism, entitled "Canadian Doctors Speak Out: Top Reasons Not to be Afraid of Covid." The (not-medical-expert) techs at YouTube ("CensorTube") deleted this expert medical testimony *in only 20 minutes,* apparently because it does not support Google/YouTube's policy of instead spreading brain-numbing Coronavirus alarmism that facilitates a philosophically *Relativist not Realist* Marxist "Great Reset." Meantime, in the Real World, this author understands that the state of Florida has been without any lockdowns or mask mandates for about 6 months at time of writing, and (as the worldwide public statistics indicated already ever since the Coronavirus "first wave"), of course they do not have any worse Coronavirus "case numbers" (now frequently asymptomatic) nor deaths (now very low) than places with strict lockdowns and mask mandates (e.g. California, where there are vast numbers of Pro-Choice Neo-Marxist Identity Politics "Cancel Culture" ideologues hoping the pandemic helps them to "reset" the world on Socialist principles). No matter how mild or how serious the novel Coronavirus is, it is certain and undisputable that the lockdowns and mask mandates and most other so-called "Coronavirus Measures" which curtail normal civil liberties and cancel normal democratic freedoms *are not scientifically nor medically effective at containing the novel Coronavirus,* but only good at getting the world population *used to what life will be like after a successful Socialist "Great Reset."*

So, the publicly available statistics and a tremendous amount of medical science expert testimony justifies life going back to normal in March 2021 when this handbook was submitted for publication (actually, the evidence is that life should have gone back to normal for the general population, just keeping up some "Focused Protection" for the elderly most vulnerable to Covid-19, at least since October 2020) – since the evidence is that the lockdowns are only good to manipulate and serve a global Marxist "Great Reset" through man-made economic desperation. Recalling the man-made desperation and starvation of my Ukrainian ethnic group in the *Holodomor* ("Murder by Starvation" or "Death Famine"), which *similarly served Marxist purposes* by *breaking the will* of very Christian rural Ukraine by killing 7-10 million Ukrainians, so those still alive could no longer resist Atheist Soviet Marxist Socialist ideology. The unscientific, unmedical, statistically proven medically useless lockdowns are similarly meant to *wear out the population, break down the citizens' collective will to resist* the transformation of the world according to Marxist Socialist principles in a globalist "Great Reset." A Marxist "Great Reset" made possible *only by a Coronavirus*

Pandemic that never ends, regardless of the statistical and scientific evidence and considerable expert medical testimony it should be long over, because *Relativist not Realist* Neo-Marxist Cancel Culture 'Big Tech' and mainstream media ideologues simply "cancel" or censor the huge amounts of evidence and expert medical testimony that life can go back to normal for the most part. Since it is *unthinking desperation* that dulls the wits of a worn-out populace, not sensible and scientifically justifiable normal life, that makes a Neo-Marxist's dream "global reset" possible to attempt.

But just like in the Socialist Soviet Union, the (*Relativist not Realist,* unrealistic) political hopes and dreams of today's Socialist-influenced Identity Politics Cancel Culture ideologues *depend upon a web of lies* (and depend upon the "cancellation" or censorship of accurate facts against the Relativist Socialist agenda. Controlling the populace – and even manipulating the good elected government representatives and leaders into supporting their never-ending lockdowns towards a "Great Reset" – by controlling the information the populace receives). But since today's Socialist agenda, like the Soviet Socialist agenda, depends upon a web of lies, deceit, and misinformation and the hiding of vital facts, **we already know what we need to do to end all this!** As even the mighty Cold War Soviet Union with its nuclear arsenal fell suddenly and bloodlessly after Solzhenitsyn boldly *spoke the truth and exposed its lies,* and after Soviet Bloc citizens in Poland *stood up together in Solidarity* for the Traditional Western Values (which undergird Free Democracy) to once again guide their country's politics, **so likewise we freedom-loving citizens of the world can end the current (witting or unwitting) Marxist/Socialist threats to human freedom by simply learning, knowing, spreading and boldly speaking the truth against their web of lies.** Which is why this HUMAN RIGHTS EDUCATION FOR LASTING FREE DEMOCRACY book series has been written, so that world citizens can know (and spread!) those facts of History, Science, Logic and Philosophy which are most pertinent to lasting human freedom.

"You will know the truth, and the truth will set you free." – Jesus Christ (John 8:32)

This author is not a medical professional myself (though as a scholar of ancient to modern documents I do know the little-known historical, logical and philosophical roots and development of all Science, including Medical Science). So, I will quote below the new alliance of medical experts, specialists, professionals in my country trying to re-establish genuine health and sanity in the midst of the mind-numbing globalist Neo-Marxist fear-manipulation of Coronavirus alarmism in support of a Marxist "Great Reset" that cares not a whit for the health and sanity of the citizens of the world because of Neo-Marxist *ideology instead of education.* These professional medical specialists (and generalists) from my country have publicly declared their collective expert medical opinions about the world's current prevailing oppressive so-called "Coronavirus Measures," as quoted below. These from my country are in essential agreement with many tens of thousands of other medical professionals and medical scientists throughout the globe who have signed the Great Barrington Declaration, or who have formed many other groups of concurring medical professionals.

47

These various collective medical testimonies all together worldwide form such an *extremely strong medical and scientific case* against Coronavirus alarmism and oppressive lockdowns (etc.) that those media and government ideologues who are so strenuously promoting lockdowns that support a Marxist "Great Reset" (and those in government whom the ideologues have fooled into going along with them) *never engage honestly (or at all)* with these tens of thousands of medical doctors and medical scientists who disagree with oppressive "Coronavirus Measures." The best the ideologues who support continuing oppressive Coronavirus measures and mandates can do is *just pretend* this vast expert testimony against their nefarious agenda *does not exist* (which their intellectually dishonest minds can easily do because they are *Relativists not Realists* with what Solzhenitsyn called "impaired thinking ability"). And the fact that there are otherwise qualified medical professionals who support the restrictive lockdowns (you know, those doctors who are *allowed* to voice their opinion in mainstream media and are not "cancelled" and erased from Big Tech's social media platforms) *is not even a case of "disagreement between qualified medical professionals."* Unsurprisingly, medical voices who are *allowed* to be heard in mainstream media usually *work for the governments imposing the lockdowns; or work for the vaccine industry that profits immensely from unscientifically exaggerated Coronavirus hysteria.* These with typical ideologue intellectual dishonesty have just *not been responding* to letters from their opposing medical peers who have nothing to gain, no agenda to promote *except practicing real medicine, real science, for the benefit of human beings.* And living the Medical Profession's ancient calling to "do no harm," articulated millennia ago in the doctors' Hippocratic Oath. For this their professional medical testimony is today "cancelled" and erased from YouTube etc. because intellectually honest medical professionals do not support the Marxist "Great Reset" that needs a Coronavirus Pandemic mind-numbing "state of emergency" that never ends. Confident in the media cancellation of opposing professional medical views, the government "health officers" imposing the lockdowns have been simply *ignoring* the letters of their honest medical colleagues challenging them to justify their oppressive policies on medical and scientific grounds.

Yes indeed, the fact there are some medical professionals allowed to speak on mainstream media channels without being censored, who have not been among the tens of thousands of ("cancelled") doctors and medical scientists who have signed the Great Barrington Declaration against lockdowns and alarmism, who instead routinely support or impose lockdowns and generally encourage "Coronavirus alarmism," *is not even a case of "disagreement between qualified medical professionals."* Because any *honest* disagreement between qualified medical professionals on a matter of grave public importance like a pandemic in a *healthy free democracy* would be handled *scientifically* (and *publicly*, before governments in session) in order to find a greater *scientific* consensus about just what might be best for public political policy. Or at least to *clearly delineate the possible options* for government policy based on the disagreeing expert sides *each making their respective scientific cases for incompatible approaches* so that the (non-expert) politicians who have to actually make the public policy can decide which side of the disagreeing experts they thought made the stronger case, which would be the better advice to follow when making public policy. But what we have *instead* of a careful and *balanced* consideration of medical science evidence and expert medical testimony before so-called "Coronavirus Measures" are decided upon, is the "cancellation," censoring and censuring of one side of the dispute among experts, *pretending* that huge numbers of expert voices against oppressive lockdowns *do not even exist*, or dismissing and villainizing the opposing scientific voices when they are (rarely) acknowledged to exist at all. What we have *instead* of honest, *balanced* medical science discussion over "Coronavirus Measures" is the blatant and completely unjustified censorship of one side, represented by tens of thousands of qualified medical experts and scientists, who are simply ignored and dismissed, while governments (wittingly or unwittingly) support a global totalitarian Marxist "Great Reset" through *politically enforced oppressive lockdown policies which destroy whole economies.* Even though "lockdowns" is a *prison* term, not a *medical* term. True medical *quarantines* isolate the *sick*, and *not the healthy!* So, in most cases the question is only whether any particular government imposing lockdowns is supporting the end of free democracy *wittingly or unwittingly*; by their own ideological design which desires a global "Great Reset," or because they have been *manipulated* by others with ideological design (especially the Marxist-influenced mainstream media controlling society by controlling information which Solzhenitsyn as a top expert in Marxism warned us about; media which makes sure that governments *not* currently led by Neo-Marxist-influenced political parties *still* support the Neo-Marxist "Great Reset" either because they:

just *never hear* the medical and scientific facts necessary to make *appropriate (and not needlessly oppressive)* "Coronavirus policy;"

or else because they remain too (spinelessly) *afraid* of being eviscerated by the powerfully influential mainstream media if they *dare* to publicly *question* or challenge the mainstream media's ideologically-motivated narrative about the "deadly" Coronavirus Pandemic (despite a statistical recovery rate of over 99%) which somehow "requires" people giving up all their normal democratic freedoms and civil rights, and sacrificing their small businesses and independent livelihood to fearful lockdowns and other fear-mongering mandates which prepare the world for worldwide Marxist Socialism.

In the Science of Logic, by the way, to quote an expert who happens to agree with your position *as if that proved your position correct*, when there is in fact controversy or disagreement *among qualified experts* in the pertinent field on the particular topic or question at hand, is called the *logical fallacy* of the *invalid appeal to authority*. It is fair enough for governments to cite experts who happen to agree with their lockdowns and mask mandates. But only letting such "agreeing" experts have their voice heard in mainstream media and considered by government policymakers, while tens of thousands of experts who disagree *are not allowed a mainstream media nor government platform to speak at all*, while their expert video testimonies are routinely erased from mainstream Internet platforms, is just the "becoming present" of the *totalitarian future led by the Marxist-influenced* which the brilliant and fiercely honest Aleksandr Solzhenitsyn long warned us was coming. So, unless you intend to act on the warning in this book (and implement the "winning strategy" described in CHAPTER 4: STRATEGY), *do not count on ever getting back all your normal democratic freedoms and usual civil liberties* they *manipulated* you into parting with for the sake of "world health," through a mind-numbing and never-ending Coronavirus alarmism which is not at all medically nor scientifically justified in continuing any longer (now that much data is available since early 2020).

There surely are many doctors just as fooled by the unjustified Coronavirus alarmism as the average person, who go along with the alarmism just because they *trust* the media and government health officials have done the research and been honest (which in a healthy democracy might be a reasonable trust; but not so in our very unhealthy democracies which long ago already moved far from *The Foundational Principles of Human Rights and Democracy* identified in this book). But, not even relying on such (unworthy) trust, regional "colleges of physicians and surgeons" in my country – the regional *government-regulated* bodies that license doctors – have apparently put "gag orders" on doctors, and some doctors testify they have been *threatened* to not dare tell their patients things which contradict the official Coronavirus Pandemic narrative that keeps the Coronavirus alarmism alive. Even gagging doctors from testifying to the reality of their patients who have been injured, some permanently, by the rushed Covid-19 vaccines. But there is no surprise here – this author's entire intellectual endeavor of tracing the history of free democracy and what threatens free democracies began precisely with anti-democratic, totalitarian-oriented *policies of a regional government-regulated college of physicians and surgeons* introduced in 2014 and enforced starting in 2015, policies to take away doctors' normal democratic freedoms of conscience and free speech and religion, and policies which make doctors betray even the most ancient and most defining principles of the medical profession.

So, there really is not much of a scientific nor medical side *for* the prevailing lockdowns and mask or vaccine mandates and so on which restrict normal democratic freedoms and civil liberties. Tens of thousands of doctors and medical scientists who disagree with lockdowns are simply "cancelled" and censored (or threatened by their government-regulated colleges) for not going along with Coronavirus alarmism. Then there are those who go along with it only because of misplaced trust. Meaning that most of the medical professionals actively "for" lockdowns quoted by the Marxist-influenced mainstream media Solzhenitsyn warned us about *either work for the governments imposing lockdowns, or work for the Big Pharma vaccine companies who stand to make immense profits from Coronavirus alarmism – especially because in many countries like the U.S., the Coronavirus alarmism has been used as an excuse to grant vaccine companies "immunity" from being sued or prosecuted for harm done by their rushed vaccine products made without anything near the normal safety testing for vaccine products.* The regional government's chief medical officer where this author lives, when asked in a January 2021 press conference to explain the *science* behind her newly-imposed "Coronavirus Measures" since November 2020, in some ways *more restrictive* even than at the early (March-April 2020) height of the Pandemic, she famously said the most honest thing to come out of her mouth, "none of this is really based on science."

In any case, the mere fact of the extremely one-sided censorship and "cancellation" of many tens of thousands of qualified medical professionals and medical scientists tells you all you need to know about the quality of the medical opinions allowed to be aired in mainstream media, the ones used to guide current oppressive lockdowns and mask mandates touted as "Coronavirus Measures" for our "safety." Scientifically and medically sound "Coronavirus Measures" would have no need to censor and de-platform from mainstream Internet services like YouTube the opposing expert medical testimonies of many tens of thousands of medical professionals. If the prevailing Coronavirus measures were scientifically and medically sound, there would be no need for their promoters to as much as possible pretend the Great Barrington Declaration or the Canada Health Alliance (and many more collaborations of medical professionals against lockdowns) *just do not exist.* There would be no need to just *never engage them in honest scientific debate.* No need to discredit, dismiss or vilify the many voices against the prevailing Coronavirus policies – all of which intellectual dishonesty is precisely what the lockdown promoters are doing. Just like *Holodomor* deniers similarly discredited and dismissed the honest testimony of honest journalists, likewise for the sake of global Marxism/Communism/Socialism which the lockdowns are excellent at preparing the world for.

But this author and Human Rights scholar, my ethnic group representing the first ten million murdered for the "glorious end" of establishing Socialism at the State level, here and now invites Big Tech, Big Pharma, mainstream media and all governments to see the global Coronavirus Pandemic *no longer* as an opportunity for a global Socialist "Great Reset" (no matter how many precious humans are harmed by it, in typical deadly Relativist Socialist thinking in which they think their proposed ideological end justifies *any* means; *any* death toll). This author invites them to instead see the current worldwide situation (wherein they are holding the whole world captive, imprisoned in their own homes by brain-numbing fear dishonestly spread by Big Tech, Big Pharma, mainstream media and governments willing to go along with them), *as their opportunity to rejoin the human race instead of trying to mold it into their own ideological and/or profit agendas.* You have nothing to lose but your intellectual dishonesty and your moral vacuum. Your dishonesty has already been exposed – so convert back to the human race (instead of trying to subjugate it) fast!

Remember – all the (non-expert) Relativist, Neo-Marxist "Cancel Culture" ideologues can do against the honest expert scientific threat to their "Great Reset" hopes is to "cancel" huge amounts of expert medical testimony against their Marxist agenda! "Cancel" – that is, censor, erase, delete from YouTube ("CensorTube") huge amounts of medical testimony like the recent (at time of publication) 11 minute March 2021 video "Canadian Doctors Speak Out: Top Reasons Not to be Afraid of Covid" which (non-medical-expert "Big Tech") YouTube erased from YouTube ("CensorTube") only 20 minutes after it was posted by medical experts! For the reader's ease of perusal, this video, along with other highly important expert medical, scientific and legal testimonies which YouTube ("CensorTube") quickly erased and "cancelled," can be accessed on this author's new webpage "Pandemic Totalitarianism" at:

Pandemic Totalitarianism | William Baptiste Human Rights and Freedoms Forever!
https://williambaptistehumanrightsandfreedomsforever.com/pandemic-totalitarianism

So, as promised above, here is the expert medical consensus of this alliance of doctors and other medical experts from my country, which accords with the expert medical testimony of 55, 500+ other medical professionals and medical scientists worldwide who (so far – the number is still growing!) have signed the Great Barrington Declaration:

Based on medical evidence, we call on all levels of government to immediately stop promoting the following measures:

- *The use of an inappropriate and misapplied test i.e. RT-PCR to determine policies*
- *Mismanagement of hospitals and other medical facilities with unnecessary COVID restrictions*
- *Lockdowns of businesses*
- *Closure of churches and other places of worship*
- *Closure of schools, daycares, gyms and special needs care centres*
- *Closure of playgrounds, parks, and other recreational facilities*
- *Inordinate and ubiquitous hand-washing with disinfectants*
- *Mandated and inappropriate physical distancing*
- *Mandated and inappropriate mask wearing*
- *Promotion or requirement of COVID-19 vaccination with inadequately trialed, experimental gene-modifying products*
- *Mandated and inappropriate social isolation*
- *Quarantine of asymptomatic people*
- *Misrepresentation of the COVID situation in the media*
- *The use of fear and other psychological manipulation to coerce the public into following harmful mitigation measures*
- *The lack of transparency and accountability of public health agencies*
- *The failure to promote evidence based preventative and therapeutic treatments*

The above measures are not based on any current medical evidence, research, human safety trials or on-going evaluations. Further, these policies are in direct opposition to medical practitioners' oaths to do no harm.

-- From https://www.canadahealthalliance.org/ [6]

Even expert medical testimonies like this are now routinely removed from YouTube, Facebook, and other mainstream Internet media. Even whole Internet news channels (like LifeSite News, which for years this author has found to be an excellent resource on current events and news of enormous significance which never appear in mainstream media) have been permanently "purged" from YouTube for daring to publish news about the existence of qualified professional voices against oppressive prevailing "Coronavirus Measures."

So remember, "This Account has been terminated for violating YouTube's Community Guidelines" now just means "this YouTube Channel account reported on expert medical testimony against Coronavirus lockdowns which support the Marxist "Great Reset," expert medical testimony which (non-expert) 'Big Tech' like YouTube/Google is determined to discredit, dismiss and pretend does not even exist, to support the global Marxist takeover using a never-ending Coronavirus Pandemic as their excuse." Marxism (and Neo-Marxism) depends upon a web of lies and hiding of the truth, the facts, as Solzhenitsyn warned the West, as Solzhenitsyn demonstrated in *The Gulag Archipelago.* So, voices which tell the truth, the full facts, have to be censored for Marxism (and Neo-Marxism) to progress. Hence, LifeSite News (and other worthy, honest news-reporting journalism) has now been permanently banned

---

[6] https://www.canadahealthalliance.org/, accessed April 22, 2021.

from YouTube ("CensorTube"). The censorship tells you all you need to know about the quality of the information you get from mainstream sources now. Just like in the totalitarian Socialist Soviet Union, journalists and authors now self-censor, edit truth out of their own work, in order to see just what they can "get past the censors" and get into print or on YouTube ("CensorTube"), before they are shut down or have their news reporting content removed from mainstream sources like YouTube. **As a representative of (only) the first ten million murdered by the Socialist ideology 'Big Tech' is now supporting a globalist "Reset" with, I here appeal to YouTube/Google and all 'Big Tech,' to change your path now (like Ebeneezer Scrooge), and so avoid being listed in future history books as major collaborators in the 2020-2021 attempted globalist Marxist "Great Reset" through widespread censorship of facts and truth for totalitarian ideological purposes. Rejoin the human race instead of trying to shape it to your ideology – ideology exposed in this handbook as among the most insidious and ultimately murderous ever known to humanity.**

Until such time as YouTube and 'Big Tech' repents, it is appropriate that hundreds of thousands are leaving YouTube for other video-posting platforms like Rumble, which do not censor truth and important facts for ideological purposes. If YouTube ("CensorTube") will not do the right thing for the sake of humanity, maybe they will eventually do the right thing because they are losing clients and money – since money seems to be all they care about, and not humanity nor Human Rights. I await their response to THE INTELLECTUAL HONESTY CHALLENGE in this book (Chapter 7), which still gives them a chance to redeem themselves and publicly commit to change their ways, even if they do not take the gentler appeal in CHAPTER 6: HUMAN RESPONSIBILITIES COME WITH YOUR HUMAN RIGHTS. In the meantime, whatever they do, the truth cannot be hidden long-term any more than it could in the Soviet Union which despite its vast military power and nuclear arsenal eventually collapsed under the immense weight of its own web of lies, as Solzhenitsyn uniquely predicted it would. Relativistic ideologies cannot last forever in the Real World. So, the important facts hidden by YouTube/Google/'Big Tech' can still be viewed, despite their intellectually dishonest "cancelling" and censorship, for example at

LifeSite | Life, Family & Culture News (lifesitenews.com)

LifeSite | Life, Family & Culture News (lifesitenews.com)
https://www.lifesitenews.com/

which has started uploading its video archives, all taken off YouTube, to Rumble, where they can be viewed at

LifeSiteNews (rumble.com)
https://rumble.com/c/LifeSiteNews

Human-life-and-freedom-lovers can take heart, in the midst of all the totalitarian and Relativist (most often Neo-Marxist) censorship and "cancellation" which was *already* taking the West to the totalitarian future Solzhenitsyn predicted long before the Pandemic accelerated it further (which is why this Human Rights scholar has been working on the HUMAN RIGHTS EDUCATION FOR LASTING FREE DEMOCRACY in this book series *since 2015*). IF the ideologues who most want the Marxist/ Communist/ Socialist "Great Reset" had an army and guns to just *force* our Western democracies into reshaping the world on Marxist principles, they would have already done it (which is how China and Russia became Marxist). They have instead been consistently using the classic Marxist "fallback" tactics, of gaining political power by *manipulation* when they cannot gain it by pure *force*. So, with Neo-Marxist Identity Politics they pretend they stand up for those they label "oppressed" with never-ending "manufactured outrage" at those they label "privileged," *manipulating* people into giving them political concessions and power, in ways described later in this book (and in *Pro-Life Equals Pro-Democracy*).

"You have to understand the nature of Communism. The very ideology of Communism, all of Lenin's teachings, are that anyone who doesn't take what's lying in front of him is a fool. If you can take it, do so. If you can attack, strike. But if there's a wall, retreat. **The Communist [Marxist/Socialist] leaders respect only firmness and have contempt for persons who continually give in to them.***"*
— *Aleksandr Solzhenitsyn*

In my country, even the more normal (non-extremist) political parties, quite pathetically, have the last few years, *whenever the (extremist) Neo-Marxist parties with their Marxist-influenced mainstream media tells them to*, started *purging from their own ranks* their members most well-versed in *The Foundational Principles of Human Rights and Democracy* identified from Human Rights History, Science, Logic, and the History of Philosophy in this book. The non-extremist parties closer to political center are terrified of taking any principled stand against the *(Skeptical) Relativist not (Scientific) Realist,* Marxist-influenced mainstream media narratives, and so the forces hurtling my country towards totalitarian oblivion (as Solzhenitsyn predicted) just grow more and more contemptuous of anyone with the Traditional Western Values upon which all Human Rights and Free Democracy depends. And ever-more contemptuous of closer-to-center parties which give in to their extremist demands and never stand on democratic principle against them. But the Neo-Marxists are not taking over with guns and armies like classic Marxists Lenin and Mao did; I honestly think most of the Neo-Marxists do not have the bloodlust of classic Marxism, even though they witlessly copy Marxist ideology and tactics, if only because Solzhenitsyn exposed the atrocities which naturally came with classic Marxism put into practice. They have been building the intricate web of lies and censorship of truth on which all forms of Marxism depend, but, I charitably think, largely without the blood-lust which Marx himself recommended, because, after Solzhenitsyn's exposé, they are still trying to prove to themselves as well as others that Marxism does not "have to" end up with millions of humans corpses like *every single attempt to establish Marxism at the State level has.* So instead, what they are using is (also typically Marxist) *lies and manipulation by fear*, burying or casting doubt on true facts and expert testimony as much they can, hoping to *fool* you into accepting their dishonesty enough to vote them into power (or to let them shut down national economies with unscientific Coronavirus *alarmism* to prepare the world for a global Marxist "Great Reset"). So, all we have to do stop them is *stand up together in Solidarity* with *Human Rights education* against their *uneducated ideology.*

♦

But until such time as people stand up together in *Solidarity* for Traditional Western Values including *The Foundational Principles of Human Rights and Democracy* to once again be the guide of public policy in "the Free West," against all the 'Creeping Totalitarianism' now accelerating us towards a global Marxist "Great Reset," we can reasonably expect that the intellectually dishonest, Relativist and Marxist-influenced in governments and media and "Big Tech" will do their best to not let the brain-numbing panic of "Coronavirus alarmism" end until they have accomplished their Marxist "Great Reset" of the whole world. Because, as explained in more detail in CHAPTER 3: PHILOSOPHY, Marxism is rooted in an underlying philosophical worldview of Skepticism and Relativism that has no use for facts, logic, or science. They deny or unreasonably doubt objective reality and only care about their own subjective opinions and ideologies. And that is why they find it so easy to pretend there are not 13,796 (and counting) medical scientists plus around 42,000 (and counting) other doctors and medical professionals united behind the Great Barrington Declaration, as well as several other unions of professionals against the brain-numbing Coronavirus alarmism which this author calls "Covidiocy."

But I reserve the invective "Covidiots" not for the many thousands fearfully trapped in their homes for a year (including some extended family members who have literally not been outside for 9 months); these are the *victims* of Covidiocy. And I do not even call "Covidiots" the thoughtless raving mobs who shame and badger and even sometimes physically attack people not wearing masks (masks which are easily proven medically ineffective and even harmful). I do not call "Covidiots" even these mobs, like the angry mob which called for my son to be "thrown overboard" on a ferry boat for not wearing a mask and did not give a damn that he had a medical condition preventing him from wearing masks; and did not give a damn that even the oppressive provincial Coronavirus regulations exempted those with such medical conditions from having to wear a mask. These are frightened people, who have been whipped into a fearful frenzy that shuts down their brain functions by endless Coronavirus alarmism in the mainstream media which they (foolishly) trust because *they have no idea* that Western mainstream media has been Marxist-influenced at least since the coverup of the *Holodomor* Genocide; and no idea that the Coronavirus Pandemic is a Marxist-influenced ideologue's dream opportunity to "Reset" the world through Relativist, unscientific Coronavirus alarmism. These shamers and angry-mob types too are victims of Covidiocy. And I suppose I cannot call the Pro-Choice Neo-Marxist Identity Politics "Cancel Culture" ideologue politicians and media moguls who *desire* the Marxist "Great Reset" and are deliberately misusing the Pandemic to bring about the Great Reset, "Covidiots," because these are calculating and evil ideologues, and not mere idiots. These (along with "Big Tech" shamelessly censoring expert medical testimony against lockdowns) are not Covidiots but evil people like those who like Socialist-sympathizing journalist Walter Duranty believe "you can't make an omelet without breaking some eggs;" who believe the Socialist end justifies any means, any deaths; who are now happily sacrificing your finances, your family business and your relatives who died due to Coronavirus *Measures* (not the virus!) all for the sake of their Marxist "Great Reset." So, instead of applying the term to any of the above, I reserve the term "Covidiots" for those in government and media and Big Tech who are *not* evil Neo-Marxists gleefully manipulating Coronavirus alarmism towards a global Marxist Great Reset but *who are nevertheless instruments and puppets of them*, taking Marxist-influenced media as gospel without any critical thinking/questioning, or at least *effectively taking orders from the alarmist Marxist media* and implementing the undemocratic and unscientific and unmedical lockdowns and mask mandates the Marxist-influenced media wants them to. Allowing themselves to be manipulated, allowing themselves to be pawns in the intellectually dishonest, Relativist and Marxist game, aiding and abetting the destruction of Free Democracy in the Marxist "Great Reset." "Covidiots" are especially those democratically elected politicians who are not utterly incompetent Pro-Choice legal-human-killing Neo-Marxists desiring a Marxist "Great Reset" but *nevertheless still do the Marxist Mainstream Media's lockdown bidding* without critical examination and without courage. History will judge them as spineless collaborators with the attempted Marxist globalist takeover of 2020-2021 unless they soon grow a spine and *start defending the democracies which they were democratically elected to represent* from the major Neo-Marxist assaults of Pro-Choice Identity Politics "Cancel Culture," and its newly weaponized never-ending Coronavirus Pandemic that simply "cancels" all expert medical science testimony against Coronavirus alarmism.

In any case, because *facts* (regarding Coronavirus or anything else) ultimately do not matter to Relativists, Solzhenitsyn near the end of his 1800-page book exposing Marxist ideological evil and ensuing atrocities, *The Gulag Archipelago,* expressed to the "ideologically lobotomized":

"All you freedom-loving 'left-wing' thinkers in the West! You left laborites! You progressive American, German and French students! As far as you are concerned, none of this amounts to much. As far as you are concerned, this whole book of mine is a waste of effort. You may suddenly understand it all someday – but only when you yourselves hear, 'hands behind your backs there!' and step ashore on our [Gulag] Archipelago."
— Aleksandr Solzhenitsyn, The Gulag Archipelago 1918-1956

Meanwhile, Marxist, Communist China – the world's largest and most influential remaining Marxist State – has just the latest Marxist genocide underway as I write this in 2021. And the human deaths caused by Marxism, in the vicinity of 100 million killed (and counting) do not even count all the additional humans killed by legal abortion, which Marxists were the first to legalize (oppressive Marxist States typically have legal abortion – in Marxist China even forced abortions against the mother's will). And all of this legal human-killing (of the born and preborn) is done in serious but utterly vain attempts to make the flawed Marxist Socialist ideology "work." Always promising but always delivering the very opposite of a classless egalitarian utopia where everyone is equal, no-one owns anything and everyone is happy as the highly centralized State equitably distributes all resources. Solzhenitsyn reflects thusly upon why Marxism, which looks so beautiful on paper, always fails so *horrifically* in practice:

"we forget that the defects of capitalism represent the basic flaws of human nature, allowed unlimited freedom together with the various human rights; we forget that under Communism (and Communism is breathing down the neck of all moderate forms of socialism, which are unstable) the identical flaws run riot in any person with the least degree

of authority; while everyone else under that system does indeed attain "equality"—the equality of destitute slaves…"
— Aleksandr Solzhenitsyn

Solzhenitsyn says that "an enormous number" of Western intellectual ideologues helped the Soviet Socialists to commit their atrocities and crimes (including genocide); that Western Marxists and Socialists (who actively refused to hear or accept evidence of Soviet crimes) helped the Soviets "cannibalize" Russia (as they refused to acknowledge the *Holodomor* Genocide in Ukraine and silenced the Western journalist whistleblowers). **These Western ideologues never went anywhere.** They are still here in the West, often teaching at universities; they or their students (including many of today's politicians) are still supporting the atrocious century-old (1920) Soviet Marxist precedent of legal abortion which denies Free Democracy's foundations in *equal human preciousness without exception*; they are still trying to cram the "Red Square peg" of Marxist/Socialist ideology into the "round hole" of the *real world* no matter how many serious attempts to implement Marxist Socialist States have consistently devolved into the most oppressive totalitarian States known to history, because they have (unrealistic) *ideology* instead of *education.* As a highly educated and intelligent member of the ethnic group from which (only) the first ten million murdered victims of Marxism came, in the *Holodomor* which was covered up by Western mainstream media *to keep Westerners unaware of the dangers of Socialism*, I am here to warn you, dear reader, that, in order to support their dream global Marxist "Great Reset" of the world (which is public, on the cover of *Time* and no longer a matter of conjecture), the Marxist-influenced ideologues Solzhenitsyn long warned us about in the mainstream media (and now in "Big Tech") and in government are doing their best as I write this to make sure you, the reader, *never hear of or at least never take seriously the tremendous and growing numbers – many tens of thousands – of qualified medical professionals and medical scientists who have joined together in various large groups of professionals against lockdowns and other oppressive "Coronavirus Measures" like mask mandates. Of these groups of doctors perhaps most notable is the Great Barrington Declaration, drafted by infectious disease epidemiologists and public health scientists from prestigious Harvard, Oxford and Stanford universities in October 2020, and since then signed by 13,796 (and counting) other medical scientists (as of March 2021) and 41,890 (and counting) doctors and other medical practitioners. These Marxist-influenced ideologues in media, "Big Tech," and governments, who do not want you to even know about the Great Barrington Declaration, do not make their decisions and Coronavirus policies based on objective facts, because Marxism is built on Relativism and subjectivism that does not believe in objective facts or science, medical or otherwise. So, they want you readers (and your elected leaders who are not Neo-Marxists themselves) to not make decisions about the Pandemic based on facts nor expert scientific medical testimony either. Therefore they are doing their best to make sure you only hear in mainstream media voices which support their oppressive Coronavirus policies which take away normal democratic freedoms and civil liberties and ultimately support the Marxist "Great Reset."* Just like in all Marxist/ Socialist countries, today's Neo-Marxist "Cancel Culture" censors or "cancels" information and voices against their agenda and otherwise controls information to manipulate the population into supporting the politicians who want to enslave them according to Marxist ideology's tenets.

Also, remember that just like classic Marxism, today's Identity Politics bifurcates society into an "oppressed class" and a "privileged class;" just like classic Marxism, Identity Politics exaggerates and fans into flames of hatred any resentments over any past or present failures (even long past injustices), motivating those labelled the "oppressed class" to one way or another overthrow or replace those labelled the "privileged class," ultimately in order to set up a seductive but unrealistically-conceived egalitarian classless Marxist utopia. Both requiring *adversarial* labels of "oppressed" and "privileged," both classic Marxism and Neo-Marxist Identity Politics have an *inherently toxic and adversarial political approach making any peaceful cooperation for the Common Good of all based on mutual respect impossible.* Which is yet another reason why **what the world needs instead of Marxist-influenced and philosophically Relativist ideology (and instead of a Marxist "Great Reset"), is a "Democracy Reboot"** that **"reloads"** into Westerners explicit consciousness *(Scientific) Realism instead of (Skeptical) Relativism* and *The Foundational Principles of Human Rights and Democracy* like *equal human preciousness without exception* and *Equal Human Rights for All Humans* and the ten *Core Principles of Lasting Democracy* identified from the disciplines of History, Science, Logic and Philosophy in this book series.

Human Life Issues are Non-Partisan

[Drawn from the author's previous book *Pro-Life Equals Pro-Democracy*]

In healthy democracies, the "Progressive Left" and the "Conservative Right" complement each other, because both at least implicitly hold the same underlying foundations as they did at the formation of our modern democracies. Within a common human-life-protecting democratic foundation, the "Progressive Left" ideally helps prevent the "Conservative Right" from "conserving" *too much* of the way things were done before; from ossifying or stagnating, holding on too long to outdated ways and structures which may not even anymore serve their original good purpose in the new context of changing times and technology and so on. And ideally the "Conservative Right" helps prevent the "Progressive Left" from "progressing" *too quickly* to change without thinking through all the consequences and "throwing out the baby with the bathwater;" from failing to *conserve* what was *essential* or *foundational* from before which remains *necessary* even with changing times and technology and so on. In a healthy democracy, at election time the "Progressive Left" and "Conservative Right" vie with each other to convince voters to vote for their particular party's platform of ideas how to approach the policy issues and questions of the day, while voters feel secure that whichever party they vote for, they live in a safe democracy that guards their freedom, and not a "DINO" – "Democracy In Name Only" - in danger of becoming a totalitarian State under extremist political parties . . .

In healthy democracies, political parties of both political Left and political Right share in common and do not compromise *The Foundational Principles of Human Rights and Democracy* like *Equal Human Preciousness Governments are Obligated to Protect.* Principles which were at least implicitly assumed by both "Left" and "Right" at the foundation of our modern democracies. In contrast, *extremist* political parties of both Left and Right, the *Extreme Left* Soviet (Marxist) Communist Party and the *Extreme Right* (Fascist) German Nazi Party, were the first modern political parties to reject the West's democracy-grounding underlying Traditional Biblical, Judeo-Christian, "Pro-Life" *Foundational Principles of Human Rights and Democracy* including *Equal Human Preciousness* and the *Inherent Human Right to Live* that means *Killing Humans Is Wrong* (originally from the Biblical Commandment, "You shall not kill"). The extremist Left Marxist Soviet Communist and Extremist Right Fascist Nazi Parties specifically rejected the West's human-protecting democratic foundations by legalizing human-killing by abortion (the Marxists legalized abortion in 1920 and the Nazis in 1934, both near the beginning of their totalitarian regimes). *Legal Abortion is inherently an extremist totalitarian political position which denies the Inherent Human Right to Live which is essential to democratic thinking and was condemned as such by the Free West at Nuremberg and Geneva in 1948. It is also prohibited by any intellectually honest and historically contextual reading of the United Nations' Universal Declaration of Human Rights produced the same year.*

Human societies have thrived and prospered under both Left-Wing "bigger governments" and Right-Wing "smaller governments," and even under the pre-democratic traditional monarchical government of "a good King," *as long as* that government was guided by or felt obligated to uphold the Traditional Western Values which include and support *The Foundational Principles of Human Rights and Democracy* like *equal human preciousness without exception* and the *Inherent Human Right to Live*. **The current bifurcation or polarization of Western societies actually has nothing to do with either political "Left" or "Right," and has everything to do with either the fundamentally democratic (loving) acceptance of *Equal Human Preciousness Without Exception* or the fundamentally totalitarian (bigoted and extremist) rejection of *Equal Human Preciousness Without Exception*** which was first embraced by the West back in the 4th Century with the original criminalization of human-killing abortion and infanticide. This 318 AD first legal recognition of *Inherent Human Rights* (due to Christian influence) started a long but logical process of development which in the end logically resulted in modern Human Rights and democratic freedoms and International Law built on essentially "Pro-Life" principles, given magnificent mature expression in 1948, with the *Universal Declaration of Human Rights.* **Human Life Issues are Non-Partisan: "Pro-Choice" Versus "Pro-Life" is NOT a Matter of Political "Left" Versus Political "Right," But a Matter of *Fundamentally Totalitarian and Extremist Thinking* Which Supports Human-Killing Versus *Fundamentally Democratic Thinking* Which Supports Human Protection. The Traditional Western "Pro-Life" Principle of *Equal Human Preciousness without Exception Which Governments are Obligated to Protect* (Which Entered Western Thought in the 4th Century Through the Christian Church) Is Not a Matter of Political "Opinion" in a *Lasting* Democracy, But Is the Very *Foundation* of Free and Lasting Democracy (and of Human Rights) . . .**

This author's country has become a world leader in Pro-Choice 'Creeping Totalitarianism' both because of a failure of the "conservative Right" to faithfully and consistently "conserve" *The Foundational Principles of Human Rights and Democracy* (sometimes in utter spineless cowardice before the Pro-Choice Left's increasing fundamentally anti-democratic transgressions); and because the "progressive Left" long ago started to "progress" without any essential mooring in *The Foundational Principles of Human Rights and Democracy*, foundations which the Left now actively and deliberately dismantles (apparently unwittingly, but, wittingly or unwittingly, in utter incompetence to lead a Free Democracy that lasts).

More generally, in the U.S. and Canada and in other countries and in the UN, not only has today's "Progressive Left" in utter ignorance of Human Rights History often "thrown out the baby with the bathwater;" they now literally throw out human babies, killing young human lives for profit in abortion clinics and now even selling their murdered corpses for "research and development" or to make health and beauty products (including some vaccines, which are a big pharmaceutical business), to make a further profit. Recalling the profitable Slave Trade which also legally devalued some human lives (Black human lives) in order to sell them for profit. And recalling the Nazi regime which before it ended also experimented with making products from the murdered corpses of millions of Jewish humans the government had legally devalued (experimental products such as lampshades and painting canvasses made from legally devalued and murdered Jewish human skin; ashtrays made from bone). And now today, officially Pro-Choice abortion-promoting political parties in power are starting to pass totalitarian-oriented laws and policies which (like the totalitarian Nazi regime) restrict the freedom of speech of and otherwise punish citizens who believe in democracy's foundations in concepts such as *killing humans is wrong* because without exception *Human Rights are for all humans.*

The "Pro-Choice Left" which considers itself "progressive" should consider this:

"We all want progress. But progress means getting nearer to the place where you want to be. And if you have taken a wrong turn, then to go forward does not get you any nearer. If you are on the wrong road, progress means doing an about-turn and walking back to the right road; in that case the man who turns back soonest is the most progressive man."
– C.S. Lewis

Legal abortion follows totalitarian legal human-killing precedents in the first place, and requires totalitarian laws against free speech, and the ultimate end of democracy, to keep such an inherently anti-human and totalitarian practice as abortion legal long-term (which is why this author can be arrested and jailed for peaceful Human Rights advocacy and for speaking established scientific facts under current totalitarian laws passed by the Pro-Choice Left while in power in his country and some its provinces). Legal abortion is the wrong road, the inevitably totalitarian road, and if the Pro-Choice Left wants to be genuinely "progressive" they have to do "an about-turn" and walk "back to the right road" – if they are up to it after so long imbibing inherently totalitarian Pro-Choice(-to-Kill-Humans) thinking . . .

The political Left in Canada and the U.S. and other countries today should not look on this non-partisan Human Rights scholar and Pro-Life author as any kind of threat to anything but the Left's current unwitting Pro-Choice (and sometimes Neo-Marxist) *politically extremist* 'Creeping Totalitarianism' which has led to the "Pro-Choice Left" unwittingly passing more and more totalitarian-oriented laws and policies in recent years. This non-partisan author is the best friend the Left has. Whenever I (nowadays frequently) hear someone say "Left," "Leftist," or "Progressive" or "Liberal" as if it was a dirty word, or as if the Left was *inherently* totalitarian and thus always *for* legal human-killing (like abortion) and always *against* Free Speech (an understandable mistake given the laws the Left in my country keep passing), I use my scholar's knowledge to clarify to them that the Left does not have to be that way. I instead clarify that the problem is that a *Pro-Choice legal human-killing abortion* Left is an unwittingly but inherently *extremist* Left. Which is indeed a great threat to Free Democracy, as much as the *extremist* Left Soviet Marxists and *extremist* Right Nazis – the first two political parties to legalize abortion – were. Because to be a Pro-Choice legal human-killing abortion Left (or Right) is to *think about human life* in ways which fundamentally reject the *equal human preciousness without exception* and *Equal Human Rights for All Humans* which Free Democracy is built on and depends on.

As a non-partisan friend of the "real" Left, I am happy to point out that in my non-partisan estimation the single greatest contributor to *Equal Human Rights for All Humans* in the last century was a politician of the Left – America's longest-serving First Lady, Democrat Eleanor Roosevelt, who guided the production of the United Nations' magnificent 1948 *Universal Declaration of Human Rights*. But it is precisely in comparison to her, "the Best of the Left," that today's Pro-Choice legal-human-killing-abortion Left is starkly revealed as an *extremist* Left which must get back to its roots and abandon its unwittingly but fundamentally totalitarian Pro-Choice thinking before the Pro-Choice Extremist Left unwittingly destroys all pretense of Free Democracy in America and elsewhere. Because the Left in America, Canada and other countries can no longer even tell the difference between totalitarianism and democracy any more, after following totalitarian legal human-killing precedents within a supposed democracy for so long. This non-partisan scholar and author and educator in this book series provides the best chance the Pro-Choice legal-human-killing-abortion *Extremist Left* has of *rediscovering its lost democratic soul*. And becoming a proper part of a healthy democracy, with progressive Left and conservative Right in healthy balance and the *Foundational Principles of Human Rights and Democracy* upheld equally by both so that voters need never fear losing their democracy to 'Creeping Totalitarianism.'

Note that this Human Rights scholar is truly non-partisan and has both harsh and healing words for the Right as well. This author's country could not have become the world leader in Pro-Choice 'Creeping Totalitarianism' that it is without a Right that itself is uneducated in the Human Rights History, Science and Logic in this book; a Right that in its ignorance is very inconsistent in its adherence to *The Foundational Principles of Human Rights and Democracy,* and too often just too spineless and cowardly to stand up against the Pro-Choice Extremist Left's "progressive dismantling" of Free Democracy before their very eyes when the Pro-Choice Left is in power.

"The price of cowardice will only be evil. We shall reap courage and victory only when we dare to make sacrifices."
— Aleksandr Solzhenitsyn

The Right in my country and others has often proven too cowardly to reverse any totalitarian-oriented legislation the Pro-Choice Extremist Left put in even when the Right is in power. So, worldwide in many places the Right also needs this Human

Rights scholar's solid *Human Rights Education* to fully recover and courageously express its democratic soul. It is not enough for Right-wing parties to merely be "big tent" enough to *accept* Pro-Lifers as party members (which the totalitarian-style "ideologically uniform" Left no longer does in this author's country; the U.S. Left in a similar trend on April 8, 2020 "purged" from the Tennessee Democrat party a 26-year incumbent African-American elected Representative and State Legislator for daring once to vote Pro-Life – like in my country, the American Left has so totally *lost* its grounding in democracy's foundations it does not even *want* people who believe in *Equal Human Rights for All Humans*).

Lasting democracy requires *both* Left and Right to finally get well-educated in Free Democracy's historical and logical foundations and *together* constitutionally enshrine and support them – as this author's books were written to help them do. *"The Winner" is always Free Democracy whenever both Left and Right uphold The Foundational Principles of Human Rights and Democracy.*

THE THINKING REVOLUTION informed by this HUMAN RIGHTS EDUCATION FOR LASTING FREE DEMOCRACY with THE INTELLECTUAL HONESTY CHALLENGE (See CHAPTER 7) given to Pro-Choice bigots WHO DO NOT OR WILL NOT THINK is necessary to correct unthinking and uneducated Pro-Choice 'Creeping Totalitarianism': Because intelligent and intellectually honest people can tell the difference between totalitarianism and democracy, and between what is and what is not political extremism. But today's Pro-Choice Left cannot make these easy distinctions from where they stand on the *extremist legal human-killing* Left. Legal human-killing is inherently politically extremist (and bigoted – bigotry, by definition, denies equal human worth or rights to some group or groups of humans, like Pro-Choicers do). Legal human-killing is bigoted and extremist, whether in Auschwitz and the Nazi Death Camps for the bigoted *Holocaust* Genocide-killing of millions of Jewish and disabled humans; whether in Ukraine for the bigoted *Holodomor* Genocide-killing of millions of this author's ethnic group; whether the bigoted abortion-killing of millions of preborn humans (a bigoted rejection of the *Inherent Human Right to Live*) starting in totalitarian Soviet Russia and Nazi Germany which first legalized abortion (and genocide); or whether today's Pro-Choice bigotry that *also* effectively says "this group of young humans has no Human Rights and can be legally killed by abortion" in Canada and the U.S. and Europe, etc.; intellectually honest and intelligent people can see that legal human-killing is always politically extremist. For the same reason that intellectually honest and intelligent people can see the difference between "choosing" parenthood, adoption, or abortion when one is pregnant.

The Pro-*Choice* Left wants people to see abortion as simply a "third option" of what a woman can *choose* whenever she finds herself pregnant. Canadian Pro-Life *Equal Human Rights for All Humans* advocate Stephanie Gray has sensibly pointed out that abortion is not simply a "third option" to parenthood or adoption, because unlike parenthood or adoption, abortion dismembers, decapitates, and disembowels a human baby, instead of raising a human baby with love into mature human adulthood, as parenthood and adoption do. Intelligent and intellectually honest thinkers can easily see this stark difference between these "choices" which are *why* in free democracies implicitly built on Equal Human Rights it has always been recognized that *choices to kill humans (whatever their age) are wrong and criminal*; which is *why* after the evil *politically extremist* Soviets and Nazis made the human-killing of millions by abortion, euthanasia, and genocide *legal*, the Free West to save humanity and democracy made the *Universal Declaration of Human Rights* which formally declared "recognition of the *inherent* dignity and of the *equal* and *inalienable* rights of *all* members of the *human family* is the *foundation* of freedom, justice and peace in the world." *Inherent, Equal, Inalienable Human Rights for All Humans* "without distinction of any kind.

"But those same hands which once screwed tight our handcuffs now hold out their palms in reconciliation: 'No, don't! Don't dig up the past! Dwell on the past and you'll lose an eye.' But the proverb goes on to say: 'Forget the past and you'll lose two eyes'"
"It is unthinkable in the twentieth century to fail to distinguish between what constitutes an abominable atrocity that must be prosecuted and what constitutes that 'past' which 'ought not to be stirred up.'"
— *Historian Aleksandr Solzhenitsyn, The Gulag Archipelago 1918-1956*

"**It is intolerable in the twenty-first century** that (while voters distracted by technology are unaware of it) Western Free Democracy is teetering on the brink of doom and this author and Human Rights scholar can be arrested and imprisoned in his supposed democracy for peacefully saying "killing humans is wrong because Human Rights are for all humans" within up to 150 meters/500 feet of a legal human-killing abortion facility.

Just because insufficiently educated and illogical Pro-Choice-to-Kill-Humans politicians (and the Mainstream Media which Solzhenitsyn warned the West was Marxist-influenced) witlessly following the genocidal totalitarian, extremist Soviet Marxist State's 1920 precedent of legal human-killing abortion (before legalizing genocide of this author's ethnicity) have **failed to distinguish between what constitutes a Democratic State (legal protection of humans as *precious*, with *inherent, equal, inalienable* Human Rights not given them by the government) and what constitutes a Totalitarian State (legal human-killing because the State is greater than humans and decides just *which* humans have *which* rights, if any).**

Western Democracy is at a critical 'tipping point' on the brink of doom because Pro-*Choice* bigots in governments and media (and "Big Tech") who (like all bigots) *choose* just *which* humans they think have worth and rights and just *which* humans they think have less or no worth, less or no rights have **failed to distinguish what constitutes an abominable atrocity that must be prosecuted (like the legal abortion first legalized by the genocidal Marxist Soviets in 1920 and then legalized by the genocidal Fascist Nazis in 1934** *because these genocidal Totalitarian States did not believe killing humans is wrong*).

All because Pro-Choice, legal human-killing abortion politicians and political parties and (Marxist-influenced) Mainstream Media and "Big Tech" have **failed to learn and understand the past which must be 'stirred up'** and understood so that we can understand our current position in the flow of *Living History* today. *This is the only way to make our future safe and free.* Abortion is the touchstone issue for determining the health and longevity of any democracy, because wherever human-killing abortion is legal, there is no legally recognized *Inherent, Equal, Inalienable Human Right to Live*, and therefore no basis for lasting Free Democracy."
— William Baptiste
Founder, *Human Rights and Freedoms Forever!*
Founder, *The Intellectual Honesty Challenge*
Proclaimer of THE THINKING REVOLUTION

"There can be no acceptable future without an honest analysis of the past."
— *Aleksandr Solzhenitsyn*

CHAPTER 1: FACTS

Science, Logic, and the TOP 6 FACTS of Human Rights History that Prove Pro-Life Equals Pro-Democracy (and Pro-Choice Equals Pro-Totalitarianism)
Legally Recognized and Protected Human Rights Began with the 4ᵗʰ Century Criminalization of Abortion because Human Life was Then First Recognized as Precious Not Cheap; Human-Killing by Abortion was First Legalized by the Genocidal Extremist Left-Wing Totalitarian Soviet Marxists in 1920; and Next by the Genocidal Extremist Right-Wing Totalitarian Nazi Fascists in 1934

"Abortion is the touchstone issue for determining the health and longevity of any democracy, because wherever human-killing abortion is legal, there is no legally recognized Inherent, Equal, Inalienable Human Right to Live, and therefore no basis for lasting Free Democracy."
– William Baptiste

"You can resolve to live your life with integrity. Let your credo be this: Let the lie come into the world, let it even triumph. But not through me."
— Aleksandr Solzhenitsyn

"I add this caveat for Pro-Choice politicians and voters: Stop the lie. Before you read this, you already knew that preborn humans are humans. You already knew that abortion kills humans. You already knew that killing humans is wrong. So all you have to do is stop lying."
– William Baptiste

"The simple step of a courageous individual is not to take part in the lie. One word of truth outweighs the world."
— Aleksandr Solzhenitsyn

[Note: CHAPTER 1: FACTS is only a very brief introduction to the facts of Science, Logic and Human Rights History most pertinent to the development and maintenance of Human Rights and Free Democracy. Each of the "Top 6 Facts" (or "clusters of facts") below is subject of an entire chapter in the author's book *PRO-LIFE EQUALS PRO-DEMOCRACY*. Science has one chapter and Logic has two chapters of that more in-depth book.]

The powerful collection of mostly well-known (at least to scholars in the pertinent fields) and mostly undisputed (even "textbook") facts of Human Rights History, Science, and Logic briefly introduced in this chapter, along with the facts of the History of Philosophy in CHAPTER 3: PHILOSOPHY, *demand a thoughtful and intellectually honest response from the reader*. And every citizen voter in every democracy should read this book's HUMAN RIGHTS EDUCATION FOR LASTING FREE DEMOCRACY so they can become *well-educated* voters, who no longer cast *uneducated* votes for *uneducated* politicians (and political parties) who are *ignorant* of these facts, and who for decades now have therefore been (wittingly or unwittingly) undermining genuine Human Rights and gradually destroying Free Democracy by passing uneducated and 'Creeping Totalitarian' laws and policies.

Anti-democratic, totalitarian-oriented policies including legalized human-killing laws witlessly following genocidal totalitarian *Extremist Left* (Soviet Marxist) and *Extremist Right* (Nazi Fascist) precedents, such as human-killing abortion and human-killing euthanasia, both expressly forbidden by the ancient doctors' Hippocratic Oath (*real doctors don't kill humans!*). Anti-democratic, totalitarian-oriented policies including the increasing number of laws in this author's country and elsewhere making peaceful "Pro-Life" *Human Rights advocacy* on behalf of democracy-grounding *Equal Human Rights for All Humans* a *crime* punishable by jail and/or heavy fines. It is obviously intolerable and unacceptable that this author and Human Rights scholar, under current laws in several jurisdictions in my country, can be arrested and imprisoned for peacefully saying "killing humans is wrong because Human Rights are for all humans;" can be arrested and *imprisoned just for speaking verifiable scientific and medical facts* in support of this conclusion; and can be arrested and imprisoned even just for "looking the wrong way" or for "staring" at a human-killing abortion clinic, which local police in this author's national capital made very clear to local Pro-Lifers would be taken as a sign of the "disapproval of abortion" which is now *illegal* to express in any fashion within up to 150 meters/500 feet of a human-killing abortion facility – under this "thought-police" law that only belongs in a totalitarian police state.

Many countries now (including the author's) have many such laws and policies which, specifically in order to provide "abortion access" completely unhindered by the pesky morals of anyone who actually believes *killing humans is wrong*, now restrict normal democratic freedoms of speech, expression, assembly, conscience and religion of those who believe in *The Foundational Principles of Human Rights and Democracy* revealed from Human Rights History, Science and Logic (and Philosophy) in this book. Not stopping there, the author's country and many others have now also passed many laws and policies against free speech and so on, restricting normal democratic freedoms in relation to other issues than abortion (other issues than *Equal Human Rights for All Humans*). In other areas too, even *speaking verifiable Science* is now a *crime* whenever Science does not support newfangled unscientific ideologies promoted by the government. Under totalitarian-oriented laws *invariably*

66

passed by Pro-Choice legal human-killing abortion-supporting politicians and parties when in power. Abortion is indeed the touchstone issue for determining the health and longevity of any democracy, because wherever human-killing abortion is legal, there is no legally recognized *Inherent, Equal, Inalienable Human Right to Live,* and therefore no basis for lasting Free Democracy.

Yes, this powerful collection of facts demands a thoughtful and intellectually honest response. THE INTELLECTUAL HONESTY CHALLENGE in Chapter 7 posits that there is no such intelligent response which allows for legal abortion to continue. Anyone currently "Pro-Choice" who disagrees is hereby *challenged* to mount an intelligent and intellectually honest response to this book's conclusions based on facts to see if they can intelligently and honestly "justify" remaining Pro-Choice, or else concede to this book's conclusions and change their position, as intellectual honesty demands, if they cannot. All those who now lean "Pro-Choice" – especially the "Pro-Choice" politicians now passing totalitarian laws with no place in a healthy democracy; and especially those in influential mainstream media and "Big Tech" who for decades have supported the "Pro-Choice" legal human-killing position against the *Equal Human Rights for All Humans* position of the "Pro-Life" movement – all those who want to continue the current legal human-killing abortion practices first legalized in totalitarian States because these evil regimes did not believe that *killing humans is wrong* have invited upon themselves THE INTELLECTUAL HONESTY CHALLENGE in Chapter 7. And now for the brief introduction to the most pertinent facts of a solid HUMAN RIGHTS EDUCATION FOR LASTING FREE DEMOCRACY . . .

Science:

Every Human Life is the Same Unique Living Individual Biological Human Organism with Absolutely Unique Human DNA Utterly Distinct from His or Her Parents at Every Age and Stage of His or Her Human Life-cycle (zygote to senior adult). All of the following terms are commonly used to describe this SAME objective scientific reality: "everyone," "people," "human," "human life," "human being," "human person," "adult," "teenager," "senior," "man," "woman," "male," "female," "child," "toddler," "baby," "pregnancy," "fetus," "embryo," "handicapped," "disabled" "healthy," "Jew," "Gentile," "Black," White." It is intellectually dishonest and logically inconsistent and unsound (not to mention *bigoted*) to treat the same objective scientific reality of a human life *differently* (having different *value* and *rights*) based on the mere choice of different *wording* to describe the same underlying human *existence* (which is what human *being* means). **Only bigots deny human *personhood* to human *beings.***

Humans, Human Beings, Human Persons – These Terms Are Equivalent in Their Meaning and Origin, and Only Ignorant Bigots Like Nazis and Slave-Owners and Misogynists and Pro-Choicers Have Ever Acknowledged a Human's Biological Human Life While Denying Their Human Personhood and Attendant Equal Human Rights

Those Pro-Choicers who try to pretend that there is some fundamental difference between a "human life" (which most, if pressed, will acknowledge cannot be scientifically denied of preborn human lives) and a "human being" or "human person" with *rights*, are just engaging in intellectually dishonest (and bigoted) wordplay, based in their utter *ignorance* of the meaning and origin of these terms.

The term "human person" is historically rooted in the Christian theology of the One God in Three *Persons* who created human life "in God's Image," such that as long as *any* humans have been called "persons," with rights, preborn humans have been called "persons," with rights. Preborn human lives/persons had legally protected Human Rights since the 318 AD criminalization of abortion and infanticide due to Christian influence, which was the first time the *Inherent Human Right to Live* of *any* human was legally acknowledged and protected.

Further, a human life or "human *being*" is literally a "human *existence*," as opposed to a "feline being" (a cat life or existence), a "canine being" (a dog life or existence), a "bovine being" (a cow life or existence), or an "elephantine being" (an elephant life or existence), and so on. All canines are canine *beings* who exist; all humans are human *beings* who exist, and who have since Christianity was adopted by the West been acknowledged as precious human *persons* with rights, rights protected from the womb by Western law or custom since 318 AD.

Pro-Choicers even say ignorant things like "it's not a human, it's a fetus" (which this author has actually heard ignorant Pro-Choicers say – one screamed it in his face). Here Pro-Choicers are merely displaying their gross *ignorance* of Science. The scientific and medical term "fetus" does not even identify what *species* it is, it only identifies what *age* (and stage of a living mammal being's lifecycle) it is. "A fetus" (which is Latin for "little one," by the way – used even as a term of endearment) can be a cat fetus; a dog fetus; a cow fetus; or an elephant fetus (and so on). So whenever the word "fetus" is used in the context of the abortion debate, it always means a *human* fetus (recalling the Latin meaning: a "little" human). That is, as opposed to a fetal-age ("little") dog or cat life, "fetus" in abortion debate context means a *fetal-age human* life; a fetal-age human *being/existence; a* fetal-age human *person.*

The murderous and genocidal totalitarian Marxist Soviets and Fascist Nazis, at opposite extremes of the political spectrum, controlled the first two modern States to legalize human-killing by abortion, *having no illusions* about the basic scientific fact they were killing humans and making it legal (the Nazis then legalized euthanasia human-killing, and both evil regimes afterwards legalized the mass killing of born humans by genocide as well). So, to make something as inherently anti-human, murderous, and totalitarian as abortion legal in a supposed Free Democracy which is supposedly built upon Human Rights, legal abortion supporters never speak with scientific honesty and accuracy about just what abortion does to just whom. As noted by Canadian *Equal Human Rights for All Humans* advocate Stephanie Gray, a *typical abortion decapitates, dismembers and disembowels a human baby.* Scientifically speaking, abortion kills a unique living individual biological human organism with absolutely unique human DNA utterly distinct from his or her parents at every age and stage of his or her human life-cycle (zygote to senior adult – but aborted human males and females never live to the senior adult stage of their human life-cycle).

As this book shows in its discussion of the History of Philosophy (see CHAPTER 3: PHILOSOPHY), all *morally relativist* ideologies, including the politically extremist and genocidal Soviet Marxist and Nazi Fascist ideologies which were the first to legalize human-killing by abortion, are rooted in the philosophically radically *Skeptical* and *Relativist* stream of philosophy which is actually opposed to the philosophical *Realism* which grounds all Science, Logic, and Technology. So, we cannot expect those who are deep-down *Relativists not Realists*, who therefore have very little grasp on scientifically verifiable *Reality* itself, to be very intelligent nor intellectually honest in how they think or in how they use words. Because they have what (Nobel Prize-winning author, historian and world-class expert on Marxism) Aleksandr Solzhenitsyn referred to as "impaired thinking ability" coming from their Relativism.

So of course, since Pro-Choicers are so extremely intellectually dishonest that they will mis-define and misuse otherwise medically accurate terms like "fetus" or "embryo" in order to effectively *de-humanize* a fetal-age, embryonic-age human enough to seemingly "justify" *killing* a human of that age by abortion, naturally Pro-Choicers do not stop there with dishonest wording intended to *hide* the scientifically verifiable *reality* of *humans* being killed by abortion. Pro-Choicers have for decades thus used the dishonest, de-humanizing term "tissue blob" to describe what is in scientific fact *a unique living individual biological human organism with absolutely unique human DNA utterly distinct from his or her parents at every age and stage of his or her human life-cycle (zygote to senior adult).* Pro-Choicers inaccurately calling a human baby a "tissue blob" is less common now because medical science has advanced so much since abortion was legalized, that we now have rich scientific evidence of the humanity of human life within the womb, with ultrasounds and with full-color spectroscopic photography and video of preborn humans living their human lives in the womb, and even responding to stimuli from the outside world (mother's or father's voice; music from headphones/speakers placed on the mother's tummy; one classic photo shows a fetal-age human arm emerging from a surgical cut and grasping the hand of a surgeon performing a delicate fetal surgery on the child). But Pro-Choicers, being so far removed from intelligence and honesty by their bad philosophy, still sometimes call young humans in the womb "tissue blobs" or use similarly dishonest de-humanizing terms for human babies.

For example, Planned Parenthood, the world's biggest abortion provider, in their literature and in their speaking to women seeking abortion frequently use the dishonest, de-humanizing term "uterine contents" to describe what they are "removing" in an abortion. To manipulate the woman pregnant with (scientifically-speaking) *a unique living individual biological human organism with absolutely unique human DNA utterly distinct from his or her parents at every age and stage of his or her human life-cycle (zygote to senior adult)* into *killing* this unique human life by abortion, they will refer to this human life about to be snuffed out by their bigotry as mere "uterine contents." But such intellectually dishonest and bigoted denial of real humanity is to be expected from Planned Parenthood. Margaret Sanger, the founder of Planned Parenthood, was a eugenicist (like Hitler), and thus Planned Parenthood originally offered abortion "services" only in *Black* American neighborhoods, specifically to ensure that there were less "undesirable" Black Americans. Bigoted Planned Parenthood abortion-killing, now extended to all races through bigotry against young, preborn humans of any race, are still disproportionately performed upon Black humans. And Planned Parenthood (and other abortion providers) still aggressively promote abortion, often against the local law, in (predominantly Pro-Life) African nations. Bigoted Planned Parenthood from its beginning just wants the world to have less Black humans, who Planned Parenthood has always considered "undesirable" – Planned Parenthood having always been completely opposed to the Pro-Life Movement's democracy-grounding principle of *Equal Human Rights for All Humans.*

[Note: Should any representative of Planned Parenthood want to dispute this book which reveals the always-totalitarian and anti-democratic, intellectually dishonest evil of the legal human-killing abortion they so aggressively promote, they are hereby given THE INTELLECTUAL HONESTY CHALLENGE in this book. To not respond to it is to tacitly admit all charges against them in particular and against legal abortion in general. They are challenged to respond without all the usual Pro-Choice intellectually dishonest tricks exposed in this book, like pretending well-established facts just do not exist, or using *logical fallacies.* This INTELLECTUAL HONESTY CHALLENGE is their chance to repent of past unjustifiable, intellectually dishonest evil and rejoin the human race instead of being one of its biggest murderous assailants.]

In review: Pro-Choicers just advertise their ignorant bigotry whenever they claim a preborn human is somehow not a "human being" or not a "human person" in order to "justify" *killing them* by abortion even though they are humans. The term "human being" just means "human existence," and the scientifically verifiable human existence of preborn, fetal-age humans (like every one of us when we were fetal-age humans) has never been in doubt. The very term and concept of *personhood* as we know it comes from Christian theology. Christians worship One Loving God in Three *Persons* who created humanity "in God's Image," and therefore precious, valuable humans "made in God's Image" are called *persons,* who have rights, starting with the *Inherent Human Right to Live.*

Christian influence in the West protected precious human life in the womb by law or custom since the 4th Century until the evil, genocidal 20th Century Soviet Marxists and Nazi Fascists first decriminalized abortion (Marxists at the Extreme Left and Fascists at the Extreme Right of the political spectrum – because legal human-killing is, of course, *extremist*). So as long as *any* humans have been called "persons" with rights, pre-born humans have been called "persons," with legally protected Human Rights since 318 AD when abortion was first criminalized due to Christian influence. And only misogynistic, slave-owning, Nazi, or other bigots who deny equal Human Rights to all humans have ever acknowledged a life's biological humanity while denying their human "personhood" and ensuing *equal Human Rights.*

From a logical standpoint, the problem is that Pro-Choicers do not define their terms, or define them dishonestly, in such a way as to *hide* the facts of the matter (like that preborn humans are humans) instead of being accurate and precise. Pro-Choicers use just about every logical fallacy in the book (see below).

If Logic had been regularly taught in high schools the last 70 years since the 1948 *Universal Declaration of Human Rights* clarified the West's long (Judeo-Christian) Traditional understanding of *equal human preciousness* and the *Inherent Right to Live* which undergirds Democracy, abortion would never have been legalised (and the UN would never have turned into today's abortion-pushing totalitarian-oriented monster the UN was originally created to fight, giving backup to every Pro-Choice totalitarian-oriented State now legislating against Free Speech of peaceful Pro-Life Human Rights Advocacy, including this author's country).

If since the 1948 *Universal Declaration of Human Rights* Logic had been taught in schools, as a core subject of knowing how to reason validly and honestly, abortion would never have been legalised, because it would be so easy to see that legal abortion had absolutely no logical merit (in addition to legal abortion being literally one of the Nazi "crimes against humanity" the Nazis were condemned for the same year of 1948, at Nuremberg).

The *Universal Declaration of Human Rights* affirmed that Human Rights were for all humans

---

"without distinction of any kind" because "recognition of the inherent dignity and of the equal and inalienable rights of all members of the human family is the foundation of freedom, justice and peace in the world."

The United Nations' *Universal Declaration of Human Rights* specifically intended to stop nations from in the future adding to bigoted government legislation which recognized a life's biological humanity while denying human personhood and attendant Human Rights, such as the following bigoted legal pronouncements through history collected by one Human Rights advocacy group:

"In the eyes of the law ... the slave is not a person"
Virginia Supreme Court decision, 1858
"An Indian is not a person within the meaning of the Constitution."
George Canfield, American Law Review, 1881
"The statutory word 'person' did not in these circumstances include women."
British Voting Rights case, 1909
"The Reichsgericht itself refused to recognize Jews ... as 'persons' in the legal sense."
German Supreme Court decision, 1936
"The law of Canada does not recognize the unborn child as a legal person possessing rights."

THROUGHOUT HISTORY, IF ANY LIFE IS RECOGNIZED AS HUMAN BUT NOT A PERSON, GRAVE INJUSTICE RESULTS

Logic:
Perfectly Sound and Scientific Logical Syllogism:
All Humans Have Human Rights.
Preborn Humans are Humans.
Therefore, Preborn Humans have Human Rights.

There is much more discussion from the Formal Science of Logic in the author's books *DEMOCRACY 101* and *Pro-Life Equals Pro-Democracy*. For now, the reader should note that *all* Pro-Choice "arguments" are logical *fallacies of distraction* which with massive intellectual dishonesty simply *avoid the question* of the Human Rights of the humans killed in abortions. That is, as a rule Pro-Choicers *avoid* ever speaking honestly about the very crux of the Abortion Debate (the Human Rights for All Humans Debate) because intellectual honesty means they lose the Debate. The simple reality is that if humans have Human Rights, then abortion, which (scientifically indisputably) kills humans, is wrong. If Human Rights are for all humans and not just some humans, then abortion, which kills humans, is wrong. Human Rights are meaningless if being human is not enough to have them. And every racist or anti-Semitic bigot, just like Pro-Choice bigots, denies Equal Human Rights to some humans. The manifest illogical silliness and blunt intellectual dishonesty of the usual so-called "major" arguments for legal abortion are demonstrated logically after the following brief review of the "Top 6 Facts of Human Rights History that Prove Pro-Life = Pro-Democracy (and Pro-Choice = Pro-Totalitarianism) – each of which "top facts" is subject of an entire chapter in this author's book *Pro-Life Equals Pro-Democracy: A Sequel to Aleksandr Solzhenitsyn's The Gulag Archipelago (Let's End 100 Years of Western Marxists Insidiously Undermining Democracy, Since Marxist Russia Legalized Abortion in 1920 to the 2020 Pandemic).*

Note that the further, deeper discussion from the Formal Science of Logic in the author's longer books includes the author's damning logical analysis of the United Nations' supremely absurd and illogical "Pro-Choice-Legal-Human-Killing" changes to its understanding of the "Right to Life" proposed in 2017 and adopted in 2018. This analysis is reproduced in *DEMOCRACY 101* and is actually available on the United Nations' own website by going to the United Nations' *Office of the High Commissioner for Human Rights* webpage:

http://www.ohchr.org/EN/HRBodies/CCPR/Pages/GC36-
Article6Righttolife.aspx

At this webpage, scroll down the alphabetical list of Non-Governmental Organization (NGO) documents and click on the link to the document of the NGO Human Rights and Freedoms Forever! (or use these links in the electronic edition of this book).

As is typical of ideologues with *ideology* instead of *education* and what Solzhenitsyn called "impaired thinking ability" due to philosophical Relativism, today's "Pro-Choice-Legal-Human-Killing" UN, which has already betrayed any intelligent and honest reading of the UN's magnificent 1948 *Universal Declaration of Human Rights* by being "Pro-Choice," simply *ignored* this feedback they asked for and even published on their own website, and went ahead and changed International Law anyway, without even addressing this feedback which proves their high intellectual dishonesty (and "ideological lobotomy"). In today's Pro-Choice (and usually Neo-Marxist) 'Creeping Totalitarianism,' since all the facts are on the Pro-Life side, it has become typical for Pro-Choice governments and organizations to in this way create the *illusion* of "democratic consultation" by asking for feedback before making a totalitarian change in law or policy, then ignore all the good feedback they get that would protect Democracy, and make the totalitarian change they intended from the beginning anyway.

The TOP 6 FACTS of Human Rights History that Prove Pro-Life = Pro-Democracy (and Pro-Choice = Pro-Totalitarianism)

Fact 1: Legal Pro-Choice Abortion and Totalitarian Government Were Both NORMAL Before There Were Any Legally Recognized Human Rights and Human Life was Cheap Not Precious and Served the Greater State.

"Popular entertainment" included torture and murder in the Roman arenas. One third of the population were slaves. Slavery meant that (adult or child) a slave could be – and often was – a sex toy for the slaveowner. **Parents had the Pro-Choice "right to CHOOSE" to raise or to kill their own human children (by abortion or infanticide),** or sell them into slavery (where they could be killed or sexually abused at the whim of the slaveowner), for the very same reason governments had the right to enslave or kill their human citizens (and human subjects not even accorded citizenship) at whim - *there were no legally recognized Human Rights governments were obligated to recognize and protect.*

Fact 2: Legal Human Rights Started with the 4th Century Criminalization of Abortion Due to the Ancient (Christian) Pro-Life Principle that All Humans without Exception are Equally Precious Not Cheap, Implicitly Establishing the Inherent Human Right to Live Which State Governments are Obligated to Protect.

Christianity introduced into the West the term and concept of *personhood,* based in the Christian theology of the one God in three *Persons* who made humanity, "male and female" equally "in God's Image" (Genesis 1:27, from the very first page of the Bible). Because Christians understand God is mysteriously three *Persons,* humans made in God's Image began to be called *persons - with inherent high value and inherent rights.* Thus, as long as *any* humans have been called *persons*, with inherent rights, *preborn* humans have been called *persons*, with an *Inherent Human Right to Live* legally protected in Western Law or custom since the 318 AD criminalization of abortion (which happened 5 years after the West stopped violently persecuting Christians in 313 AD and started listening to them).

Note: As discussed more thoroughly in the author's books (in the HUMAN RIGHTS EDUCATION FOR LASTING FREE DEMOCRACY book series) *Pro-Life Equals Pro-Democracy* and *DEMOCRACY 101* – Western *Christian* Civilization from the 4th Century to the first half of the 20th Century provided the necessary background for the logical development of Modern Human Rights. Legally recognized Human Rights started with the 4th Century criminalization of abortion and infanticide due to Christian influence, and culminated in the UN's 1948 *Universal Declaration of Human Rights*, produced under the direction of a devout Christian at a time when most in the "Free West" were baptized Christians and attended a Christian Church (see Fact 4 below). In addition to *personhood*, ancient Christians also introduced the West to *charity* to look after basic human needs. As they do to this day, Christian missionaries and religious orders provided free health care and education to as many humans as possible (Christian or not), raising the *quality* of human life in order to best serve the great dignity of humans "made in God's Image." Christians invented hospitals and universities as an outgrowth of these pursuits in recognition of the Christian belief in *equal human preciousness* - which is one of *The Foundational Principles of Human Rights and Democracy* described in CHAPTER 2: PRINCIPLES. Note also – as discussed more thoroughly in the author's books *Pro-Life Equals Pro-Democracy* and *DEMOCRACY 101,* excerpts from the former appearing in CHAPTER 3: PHILOSOPHY below – that Modern Science and the Modern Scientific Method were developed by devout Christians, some Catholic (Nicolaus Copernicus, Johannes Kepler, Galileo Galilei), some Protestant (Sir Francis Bacon, Sir Isaac Newton) in the Christian universities of Christian Europe, the world's first stable, long-term community of scientific scholars, logically building Science as we know it upon *First Principles* gleaned from the Bible - that the universe is an *ordered cosmos*, with an intelligent orderer/Creator God, and *not* an ultimately random, *undirected chaos* - which is *why* it is worth looking at Nature for underlying patterns of *order*, the sign of an ordering intelligence, as Science does. Science never developed wherever an ordering intelligence was not assumed as *First Principles*, and all the major figures of the Scientific Revolution which established Modern Science and the Modern Scientific Method were devout Christians. Later on, colonists from Christian Europe wherever they went typically ended indigenous wars and indigenous Human Rights abuses like human sacrifices, cannibalism, widow-burning, and giving children over to be temple prostitutes, in accordance with the Christian principles that underlie Human Rights. Unfortunately, colonists may not be the most devout Christians themselves and did not always show proper Christian love and respect for every indigenous human "made in God's Image." So, devout Christians became the Founders of *International Law* to help make up for this lack. All the Founders of International Law were devout Christians, some Catholic (Friar Francisco de Vitoria; Father Francisco Suárez), some Protestant (Alberico Gentili, Hugo Grotius). Devout Christians founded International Law in order to protect humans and their inherent rights to life and property no matter where they were, whether they were Christian or not, and however primitive their civilizations might be compared to Europe. Most of the greatest social reformers in history, such as William Wilberforce ending slavery in the British Empire, were devout Christians specifically trying to have Christian principles like *equal human*

74

preciousness without exception better put into practice in their country. Non-Christian social reformers like Gandhi were educated in the Christian West, well-versed in the Judeo-Christian Bible, and heavily influenced by Christian principles.

Bulverism: A Major Democracy-Destroying Logical Fallacy Now Widespread

---

"Nothing worthy can be built on a neglect of higher meanings and on a relativistic view of concepts and culture as a whole."
"The generation now coming out of Western schools is unable to distinguish good from bad. Even those words are unacceptable. This results in impaired thinking ability."
"... We have arrived at an intellectual chaos."
— Aleksandr Solzhenitsyn

The "impaired thinking ability" which Solzhenitsyn notes is related to Atheist Moral Relativism – the moral relativism which led the Atheist Soviets to be the very first to legalize human-killing by abortion (and later by genocide) – can be seen from any consideration of Logic. This author has taught courses in Logic, and will later show how literally *all* of the arguments used by Pro-Choicers (including most Atheists) to support legal human-killing abortion are logical fallacies, which not only do not prove any Pro-Choicer's case for legal abortion, but actually prove that Pro-Choicers do not know how to argue logically nor with intellectual honesty at all. But there is another logical fallacy typically used by Pro-Choicers (and Atheists), which entirely shuts off their brains before rational argument ever even takes place, which it is appropriate to briefly introduce here after introducing the Christian origins of Western freedom.

This author's books make it clear how Traditional Western, Judeo-Christian Pro-Life Family Values and principles include and support *The Foundational Principles of Human Rights and Democracy*. This is why:

Anti-Christian and Pro-Choice Bigotry Can Destroy Democracy Which Depends on Christian and Pro-Life Principles:
Today's Uneducated and Unintelligent Anti-Christian and Pro-Choice Bigotry Uses What the Science of Logic Calls "the Genetic Fallacy" Combined with "Circular Reasoning" Known as "Bulverism" to Simply Dismiss or Ignore a Pro-Life or Christian Opponent's Argument Merely *Because* it is Christian or Pro-Life (Turning Off the Brain and Ignoring the Overwhelming Facts of Human Rights History, Science, and Logic Which Show that Pro-Life = Pro-Democracy and that at Least *Respecting* the Christian Origins of Human Rights is Essential for LASTING Democracy – Dismissing Established or Verifiable Facts Merely Because it is a Christian or Pro-Lifer Who is Presenting the Facts, Which is Bigoted and Unthinking).
Anti-Christian and Pro-Choice Bigotry and Illogical "Bulverism" in Politicians, Political Parties, Legislators and Judges is Extremely Dangerous for Free Democracies, because Free Democracy and Human Rights are Demonstrably, Literally, Historically, and Logically Built on Fundamentally

Christian and Pro-Life Principles Which Christians Introduced into the West, and Free Democracy *Cannot Possibly Last* Without Maintaining its Fundamentally Christian and Pro-Life Foundations. This is Not a Prediction. It is Already Evident in the Increasing Compromises of Normal Democratic Freedoms Coming from Pro-Choice Politicians and Political Parties, and from Judges on High Courts Upholding Bigoted Decisions Against Christians and Pro-Lifers in Pro-Choice Judges' Uneducated Ignorance of Key Facts of Logic and Science and Human Rights History.

Because most Pro-Lifers are Christians (because there are over two billion Christians in the world, and because it was Christians who first taught the brutal ancient West and the whole world the "Pro-Life" principle that *killing humans is wrong*), Pro-Choice human-killing bigotry against preborn humans and anti-Christian bigotry frequently go together – and involve the same ignorance of facts and the same logically fallacious thinking behind their bigotry.

Pro-Choice bigots and Anti-Christian bigots (and Illogical "Bulverists" – who are often the "ideologically lobotomized," especially lobotomized by Atheist Marxist ideology which has killed more humans than anything else) invalidly "justify" their unintelligent bigotry without considering any facts or logic by reasoning in a circle of the general nature: "Christian/Pro-Life opinions are not worth considering. Your opinion is not worth considering because you are a Christian/are Pro-Life." "Christians/Pro-Lifers are not worth listening to because they are wrong. Christians/Pro-Lifers are wrong because they are not worth listening to." Circular reasoning can be hard to spot (meaning we can even fool ourselves with it) because it usually uses different wording that *assumes* the *conclusion*, but the different wording still boils down to assuming one's conclusion at the outset without proving or demonstrating it. In this case the effective (and bigoted) and ultimately circular reasoning is the tautology "Christian/Pro-Life opinions are not worth considering because Christian/Pro-Life opinions are not worth considering."

This logically fallacious approach also commits what the Science of Logic calls the "genetic fallacy" ("oh, you just believe that because you're a Christian"). This means discounting an opponent's position out-of-hand only because of the "genetics" or probable "source" of that belief. While it may indeed be true that a Christian got his or her Pro-Life (or other traditional Christian) beliefs from being raised a Christian, this "genetic source" in no way justifies dismissing their position as if it was not supported by facts, evidence, and sound logic (which a Pro-Life position is – super-abundantly – as this HUMAN RIGHTS EDUCATION FOR LASTING FREE DEMOCRACY book series demonstrates). Pro-Choice "arguments" are just a compendium of intellectually dishonest logical fallacies (as demonstrated in the chapters on the Science of Logic in *Pro-Life Equals Pro-Democracy*, and below). The genetic fallacy is yet another Pro-Choice *fallacy of distraction* which dishonestly *avoids the question* of the Human Rights of the humans killed in abortions. Illogical Pro-Choice "Bulverists" do not even engage their brains in a rational argument with a Pro-Lifer over the *Human Rights for all humans* abortion debate – instead of thinking or considering evidence Pro-Choice "Bulverists" just assume their opponent is wrong without proving it (circular reasoning) and condescendingly blame the assumed-but-not-proved wrongness on their Christian faith (the genetic fallacy).

Chapter 1: Facts

All of this is highly bigoted. But all bigotry is based in ignorance or *lack of education and knowledge*, and Pro-Choice anti-Christian bigots have to be about the most ignorant people out there – at least, the most ignorant of/uneducated in the most pertinent facts of Human Rights History, Science, and Logic which prove Pro-Life = Pro-Democracy!

Likely the biggest group of illogical Bulverists unwittingly undermining free democracy after Pro-Choicers are Atheists with their particular (and often rabid) Anti-Christian bigotry. But of course, it was Atheists who first de-criminalized human-killing by abortion in 1920 Soviet Marxist Communist/Socialist Russia (not long before legalizing the *Holodomor* Genocide of this author's ethnic heritage group). Pro-Choice human-killing abortion is typically a feature of Atheist States, which are also typically among the most brutally oppressive totalitarian States ever known to humankind (the scholarly *Black Book of Communism* estimates Atheist Communists killed over 94 million born humans in the 20th Century; they also started the trend of killing pre-born humans by abortion). Although few people are truly dedicated Atheists, because Atheism is so unsatisfying because it ignores the entire spiritual dimension of human life, Atheism still exerts an immense influence in the West through being the cause of Secularism, which adopted Atheism's rejection of Christian "Guiding Principles for Public Policy" in favour of Atheism's principle of *Moral Relativism* (which cannot accept the Christian *Foundational Principles of Human Rights and Democracy* like *equal human preciousness* nor the *Inherent Human Right to Live* nor the Biblical commandment "you shall not kill" as moral absolutes. Without these foundations, Free Democracy cannot be maintained long-term). Secularism depends on the *doubt* of Traditional Christianity's value as the traditional Source of the West's "Guiding Principles for Public Policy," a doubt historically sown by intellectually dishonest Atheists entirely uneducated in the Biblical, Judeo-Christian foundations and history of Science itself, nor educated in the history of Human Rights and Democratic Freedoms.

Many Atheists can be "nice" people – usually because they "borrow" Traditional Western, Judeo-Christian values which do not come from their Atheism and are inconsistent with it ("nice" Atheists cannot win arguments with their fellow Atheists running oppressive Totalitarian States, to convince them to be nicer to humans, based on their common Atheism). This author respects intellectually honest Atheists and is happy to have intelligent dialogue with them. Recently, the more intellectually honest Atheists, especially those well-versed in history, faced with the accelerating degradation of Western freedom as Western society becomes ever more "Post-Christian," have come to admit, if sometimes grudgingly, that Christianity is nowhere near as bad as they used to say it was; is far preferable to where society is going without it, and may well be *necessary* for the *survival* of Western Civilization whether or not they are personally convinced Christianity is true. Historian Tom Holland's book *Dominion: How the Christian Revolution Remade the World* is a notable example. At some point such Atheists may find themselves in the same situation as the devout Atheist Marxists nevertheless sent to the gulag, described in (former Atheist Marxist) Aleksandr Solzhenitsyn's book *The Gulag Archipelago*. Where they have to face the fact that the anti-Christian Atheism they once strenuously promoted has now taken away their very freedom, because Christianity is the religion of Freedom.

This author respects and is happy to respectfully engage with such intellectually honest Atheists. But unfortunately, many other Atheists take their intellectually dishonest "Bulverism" to the next level: not only do they turn off their brains instead of engaging them in honest intelligent argument with Christians or Pro-Lifers who they at the outset merely assumed were wrong without proving it. They often go further, and actually arrogantly, condescendingly disparage and belittle and insult religious believers as if all traditional religious believers were "backwards" and "stupid" for believing differently than Atheists do – without having actually demonstrated their opponents are wrong, nor even having engaged in any intellectually honest argument to attempt to prove them wrong. This author in his book *DEMOCRACY 101* coined the term "Atheistic Flatulence" to describe the unsubstantial but pungently unpleasant extreme intellectual dishonesty of so many Atheists, who thus condescend to and belittle those who disagree with them, because they cannot win an argument on legitimate grounds. Like Pro-Choice opinions for legal abortion, which was first legalized by Atheists in 1920, Atheist opinions in general also depend on a tremendous amount of *ignorance* and *lack of knowledge* of established facts. Atheist and Pro-Choice positions are opinions which only seem reasonable (and only seem *safe*) when you know almost nothing about the history and logical development of Science and of Human Rights (See more on Atheism/Secularism in relation to Christianity – and their very different natural fruits in Western Societies – in CHAPTER 3: PHILOSOPHY below and in the author's next book *Killing Humans Is Wrong*).

◆

Note, as discussed in more detail in CHAPTER 3: PHILOSOPHY below, that there were never any significant numbers of Atheists denying any Ordering Intelligence (Creator God) of the universe before Western Philosophy became *unhinged from Reality itself* through Radical Skepticism which *seriously doubted or denied that even the universe existed*. After most of the (all devout, practicing Christian) scientists of the Scientific Revolution (in the Christian universities of Christian Europe) had already made their vast contributions to Modern Science and the Modern Scientific Method, only after then "Modern Philosophy" began, with Descartes, "the Father of Modern Philosophy" *seriously doubting anything external to his own mind even existed*. No-one can even live for long if they consistently hold such philosophical *Radical Skepticism* that seriously doubts or denies all Common Sense (they will get hit by buses they are not even sure exist). No-one can stay sane for long if they consistently hold such philosophical *Radical Skepticism* that seriously doubts or denies all objective facts and Science which are grounded in philosophical *Realism* that accepts the universe we humans commonly perceive with our senses as *real, which is why Science studies it to discern the patterns of Order that govern the intricately Ordered Cosmos*. Thus Descartes, himself a good Christian and far too intelligent to stay *divorced from reality*, grew beyond this absurd radically skeptical silliness which was fair enough to explore as an intellectual "Meditation" (just one of six in his 1641 book *Meditations*). But he "let the genie out of the bottle" and since then "Modern Philosophy" has been dominated by Radical Skepticism (and the series of problematic philosophies dependent upon it listed in CHAPTER 3: PHILOSOPHY below, which have perhaps inexorably led the West to the current crisis which threatens Western freedom and Science itself).

In any case, as there were not significant numbers of Atheists denying any Ordering Intelligence (Creator God) of the universe before Western Philosophy became *unhinged from Reality* through Radical Skepticism which seriously doubted or denied that *even the universe existed* (the incredibly foolish *denied reality itself*, and only then did Atheism which denied Reality's Orderer become popular), so likewise there were not any Moral Relativists to speak of before there were Relativists. So likewise there were not Moral Relativists who thought every individual could subjectively "choose" or "create" their own "moral truth," before there were Relativists who ridiculously thought every individual could subjectively "choose" or "create" their own "factual truth" *because they ridiculously denied any objective facts or truth.* Again, all of this silliness, which now has direct political consequences, is rooted in absurd philosophical *Radical Skepticism* which doubts or denies any knowable existence beyond one's own mind; this is the underlying silliness which precedes and leads directly to Moral Relativism, which claims there are no Moral Absolutes like *killing humans is wrong* (which means human-killing abortion is wrong). It is a *hypocritical* silliness, since every Skeptic, Relativist and Moral Relativist can only get through a day without dying stupidly by following Common Sense and therefore treating the universe we humans commonly perceive as *real* – as does Science, rooted thoroughly in the philosophical *Realism* which is opposed to philosophical *Skepticism.* Hence CHAPTER 3: PHILOSOPHY below draws conclusions showing how the current politically destabilizing bifurcation and polarization in the West can be traced to the two sides at root accepting either *Realist and Scientific* or *Skeptical and Relativistic* underlying philosophical worldviews.

"One world, one mankind cannot exist in the face of... two scales of values: We shall be torn apart by this disparity of rhythm, this disparity of vibrations."
— Aleksandr Solzhenitsyn

This philosophical disparity has real political consequences like half of America the last twenty years consistently voting for Pro-Choice-to-Kill-Humans extremist Leftist Moral Relativists who witlessly follow the Extremist Left Soviet Marxist Relativist precedent of legal human-killing abortion (now also following the Extremist Right Nazi Relativist precedent of legal human-killing euthanasia – note both political extremes were influenced by German Atheist Relativist philosophers, the Extreme Left Marxist Socialists by Karl Marx, the Extreme Right Nazi Fascists by Friedrich Nietzsche). Today's nations suffer real political consequences like this author's country putting into political power anti-scientific and moral Relativists who have made it a crime punishable with jail and/or fines to speak verifiable scientific facts which do not support various unscientific ideologies of the Pro-Choice legal human-killing extremist Left in my country, who have long forgotten what it means to be a *real* "Progressive Left" that *belongs* in a healthy democracy, balanced with a *real* "Conservative Right," both sides sharing and supporting in common *The Foundational Principles of Human Rights and Democracy* embedded in Traditional Western Values. Sadly, at present the "Conservative Right" in my country, while (unlike the extremist Left) still "accepting" Pro-Lifers with democracy-grounding Traditional Western Values, are themselves so uneducated in the overwhelming facts of Human Rights History, Science and Logic in this book which prove its title *Pro-Life Equals Pro-Democracy*, that they up until now have been too *terrified* to practically oppose in any meaningful way the Pro-Choice Extremist Left with their Neo-Marxist "manufactured outrage" at anyone who disagrees with them – allowing all the anti-democratic and totalitarian-oriented Extremist Left legislation to remain in place even when the "Conservative Right" manages to get into power. Hopefully, this book's HUMAN RIGHTS EDUCATION FOR LASTING FREE DEMOCRACY will help them to finally become *confident* to stand up to the Pro-Choice legal human-killing Extremist Left (and hopefully, the Pro-Choice Extremist Left themselves will actually start *thinking* with a modicum of *intellectual honesty* after exposure to this book's powerful *education in democratic foundations*, and eventually become once again a "Real" Left that belongs in a healthy, balanced democracy. Free Democracy and *Equal Human Rights for All Humans* will only be safe for the long-term future when *both* political Left and Right, *both* properly educated in *The Foundational Principles of Human Rights and Democracy* identified from Science, Logic, and Human Rights History in this book, in a *bi-partisan* effort constitutionally enshrine some articulation of *The Foundational Principles of Human Rights and Democracy* in their federal constitutions).

In any case, both sides (political Left and Right) should note that the Atheist belief in Moral Relativism (believing in no human-loving God of Judaism and Christianity to set any moral absolutes for humans such as "you shall not kill" nor *equal human preciousness* nor the *Equal Human Rights for All Humans* implied by *equal human preciousness*) is *integrated into all the ideological frameworks built by Atheists in their attempts to organize political society* – Marxism (Communism, Socialism, Leninism, Maoism) and the new twist on Marxist "class struggle" politics which is Identity Politics. Identity Politics just substitutes a divisive "race/identity group struggle" which is just as poorly conducive to Free Democracy as all the other forms of Atheist/Marxist/Socialist ideology. Identity Politics in fact guarantees conflict and struggle and the bifurcation or polarization of society which we now in fact see in most countries, where the Pro-Choice extremist Left has adopted an Identity Politics approach, ultimately rooted in Atheist Marxism, instead of mutual respect between *equally precious* groups of humans (Atheist Marxists having also entirely rejected democracy-grounding *equal human preciousness* by being first to legalize abortion 100 years ago in 1920 Soviet Russia).

Despite the common human failings and imperfections of Christians, today the Christian ideal of *equal human preciousness* we in fact can see more or less in practice in most of the 2.3 billion Christians worldwide, the largest and most diverse group of humans on the planet, coming from almost every other grouping of humans (from almost every racial/ethnic/national groupings; language; sex/gender; social status; ability or disability groups of humans). Despite the frequent squabbling among Christians over comparatively minor doctrinal conflicts between some groups of Christians rooted in long-past history, today this is almost never violent because of the Christian value of *equal human preciousness*. It is largely the squabbling of *family* (what family does not have disagreements?) and as a rule this author can go anywhere in the world and be welcomed lovingly as *Christian family* even where I do not speak the local language or know the local culture.

(Each of The "Top 6 Facts" is Subject of an Entire Chapter In the Book *Pro-Life Equals Pro-Democracy*)

Fact 3: Preborn Human Rights Were Protected for Centuries Until the Evil, Genocidal Soviet Marxist & Nazi Fascist Extremists Legalized Abortion

CHAPTER 1: FACTS

Preborn Humans' Inherent Human Right to Live Was Generally Protected by Western Law or Custom from the 4th Century Criminalization of Abortion Until the 20th Century De-Criminalization of Abortion First by the Evil Soviet Communist and Nazi Fascist Regimes – Totalitarian States Threatening the Lives and Freedoms of Citizens Just Like Those Back When Legal Abortion Was the Ancient Norm.

Preborn Humans Were Protected in the Womb for Many Centuries until Abortion Was Legalized First by the Evil Extremist Left (and Atheist) Soviet Communist Party, then the Evil Extremist Right (and led by occultists) Nazi Party - "Pro-Choice" vs. "Pro-Life" is NOT a Matter of Political "Left" vs. "Right," But a Matter of Fundamentally Totalitarian, Extremist Thinking Which Supports Human-Killing vs. Fundamentally Democratic Thinking Which Supports Human Protection.

The first two modern nations to de-criminalize abortion (allowing the legal killing of preborn humans) since the 4th Century were the oppressive and totalitarian (total-control, belief-control) Soviet (Marxist) and Nazi (Fascist) regimes – shortly before these two governments perpetrated the two largest genocides of born humans in history. First, the Soviet *Holodomor, ("Death Famine"* or *"Murder by Starvation")* – the forced starvation to death of 7-10 million Ukrainian humans (this author's ethnic heritage) in 1932-33, just as the Nazi *Holocaust* of 6 million Jewish humans (plus handicapped humans) was getting started.

The Nazis kept abortion illegal for healthy German humans, whom the Nazis valued, but encouraged abortion for Jewish humans and other humans they considered "inferior," especially disabled/handicapped humans. The same bigotry against disabled human lives as "not worth living" led the Nazis to be first to legalize euthanasia for born disabled humans – initially using "prevention of suffering" as the excuse for legalizing the killing of humans by euthanasia – just like today's euthanasia advocates also violate the ancient non-killing Hippocratic Medical Tradition and hide their bigotry in feigned compassion. Because it follows Nazi precedent and bigoted Nazi reasoning that denies *equal human preciousness* and the *Inherent Human Right to Live*, euthanasia-killing has gotten out of control in every place in the West euthanasia has been legalized. More and more people with more and more conditions – even conditions as simple as "loneliness" – are now legal to kill by euthanasia (with or without the person's knowledge or consent) in more and more countries which followed the Nazi precedent of legal human-killing euthanasia (usually giving it nicer-sounding terms like "Medical Assistance in Dying" or "Assisted Suicide"). In European countries where human-killing by euthanasia has been legal longest, people come up to parents of disabled children in the streets and (dripping with the Nazi-style bigotry which first legalized euthanasia) ask them why they have not yet euthanized their annoying handicapped child. Groups of disabled humans (like "Not Dead Yet") have had to band together against this bigotry that, rejecting the *equal human preciousness without exception* which grounds free democracy, assumes that disabled human lives are not worth living and now repeatedly "offers" to "assist the suicide" of those with disabilities. Imagine how it makes a disabled person feel to (unbidden) be repeatedly "offered help" *to commit suicide* by so-called "medical professionals" who have abandoned the ancient doctors' Hippocratic Medical Tradition to "do no harm," the oldest forms of the doctors' Hippocratic Oath specifically prohibiting both human-killing abortion and human-killing euthanasia. The medical profession was "Pro-Life" for many centuries while ancient totalitarian governments were "Pro-Choice" and were often the biggest threat to the human lives and freedoms of those governed.

Both the genocidal extremist regimes which were first to legalize abortion, the Soviet Marxists and Nazi Fascists (see CHAPTER 3: PHILOSOPHY for more details) were strongly influenced by German Atheist, *Relativist-not-Realist* philosophers who did not believe in the Traditional Western Values which undergird Western Human Rights and freedoms (the Nazi Fascists were influenced by Friedrich Nietzsche, the Soviet Marxists were heavily influenced by Karl Marx and followed his sophisticated but *unrealistic* system). Both totalitarian regimes were led by those who explicitly rejected the (philosophically *Realist-not-Relativist*) Traditional Christianity which furnished the underlying principles modern Human Rights and freedoms are built on, embracing other, contrary philosophical worldviews and religious ideals instead. The Soviet Marxists who first legalized human-killing by abortion (and later by genocide) in denial of any *Inherent Human Right to Live* were formal Atheists like Marx who despised Christianity. Atheist Nietzsche also despised Christianity, specifically for its concept of *equal human preciousness.* In rejection of this democracy-grounding principle, Nietzsche disparagingly called the Biblical, Judeo-Christian morality a "Slave Morality" and, as a Moral Relativist, Nietzsche promoted in its place a "Master Morality" to be created by exceptional people (including himself, of course); morality determined (and ultimately enforced in politics) by a superior elite. The Nuremberg War Crimes Trials of the many Nazi atrocities after World War II specifically noted the influence of Nietzsche on Nazi thinking. But Hitler and the top level Nazi Fascists who (after the Soviet Marxists) were next to legalize human-killing by abortion (and later by genocide), encouraged by Nietzsche's elitist "Master Morality," were also *occultists*, holding many anti-Christian views, including the Nazi idea of an "*Aryan* Master Race" which they promoted through legal human-killing by legal abortion, by legal euthanasia, and by legal genocide in the Nazi Death Camps. In rejection of the Biblical, Judeo-Christian belief that God created every human life "in God's Image," making each human uniquely special, valuable, and infinitely loved by God, the Nazis held to an occultic mythology from which the Nazis got their bigoted idea of a mythological superior "*Aryan* Master Race."

[*Digressio*: The "Aryan Master Race" myth was bolstered by the then-popular pseudo-science of Eugenics; fake science which in addition to inspiring the Nazis to legalize abortion and exterminate Jewish humans, disabled/handicapped humans and other humans deemed "inferior," also inspired Margaret Sanger to found Planned Parenthood, today the world's biggest abortion provider, initially offering abortion "services" only in Black American neighborhoods in order to reduce the number of Black humans which they see as undesirable. Today Planned Parenthood still disproportionately offers and performs human-killing abortion on Black humans, and also lobbies and manipulates African countries, which are mostly officially Pro-Life, to accept Planned Parenthood's ideal of legal human-killing abortion. In the meantime Planned Parenthood (and other abortion providing organizations) illegally perform abortions in Pro-Life Africa with no more regard for democracy-grounding Traditional Western Pro-Life Family Values (like *equal human preciousness without exception*) than the (also bigoted Eugenicist) Nazis had.

But not only do Pro-Choice human-killing abortion providing organizations like Planned Parenthood aggressively try to reduce the number of Black humans by lobbying for legal abortion in Pro-Life Africa. Western nations run by Pro-Choice legal human-killing abortion political parties also put pressure upon African nations to give up their Pro-Life belief in *Equal Human Rights for All Humans* by making African Relief Aid (more recently including Coronavirus Pandemic Relief Aid) *contingent upon Africans accepting abortion in their nations.*

There has been response to this by Obianuju Ekeocha, an African (Nigerian) woman this author has met who works as a specialist biomedical scientist in the UK and is author of the book *Target Africa: Ideological Neo-Colonialism of the Twenty-First Century* (she is also producer of the film *Strings Attached* which describes the foreign relief aid now offered to Africa). She mentioned the author's Prime Minister by name (a scurrilous representative of the scurrilous lot of Western nations trying to coerce Africa into accepting their legal human-killing evil) in a May 14, 2020 interview (on the day which marked precisely 51 years of the author's country legally eradicating the *Inherent Human Right to Live* by legalizing abortion). She said Western nations are forcefully pushing abortion on Africa which does not want it,

> *"Because Abortion is an issue that indicts ... If someone will go so far as rejecting the reality of human life (... Science continues to show us day by day just how human a baby in the womb is and so should be protected) ... if people within certain Western communities have decided to completely ignore that, but not only ignore it, they deny it actively, and not only that, they promote the denial of it and they make it completely illegal to even object in certain quarters (we know about all the "bubble zones" that have happened in some places within Western countries ... so they are going as far as making our Pro-Life advocacy illegal) ... If they do that, if they go that far, I think it's an indictment then when somebody in a neighboring country or in another country would look at the same baby in their country and say, you know, this baby is also part of our community, and we are going to protect this child ... when one completely abandons the duty to protect the most vulnerable ones within our society, it will then be an indictment when you look and you see perhaps a poorer country struggling and all that, not as glamourous as your country, going as far as saying that this child that is within the womb is one of us and we are going to protect this child. This is what every country has the duty of doing in the first place. But if you have abdicated your duty to protect these little ones [which is what "fetus" means in Latin, by the way], it's an indictment to see someone else doing that [protecting the humans you kill]. So I believe that's why abortion activists, abortion-promoting politicians [like the author's Prime Minister who she mentions by name], abortion-supporting politicians, abortion organizations, that's why they go all-out to fight these battles in countries that have not legalized abortion. Because they want to completely silence the voice anywhere in the world that is raised [on behalf of the unborn child], the voice that says that the child in the womb is one of us, and in fact is the most vulnerable of us and so should be protected."*
> *-- Obianuju Ekeocha*

Obianuju Ekeocha's above testimony against the ideological bribery of foreign aid with "strings attached" indicates that any country, like most African countries, that says "we believe in *Equal Human Rights for All Humans* and so we will not kill young humans still in the womb" indicts or incriminates those countries which do kill young humans still in the womb, exposing their legal human-killing evil which, as this book abundantly proves, simply has no intelligent nor intellectually honest justification in the light of Science, Logic, and History (nor in the light of the millions of born humans also murdered by the very same evil regimes which were first to legalize abortion – the Soviet Marxists and Nazi Fascists). Therefore, to "justify" their own legal human-killing abortion evil, Western nations spearheaded by the author's own Prime Minister through the bribery of "strings attached" poverty aid (and Coronavirus Pandemic aid) are trying to *stop* financially poor Africa from protecting human life in the womb out of Africa's morally superior belief in democracy-grounding *Equal Human Rights for All Humans*. **Officially Pro-Choice federal and provincial governments through totalitarian-oriented laws and policies** *are trying to stamp out Free Democracy's Pro-Life foundations wherever they find them, inside or outside of their own country.* Hence the author's national leader is pressuring Africa to compromise their Pro-Life stance in order to get needed medical aid, and within the country Pro-Lifers now suffer the international embarrassment of living in a country with expanded "no-free-speech-on-behalf-of-equal-Human-Rights-bubble-zones" (where you can be arrested for saying "killing humans is wrong") in an increasing number of its provinces (Ekeocha from across the world noting above "we know about all the "bubble zones" that have happened . . . so they are going as far as making our Pro-Life advocacy illegal"). *End Digressio*]

It is very significant that before both evil extremist totalitarian regimes (the Soviet Marxists and Nazi Fascists) legalized genocide also, *de-criminalized abortion had already established in the Union of Soviet Socialist Republics (USSR) and Nazi Germany that there was no longer* any legally recognized *Inherent Human Right to Live* as had been recognized by Western law or custom since 318 AD, and so logically these governments no longer felt any *obligation* to protect or serve born humans either, logically leading them to descend back into the oppressive governmental totalitarianism *that was NORMAL in ancient times back when legal abortion was NORMAL.*

Note: Legal human-killing is inherently extremist. So, current Pro-Choice political parties which now unwittingly follow the Extremist Left Soviet Communist Party and Extremist Right Nazi Party precedents of legal abortion as a "party value" incompatible with the *Inherent Human Right to Live* are now inherently *extremist* political parties and some have already proved it by passing totalitarian laws and policies suppressing Free Speech and other democratic freedoms (especially of Pro-Life Human Rights advocates and doctors who will not kill. It is so significant that it is worth repeating that *this author can be arrested and jailed in his country for any peaceful Pro-Life Human Rights advocacy within blocks of an abortion facility in some provinces. This author can be arrested for saying "killing humans is wrong because Human Rights are for all humans;" for speaking scientifically verifiable facts supporting this conclusion; or just for "staring disapprovingly" at an abortion clinic where humans are legally killed following totalitarian Soviet and Nazi precedents).* **This non-partisan author and Human Rights scholar notes that political parties being "officially Pro-Choice" (and thus unsurprisingly passing totalitarian-oriented laws) is a recent trend, and today's Pro-Choice political parties should immediately distance themselves from the uneducated and extremist Pro-Choice legal** human-killing abortion position and get back to their party's roots, which ("Left" and "Right") at the foundation of our modern democracies at least implicitly recognized the ancient Christian "Pro-Life" principle of *equal human preciousness without exception*, which grounds all Western Democracy. As more and more voters get a solid *Human Rights Education* in the Pro-Life *Foundational Principles of Human Rights and Democracy*, political parties which do not immediately recant their uneducated Pro-Choice position on Human Rights principle will eventually find it harder and harder to get votes from the increasing number of Human-Rights-educated voters.

Fact 4: In 1948 the Free World Condemned Legal Abortion as "A Crime Against Humanity" at Nuremberg; Affirmed that Doctors Do Not Kill Humans "From the Time of Conception" in the Declaration of Geneva; and the United Nations' Universal Declaration of Human Rights Declared Human Rights are for ALL humans "without distinction of any kind" because "recognition of the inherent dignity and of the equal and inalienable rights of ALL members of the human family is the foundation of freedom, justice and peace in the world;" In 1948 the West Still Knew Killing Humans Is Wrong and That Human Freedom from Totalitarianism Depends on These "Pro-Life" Values.

The *Universal Declaration of Human Rights* with its detailed explicit articulation of Human Rights brought to mature fruition the long but logical process of development of Human Rights in the Christian West, begun precisely 1630 years earlier with the first legal recognition of an implicit *Inherent Human Right to Live* with the initial criminalization of abortion and infanticide in 318 AD, specifically because Christianity had then taught the West that human life is *precious not cheap* - and that governments are *obligated* to protect human life because governments are *accountable* to something higher than the government for how it treats the humans it governs. Not surprisingly, *The Universal Declaration of Human Rights* was produced under the direction of another devout, Bible-reading, church-attending, praying Christian, who often shared the insights of her Christian faith in her regular newspaper columns: Eleanor Roosevelt, the U.S.'s longest-serving First Lady. Roosevelt had previously written in her 1940 book *The Moral Basis of Democracy* that

---

"we must acknowledge that the life of Christ was based on principles which are necessary to the development of a Democratic state" and wrote that if we "develop the fundamental beliefs and desires which make us considerate of the weak and truly anxious to see a Christ-like spirit on earth ... we will have educated ourselves for Democracy."[7]

---

[7] Cited in the article "God and Mrs. Roosevelt" by Mary Ann Glendon, the Learned Hand Professor of Law at Harvard University. Her entire article can be viewed at https://www.firstthings.com/article/2010/05/god-and-mrs-roosevelt (accessed Sept.28, 2017).

Of course, *The Universal Declaration of Human Rights* was produced at a time, 1948, when most in the "Free West" were baptized Christians and attended a Christian Church. And of course, all of the representatives of Atheist governments (under Soviet influence) who were on Roosevelt's original UN Human Rights Commission refused to even vote on the *Universal Declaration of Human Rights*, because as Atheists who believe in Moral Relativism (Atheists believe in no Christian human-loving God to set any Moral Absolutes for humanity), they could not accept any Moral Absolutes like the *Inherent Human Right to Live* nor any other inherent Human Rights; nor any Moral Absolute like *killing humans is wrong* nor any of *The Foundational Principles of Human Rights and Democracy*. As Atheists, they could not accept anything higher than the State government, to which the State government is *accountable* for how it treats the humans it governs. This is why every Atheist State in history has been totalitarian, and oppressive to human life and freedom. The academic tome *The Black Book of Communism: Crimes, Terror, Repression* makes scholarly estimates that Atheist Communist States killed an astonishing *over 94 million people* in the 20th Century (born humans; this figure does not account for the fact that Atheist Communist Soviet Socialist Russia began the 20th Century trend of legal human-killing abortion in 1920 - because it did not believe that *killing humans is wrong).*

If you did not know this fact and you are "Pro-Choice," this fact alone should make you re-think your position for the sake of all humanity. If you did not know this fact, or any of the other "Top 6" facts, then your "Pro-Choice" position is based on *ignorance* and *lack of knowledge* of the most pertinent facts. So unless you are selfish and/or evil, you likely never would have been silly enough to choose a Pro-Choice position in the *Human Rights for All Humans Debate (the Abortion Debate)* IF you had first at least known the "Top 6 Facts" of Human Rights History which prove *Pro-Life=Pro-Democracy*. So, for the sake of all humanity you need to get a solid *Human Rights Education* and choose an *educated* "Pro-Human-Right-to-Live" or "Pro-Life" position . . .

(Each of The "Top 6 Facts" is Subject of an Entire Chapter In the Book *Pro-Life Equals Pro-Democracy*)

Fact 5: Pro-Choice Political Parties Pass Totalitarian Laws & Policies Against Normal Democratic Freedoms

The "Free West" Uneducated in the Above Facts of Human Rights History Ignorantly Followed the Totalitarian Precedent of Legal Human-Killing Abortion and is Now Showing the Logical Totalitarian Fruit with Pro-Choice Political Parties in Power Passing Totalitarian Laws & Policies Against Normal Democratic Freedoms of Speech, Expression, Assembly, Conscience and Religion. And Policies Putting the Government in between Parents and their Own Children, Like in Totalitarian States. And in Schools Enforcing Indoctrinating "Education" in New-fangled Values with No History in the Culture and in Unscientific Ideologies with No Grounding in Real Science, Like in Totalitarian States.

There are Now Laws & Policies Against Speaking the Traditional Western (Judeo-Christian) Pro-Life Family Values Which Democracy is Historically and Logically Built Upon and Cannot Last Without (and Even Laws Against Speaking Established Facts and Science which Do Not Agree with Pro-Choice and other New-

fangled Ideologies Held by Pro-Choice Political Parties). By Ignorantly Adopting the Extremist, Totalitarian Marxist Soviet Communist Party and Fascist Nazi Party Precedents of Legal Abortion as a "Party Value" Wholly Unscientific and Completely Illogical, and Entirely Incompatible with the Inherent Human Right to Live Which Grounds Democracy, Pro-Choice Political Parties are Now Extremist Political Parties and are Demonstrating This Through Totalitarian Laws and Policies Suppressing Free Speech and More.

The "Free West" ignorantly followed the Totalitarian Soviet Communist Party and Nazi Party precedent of de-criminalizing the abortion-killing of preborn humans (thereby cancelling out the legally recognized *Inherent Human Right to Live* which is the foundation of all Human Rights and Freedoms). **As any thinking person would totally expect once knowing the above facts, of course this means the "Free West" decades ago in fact introduced 'Creeping Totalitarianism' into Western democracies**, gradually but logically undermining Human Rights and Democratic Freedoms and making Western democracies gradually take on more and more characteristics of Totalitarian States. As after decades this process is coming to maturation, it is merely logical, to preserve human-killing "abortion access" without anyone complaining about humans being killed, that Pro-Choice political parties in power worldwide today are starting to pass anti-democratic laws and policies such as: taking away Pro-Life doctors' Freedom of Conscience and Freedom of Religion to not kill humans by abortion and euthanasia; making peaceful and scientific Pro-Life Human Rights Advocacy a crime subject to heavy fines and/or jail time; putting the government in between parents and their own children (one government gave itself the right to take children away from their parents for *traditional childrearing* in the Traditional Western Values which undergird Democracy, values which the Pro-Choice and therefore "Creeping Totalitarian" government no longer considers "in the best interest of the child;" even making criticizing the government a crime (like in totalitarian States); and otherwise starting to pass laws restricting democratic Freedom of Assembly and Freedoms of Speech and Expression (even of verifiable scientific facts – **Science is a crime when it does not support the Party Ideology of Pro-Choice Political Parties which no longer uphold the Traditional Western Values which include and support *The Foundational Principles of Human Rights and Democracy*).**

In France you can be arrested, jailed *and* heavily fined for making a Pro-Life website. Under current laws *this author and Human Rights scholar can be arrested and jailed in his country* for any kind of peaceful Pro-Life Human Rights advocacy including just for saying "killing humans is wrong because Human Rights are for all humans;" or for speaking scientific and medically verifiable facts about abortion; or just for "staring" at an abortion clinic, which the police said would be taken as a sign of "disapproval of abortion" which it is now *illegal* to show in large "no-free-speech-bubble-zones" around human-killing abortion facilities where Human Rights advocacy is most pertinent. **We can lose our democratic freedoms so fast that one such law was passed after *only 3 weeks* in the regional legislature. Police were on the scene *within half an hour of the totalitarian bill being signed into law*, to disperse the praying Christians on about Day 30 of a "40 Days for Life" peaceful silent prayer vigil. Police told the praying Christians they no longer had the democratic freedom to silently pray for human life to be respected across the street from the legal human-killing abortion facility within blocks of the National Parliament Buildings of a supposed democracy!** This author spoke on the phone with the organizer of that "40 Days for Life" peaceful silent prayer vigil right after this happened. The organizer cancelled the peaceful protest in defense of the Pro-Life *Foundational Principles of Human Rights and Democracy* early *for fear of arrest by police for silently praying for the value of human life to be recognized –* something which should only happen in a totalitarian Police State!

In 2018 this author gave a eulogy at the funeral of a 70-year-old man born in 1948 – when all those wonderful protections of *Human Rights from the womb* were introduced (see Fact 4 above). *This man died while awaiting unjust trial after having been twice arrested not for breaking the new totalitarian law against Pro-Life speech, but just for being a "KNOWN PRO-LIFER" carrying signs reading "FREEDOM OF EXPRESSION AND RELIGION. NO CENSORSHIP" and "GOD SAVE OUR CHARTER RIGHTS."* (See the above News Editorial after his first arrest – even the self-described "Pro-Choice" editorial staff saw this Pro-Choice law threatened democratic free speech.)

Such Pro-Choice totalitarian laws ending Free Democracy are the only way Pro-Choice political parties can keep abortion legal long-term - since, as introduced in this "TOP 6 FACTS" chapter, all the most pertinent facts of Science, Logic, and Human Rights History prove that Pro-Life = Pro-Democracy (and Pro-Choice = Pro-Totalitarianism) . . .

(Each of The "Top 6 Facts" is Subject of an Entire Chapter In the Book *Pro-Life Equals Pro-Democracy*)

***Fact 6:** Legal Slavery and Legal Abortion Are Both Fundamentally Incompatible with Democracy Since Both Deny the Equal Human Preciousness and Equal Human Rights for All Humans Which Ground Democracy. As with*

Slavery, Either Legal Abortion or Democracy Will END Because They are Entirely Incompatible

To Elaborate: Legal Abortion (with its profitable Abortion Industry) is every bit as fundamentally incompatible with Democracy as Legal Slavery (with its profitable Slave Trade) was, for precisely the same reason: Both (like the Nazis) deny Human Rights to some humans (making "Human Rights" meaningless if not all humans have them) and both violate the same traditional *Foundational Principle of Human Rights and Democracy* that every human life without exception is *equal* and *precious*, which is the underlying reason Western governments stopped being oppressive and totalitarian, ended slavery and eventually gave every adult human a vote or democratic say in his or her own governance, in the first place. Legal Abortion needs to be abolished for precisely the same reason Legal Slavery did. It is fundamentally anti-human and anti-democratic. The fundamental incompatibility between democracy (where every human is understood as equal and valuable) and legal slavery or legal abortion (both of which deny equal Human Rights to some humans) is so great that in the end we will either have to keep democracy and lose legal abortion (as we lost legal slavery), or keep legal abortion and lose democracy. Lose democracy starting as where the author lives, where under current laws and policies citizens can already be arrested and jailed just for speaking scientifically verifiable facts against various unscientific ideologies of officially Pro-Choice political parties in power.

The Slave Trade, like the Abortion Industry, profited highly from denying Human Rights to some humans, motivating great political resistance to abolishing the Slave Trade even though, like the Abortion Industry, it violated even the *Inherent Human Right to Live* which undergirds Democracy.

Legally devalued Black humans by the tens of thousands died tightly chained together in their own waste on slave ships before they even got the chance to be slaves, at plantations with poor safety standards where many died working as slaves, just as **legally devalued** Jewish humans were killed in the millions in Nazi Death Camps and just as **legally devalued** preborn humans are today killed in the millions in abortion clinics. The original Abolitionists called for the Abolition of Legal Slavery for the sake of **equal human rights for all humans** which is the foundation of Democracy. **"Pro-Lifers"** are literally the *New Abolitionists*, calling for the Abolition of Legal Abortion because they are championing **precisely the same** *Foundational Principle of Human Rights and Democracy* that every human without exception – whether Black, Jewish, or preborn – has Equal Human Rights including an *Inherent Human Right to Live.*

Only ignorance and bigotry ever denies Human Rights to some humans, and the age-bigotry of Legal Abortion is every bit as vile as the race-bigotry of Legal Slavery or Nazi Death Camps; worse, it is the bigotry against the Human Race itself, **eradicating the *Inherent Human Right to Live* of everybody**, since every one of us used to be a fetal-age human who (in the perspective of Legal Abortion) could have been legally killed at fetal age and therefore *none of us* have any legally recognized *Inherent Human Right to Live* since abortion was de-criminalized. Even the Nazis, who had no *illusions* that they were not in fact killing humans by abortion (they did not unscientifically pretend that a fetal-age human was anything other than a human), actually valued SOME humans – the Nazis kept abortion *illegal* for healthy Germans whom the Nazis *valued*, while making abortion legal for Jews and other races considered "inferior," and for handicapped Germans, since their Nazi bigotry considered anyone handicapped or disabled in any way to be "less valuable" than perfectly healthy human beings. *Today's Pro-Choicers are even more bigoted than the Nazis, since they do not value ANY humans enough to protect them from the start of their utterly unique human lives in the womb.* To today's Pro-Choice bigots, not even "healthy Germans" are protected from the beginning of their unique human lives; no human whatsoever has an *Inherent Human Right to Live*; but every single one of us humans was only "allowed" to live, in violation of the clear intention of the 1948 *Universal Declaration of Human Rights* to apply Human Rights to all humans

"without distinction of any kind" because "recognition of the inherent dignity and of the equal and inalienable rights of ALL members of the human family is the foundation of freedom, justice and peace in the world."
– Universal Declaration of Human Rights

If you did not know this fact and you are "Pro-Choice," this fact alone should make you re-think your position for the sake of all humanity. If you did not know this fact, or any of the other "Top 6" facts, then your "Pro-Choice" position is based on ignorance and lack of knowledge of the most pertinent facts. So unless you are selfish and/or evil, you likely never would have been silly enough to choose a Pro-Choice position in the *Human Rights for All Humans Debate (the Abortion Debate) if* you had first at least known the "Top 6 Facts" of Human Rights History which prove Pro-Life=Pro-Democracy. So, for the sake of all humanity you need to get a solid Human Rights Education and choose an *educated* "Pro-Human-Right-to-Live" or "Pro-Life" position.

Addendum: Recent Bombshell News Means Some of the Most Hidden Disturbing Facts of Abortion Industry Evil are Now Matters of Public Court Records

"Abortion is not a 3rd option [to parenthood or adoption] because [unlike parenthood or adoption] it dismembers, decapitates, and disembowels a baby."
– Stephanie Gray

"Violence does not and cannot flourish by itself; it is inevitably intertwined with lying."
— Aleksandr Solzhenitsyn

"Let us not forget that violence does not live alone and is not capable of living alone: it is necessarily interwoven with falsehood. Between them lies the most intimate, the deepest of natural bonds. Violence finds its only refuge in falsehood, falsehood its only support in violence. Any man who has once acclaimed violence as his method must inexorably choose falsehood as his principle."
— *Aleksandr Solzhenitsyn*

BOMBSHELL NEWS: Several Officials of World's Biggest Abortion "Service" Provider (Planned Parenthood) Admit Under Oath in Court to Illegal Selling of Aborted Fetal-Age Human Baby Body Parts for Money (and Reveal Other Disturbing Things about the Abortion Industry Which Should Surprise No-One; Abortionist Industry People Make Their Living by Killing Human Babies; to Keep Making Money They Support Totalitarian-Oriented Legislation that *Denies Equal Human Rights* to the Humans They Kill for Money; So Literally Nothing is Beneath Them); California's Most Experienced Abortionist (who has personally performed over 50,000 abortions and readily admits the scientific fact that abortion kills human beings), Motivated By His (Surprising) Moral Superiority to Planned Parenthood, as an Expert Witness Testifies in Court that Planned Parenthood Frequently (Unlike him) Puts the Mother at Greater Health Risk by Using a Procedure and Drug Combination that Induces Tumultuous Rapid Labor So the Baby is Usually Born Alive, So That the Baby's Organs are "Fresher and in Better Condition" and Worth More Money for Sale after the Human Baby is Illegally Murdered to Harvest His or Her Organs (yes, murder laws now apply because the baby was born alive).

"Violence does not necessarily take people by the throat and strangle them. Usually it demands no more than an ultimate allegiance from its subjects. They are required merely to become accomplices in its lies."
— *Aleksandr Solzhenitsyn*

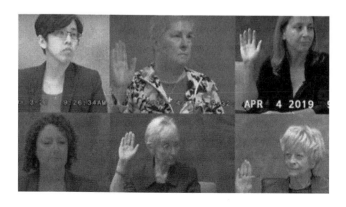

The above photo shows several Planned Parenthood officials giving sworn testimony in court which reveals much hidden abortion industry evil. For more details, see the footnoted news articles.[8]

Over the years, this author (or my dear Bride of 23 years) have heard or read various testimonies of former abortionist doctors and other abortion industry workers. Those who got out of the Abortion Industry typically testify that it really is a big money-maker, because they can charge the women (or charge the government "Non-Hippocratic 'healthcare' that intentionally kills humans") for performing the abortion, and then possibly (not always) sell the human corpses of the aborted human baby (or body parts of the aborted baby). One abortionist testified her clinic would often tell teenage girls and women who came in for abortions to "come back on this particular week" and schedule the abortion for a specific time that that woman's *in utero* baby would be the specific age they needed to sell a specific baby body part to a specific buyer (for their research or making health and beauty products, including some vaccines).

One former abortionist testified it was their clinic's practice, when a girl/woman who came in to their abortion clinic for a pregnancy test turned out not to be pregnant after all, to tell them they were pregnant, schedule their abortion appointment and collect their $300 or whatever abortion fee. Then scrape their empty uterus with abortion tools so it would seem like they had had a medical procedure to abort their non-existent baby, and the girl would leave a satisfied customer having paid them hundreds of dollars to "solve" a "problem" they did not even have!

Another abortionist who left the industry testified she used to go into schools supposedly teaching about birth control, handing out condoms and encouraging the girls to practice "safe sex," and making sure they knew where to go if they did become pregnant after all. But she had sabotaged the condoms with tiny holes to make sure the condoms would not work – so that the girls would call their clinic when they got pregnant.

Because literally nothing is "beneath" anyone who kills human babies for a living, these above testimonies are just *typical* dishonest and money-grubbing practices of "nice" abortionists. The perverted, sick and evil practices of abortionists can be much worse, such as 30-year abortionist Kermit Gosnell, one of the worse ones who eventually got caught, in Philadelphia. He had aborted baby bodies and parts all over his property as "trophies," like a classic serial killer (like 47 bodies in containers, including a kitty litter box; baby feet in jars marked with the mother's name). When babies were (frequently) born alive, he cut their throats with scissors. He was convicted of killing babies after they were born; as well as killing one of two mothers who died (a manslaughter charge); and numerous late-term abortions illegal in his state (of many hundreds performed). For 30 years, no medical regulating body had investigated or checked on Gosnell's abortion clinic. **But even abortion clinics**

---

[8] https://www.liveaction.org/news/bombshell-planned-parenthood-admits-oath-aborted-parts/, accessed June 1, 2020. (Article Published May 26, 2020).
https://www.washingtonexaminer.com/opinion/abortion-doctor-admits-sold-baby-parts-often-came-from-babies-born-alive, accessed June 1, 2020.
https://www.lifesitenews.com/news/abortionist-testifies-at-daleiden-hearing-no-question...some-of-these-fetuses-were-live-births, accessed June 1, 2020.

which perfectly follow local laws are still following *originally totalitarian, extremist legal human-killing laws which have no place in a healthy democracy because they legally eradicate the Inherent, Equal, Inalienable Human Right to Live which is part of the essential foundation of Free Democracy, unleashing 'Creeping Totalitarianism' and therefore Western democracies are now failing without their essentially "Pro-Life" foundations* – as demonstrated by more and more laws against normal democratic Freedoms of Speech, Expression, Assembly, Conscience and Religion passed by "officially Pro-Choice" political parties in power, such as those current laws which mean this author can now be arrested and imprisoned many places in his country just for saying "killing humans is wrong because Human Rights are for all Humans."

"it is essential . . . that human rights should be protected by the rule of law"
-- The Universal Declaration of Human Rights

A logical consequence of the overwhelming facts (of History, Science, Logic, Philosophy and so on) that compellingly prove *Pro-Life equals Pro-Democracy* and *Pro-Choice equals Pro-Totalitarianism* is that, if Free Democracy is to last at all, it will only do so if countries soon *explicitly* restore Democracy's *implicit* foundations in Traditional Western Values like *equal human preciousness without exception which governments are obligated to protect;* values which have already been more than adequately defined and elaborated in the United Nations' magnificent 1948 *Universal Declaration of Human Rights.* Only severe intellectual dishonesty brought on by outright evil or by Relativist and/or Marxist "ideological lobotomy" or by what Solzhenitsyn called the "impaired thinking ability" of (anti-scientific, skeptical) philosophical *Relativism* (versus *Realism*) leads today's Pro-Choice United Nations to violate and defecate all over the *Universal Declaration of Human Rights* by aggressively promoting the legal human-killing abortion evil which (the same year of the *Universal Declaration*) at Nuremberg was literally condemned as

---

"an inhumane act," an "act of extermination," and a "crime against humanity."
— Records of the United States Nuremberg War Crimes Trials, United States of America v. Ulrich Greifelt Et Al (Case VIII), October 10, 1947 March 10, 1948; The National Archives, Washington, D.C.

You do not have to be genius to be intellectually honest enough to realize that even despite the (in retrospect) unfortunate wording in the *Universal Declaration's* Article   1, "All human beings are born free and equal in dignity and rights," this cannot possibly mean that preborn humans (exactly like every one of us at their age) somehow have no Human Rights at all and can be legally killed. One must remember the historical context of the 1948 *Universal Declaration,* wherein at the time, throughout all previous history only the evil, genocidal Soviet Marxist Extremists and the evil, genocidal Nazi Fascist Extremists (the latter under trial for Human Rights abuses *including legal abortion* in Nuremberg that same year) had ever formally legalized abortion. There is no intelligent nor intellectually honest (nor historically contextual) way to interpret the *Universal Declaration of Human Rights* that allows for legal human-killing by abortion (as discussed in great detail in the author's *DEMOCRACY 101*). Any such bizarre interpretation would make the *Universal Declaration of Human Rights* a meaningless scrap of paper when it clearly affirms (in Article 2 and in the Preamble preceding Article 1) that Human Rights are for all humans:

"without distinction of any kind" because "recognition of the inherent dignity and of the equal and inalienable rights of all members of the human family is the foundation of freedom, justice and peace in the world"

If preborn humans (which all of us were when we were younger) have no Human Rights and so can be killed legally by abortion, then there is no such thing as "inherent," "equal," "inalienable" Human Rights after all, and the *Universal Declaration of Human Rights* is a meaningless farce. Of course the legal abortion of preborn humans is precisely one of the "barbaric acts" committed by the Nazi Fascist regime (for which it was on trial in 1948 at Nuremberg) which the Preamble of the 1948 *Universal Declaration of Human Rights* indicates the *Declaration* was written to prevent in future! Only severe intellectual dishonesty or "ideological lobotomy" (or perhaps simple lack of intelligence) could suggest otherwise.

With all the increasing 'Creeping Totalitarianism' now accelerating in the West (as in Fact 5 above), much of it specifically in service of expanded "abortion access" at the expense of usual democratic freedoms, and much not specifically concerning abortion *but always promoted by officially Pro-Choice abortion political parties*, it is clear that Western democratic society will by necessity have to end its love affair with the legal human-killing by abortion (and euthanasia) started by the evil, genocidal totalitarian Extremist Left Soviet Marxists and the evil, genocidal totalitarian Extremist Right Nazi Fascists, if Western Human Rights and Democracy are to survive at all. Just as at the Nuremberg War Crimes Trials of Nazi atrocities, "it was legal in my country" will not be any kind of defense for promoting or participating in legal abortion (or any other legal human-killing atrocities), because Nuremberg implicitly established, for the sake of human safety everywhere for all time, that Human Rights necessarily come with *Human Responsibilities* to recognize what the *Universal Declaration of Human Rights* called the "Inherent," "Equal," "Inalienable" Human Rights of all humans. Therefore, to fail to protect the Human Rights of some other humans, or to actively violate the Human Rights of some other humans, is a *criminal* dereliction of human duty to the human race itself, and this is why Nazis were put on trial at Nuremberg for legal abortion, legal euthanasia, legal genocide in the Death Camps, all called "crimes against humanity." It is *criminal* to shirk one's Human Responsibilities to recognize and protect the Human Rights of other humans, even if, as in Nazi Germany, killing other humans of any age or race, ability or disability, is "legal in my country."

Moreover, literally all of the usual "arguments" given for legal abortion are below proved to merely be intellectually dishonest *logical fallacies* which not only do not prove anyone's position for legal abortion, but actually prove Pro-Choicers do not know how to argue logically nor honestly at all. Nevertheless, **in THE INTELLECTUAL HONESTY CHALLENGE in Chapter 7, the author respects an honest attempt** to defend any Pro-Choice politician or voter's position against the mountain of evidence that Pro-Life = Pro-Democracy collected in this book (and the other, longer books in the HUMAN RIGHTS EDUCATION FOR LASTING FREE DEMOCRACY book series). As Pro-Choicers who disagree with the conclusions of this book (and book series) send their responses to

HonestyChallenge@WilliamBaptisteHumanRightsAndFreedomsForever.com

the author will be very happy to continue respectful dialogue with Pro-Choice politicians and voters honest enough to try to defend themselves in the light of facts, without just pretending facts do not exist and/or spouting intellectually dishonest logical fallacies like Pro-Choicers usually do. Any Pro-Choicer in influential positions in government, media, or "Big Tech," who have wittingly or unwittingly been helping disable and dismantle Free Democracy by being Pro-Choice-to-Kill-Humans (instead of without exception affirming *Equal Human Rights for All Humans*), must take THE INTELLECTUAL HONESTY CHALLENGE, or else they too tacitly concede that they have no honest nor intelligent reason to remain Pro-Choice. If they really think legal abortion is at all reasonable in light of established facts and sound logic, Pro-Choicers should have no fear of defending their position against THE INTELLECTUAL HONESTY CHALLENGE – and this author awaits your honest and intelligent attempts to justify the Pro-Choice legal abortion position, sent to the above address.

Intending to be the world's informal "Professor of Human Rights," this author considers no opponent an enemy, but a precious human being who, it is hoped, will become convinced to treat all other humans as precious. **This is our Human Responsibility which comes with our own Human Rights: to recognize** *"inherent," "equal," "inalienable"* **Human Rights in all other humans, "without distinction of any kind," in the words of the** *Universal Declaration of Human Rights.* If you are intellectually honest enough to discover the attempt to refute this book (by taking THE INTELLECTUAL HONESTY CHALLENGE) forces you to change your position from "Pro-Choice" to "Pro-Life," as, the author posits, intellectual honesty demands, then please also email the results of your attempt to *The Intellectual Honesty Challenge* at the above email address.
    ***End Addendum.*]

The above "Top 6" facts (or "clusters of facts") alone (there are many more in William Baptiste's books in the HUMAN RIGHTS EDUCATION FOR LASTING FREE DEMOCRACY book series) prove far beyond reasonable doubt that "Pro-Choice Abortion" philosophy with its "right-to-kill-humans" has since ancient times been the enemy of Human Rights and Freedoms; has already eliminated everyone's legally recognized *Inherent Human Right to Live*; and is currently destroying genuine democracy through "Pro-Choice" "Creeping Totalitarian" policies restricting freedom of speech and expression; restricting freedom of conscience and assembly and religion and other freedoms all specifically to ensure completely unimpeded "abortion access" at the high cost of Human Rights and Democratic Freedoms. **The inescapable conclusion:** *Pro-Life = Pro-Democracy.*

This conclusion based on the above Human Rights history is also supported by Biological Science and the Formal Science of Logic, as also elaborated but more thoroughly in William Baptiste's books *Pro-Life Equals Pro-Democracy* and *DEMOCRACY 101.*

The above facts suggest that, for the sake of intellectual honesty (and lasting democracy), it is time we adopt:

Accurate Terms to Clarify the Central Dispute of our Time: Where Do You Stand on the Current Human Rights for All Humans Debate?

Do you believe in *Equal Human Rights for All Humans*, or do you believe Human Rights can and should be denied to some humans (as with slavery, Death Camps, human-killing abortion and human-killing euthanasia)? That is, are you 'Pro-Human-Right-to-Live' or 'Pro-Choice-to-Kill-Humans'? Are you a 'Pro-Life Human Rights Advocate' or are you a 'Pro-Choice Bigot' who (like all bigots) *chooses* just *which* humans you accept as humans with equal human value and rights and *which* humans you do *not* value equally? These more accurate terms leave less room for the Pro-Choice(-to-Kill-Humans) side's intellectually dishonest tendency to be illogical and unscientific and pretend that humans are not killed in abortions.

INTELLECTUALLY INDEFENSIBLE: ALL Pro-Choice Abortion "Arguments" are Intellectually Dishonest Uses of What the Science of Logic Calls Fallacies of Distraction Which Avoid the Question of the Human Rights of the Humans Killed in Abortions

---

"What good fortune for governments that the people do not think."
– Adolf Hitler

"Logic needs to be compulsory in high schools to ensure future voters and future politicians both know how to think clearly, logically and with intellectual honesty, so they can vote and govern intelligently and not be so easily fooled (even by textbook logical fallacies) into destroying the foundations of their own freedom. When citizen voters and politicians know neither The Foundational Principles of Human Rights and Democracy, nor how to think clearly, consistently, and logically (nor how to avoid logical fallacies of reasoning), Free Democracy is sure to fail and not last."
- William Baptiste,
Founder, Human Rights and Freedoms Forever!
Founder, The Intellectual Honesty Challenge
Proclaimer of THE THINKING REVOLUTION

"Women's Reproductive Rights" Actually Means "Women's-Right-to-Kill-Humans" INSTEAD of Human Rights Which are Logically Incompatible with a "Woman's-Right-to-Kill-Humans-in-Her-Womb" (It is "Women's Rights" OR Human Rights – You Cannot Have Both Because They are Mutually Exclusive; "Women's Rights" are Only Ever Cited to Dishonestly DISTRACT from the Human Rights of the Humans Killed in Abortions)

Listening to Pro-Choice "arguments" is like reading a logic textbook highlighting logical fallacies or errors. Pro-Choicers use distracting "red herrings" and "diversions" that take attention away from the actual heart of the abortion issue (Human Rights), diverting distractions like "women's reproductive rights," which logically can only exist *instead of* Human Rights, because they are mutually exclusive. If a woman has a "reproductive right" to kill her preborn human child, then there is no *Inherent Human Right to Live*, the fountain of all other Human Rights, for either the child, the women herself, nor anyone else – all of whom could have been legally killed by their mothers. And this is certainly not an "equal right" – men do not have a "right-to-kill-humans," nor to deny Human Rights to other humans, so why should women?

Nothing is more logically self-contradictory and stupid than to speak of a "Human Right to abortion" which kills humans, violating their Human Rights. Avid Pro-Choicers are not generally known for their intelligence, however, so even at the UN, some Pro-Choicers are unintelligent enough – or, more likely, intellectually dishonest and therefore "willfully stupid" enough to actually use this language. Still, as a rule you never hear a Pro-Choicer speak of "women's reproductive rights" and "Human Rights" at the same time, because that would expose their deceit. Rather, committed Pro-Choice politicians are so intellectually dishonest they will practically scream "women's reproductive rights" in attempt to *avoid* ever seriously engaging the question of Human Rights, which is the actual crux of the Abortion Debate (The

Human Rights for All Humans Debate) – and on which basis they would lose the Abortion Debate, since humans have Human Rights, and preborn humans are humans.

The Rape "Argument" : Several Intellectually Dishonest Logical Fallacies and Propaganda Techniques Rolled into One

Pro-Choicers also distract from the Human Rights issue with irrelevancies like rape. Of course we have sympathy for victims of rape, and we must, but this is irrelevant to the key question of whether humans have Human Rights or not. If humans have Human Rights, then the abortion-killing of humans is wrong, even in the rare instances where a human is conceived through a rape. As one such human woman conceived in rape has said, "*I did not deserve the death penalty for my father's rape of my mother.*" Responses to the problem of rape that maintain the *Inherent Human Right to Live* must be sought – like combatting today's "rape culture" with its immature and irresponsible sexual practices, fueled by women-objectifying pornography – rather than by copying Nazi War Crimes condemned at Nuremberg, such as legalized human-killing abortion.

The "rape" argument for abortion actually has elements of several kinds of logical fallacies rolled into one, it is not just a *fallacy of distraction*. It is a *non-sequitur*: it *does not follow* that abortion, even if it is allowed in the rare sympathetic cases of rape, should in any way justify the current *abortion-on-demand*, where humans are killed by abortion by any woman for any reason (even killing a unique human life just because "I had plane tickets close to my due date").

Anyone who cites the rape example when they really want *abortion-on-demand* (not just exceptions to the rule *killing humans is a crime* for rape victims) are just being dishonest and illogical. Any Pro-Choicer who *would not be satisfied* with an abortion law which allowed abortion in the case of rape but would not allow abortions for any reason, who brings up the rape example, is *not genuinely compassionate to women, but rather is very dishonest and is scandalously misusing the great misfortune of rape victims to try to prop up their dastardly support for the Human Rights abuse of abortion for any reason.* Pro-Choicers who cite rape as "justification" for abortion when they actually want *abortion on demand* should be immediately and harshly reprimanded for so callously and dishonestly misusing the plight of raped women to prop up their uneducated Pro-*Choice* bigotry that (like all bigotry) does not believe in *Equal Human Rights for All Humans* but instead *chooses* which humans they think have equal Human Rights and which humans they think do not have equal Human Rights with themselves. Note that intellectually dishonest European Pro-Choicers harshly criticize Pro-Life Poland's abortion laws as somehow "draconian" for protecting *Equal Human Rights for All Humans* better than any other European nation, *even though Poland has compromised with Pro-Choicers and expressly allows abortions in the cases of rape* and when the mother's health is threatened. So, many typical Pro-Choicers are themselves dishonest and do not believe in the rape argument themselves. They effectively and actually believe in "*abortion on demand, Human Rights for All Humans be damned,*" but because this accurate slogan reveals their evil disdain for Human Rights, they instead use the "rape argument" so they can pretend to be "compassionate" when they are really just selfish bigots who care nothing for Human Rights.

The rape "argument" also fits the profiles of several logical *fallacies of distraction* and propaganda techniques. Instead of actually engaging the critical question of Human Rights of preborn humans, and dishonestly trying to avoid it, Pro-Choicers citing rape are committing "special pleading" fallacy, whereby (assuming they hold that *killing humans is wrong* at all) they plead a "special case" for women who have been raped. This is like saying, "The law against killing humans applies to everyone else but not to them. I know that killing humans is wrong for most people, but I think raped women should have the right-to-kill-humans when the human in question is in their womb." As if one violent crime cancels out another.

The rape argument also fallaciously distracts the mind from the Human Rights question through the "emotional appeal" fallacy, shutting down the brain by appealing to the emotions (this also fits the profile of the propaganda technique known as "appeal to pity" – instead of appealing to facts and sound logic). By emphasizing the genuinely sympathetic condition of the raped woman while ignoring facts of Science and Human Rights History, Pro-Choicers dishonestly avoid engaging the issue of the human baby conceived in rape's Human Rights. The rape argument is also a "red herring" logical fallacy or "diversion" that makes the argument about rape, instead of about the central abortion question of preborn Human Rights (when rape is not involved in the vast majority of abortions and is entirely irrelevant to the *Human Rights for all humans* issue raised by currently legal *abortion on demand*).

All of these different kinds of *fallacies of distraction* involved in the rape argument have the intellectually dishonest purpose of *distracting* from and *avoiding* the whole question of the Human Rights of the humans undeniably killed in abortions – which is the crux of the Abortion Debate! (which is really the Human Rights for All Humans Debate). But humans do have Human Rights. That is why *killing humans is wrong*, whether by abortion or any other means – and whether the person wanting an abortion was raped or not (most abortions are *not* performed for cases of rape).

The "Argument" for Legal Abortion to Prevent Illegal Abortions - The Logical Fallacy of False Dilemma (and others)

Pro-Choicers also deceitfully distract from addressing the Human Rights issue by claiming abortion needs to be legal to prevent women from being harmed during illegal abortions. This argument is bigoted from the outset, because it assumes that the human baby has less worth than the human mother, instead of both being precious human lives.

Moreover, it dishonestly "forgets" that the precious human baby is always denied Human Rights and killed by his or her own mother effectively hiring a "hitman" (abortionist) in these extreme cases. But women seeking dangerous illegal human-killing abortions in democratic countries where the Human Rights of all humans are protected by law is an extreme act of criminal desperation. Basic respect for the law that protects everybody's rights means that there is no other crime that we would ever consider de-criminalizing just so that criminals do not harm themselves while committing their crimes. Why would we de-criminalize the "crime against humanity" of abortion which was condemned as such at Nuremberg after World War II, back when the Nazi atrocities (including legal abortion) had made everyone more highly aware of Human Rights (and how they can be violated) than Western society had ever been?

Even if some people get criminally desperate enough to steal for sympathetic reasons (like feeding their poor family), it would be foolish to *de-criminalize stealing* for everybody, such that no-one's property is safe, just to prevent a few sympathetic desperate criminals from harming themselves while committing their crime (say, by falling from of a third story window they were breaking and entering). It is just as foolish to *de-criminalize human-killing abortion* for everybody, such that no-one's *inherent Human Rights* are intact, and our society is exposed to 'Creeping Totalitarianism,' just to prevent a few sympathetic but criminally desperate women from risking self-harm while killing their own children.

This bad logic has already resulted in millions of people who were not criminally desperate at all (and so would not have risked harming themselves while committing a crime against humanity), and/or who have no sympathetic circumstances at all, now easily and legally hiring a "hitman" to kill their human child by abortion for reasons as thin as "I had plane tickets around my due date" or as bigoted as "my family didn't want to have a girl."

It is in any case the logical fallacy of "false dilemma" (also known as "false binary" or "either/or fallacy") to claim that abortion "must" be legal "or else" many women will die from illegal abortions – as if there were no intermediate options or alternatives. This argument is also a logically fallacious "appeal to emotion" (and propagandist "appeal to pity" instead of to facts and logic) while turning off the brain's ability to seek alternatives. There are surely very many ways that a democratic society which assumes *every human life is equally precious* can build various social supports which prevent precious pregnant women from becoming *criminally desperate* enough to risk self-harm while killing their precious human baby. We can start by developing services which connect the long waiting lists of infertile and other couples wanting to adopt with the unhappily pregnant. In any case, against all human ingenuity for problem-solving the false logic of the "illegal abortions" false dilemma implies we "must" alleviate the distress of the sympathetic few criminally desperate *by any means necessary*, even by means of de-criminalizing human-killing abortion which was criminalized for good reason in the 4th Century – because humans are *precious not cheap* (and have Human Rights).

Obviously, implementing better social supports which prevent women from getting criminally desperate enough to risk harming themselves in an illegal abortion is far smarter than unleashing ultimately democracy-destroying 'Creeping Totalitarianism' into the West by following the totalitarian Soviet and Nazi precedents of de-criminalizing abortion.

The 2500-year-old Hippocratic Oath, Foundational to the Medical Profession, Specifically Prohibited Abortion and in Fact There Is No Such Thing as a "Medically Necessary Abortion" – A Medical Procedure to Save the Precious Mother's Life that the Precious Baby Will Not Survive (as an Unintended Side Effect) Is Simply a Matter of the Rare Case Where Medical Science Cannot Save BOTH Precious Mother AND Precious Baby, and One or the Other Will Die Due to the Limits of Medical Science (Either One a Human Tragedy). It is Completely Unnecessary and Completely Illogical to Legally Devalue Preborn Human Lives Through Legalized Abortion (Thereby Legally Eradicating the Inherent Human Right to Live Which Grounds Democracy) to "Cover" this Rare Sympathetic "Hard Case."

Devoid of logic and not used to ever thinking anything through, Pro-Choicers will even distract from addressing the human baby's Human Rights by making the ridiculous claim that abortion somehow "needs" to be legal in case it is "necessary to save the mother's life." But many surgeons testify abortion is never "medically necessary," because a medical procedure to save the precious mother's life, which the precious baby will not survive, does not have to deliberately target the baby for death the way an abortion does (even if the baby's death is an unfortunate side-effect).

It most certainly is not "necessary" to legalize human-killing abortion, thus legally eradicating the *Inherent Human Right to Live* of everyone (who then could have been legally aborted), in order to cover the rare cases where current medical science cannot save *both* precious human mother *and* precious human baby. All that is necessary is to recognize the obvious fact that sometimes medical science is unable to save all the precious humans involved and has to focus on saving one and letting another die (without deliberately killing the other).

This is in fact commonplace in emergency medical clinics on battlefields or in disaster areas: In these places, constraining factors frequently mean that doctors have to make the terrible decision to save one precious human life and not another, usually the one understood to have "the best chance of survival" being chosen. This commonplace battlefield medical practice is all that is necessary to cover the rare cases where current medical science is unable to save both precious mother and precious baby.

So, there is no need to violate the non-killing integrity of the medical profession, which when it began about 2500 years ago explicitly prohibited abortion in the oldest known forms of the doctors' Hippocratic Oath; there is no need at all to legally devalue some humans in order to legally abort them and so legally eliminate the *Inherent Human Right to Live* which is the foundation of all Human Rights and Democratic Freedoms; one needs only to simply acknowledge that regrettably, sometimes the medical profession is unable to save all the precious humans it treats.

Intellectually Dishonest Pro-Choicers Only Ever Bring Up Sympathetic But Rare "Hard Cases" Like Rape and the Misnamed "Medically Necessary" Abortions for the Intellectually Dishonest Purpose of Misusing Rare Sympathetic Cases as a "Springboard" to Current Legal Abortion On Demand, Which Does Not Logically Follow (Even If Abortions were Legal for These Rare Sympathetic Cases, as Long as Humans Have Human Rights it Must Be Admitted that Abortion on Demand Always Treats Preborn Fetal-age Humans Unscientifically and with Great Bigotry, as If They Were Not Humans, and Valueless, without the Human Rights which Humans Have)

The intellectual dishonesty of committed Pro-Choicers is so pronounced, that after bringing up these genuinely sympathetic but *rare* cases of:
- an unwanted child conceived involuntarily through rape;
- a woman (for sympathetic or unsympathetic reasons) criminally desperate enough to risk harming herself in an illegal abortion in order to kill her unwanted child;
- a woman whose life medically cannot be saved without her baby dying;

they actually try to illogically stretch abortion allowed for these rare sympathetic "hard cases" into unrestricted *abortion on demand* (as if there were no such thing as Human Rights and so society does not even need to have a sympathetic excuse like these three reasons to kill humans by abortion).

But, again, these rare cases, even if they were to be allowed as "exceptions" to the democracy-grounding rule that Human Rights are for all humans and therefore *killing humans is wrong* and illegal, in no way offer any logical justification for *abortion on demand* which always treats preborn fetal-age human babies unscientifically and with great bigotry, as if they were not humans, and so valueless, without the Human Rights which humans have.

Logical fallacies abound in Pro-Choice thinking. These "big three" Pro-Choice arguments are all (among other fallacies) "appeals to emotion" (at the expense of the mind) which the Science of Logic specifically lists as one of many forms of the "fallacies of distraction" (as well being the propaganda technique of "appeal to pity" - getting someone to side with your opinion merely on the basis of pity, without any reference to facts or sound reasoning). These three genuinely sympathetic cases are dishonestly cited to stir emotional compassion while distracting the mind from actually thinking things through – and dishonestly *avoiding* the key *Human Rights* question at the center of the Abortion Debate (which is really the *Human Rights for All Humans Debate*).

Typically, committed Pro-Choicers only ever bring up these three rare sympathetic "hard cases" *for the intellectually dishonest purpose* of using them as the "thin edge of the wedge" towards *legal abortion on demand*, even though there is no logical justification to go from the one to the other, as long as humans are understood to have Human Rights.

It is what the Science of Logic calls a "non-sequitur" (Latin: "it does not follow"), to say that if abortion is allowed in these rare sympathetic cases, then abortion should be allowed "on demand," by any woman for any reason. But if abortions were only allowed in these rare cases, hardly any abortions would ever be performed. A child conceived through rape is truly rare, as the woman would have to be raped during the two days of her monthly cycle she can conceive (a less than 7% chance), and violent rape lacks the bio-chemical environment healthy lovemaking has which enhances the chances of conceiving a child.

Most women most of the time are law-abiding, and not so immature and irresponsible (or psychologically unbalanced) as to be so criminally desperate to kill their unwanted human child (rather than give the child up for adoption) that they would risk bodily harm through an illegal abortion. And the very rare pregnant woman with extreme medical complications whose life cannot be saved without losing her baby does not *need* a legal abortion at all to live; she only needs a medical procedure which the baby is not likely to survive (and the doctor's report can simply explain why they were medically unable to save the valuable little patient, as doctor's reports every day have to explain why a patient died despite the doctors' best efforts at treating *valuable human beings*).

That said, there actually is no good logical reason to make abortion legal even just for the first two rare cases, according to the perfectly scientifically and logically sound categorical syllogism of Formal Logic *All humans have Human Rights. Preborn humans are humans. Therefore, preborn humans have Human Rights.* Since Human Rights are the highest values we have in Western Society; and since they are the historically and logically necessary foundation of *lasting* Democracy (see *DEMOCRACY 101* and *Pro-Life Equals Pro-Democracy* for even more details than in this book); and since, as shown by the current worldwide crisis of 'Creeping Totalitarianism' compromising legitimate democratic freedoms which has been logically leading up to this point ever since human-killing abortion was de-criminalized following the totalitarian Soviet and Nazi precedents – there is actually no good reason to compromise on Human Rights by legally allowing abortion in *any* circumstances, even the rarest of cases like a child conceived in rape or to prevent a few criminally desperate and unstable women from harming themselves while killing their precious human child.

Both of these rare circumstances become even rarer, and less problematic when they do occur, if instead of compromising our highest Western values of Human Rights we *educate* Westerners in the Pro-Life *Foundational Principles of Human Rights and Democracy* and start to rebuild a true 'Culture of Life' to replace the current 'Culture of Death' which is now cancelling Human Rights and undermining Democracy at an unprecedented rate. With this kind of solid Human Rights Education (as that provided first in *DEMOCRACY 101* and introduced in this book), Western culture would become generally so consciously aware of the *Inherent Human Right to Live* which historically and logically grounds our whole free and democratic Western way of life, that women in those two rare extreme cases will be advised and supported in having their babies and if necessary giving them up for adoption, so that they are much less inclined to become criminally desperate enough to hire killers to kill their precious preborn human children at risk to themselves also.

Human life-affirming government programs could facilitate this. This author is amazed that already no one in government has thought of setting up a service whereby those with unwanted pregnancies (unwanted *human children*) get connected with the long waiting-lists of couples wanting to adopt children. Whether an unwanted pregnancy (unwanted human child) exists because of rape, which is very rare, or exists because of immature and irresponsible sexual practices (like irresponsibly engaging in nature's way of generating the next generation of human children without any intention of doing so), a culture that affirms life – the only kind of culture that can support *lasting* democracy – will offer support and encouragement to a woman pregnant with a unique and precious human child who she for whatever reasons does not want to (or feels unable to) raise to healthy mature human adulthood herself. Other humans who believe in *Equal Human Rights for All Humans,* which is part of Free Democracy's very foundation, do want to help the precious woman and the precious child.

Human ingenuity knows no bounds (if one is not a dull-witted Pro-Choicer with what Solzhenitsyn called "impaired thinking ability" due to being Moral Relativists - these seem to think that the answer to every complex human social problem is to kill more humans). Once the terrible, inhuman and ultimately anti-democratic option of human-killing abortion (first legalized by genocidal Soviets and Nazis) is re-criminalized, for the sake of *lasting* democracy and uncompromised Human Rights and to end 'Creeping Totalitarianism,' many creative human-life-affirming solutions to the rare sympathetic cases of mothers who do not want to be mothers will be found. It is certainly not necessary to follow totalitarian precedents (and unleash 'Creeping Totalitarianism') by legally devaluing some human lives (as totalitarian States do) and allowing mothers to be killers by abortion.

Against the mountain of evidence from the disciplines of Human Rights History, Science, and Logic that Pro-Life = Pro-Democracy, Pro-Choicers only use distractions and invalid arguments to dishonestly avoid even engaging the critical question of the inherent Human Rights of preborn humans; they refuse to even discuss the very crux of the Abortion Debate (the *Human Rights for All Humans Debate*). Pro-Choice "arguments" read like a Logic textbook's examples of bad reasoning, with Pro-Choice voters and politicians primarily using logical fallacies of distraction distracting away from the crux abortion question of preborn Human Rights, such as the above-refuted rape or so-called "medically necessary" arguments or the "red herring" of "women's rights." So-called "women's rights" which as human-killing abortion supporters define them are completely incompatible with Human Rights, because they effectively mean a "woman's right-to-kill-humans" which effectively cancels out the *Inherent Human Right to Live.* **By using only these and other equally illogical "arguments" all in an intellectually dishonest attempt to "justify" being Pro-Choice (and thereby supporting legal human-killing by abortion), not only do Pro-Choicers not prove their case for legal abortion:** *they rather prove that they do not know how to argue logically nor honestly at all.*

◆

Pro-Choice Voters and (Even More Influential) Pro-Choice Politicians, Political Parties, Judges, Civil Servants/Government Employees (Who Have Influence Over Public Policies and Laws); as well as Influential Billionaires, Media Moguls, Journalists and "Big Tech" Employees (Who Have Influence Over News and Media and Thus Control Public Access to Information) NEED TO REALIZE THAT THEIR PRO-CHOICE STANCE MARKS THEM (TO THE HUMAN-RIGHTS EDUCATED AND TO FUTURE HISTORY BOOKS) as Among the Most Bigoted and Least Intellectually Honest People on the Planet Earth Throughout All Human History

As this thoughtful, highly educated and intelligent and intellectually honest book series reveals, self-described "Pro-Choicers" are among the most hypocritical, most bigoted and least intellectually honest people on the planet. The most bigoted, because they copy the genocidal (philosophically *Relativist not Realist*) Marxist/ Socialist ideologue bigots who *first* legalized human-killing abortion in modern times and *then* legalized the human-killing genocide of millions of my ethnic group, *just like all bigots deny Equal Human Rights to some humans.* Today's self-described Pro-Choicers are also the *least intellectually honest people on the planet* because (see Chapters 7-9 of this author's longer book *Pro-Life Equals Pro-Democracy* for many more details) they justify their beloved legal human-killing abortion following totalitarian Marxist precedent *only by absurdly denying the plain Science* that preborn humans are humans (so Abortion kills humans). And also by *using nearly every intellectually dishonest logical fallacy* in a Logic textbook to try to *dishonestly* wiggle out of *admitting* that *killing humans is wrong,* which is a principle they usually pay insincere "lip service" to, of course *applies to the preborn humans of any age they are eager to kill for their own convenience.*

"Pro-Choicers," whatever their level of societal influence (as above) need to realize that their Pro-Choice position logically implies other things about them they probably do not wish others to think of them (which is the result of foolishly associating themselves with a Pro-Choice position/opinion that involves *killing humans* without first thinking it through scientifically and logically):

1. Being Pro-Choice logically means you do not believe that *killing humans is wrong* (so you are like evil and violent criminals and dictators).

2. Being Pro-Choice logically means you do not believe in *Equal Human Rights for All Humans* (so you are like every bigot or slaveowner).

3. Being Pro-Choice logically means you do not believe *in the science of human life nor the science of logic,* since science confirms preborn humans are humans, and logic confirms they therefore must have Human Rights (so you are *like the uneducated and ignorant*).

4. Being Pro-Choice logically *means you do not know how to think scientifically nor logically nor honestly* (suggesting you may be like *the unintelligent or mentally deficient –* or perhaps simply *dishonest.* Actually, many people who because of developmental disorders are in fact unintelligent or mentally deficient can still *honestly grasp the truths* that *humans are equally precious* and that *all humans have Human Rights*).

So, Pro-Choice voters, politicians, political parties, billionaires, journalists, judges and "Big Tech" employees who are now intertwined with the Mainstream Media which Solzhenitsyn (the Nobel Prize-winning historian of brutally totalitarian Soviet Marxism/Socialism) repeatedly testified (after living 18 years in the U.S.) was Marxist-influenced, NEED to REALIZE:

When you say, "I believe in a woman's right to CHOOSE to have her baby (or terminate her pregnancy)" you are saying *you do not actually believe in Human Rights* (which are incompatible) and you do not realize you are saying you do not know how to think consistently, honestly, nor logically (or else you would know they are incompatible).

Your Pro-Choice position says a lot of awkward and embarrassing things about you that you did not realize you are advertising whenever you say that you are Pro-Choice. From now on, get used to EDUCATED people calling you on it and embarrassing you if you are ignorant, unintelligent, or evil and bigoted enough to stay Pro-Choice after exposure to the now readily available HUMAN RIGHTS EDUCATION FOR LASTING FREE DEMOCRACY delineated in this book series from mostly undisputed facts of Human Rights History, Science, Logic, and the History of Philosophy (and of Science).

Some Useful Terms (Discussed More Fully in Pro-Life Equals Pro-Democracy)

FEMALE GENDERCIDE: Legal abortion has brought back the ancient deadly misogynistic bigotry against females, who are now once again killed just for being females (now by abortion; before by infanticide) – The refusal of Pro-Choice so-called "Feminists" (and their male "Women's Rights" supporters) to fight this affront to genuine women's rights (which are Human Rights) for the sake of keeping their Pro-Choice abortion "Women's-Right-to-Kill-Humans" exposes that such "Pro-Choice Feminists" (and their male "women's rights" supporters) are *not interested in genuine women's rights at all.* All genuine "women's rights" of course fall under the umbrella of *Human Rights* and cannot possibly contradict and eradicate any human's *Inherent, Equal, Inalienable Human Rights* the way legal human-killing abortion does. In the author's country, even though most people polled agree that female gendercide/sex-selective abortion of females is wrong, and females should not be killed by abortion just because they are females, government bills to end female gendercide have not been supported by Pro-Choicers, revealing their true allegiance is to legal human-killing abortion and not to Human Rights nor to any genuine women's rights, which cannot contradict Human Rights.

BULVERISM: Intellectually dishonest, bigoted anti-Christian and Pro-Choice "Bulverism" first assumes that Christians and Pro-Lifers are wrong and then "justifies" turning off the brain and not listening to facts and logic presented by Christians and Pro-Lifers merely on the basis of the "wrongness" assumed but not proved (circular reasoning). Intellectually lazy Bulverists say things like "you only believe that because you're a Christian/Pro-Lifer," as if the origin or "genetics" of their opponents' belief justify simply dismissing their position (the genetic fallacy), without any regard to the overwhelming facts of Science, Logic, and Human Rights History (and the History of Philosophy) which support the conclusions that Pro-Life = Pro-Democracy and that Christianity, if it need not be individually embraced, must at least be respected by governments as the origin and source of the underlying Foundational Principles of Human Rights and Democracy, in any country that wants to remain a free democracy and not eventually fall to current 'Creeping Totalitarianism' now undermining Democracy from its very foundations.

INTELLECTOPHOBIA: The fear of respectful, intellectually honest, rational, scientific and rigorously logical argument and debate which today leads anti-traditional people and politicians (including Pro-Choice and Neo-Marxist Identity Politics "Cancel Culture" ideologues) to label traditionalists who disagree with their weakly-grounded opinions some kind of "phobes" or "haters" (to be "cancelled" or censored) in an intellectually dishonest attempt to AVOID any honest scientific and logical debate over their opinion which they would LOSE based on objective facts of science, logic, and history etc. (Facts which overwhelmingly show that all Western Human Rights and Democratic Freedoms depend historically and logically on the Traditional Western Values they were historically and logically built upon). If you ever hear someone call their opponent who disagrees with them some kind of a "phobe" or "hater," or "fascist" or "racist" or other intimidating names, it means most likely that the name-callers are too scared to engage in respectful, intelligent debate with those who disagree with them because they do not think their position is strong enough to win a fair intellectual and scientifically grounded debate, while at the same time the name-callers are too intellectually dishonest to change their position even if verifiable scientific or historical facts and sound logic do not support it. SPEAKING VERIFIABLE FACTS IS IN NO WAY "HATE SPEECH," BUT ONLY THE RESULT OF AN HONEST INTELLECT; BUT INTELLECTOPHOBES EVEN CALL VERIFIABLE FACTS OF SCIENCE OR HISTORY ETC. "HATE SPEECH" OR "PHOBIAS" WHEN FACTS DO NOT AGREE WITH AN INTELLECTOPHOBE'S UNSCIENTIFIC OR OTHERWISE UNEDUCATED POLITICAL IDEOLOGY (Especially divisive and toxic Neo-Marxist Identity Politics with its "Cancel Culture" attempting to silence all facts against their vacuous ideologies). Intellectophobia is a major threat to Free Democracy, and today intellectophobe Pro-Choice government lawmakers have even made totalitarian laws which make it a crime to speak scientifically verifiable facts which do not support their political party's Pro-Choice or other unscientific ideologies.

To the legal human-killing Pro-Choice *extremist*, Neo-Marxist Identity Politics "Cancel Culture" ideologues who have corrupted and largely taken over the once-healthy political Left, there is no more classic democratic notion "Though I disagree with what you say, I will defend to the death your right to say it." They instead live by "if I disagree with what you say, I will paint it as *hate speech,* and I will fight to the death your right to even have your say." Wherever they can get away with it, these ideologues in "Big Tech" and mainstream media "cancel" or censor facts and voices against their ideological agenda. Wherever they can get away with it, such

"Intellectophobes" in government legislate away your democracy-grounding right to Free Speech.

Pro-Choice Legal Abortion is a Not-Even-Remotely Intellectually Defensible Position

It is important to understand that Pro-Choice legal abortion is a not-even-remotely intellectually defensible position for any honest intellect which has been properly educated in Science, Logic, and Human Rights History (and the History of Ideas/Philosophy – see CHAPTER 3: PHILOSOPHY). And a Pro-Choice position is a completely untenable position **in a free democracy which claims to uphold Human Rights.** As shown in the HUMAN RIGHTS EDUCATION FOR LASTING FREE DEMOCRACY book series by William Baptiste, Founder of *Human Rights and Freedoms Forever!* and *The Intellectual Honesty Challenge;* proclaimer of THE THINKING REVOLUTION to replace current widespread Pro-Choice and Neo-Marxist *ideology* with *education.*

Casual Pro-Choicers may be simply uninformed (easily remedied by reading one of the books in this book series). But one has to be staggeringly intellectually dishonest (if not simply unintelligent or evil!) in order to be politically dedicated to the Pro-Choice position, as shown in this book series. Therefore, the author naturally concludes anyone who is Pro-Choice is incompetent to lead a free democracy – they simply have no foundation for democracy. Anyone who disagrees must take THE INTELLECTUAL HONESTY CHALLENGE in Chapter 7 and see if they still disagree.

CHAPTER 2: PRINCIPLES

The Foundational Principles of Human Rights and Democracy;
The Core Principles of Lasting Democracy;
The Pledge of Allegiance to Democracy;
The Necessity to Constitutionally Enshrine Equal Human
Rights for All Humans to Ensure Lasting Democracy.
Announcing the Flag of Democracy and the Global Solidarity
Movement for Traditional Western Values in Public Policy to
Ensure Human Rights and Freedoms Last Forever on their Firm
Traditional, Historical, Logical Foundations (Including
Philosophical Realism Which Grounds Science instead of
Relativism Which Grounds Politically Extremist Legal Human-
Killing Marxism, Nazism, and All Current Threats to Free
Society – Notably Legal Human-Killing by Abortion Which Was
First Legalized by Genocidal Relativist Marxists and Nazis)

"Democracy Pledgers" (or, More Poetically, "Knights of Human
Rights" and "Ladies of Lasting Democracy") and the Global
Solidarity Movement - Definition

---

*"Democracy Pledgers" (or, more poetically, "Knights of Human Rights" and "Ladies of
Lasting Democracy") are people who take responsibility for Human Rights and Democratic
Freedoms for everyone rather than taking them for granted. People who bother to learn
where they come from so they can protect these rights and freedoms for future generations.
Rather than not even knowing where they come from and so not being vigilant to maintain
their foundations, and thus being prone to ignorantly compromise Human Rights and
undermine Democracy without even realizing it. Such uneducated ignorance on a wide
scale in both politicians and voters (and judges; journalists; influential employees of
government bureaucracies, media and "Big Tech") has brought on the current worldwide*

threat of 'Creeping Totalitarianism' now accelerating. This global crisis has necessitated, to combat this uneducated ignorance, the writing of the HUMAN RIGHTS EDUCATION FOR LASTING FREE DEMOCRACY educational book series (including DEMOCRACY 101; PRO-LIFE EQUALS PRO-DEMOCRACY; KILLING HUMANS IS WRONG; NO FRUIT WITHOUT ROOTS; THINKING REVOLUTION: THE INTELLECTUAL HONESTY CHALLENGE; EQUAL HUMAN RIGHTS FOR ALL HUMANS; and the handbook KNIGHTS OF HUMAN RIGHTS, LADIES OF LASTING DEMOCRACY: Handbook Manifesto of the Educated <u>Global Solidarity Movement</u>
Against Uneducated Global 'Creeping Totalitarianism' Now Accelerating; with more books to come).
"Democracy Pledgers" (or "Knights of Human Rights" and "Ladies of Lasting Democracy") read from the HUMAN RIGHTS EDUCATION FOR LASTING FREE DEMOCRACY educational book series and its Pledge of Allegiance to Democracy (which identifies The Foundational Principles of Human Rights and Democracy and 10 Core Principles of Lasting Democracy from the disciplines of History, Science, Logic, and Philosophy) in order to learn Democracy's historical and logical and philosophical foundations and then spread knowledge of these to others who spread them to others, until there are enough EDUCATED citizens in their country (who no longer take Human Rights and Freedoms for granted) to ensure they last long-term.
"Democracy Pledgers" (or "Knights of Human Rights" and "Ladies of Lasting Democracy") "take the Pledge of Allegiance to Democracy" simply by reading to get this HUMAN RIGHTS EDUCATION FOR LASTING FREE DEMOCRACY <u>and spreading it to others</u> as part of a worldwide grassroots movement (the Global Solidarity Movement) to make sure Human Rights and Freedoms last forever on their firm traditional, historical, scientific and logical foundations – until enough citizens in their country understand and stand up together in Solidarity for the constitutional enshrinement in their country of the essential content of The Foundational Principles of Human Rights and Democracy and The Core Principles of Lasting Democracy. These are contained within Traditional Western Values and they are identified from History, Science and Logic (and Philosophy) in the Pledge of Allegiance to Democracy initially published in <u>DEMOCRACY 101</u> (additional Core Principles and the most pertinent facts of Philosophy initially published in <u>Pro-Life Equals Pro-Democracy</u>). A short form of the Pledge and these key principles are included in all other books of the HUMAN RIGHTS EDUCATION FOR LASTING FREE DEMOCRACY series, so that they may easily be learned and spread.

Human Rights and Free Democracy are non-partisan, and therefore "Democracy Pledgers" (or "Knights of Human Rights" and "Ladies of Lasting Democracy") may be politically "progressive Left" or "conservative Right" (in healthy democracies these can work together fruitfully) <u>but not extremist</u> (political extremism, Left or Right, is easily identified by its attitude towards human life and its approach to Science and Objective Reality). The Foundational Principles of Human Rights and Democracy and the philosophical objective Realism (versus subjective Relativism) which grounds Science, Logic, and Technology are both incorporated into Traditional Western Values, which therefore remain the best guide for public policy, and are promoted as such by the Global Solidarity Movement.

All of the various threats to human life and democratic freedom today come from people having ideology instead of a solid education in the History, Science, Logic, and Philosophy most pertinent to lasting Human Rights and freedoms, and all these threats can be traced to a predominantly Relativistic and Subjective instead of predominantly Realistic and Objective view of the universe in one's (usually unconscious) underlying philosophical worldview.

Today's many threats to Human Rights and democratic freedoms are ultimately rooted in philosophically (Skeptical) Relativism (which ultimately doubts or denies there even are any objective facts or science which can be certainly known, but everything is "subjective" and "relative") instead of (Scientific) Realism. Thus, a basic philosophical worldview which accords with the Traditional Western philosophical Realism which implicitly underlies the Common Sense which daily prevents humans from dying stupidly, and which explicitly grounds all Science, Logic, and Technology, is also ultimately vital to lasting democracy. Because education in the History, Science, Logic and Philosophy most pertinent to lasting Human Rights and democratic freedoms reveals that all Science, Logic,Technology and Human Rights and Free Democracy are grounded in the same underlying philosophical worldview framework of philosophical Realism, which is opposed to the philosophical Relativism which grounds (Extremist Right) Fascism/Nazism, (Extremist Left) Marxism/Communism/Socialism and all current politically extremist (Left or Right) threats to Human Rights and freedoms, "Democracy Pledgers" (or "Knights of Human Rights" and "Ladies of Lasting Democracy") quickly become educated confident champions of human life and freedom, finding that those most against their democracy-grounding Traditional Western Values are also those most uneducated and those most against the Realistic and Objective foundations of Science, Logic, and Technology itself.

An educated electorate of voting citizens in today's compromised democracies will no longer make uneducated votes for uneducated politicians (and political parties) who have no clue where Human Rights and Free Democracy (and Science!) come from, nor how to maintain them. Thus, as many citizen voters as possible getting and spreading to others this HUMAN RIGHTS EDUCATION FOR LASTING FREE DEMOCRACY is part of The WINNING STRATEGY for the 'Culture of Life' (and Philosophical Realism) to WIN the 'Cultural War' with 'The Culture of Death' (and Philosophical Relativism) to Save Humanity Forever from Bigotry and 'Creeping Totalitarianism' Now Accelerating.

The Pledge of Allegiance to Democracy
(Which Identifies The Foundational Principles of Human Rights and Democracy and 10 Core Principles of LASTING Democracy)

"The foundation stones of a great building are destined to groan and be pressed upon."
— Aleksandr Solzhenitsyn

I pledge allegiance to Democracy, and to the implicit foundational principles on which Democracy is historically and logically built and which it needs to explicitly restore in order to survive currently escalating and accelerating 21st Century worldwide trends of 'Creeping Totalitarianism' and last long-term on its foundations (I pledge allegiance to . . . The Foundational Principles of Human Rights and Democracy) . . .

FOUNDATIONAL PRINCIPLE OF HUMAN RIGHTS AND DEMOCRACY #1: EQUAL HUMAN PRECIOUSNESS

Every human life without exception, without discrimination and "without distinction of any kind" is *supremely* and *equally* valuable and precious, *obligating* governments to protect and serve *all* precious humans who have "inherent . . . equal and inalienable [human] rights," [quoted phrases are from the United Nations' *Universal Declaration of Human Rights* which clarifies that "recognition of the *inherent* dignity and of the *equal* and *inalienable* rights of *all* members of the *human family* is the *foundation* of freedom, justice and peace in the world"] . . .

FOUNDATIONAL PRINCIPLE OF HUMAN RIGHTS AND DEMOCRACY #2: FREEDOM OF BELIEF/ THOUGHT/ RELIGION/ SPEECH

Every human must be FREE from government coercion in matters of belief (must have Freedom of Thought/Religion, and Speech) so they can without impediment hear, learn and speak the *equal human preciousness* that grounds Human Rights and Democracy . . . These two principles together are the implicit underlying *First Principles* or logical starting point of both Human Rights and Democracy as we know it . . . [which entered Western consciousness in the 4th Century through the Christian Church]

CORE PRINCIPLE OF LASTING DEMOCRACY #1: UNCOMPROMISING LEGAL RECOGNITION OF THE INHERENT HUMAN RIGHT TO LIVE

Lasting Democracy requires full and uncompromising legal recognition of *The Inherent Human Right to Live* and the traditional Western belief expressed in the simple maxim *killing humans is wrong*, because *Human Rights are for All Humans* or else they are meaningless (if being human is not enough to have them) . . . Therefore, human-killing abortion *must* be re-criminalized in any *lasting* democracy as a necessary condition of democracy lasting long-term . . .

CORE PRINCIPLE OF LASTING DEMOCRACY #2: TRADITIONAL WESTERN PRO-LIFE FAMILY VALUES

Traditional Western "Pro-Human-Right-to-Live" or "Pro-Life" Family Values Include and Support *The Foundational Principles of Human Rights and Democracy* which make governmental totalitarianism unthinkable, and must be promoted in any LASTING democracy . . . Traditional Family Values when followed ensure every human is born into stable loving *families* where humans are always treated as precious human *persons*, never as mere *objects* or *tools* to be used (or thrown away), and raised to healthy human maturity within these *stable loving families* which are the building blocks of *stable caring societies* . . .

CORE PRINCIPLE OF LASTING DEMOCRACY #3: JUST CRIMINAL LAWS

Lasting Democracy does not grant *unqualified* freedom to individual humans, but Lasting Democracy restricts individual freedom with just criminal laws which uphold *The Inherent Human Right to Live* and the maxim *killing humans is wrong;* laws which protect the Human Rights and property of other humans and encourage *mature respect for all humanity* which ensures that humans are always treated as precious *persons* not as mere *tools* or *objects* to be *used* or thrown away. For lasting world peace nation-States also need to be guided by just International Laws which similarly uphold *The Inherent Human Right to Live, Equal Human Rights for All Humans* and the maxim *killing humans is wrong . . .*

CORE PRINCIPLE OF LASTING DEMOCRACY #4: CONSTITUTIONAL ACCOUNTABILITY TO FOUNDATIONS

Lasting Democracy does not grant an *unqualified "anything* the majority asks for or accepts from the government," but Lasting Democracy MUST hold its citizens and its politicians (and judges, unelected bureaucrats, elected political parties and police) constitutionally *accountable* to *The Foundational Principles of Human Rights and Democracy* including the *Inherent Human Right to Live* and the maxim *killing humans is wrong* because *Human Rights are for All Humans,* or else genuine Democracy can easily be lost to 'Creeping Totalitarianism' wherein democracies (like 1930s Germany) gradually but increasingly take on the characteristics of totalitarian States (all of which deny *killing humans is wrong* and all of which think the *government* decides *which* humans may or may not be legally killed instead of recognizing lasting *democratic* government's *foundation* that governments are *obligated* to always protect and serve *always-precious human lives* because *Human Rights are for All Humans*) (Hitler's Nazis were democratically elected by voters who did *not* hold government accountable to *human equality*) . . .

CORE PRINCIPLE OF LASTING DEMOCRACY #5: HUMAN RIGHTS EDUCATION

Lasting Democracy requires that all citizens as part of their basic education as citizens of a Free Democracy be taught and know *The Foundational Principles of Human Rights and Democracy* which all Human Rights and democratic freedoms are historically and logically built on and cannot last without (which is why they should also be *constitutionally enshrined* for accountability in any democracy which wants to last, as per Core Principles #4 and #7. But our modern democracies have failed on both counts!). *Uneducated ignorance of the foundations of Free Democracy guarantees its eventual failure.* Basic Human Rights Education in *The Foundational Principles of Human Rights and Democracy* equips all citizens to guard and protect their own freedom even from uneducated politicians. This education makes citizens of democracies too educated to unwittingly cast votes for extremist politicians and extremist political parties who (wittingly or unwittingly) do not even uphold *The Foundational Principles of Human Rights and Democracy,* but who in their own uneducated ignorance may even follow the totalitarian legal human-killing precedent of the *Extremist Left* Atheist Marxist Soviet Communist Party which first legalized human-killing abortion, or of the *Extremist Right* German Nazi Party (full name: The National Socialist German Workers' Party under Adolf Hitler) which first legalized both human-killing abortion and human-killing euthanasia (legal human-killing is of course *inherently extremist. It is no surprise that the first two governments to legalize human-killing by abortion also later committed the two biggest genocides in history – also making the mass-killing of humans by genocide legal. The legal abortion-killing of humans had already established that extremist Left Soviet Russia and extremist Right Nazi Germany did not believe in the Inherent Human Right to Live which grounds Democracy*). In democracies "of the people, by the people, for the people," citizens *govern themselves*, through their elected representatives. **This means the responsibility of governing well and** maintaining Free Democracy on its historical and logical foundations ultimately rests with each citizen voter, which is why each citizen voter *must* be *educated* in Democracy's foundations (why would any political system last if its foundational *First Principles* are not even taught to those who live under it and are supposed to be part of it?). Citizens cannot possibly govern themselves well and democratically, through intelligently elected representatives who govern well and avoid totalitarianism for the long-term, if neither the citizen voters nor their elected representatives even know *The Foundational Principles of Human Rights and Democracy*, nor are even held constitutionally accountable to uphold them.

To further assist lasting Free Democracy, Logic needs to be compulsory in high schools to ensure future voters and future politicians both know how to think clearly, logically, scientifically and with intellectual honesty, so they can vote and govern intelligently and not be so easily fooled (even by textbook *logical fallacies*) into destroying the foundations of their own freedom, as they have been up until now. For example, every single argument proposed to defend in democracies the totalitarian extremist (originally Soviet and Nazi) policy of legal abortion uses one or more textbook logical fallacies (which voters would know better than to be fooled by if they were actually educated in Logic). Totalitarian policies breed more totalitarian policies to protect them, and now democracies (including the author's country) which are compromised by illogical and totalitarian abortion policies are starting to pass more totalitarian laws against normal democratic freedoms of speech, expression, assembly, conscience and religion of Pro-Life doctors and Pro-Life Human Rights advocates. Having no justification for legal abortion from Science nor Logic nor Human Rights History, in order to keep abortion legal Pro-Choice legal abortion-supporting governments today are *restricting normal democratic freedoms specifically for the sake of "abortion access"* completely unhindered by the free speech (even of scientific facts) of those who believe in the Pro-Life *Foundational Principles of Human Rights and Democracy* which say that *killing humans is wrong* because humans have *Inherent Human Rights* (this author can be arrested and imprisoned under current laws in his country for saying this). When citizen voters and politicians know neither *The Foundational Principles of Human Rights and Democracy*, nor how to think clearly, consistently, and logically (nor how to avoid logical fallacies of reasoning), Free Democracy is sure to fail and not last.

As discussed at length in the Philosophical "Phootnote" to the author's book *Pro-Life Equals Pro-Democracy* (which first really got to the bottom of the problem and traced it back to the 17th Century), and as discussed at length but somewhat differently in CHAPTER 3: PHILOSOPHY of the author's book *Knights of Human Rights, Ladies of Lasting Democracy: Handbook Manifesto of the Educated Global Solidarity Movement Against Uneducated Global 'Creeping Totalitarianism' Now Accelerating*, all of the various threats to human life and democratic freedom today come from *ideology* instead of *education*, and can be traced to a predominantly *Relativistic* instead of predominantly *Realistic* view of the universe in one's (usually unconscious) underlying philosophical worldview. Today's many threats to Human Rights and democratic freedoms are ultimately rooted in philosophically (Skeptical) *Relativism* (which ultimately doubts or denies there even are any objective facts or science which can be certainly known, but everything is "subjective" and "relative") instead of (Scientific) *Realism*. Thus, a basic philosophical worldview which accords with the Traditional Western philosophical *Realism* which *implicitly* underlies the Common Sense which daily prevents humans from dying stupidly, and which *explicitly* grounds all Science, Logic, and Technology, is also ultimately vital to lasting democracy.

"One world, one mankind cannot exist in the face of... two scales of values: We shall be torn apart by this disparity of rhythm, this disparity of vibrations."
— *Aleksandr Solzhenitsyn*

Opposed to the *(Skeptical) Relativism* which gave the world *solipsism* (the demented belief that nothing outside one's own mind certainly exists – a philosophy that mimics a mental disorder) and Marxism (which has killed more people than anything else – over 94 million deaths caused by Marxist policies in the 20th Century alone), *(Scientific) Realism (Aristotelian* and *Scholastic* or *Thomist,* as used in the European universities which developed Modern Science and the Modern Scientific Method), is also the philosophical framework within which *The Foundational Principles of Human Rights and Democracy* were historically and logically developed.** Therefore, a HUMAN RIGHTS EDUCATION FOR LASTING FREE DEMOCRACY includes some solid introduction to the most pertinent facts of the History of Philosophy, as in the above-mentioned books.

CORE PRINCIPLE OF LASTING DEMOCRACY #6: HUMANS ARE EQUAL; IDEAS ARE NOT EQUAL
Nothing could be more obvious than that holding that *people* are equal does *not* make the *ideas* people have equal. *Ideas and opinions can be tested against objective standards like Science and Logic and established facts of History. Pro-Choice opinions are proven extremely uneducated and unintelligent opinions when tested against these standards* (as well as politically dangerous to democracy, as they literally follow totalitarian precedents), as shown in the author's books in the HUMAN RIGHTS EDUCATION FOR LASTING FREE DEMOCRACY Series (*DEMOCRACY 101; Pro-Life Equals Pro-Democracy; Killing Humans Is Wrong; No Fruit Without Roots; THINKING REVOLUTION: THE INTELLECTUAL HONESTY CHALLENGE; Equal Human Rights for All Humans; and (the Handbook Manifesto) Knights of Human Rights, Ladies of Lasting Democracy*).   It is the historic "Pro-Life" principles of *equal human preciousness without exception* underlying Democracy that say that *every human is equal* in the first place – so "Pro-Choicers" are *borrowing* from what they *deny* when they want to have their Pro-Choice opinion treated as if it was "equal" to someone else's Pro-Life opinion (human equality is a traditional, Judeo-Christian, "Pro-Life" assertion effectively denied by "Pro-Choicers" who believe they should have the *choice* to legally kill humans by abortion, effectively denying any Pro-Life, democracy-grounding *Inherent Human Right to Live*).   But it is manifestly true that *not all ideas and opinions people have are equal* in value; in quality; even in conformity with objective, verifiable reality; and it is obviously the case that ideas and opinions are not equal even if humans themselves are equal in value and rights (which is a Pro-Life assertion, not a Pro-Choice one).   Nothing could be more obvious than that uneducated Pro-Choice opinions are not equal with educated Pro-Life opinions.

Educated Pro-Life opinions are backed up by all the most pertinent facts of Science, Logic, and Human Rights History, while Pro-Choice opinions can only be held by the uneducated, intellectually dishonest (or unintelligent; or "ideologically lobotomized" and thus "willfully unintelligent") who can and do only defend legal abortion by denying established facts of Science (like that preborn humans are humans) and/or by using textbook *logical fallacies* of reasoning (see the above book series and Chapter 1 above).

CORE PRINCIPLE OF LASTING DEMOCRACY #7: PRIVATE INDIVIDUAL FREEDOMS CAN ONLY BE GUARANTEED BY PUBLIC POLICIES/LAWS BEING CONSTITUTIONALLY ACCOUNTABLE TO UPHOLD THE FOUNDATIONAL PRINCIPLES OF HUMAN RIGHTS AND DEMOCRACY

To prevent poor, illogical, uneducated thinking among the population making a democracy slip gradually towards becoming a totalitarian "Police State," and

to protect the private individual freedoms of all citizens, Lasting Democracy requires that democratic governments and their elected politicians and political parties and unelected bureaucrats/civil servants and police and judges be sworn to uphold the constitutionally-enshrined *Foundational Principles of Human Rights and Democracy* as the guide of public policy, so that government public policies and laws (and police enforcement of them) are always accountable to them and never undermine the foundations of Free Democracy (no matter what uneducated, stupid, senseless or dangerous ideas and opinions may be held by some, even many, individual citizens as they exercise their *individual private freedom of belief* which is guaranteed only by educated and genuinely democratic *public* policies and laws).

This individual human Freedom of Belief/Thought/Religion/Speech articulated in FOUNDATIONAL PRINCIPLE OF HUMAN RIGHTS AND DEMOCRACY #2 is itself built upon FOUNDATIONAL PRINCIPLE OF HUMAN RIGHTS AND DEMOCRACY #1, *equal human preciousness without exception and the Inherent Human Right to Live which governments are obligated to protect.* **This means that publicly promoting or enforcing privately-held beliefs (such as Pro-Choice beliefs) *contrary* to the equal human preciousness which grounds individual freedom of belief in the first place *is logically self-destructive to lasting human freedom and democracy.*** There is a grave potential danger of individual citizens in a Free Society freely holding or expressing uneducated or unintelligent, dangerous, or anti-democratic opinions which gradually undermine Free Society. This danger is especially present if, as so often today, citizens were never educated in *The Foundational Principles of Human Rights and Democracy* in the first place, such that uneducated and anti-human, ultimately anti-democratic opinions took root instead. Ultimately anti-democratic and totalitarian-oriented opinions like racist Neo-Nazi opinions or bigoted legal human-killing abortion opinions which follow totalitarian Soviet Marxist (Extreme Left) and Nazi Fascist (Extreme Right) precedents.

Note that most insidious and deadly dangerous of all are Marxist opinions, more recently re-cast in the form of today's Neo-Marxist Identity Politics opinions which, (following Karl Marx's example) unrealistically and simplistically reinterprets all political history in terms of toxic, adversarial class struggles between those given Marxist labels of "oppressed class" and "privileged/oppressor" class, fomenting resentment and hatred between groups in order to create enough political instability to assist a Marxist takeover, in order to attempt the seductively beautiful but utterly unrealistic "Marxist egalitarian Utopia" (which Marx himself said could only be achieved through bloody revolution). Marxism in practice to date has killed more people than anything else in history, with over 94 million people killed under Marxist policies in the 20th Century alone. The first ten million of these victims of Marxism were of the author's ethnic heritage – which is why the author is duty-bound to warn the West of the insidious dangers of Marxist ideology. As did Aleksandr Solzhenitsyn, who lived 18 years in the West (USA) after being exiled from Marxist Soviet Russia for exposing its atrocities in his book *The Gulag Archipelago*. Solzhenitsyn, whose mother was also of this author's ethnic heritage, likewise warned the West that the same Marxist ideology which destroyed his beloved Russia had also firmly planted itself in Western education and media and was taking the West slowly to the same totalitarian ends as Soviet Russia, just by a different route. Decades later, Solzhenitsyn's warning has proven true, right before our eyes, to those properly educated and not "ideologically lobotomized" by the Marxist-influenced "education" Solzhenitsyn warned the West of. Any Marxist-type thinking always pitting "oppressed" against "privileged" makes impossible mutual respect and cooperation between groups for the Common Good of all, which is based instead in the *equal human preciousness* incorporated into *The Foundational Principles of Human Rights and Democracy*. The officially Pro-Choice legal human-killing (following Soviet Marxist precedent) Neo-Marxist Identity Politics organization calling itself Black Lives Matter (which gets angry and even violent if anyone suggests "all lives matter," because you cannot cause Marxist mayhem and political instability on that *Equal Human Rights for All Humans* principle), is run by *self-described Marxists* who are deliberately leading riots and looting and burning of cars in the U.S. while these words are being written, precisely for anti-democratic Marxist purposes.

But the very real, and now very present *danger to Democracy* posed by citizens being *free* to in private believe anything at all, free to be stupid, free to be Neo-Marxist or Neo-Nazi or whatever, is greatly reduced *as long as the government and its agents (including elected politicians/parties, unelected bureaucrats/civil servants and police and judges) are held constitutionally accountable to set and enforce actual public policy* only according to *The Foundational Principles of Human Rights and Democracy* like *equal human preciousness* which is the actual foundation *of* individual freedom of thought (which is *why* individual freedom of thought cannot compromise *equal human preciousness* without ultimately damaging freedom of thought/religion/speech as well). Freedom of Belief/ Thought/ Religion is then both a *privilege* and a *responsibility* to think with intellectual honesty and logical clarity, taking care to avoid *bad/illogical thinking* and taking care to maintain *The Foundational Principles of Human Rights and Democracy*, because one's democratic Freedoms of Thought and Speech themselves can only last upon their foundation of *equal human preciousness* maintained with intellectual honesty and logical discipline.

Free democracies indeed include individual Freedom of Belief/ Thought/ Religion/ Speech/ Expression, such that Freedom of Belief does technically mean that individual citizens of a Free Democracy have the personal, private freedom to hold even stupid, uneducated and dangerous opinions (like Pro-Choice Abortion which comes from an anti-democratic, totalitarian-oriented and illogical human-killing mindset which is not mindful of avoiding intellectually dishonest logical fallacies). But **to stay Free, Free Society must not give such *objectively inferior and uneducated opinions* expression in public policy. Public policy must rather be always guided by *The Foundational Principles of Human Rights and Democracy*** which are informed by established facts of the disciplines of History, Science and Logic (and Philosophy).

Further Reflection: **The great irony is that current Western Society has this exactly backwards:** Today we are told that the Pro-Life *Foundational Principles of Human Rights and Democracy* may be "privately believed at home or in church or synagogue" but "have no place in the public sphere" and "must not influence public policy" because they are rooted in Biblical, Judeo-Christian religious beliefs like the *equal human preciousness* of every human, "male and female" without exception made "in the Image of God" (Genesis 1:27 in the very first chapter and page of the Bible) and like the *Free Will* God gave to humanity (which means people should have *religious freedom* to *choose* whether or not to become Christians, because becoming a Christian must be *a free act of love for God*). But officially "Pro-Choice" political parties in power today can and are passing laws and policies in the public sphere to encourage and even aggressively enforce uneducated Pro-Choice legal human-killing abortion opinions (ignorantly following totalitarian Soviet and Nazi precedents) among a population woefully uneducated in Human Rights History, Science, and Logic (which is why under current laws this author can be arrested and jailed in some provinces in his country just for saying "*killing humans is wrong* because *Human Rights are for all Humans*" or even just for "staring" at an abortion clinic in his national capital, which the local police told local Pro-Life Human Rights advocates would be taken as a sign of the "disapproval of abortion" that is now *illegal* to show anywhere within up to 150 metres (500 feet) of a legal human-killing abortion facility, precisely where such peaceful (but now illegal) Human Rights Advocacy is most pertinent).

Lasting Democracy requires that the police who enforce the laws and policies (and the politicians and parties who make them) must *all* be held *accountable* to *The Foundational Principles of Human Rights and Democracy* - and that police are *not* strictly accountable to *unthinkingly* enforce the State government's policies *whatever they are, as police are in any totalitarian "Police State."* For example, it is democratically unacceptable that the police in this author's national capital and most populous province, even after receiving from this author a scholarly handout describing this Core Principle of LASTING Democracy, believed that they had "no choice" but to *unthinkingly* and *without complaint* enforce new totalitarian laws against Freedom of Assembly, Speech and Expression of (democracy-grounding) Pro-Life views, and actually told peaceful Pro-Life Human Rights Advocates that they could be arrested just for being "known Pro-Lifers" near an abortion clinic or for "staring" at an abortion clinic, and the police in the national capital in fact arrested peaceful, elderly Pro-Lifers just for holding signs reading "FREEDOM OF EXPRESSION AND RELIGION. NO CENSORSHIP," "GOD SAVE OUR CHARTER RIGHTS," and "THE PRIMACY OF FREE SPEECH: CORNERSTONE OF WESTERN CIVILIZATION." This author gave a eulogy at the funeral of one of these elderly *Equal Human Rights for All Humans* Advocates who *died* while awaiting unjust trial weeks after his two *arrests* for *upholding Free Speech* in a *supposed democracy*! Police and politicians both should be so *sworn to uphold The Foundational Principles of Human Rights and Democracy* that uneducated politicians never put the police into such *democratically unacceptable situations* where police have to *choose* between their obligation to "protect and serve the public" and their obligation to enforce the policies of politicians who pay them. This kind of unacceptable conflict will not happen in a *healthy* democracy whose agents (politicians, bureaucrats, judges and police) are all *accountable* to uphold democratic foundations, so they can remind each other of this duty if one of these government agents forgets and starts compromising democratic foundations. For example, before arresting peaceful Human Rights Advocates under anti-democratic, totalitarian laws, police in this author's country ideally should have been able to formally complain and *remind* the government lawmakers that police are bound by oath to uphold democratic foundations and thus they cannot enforce badly made laws which clearly compromise them; if the politicians still refused to accept this friendly reminder, a judge, likewise accountable to uphold democratic foundations, should have upheld such a police complaint to settle the dispute. **But unfortunately, in the author's country where neither judges, politicians nor police swear any oath to uphold** *The Foundational Principles of Human Rights and Democracy*, **politicians make undemocratic laws; police blindly enforce them as if it was a totalitarian Police State; and judges uphold in court badly-made, totalitarian laws and policies that even make speaking science a punishable offense, in the increasing number of areas where well-established science contradicts current ruling party unscientific ideologies** (to help explain how such extremely unscientific, totalitarian, and colossally stupid laws and policies keep getting made all over the West, note that such Pro-Choice political parties are actually in the stream of bad thinking identified in CHAPTER 3: PHILOSOPHY below, which literally gives Pro-Choicers a *poor grip upon scientifically verifiable Reality itself*).

The "seedy underbelly" of a Free Society *only because of The Foundational Principles of Human Rights and Democracy* is technically "free" to be stupid, uneducated, immature and addicted *in their private life*, if they foolishly use the freedom that *The Foundational Principles of Human Rights and Democracy* give them to remain uneducated and addicted (to drugs or alcohol or to sex and pornography, which more and more scientific studies are identifying as fundamentally *addictive* in their character when sex is pursued *without mature responsibility* and *without reference to the scientific, biological purpose of sex* – reproduction of the human species. This author has been informed there are now scientific studies which (unsurprisingly) demonstrate that pornography literally so *objectifies* women as "things" rather than "persons." Brain scans of men watching pornography apparently literally show that the same parts of their brains are stimulated as are stimulated by hamburgers or other *objects*, rather than the parts of their brains being stimulated as are stimulated by interactions with *other human persons*).

But democratic freedom does not mean freedom to be immature and selfish and uneducated and stupid. In fact, it must not, or else everyone's freedom cannot be sustained long-term. Because Free Democracy's foundations are principles which require maturity and selflessness or at least *a concern and care for all other humans as equally valuable as yourself* (which is a Biblical principle, as are *The Foundational Principles of Human Rights and Democracy*). Immaturity and selfishness in some may be *tolerated* in some; in the "seedy underbelly" of selfish, self-centered and greedy people that exists in any society, who among other things use their precious-human-generating sexuality for personal pleasure without treating their sex partners with maturity, as precious humans and life partners. But to make public policy *promote* immaturity and selfishness, as the immature-sex-soaked Pro-Choice West now does, is to put the "seedy underbelly" at the top, which will surely unbalance the whole free democratic society until it falls down – which is precisely the anti-democratic process that is right now threatening Free Democracy in the West.

A certain amount of immature, irresponsible and uneducated behavior – such as *sexual promiscuity* which treats sex partners as *objects* to be *used* for pleasure instead of treating them as precious human *persons* and life-partners – may be *tolerated* within the "seedy underbelly" of a Free Society. Just because *individual human maturity* cannot be "forced." But to *stay Free*, Free Society must *encourage maturity and responsibility* and must not give such *objectively inferior and uneducated opinions and immature and irresponsible practices (which degrade some humans) expression in public policy or in public education of impressionable young humans.*

Public policy, rather than promoting unscientific and irresponsible attitudes must rather be always guided by *The Foundational Principles of Human Rights and Democracy* which are informed by established facts of the disciplines of History, Science and Logic.

[There is more discussion of the above Core Principle #7 in the author's book *Pro-Life Equals Pro-Democracy*]

CORE PRINCIPLE OF LASTING DEMOCRACY #8: NO FRUIT WITHOUT ROOTS (RESPECT FOR THE CHRISTIAN ORIGINS OF WESTERN HUMAN RIGHTS AND FREEDOMS IS NECESSARY)

Core Principle: *There is No Fruit Without Roots.* **Regardless of what percentage of a democratic country are practicing Christians, *lasting* democracies must minimally maintain a proper, healthy respect for Christianity as the historical root and Source of *The Foundational Principles of Human Rights and Democracy.* Government persecution or restriction of Christian belief or practice is a sure sign of ultimately Democracy-ending 'Creeping Totalitarianism.'**

Western Civilization was viciously brutal before Christianity, entirely lacking any concept of human equality or Inherent Human Rights. The very first Chapter and page of the Judeo-Christian Bible provided the West with the historical foundation of the *equal human preciousness* which grounds Free Democracy: In the Bible's first Book, Genesis, Chapter 1 verse 27, the Bible declares that humans, "male and female" are equally created "in God's Image." *The Foundational Principles of Human Rights and Democracy* are also rooted in the Judeo-Christian Bible's Commandment, "you shall not kill," and the Biblical testimony that "God is Love" (1 John 4:8, 16). This made Love for every precious human "made in God's Image" *the highest Western value* Europeans (for all their human imperfections) were motivated to strive for. Just the *striving* for this extremely high and difficult goal (to overcome human selfishness and prejudice) and often failing, *just in the effort* made Western Christian Civilization gradually better and better, as Europeans attempted to live the Bible's way of "loving your neighbor as yourself" (Jesus confirming that one's "neighbor" includes any human who needs help).

Furthermore, the very term and concept of precious human *personhood*, with its attendant *equal Human Rights*, is rooted entirely in the Christian Theology that the One God mysteriously exists eternally as a Trinity of Three "Persons" – this One God in Three *Persons* created humanity "In God's Image" and thus humans are now also said to be "*persons.*" Historically God was called "Three Persons" before humans were ever called "persons." Christianity changed cheap-not-precious humans who served greater States into precious-not-cheap *persons* whom the State is obligated to *protect* (and ultimately *serve* – which is why Modern Democracy – as well as Modern International Law and Modern Human Rights – only ever developed in Western *Christian* Civilization which had this background of Christian principles).

It must be stressed that this concept of human equality and human preciousness which together ground Free Democracy and Human Rights come from Christianity and nowhere else. Humans are manifestly *not* equal in physical or intellectual traits or prowess, abilities (or disabilities). We are each wonderfully and individually divergent, with a unique combination of physical and mental traits, talents, interests, abilities (and disabilities), strengths (and weaknesses). But we are all equally *human* (and not some other species), and Christianity teaches we are all *equally precious to God*, regardless of our race/ethnicity, sex/gender, social class or status, and regardless of our abilities and disabilities.

The latter consideration is one of the reasons that while democratic societies built on Christian principles properly seek to create "equality of opportunity" for success in different fields or professions, it is characteristic of *unrealistic* Neo-Marxist Identity Politics thinking (rooted in the flawed philosophy exposed in CHAPTER 3: PHILOSOPHY below) to dismiss the *facts* of different individual human capacities and interests and seek to force an "equality of outcome." As if one could possibly get perfectly equal ratios of males, females, races or other (always-multiplying) "identities" represented in every (or any) field or profession (elected representatives; nurses; plumbers; professors; mechanics; teachers; farmers; secretaries and so on). This author's late father was a high school principal (in Canada, where Black American slaves went to be *free*) whose habit was to hire women and minority women as well as men, all according to their *competence* for particular teaching positions, and he commented how strange it was when he was suddenly under political *pressure* to hire women and minorities (which he already did based on merit, but was suddenly expected to in order to produce "equality of outcome"). This author's fellow "Canadian intellectual for Free Speech" Jordan Peterson has every ably commented on how functioning societies function precisely by building "hierarchies of competence," where the most competent people for a particular job do that particular job (regardless of their sex/gender or race or other features unrelated to their job competence), and how the lights stop working if you do not put the most competent people for the position in the position (even if an electricity provider did miraculously manage to produce true "equality of outcome" and hire a "perfectly evenly balanced ratio" of male, female, Black, White, Hispanic, Chinese, Japanese, Korean, Ukrainian, Native American, Italian (and so on) employees). Peterson notes,

"Western culture, which is by no means perfect, and certainly has tyrannical elements like all cultures do, is the least tyrannical society that has ever been produced, and certainly the least tyrannical society that exists now ..."

Peterson thus points out that people call male plumbers (most of whom are males) for their *competence* in their profession (how many women are even interested in being plumbers?), and that there are not raving bands of tyrannical plumbers going about dominating Western society with a "tyrannical patriarchy" that "must be opposed" by Neo-Marxist Identity Politics so-called "Social Justice Warriors." This is not an issue of human equality. It is a matter of both interest and competence. Those women who are interested in this field of employment are more likely to become competent at it, and if they make a living off of it, it will be because of their *competence*; it is not an issue of equality.

Because the only ways humans have ever been *equal* is in being equally members of the human species; and *equal in precious human worth and value to God who created humans, male and female, "in God's Image."* This is why only Christian Europe gradually but logically over many centuries developed Modern Free Democracy, as described in Chapter 2 of *Pro-Life Equals Pro-Democracy* and reviewed below.

Not just human equality, but *equal* human *preciousness* as taught by Christianity, is necessary for Human Rights and Democratic Freedoms, as demonstrated not only by positive example (only Christian Europe developed Modern Democracy), but by the negative examples of the consistent and colossal failures of Atheist, philosophically Relativist Marxism to even in the slightest way accomplish Marxism's seductive "classless egalitarian ideal."

Marxism is by far the most sophisticated and popular of Atheist, Relativist political approaches, today still very popular in the West, as Aleksandr Solzhenitsyn warned, notably in the form of Neo-Marxist Identity Politics (which Solzhenitsyn described in 1983 without using the term) informed by the radically skeptical Postmodernism developed by Marxists — and all following the 1920 totalitarian Marxist Soviet precedent of legal human-killing by abortion. Because Marxism is thoroughly rooted in the radically skeptical stream of Western Philosophy identified in CHAPTER 3: PHILOSOPHY below, which ultimately has a *poor grasp on reality*, the Marxist take on "equality" is ultimately *unrealistic*, treating human males and females "equally" in foolish ways that ignore real biological differences, and in any case, in the end all Marxist States just treat all humans "equally badly" — Aleksandr Solzhenitsyn stating Marxism only ever achieves "the equality of destitute slaves" — backed up by the well-documented deaths of many tens of millions of human deaths due to Marxist policies wherever Marxism has been implemented. Marxists and today's Western Neo-Marxist Identity Politics "Cancel Culture" ideologues, both rooted in the absurd philosophical error described in CHAPTER 3: PHILOSOPHY below, have *so little grip on Reality, Science, facts,* that it does not matter how many of millions have been murdered by Marxist States as they attempt to build their seductive "egalitarian Marxist utopia," they undaunted keep trying to cram the "Red Square peg" of Marxist thinking into the "round hole" of Reality, with consistently bloody results.

But the model development of Modern Democracy (without any bloody revolution) happened in Christian Britain, where starting with the 1215 *Magna Carta* (followed by the creation of *representative government* in the 1265 first London Parliament), the King recognized the rights of his subjects and started sharing his power with some of them. Initially just with the barons, but slowly, progressively sharing power in ever-widening circles until today, when all adult humans in the British Commonwealth of Nations have an equal say or vote in their own governance; they are governed by representatives they elected; and the Monarch's power is only titular. This entire development happened because Christian Britain understood from the Bible that *before God a King/Queen and a peasant were equal, and equally loved by God.*

The "Father of International Law" (in 2006 also named the "Founder of Global Political Philosophy), Friar Francisco de Vitoria - and all the other later "Founders of International Law" like Father Francisco Suárez, Alberico Gentili and Hugo Grotius - were dedicated Christians (some Catholic, some Protestant) working logically from the Biblical, Christian, and 'Pro-Life' foundations of Christian Europe to help ensure Human Rights were respected wherever humans were (even outside of Christian nations). Thus the various colonizations from Christian Europe, for all their sad failures to best live the extremely high Christian standards of Love for every human and their lack of respect for some indigenous cultures considered "primitive" and "inferior" (failures which Friar Francisco de Vitoria had "fathered" International Law specifically to counteract), still also imported these Christian values of Human Rights and Freedoms worldwide, these taking root to greater or lesser degree in the colonies. Note that the European Christian colonists, whatever their imperfections and failures to live the extremely high Christian ideals, still *stopped all indigenous Human Rights abuses* like human sacrifice, cannibalism, infanticide, widow-burning and giving girls over to be Temple prostitutes – and stopped longstanding wars between indigenous tribes. All out of the *Christian* belief in *equal human preciousness* and the *Inherent Human Right to Live.* It is only today's ignorant and insufficiently educated Neo-Marxist Identity Politics ideologues (and those they have fooled) who try to paint past Western colonialism as if it was exclusively negative. And they only do this for the dishonest purpose of burying the Traditional Western (Judeo-Christian) culture and values which include *The Foundational Principles of Human Rights and Democracy,* so they can remake society according to ultimately Atheist Marxist principles which have time and time again proven to ultimately result in *violent, oppressive totalitarian States,* because of Marxism's serious flaws and unrealistic, simplistic reinterpretation of all history and politics as inevitable toxic struggles between "oppressed" and "privileged." Toxic conflicts based on past or present *resentments* which both Marxist and Neo-Marxist Identity Politics ideologues *deliberately exaggerate and foment into hatred* for the purpose of those they label "oppressed" politically overthrowing those they label "privileged," so that a Marxist-based government can replace the existing political structure, whatever kind it is.

But these inherently divisive and toxic (and in practice often bloodily violent) Marxist mechanisms for societal change, which make mutual respect and cooperation for the Common Good impossible, are completely unnecessary.

Because in fact, most of the greatest social reformers in history were devout Christians specifically seeking to have Biblical, Christian principles of God's infinite love for every human "made in God's Image" *better put into practice* in their time and place, like William Wilberforce ending slavery in the British Empire (and even non-Christian social reformers like Gandhi were educated in the Christian West and very familiar with the Bible, and steeped in its principles).

To this day Human Rights including Freedom of Belief/Religion and Freedom of Speech do not exist in the most markedly non-Christian countries, those countries least influenced by *The Foundational Principles of Human Rights and Democracy* which Christianity introduced into the West. Neither do Western Human Rights and Freedoms exist in the non-Christian countries least influenced by International Law which was founded by devout Christians putting Christian principles into practice worldwide. Atheist States and the most traditional Muslim States typically have no religious freedom and are profuse with other violations of Human Rights – and they typically persecute the Christians within their borders, who believe in *The Foundational Principles of Human Rights and Democracy. Most successful democracies are in traditionally Christian countries which thus have the background needed for Human Rights and Democracy.* Though Christian Britain spread these concepts worldwide where they took root in greater or lesser degree in the various British colonies, in many nations without a Christian background in which the West has tried to implement democracy, it does not take root well, and people are threatened by thugs into voting a certain way, or typically have other major compromises of the democratic ideal.

This is because *human equality, equal human preciousness which governments are obligated to protect* and *Freedom of Belief/ Thought/ Religion/ Speech* have never been political givens. These wonderful things have only existed as guiding principles for the governance of humans since these underlying *Foundational Principles of Human Rights and Democracy* were adopted by the West *from the Christian Church* when the West stopped persecuting Christians in the 4th Century.

Christianity's principles mean without compromise that *killing humans is wrong* because all humans without exception are *equally precious* and have Inherent Human Rights beginning with *The Inherent Human Right to Live.*

Anti-Christian bigotry and illogical "Bulverism" that dismisses ideas just because they are Christian, is the surest route to eventual totalitarian oppression, because these fail to maintain the essentially Biblical, Judeo-Christian (and Pro-Life) *Foundational Principles of Human Rights and Democracy.*

Thus, **any LASTING Democracy must at least respect (if not embrace) Christianity as the Source of** *The Foundational Principles of Human Rights and Democracy*, **and never persecute Christianity, no matter what percentage of the country's population are practicing Christians.**

Note that all *The Foundational Principles of Human Rights and Democracy* like *equal human preciousness without exception which governments are obligated to protect* and the *Inherent Human Right to Live* which means that *killing humans is wrong*, are all *moral absolutes.* Atheist Moral Relativists (including Marxists) who believe in no human-loving God of Christianity to set any such moral absolutes for human behavior, cannot abide nor consistently practice any of the *Foundational Principles of Human Rights and Democracy*, which is why all the representatives of Atheist Marxist Communist States on the original United Nations Human Rights Commission refused to even vote on *The Universal Declaration of Human Rights. As Atheists they could not accept any moral absolutes like any Human Rights the government had to respect;* in fact, as Atheists, they could not accept *anything* higher than the government, to which the government is *accountable for how it treats the humans it governs.* Which is exactly why all Atheist governments in history have been totalitarian and oppressive to human life and freedom.

Starting with Atheism's first foray into politics: the French Revolutions' *Reign of Terror* which first killed Christian leaders (and even mild nuns) in large numbers and attempted to enforce on the still mostly Christian population an Atheistic government-led "Cult of Reason" (actually converting Christian churches into "Temples to Reason"). The Mexico of Atheist Plutarco Elias Calles was similarly oppressive and deadly, and Atheist Communist governments killed an astonishing over 94 million people in the 20th Century, according to the large scholarly tome *The Black Book of Communism: Crimes, Terror, Repression.* Note that the politically *extremist Left* Marxist Atheist Soviet Communist Party *both* committed the largest Genocide in History, the *Holodomor* ("Murder by Starvation") Genocide of an estimated 7-10 Million Ukrainian humans in 1932-33, *and* was the first political party to legalize human-killing by abortion in 1920. *Both* because as Atheist extremists they did not believe in any human-loving God of Christianity nor any moral absolutes like an *Inherent Human Right to Live.* Note that 1933 also saw the opening of Dachau, the first of the Concentration Camps used in the politically *extremist Right* German Nazi Party's *Holocaust* Genocide of 6 million Jewish humans plus disabled/handicapped humans. And the occultic extremist Nazis (the top Nazis followed an occultic mythology from which they got the myth of the "Aryan Race") also legalized abortion, in 1934.

Like the Soviets, they were totalitarian extremists who both committed Genocide and legalized abortion because they did not believe in the *Inherent Human Right to Live* which grounds Democracy. The extremist Nazi Party (influenced by Marx's fellow German Atheist Relativist Nietzsche to abandon Traditional Christian morality from the other extreme of the political spectrum) was the first to legalize human-killing by both abortion *and* euthanasia. Note that today's Secularism exists by borrowing the Atheist principle of Moral Relativism, and doing so in response to groundless Atheist claims doubting the value of Traditional Christianity as the source of the West's "guiding principles for public policy." Secularism then follows the Atheist Soviet Marxist and Nazi precedents of legalizing human-killing by abortion out of disrespect for the Traditional Western, Biblical, Judeo-Christian Pro-Life Family Values that the West's Free Democracy was built upon. And now this Human Rights scholar and author can be arrested in his secularized country for saying "killing humans is wrong because Human Rights are for all humans," because without Judeo-Christian Pro-Life values there is no *basis* for a Free Democracy.

But the Traditional Western, Biblical, Judeo-Christian, Pro-Life Family Values which Western Human Rights and Democratic Freedoms were historically and logically built upon, *when followed*, guarantee that each human is born into stable, loving human *families* which are the building blocks of stable, loving human *societies.* The Biblical, Judeo-Christian principle of *equal human preciousness (without exception; which governments are obligated to protect)*, when followed, not only furnishes the first of *The Foundational Principles of Human Rights and Democracy,* but it is also the antidote to all forms of prejudice and bigotry and racism which treat some humans as of less worth or value or rights than other humans.

The Christian principle of *equal human preciousness* is exactly the reason *there is no larger nor more diverse group of humans on the planet than Christians.* Christians are an identifiable group of 2.3 billion humans from almost every other racial, ethnic, national, cultural, language, sex/gender, or social class group, of every ability or disability/disorder. A huge group of *unparalleled diversity* that understands itself as God's adopted Family, and thus most Christians hold *loving Christian Family unity* as an ideal to strive for, even where long-past historical divisions and disagreements have separated different Christian communities from each other (but what *family* does not have disagreements?).

As another logical outflow of *equal human preciousness*, Christians understand the planet Earth (and by extension the entire created universe) as the "Family Home" which God created for God's beloved adopted human children to live in, providing motivation *to take good care of the environment* which all equally precious humans live in, so that it remains a good Family Home for future generations of *equally precious humans*. Without succumbing to the Pro-Choice, Neo-Marxist Extremist Left's typical climate *alarmism*, with its fear-mongering and its distinctly Marxist flavor of pitting the "oppressed Earth" against "oppressor humans" who are a herd to be culled and reduced (something Marxists have proven themselves very good at) — like all Marxists completely missing the human *preciousness* which is the legitimate *reason* the environment should be well (and sensibly) taken care of.

Traditionally, Christians are just as likely to lean "politically progressive Left" as "politically conservative Right," and relatively near the Center. Healthy democracies keep an appropriate balance between "progressing" as necessary to deal with new, unprecedented situations, while "conserving" what is foundational and necessary to maintain free democracies. Human nature is imperfect and Christians (as much as non-Christians), both individually and in societies, *struggle* to live their own highest ideals ("Israel" in the Bible means "struggle with God" – both Jews and Christians are Biblically-based communities which "struggle with God" so they may live better lives and make the world/universe which *equally precious humans* live in a better place). Most of the greatest social reformers of history have been devout Christians struggling precisely to *better implement* in their time and place the high Christian ideals of lovingly taking care of every equally precious human loved immensely by God; ideals which are part of *The Foundational Principles of Human Rights and Democracy* (and the great non-Christian social reformers, like Gandhi, were also educated in the Christian West and steeped in Biblical, Judeo-Christian ideals).

Unfortunately, as mentioned, Atheist Marxism (Socialism and Communism) at the Extreme Left of the political spectrum has proposed a powerfully seductive "ideal egalitarian utopia" which Atheist Marxism seeks to create without Christian principles. Not only has Marxism never succeeded, it has in practice consistently created among the most oppressive totalitarian States ever known to humankind, Marxist policies killing many tens of millions of humans in the USSR/Soviet Bloc countries, China, Cambodia, Vietnam, North Korea and so on. To continue in the face of the *objective facts* of such obvious and consistent failures, Marxism has more recently been "reimagined" by Marxist philosophers like Jacques Derrida, ultimately yielding

1) today's Postmodernist philosophy (which denies or doubts all *objective facts* and Science, reducing everything to *subjective* will and power – thereby "melting the brains" and destroying any critical thinking skills in Postmodernists, who give priority to their *subjective feelings* and opinions and reject any *objective reality* such as that which underlies Science and Common Sense; and

2) Identity Politics. Again, today's Neo-Marxist Identity Politics ideologues copy classic Marxism's simplistic and unrealistic reinterpretation of all history as adversarial and toxic "class conflict" between those labelled "the

oppressed" and those labelled "the privileged oppressor." Like classic Marxism, Neo-Marxist Identity Politics requires resentment and hatred between the "oppressed" and the "privileged" to create enough political instability to one way or another overthrow or overpower the current government (perhaps by manipulating and "guilting" the "privileged" into political concessions, for those unwilling to pursue the revolutionary violence which Marx considered necessary), so that some form of the Marxist egalitarian utopia can be attempted in its place. Marx himself knew that his Marxist ideal, which includes the elimination of personal property and the elimination of the traditional Family, was so radical that most people would have to be *forced* into accepting it at first, and he planned for violent overthrow of the current government as the usual first stage of implementing Marxism. To achieve the necessary violence, Marxism has to exaggerate or invent resentment and incite hatred between those labelled the "oppressed" and the "privileged oppressor," meaning Marxism (and its new form of Identity Politics with its "Cancel Culture" which discourages any free speech of opposing views) is totally unsuited to any kind of cooperation or working together for the Common Good based on mutual respect, because, while claiming to promote "equality," Atheist Marxism rejects Christianity's principle of equal human *preciousness* (thus Solzhenitsyn noted that in the end Marxism/Socialism only ever achieves "the equality of destitute slaves" – with the Marxist government treating its citizens *equally badly*).

What Marx did not anticipate is that his seductive utopian egalitarian ideal was so radical, and so against actual human nature, that in practice Marxism never gets beyond having to *force* people to be Marxist Socialists – hence the tens of millions of murders and genocides consistently coming out of every attempt to implement the Marxist ideal.

Thus, Leftist Marxism, and Neo-Marxist Identity Politics (with its attendant "Cancel Culture" to censor, censure, and silence those who disagree with Identity Politics ideologues), ultimately just makes a sad, sick parody of what the Left in any country could be and should be. All the good-sounding ideals which today's (Pro-Choice and Neo-Marxist, extremist) Left have, they approach in a way tainted with inherently adversarial and toxic Marxism.

Probably most who today have been fooled by Neo-Marxist Identity Politics' claim of seeking "equality" and "social justice" are not consciously seeking to implement classic Marxism according to Marx and Engel's *Communist Manifesto* which called for explicit violence (even though Marx himself mocked as "castles in the air" all pre-Marxist visions to create a Socialist State without the violence of a bloody revolution; and no Socialism since has been without the influence of Marx). But nevertheless, even if they claim to shun violence, today's Neo-Marxist Identity Politics ideologues still take the *venomous, adversarial* approach of classic Marxism which sabotages any possible positive outcome.

Identity Politics ideologues in one way share the above good Christian ideals that every human child should be wanted and loved; that there should be no racist bigotry; that the environment should be cared for. But they approach all of these good things without the Christian foundation of *equal human preciousness*, and instead with a distinct adversarial Marxist flavor of pitting "oppressed" against "privileged oppressor" which is wrong-headed and which destroys any positive outcome.

Instead of seeking that every human child should be wanted and loved *because all humans are equally precious,* and instead of thus promoting Traditional Western, Judeo-Christian, Pro-Life Family Values because *when followed,* these guarantee that each human is born into stable, loving human *families* which are the building blocks of stable, loving human *societies* – Neo-Marxists instead, in Marxist fashion, absurdly pit the "oppressed mother" against the "oppressor baby" whose very existence threatens the "convenience" or "range of choices" of the mother. Even to the point of unscientifically calling a unique and utterly innocent new human baby a "parasite" — a "parasite" which, then, needs to be *killed* by abortion to "free" the "oppressed mother."

Marxism at bottom is all about *blaming someone else for your troubles and taking your violent revenge upon them,* and never taking mature, personal *responsibility* for one's own actions. So, completely ignoring the scientific fact that in almost all cases the new human baby was brought into existence by the (Pro-Choice) mother immaturely and irresponsibly *choosing* to engage in Nature's way of reproducing the human species without any intention of doing so, such that a (biologically-speaking) "successful" sexual encounter resulted in the procreation of the next generation of the human species (which is the biological purpose of sex), Neo-Marxists are fine with simply murdering the unique new human life brought about by their own immature irresponsibility – thus reinforcing the pre-Christian, pre-democratic notion that human life is *cheap not precious.*

Instead of taking good care of the environment for the future *because it is the home of equally precious humans,* Neo-Marxists, who might regard humans as *equal* but not as *precious,* in typically Marxist fashion pit the "oppressed environment" against the "oppressor humans." Even to the point of referring to humans as "parasites" or as a "disease" of the Earth; advocating for reductions in the human population (including more totalitarian legal human-killing like abortion and euthanasia to "cull the herd"). And they are very willing to sacrifice the economic and other legitimate needs of humans for what they perceive as the good of the environment (often according to dubious or unproven science – remember, today's Pro-Choice Left is an unhealthy and intellectually dishonest, extremist, legal human-killing abortion Left, that does not even understand enough Science or Logic to understand that *preborn humans are humans*; that *abortion kills humans*; nor that *killing humans is wrong.* So, they have no genuine understanding of Science, and are easily manipulated by climate alarmists. Even though such climate alarmists for years claimed "Global Warming," and, when actual facts did not support their claims, they dishonestly kept up the *alarmism* by instead claiming the more generic term "climate change" – generic enough to not really mean anything definite, but this does not stop Neo-Marxists from fear-mongering, and trying to manipulate people into doing what they want (even on the basis of very sketchy science) for the sake of the ("oppressed") environment, without much regard for how humans are affected. Which totally misses the point that caring for the environment *is* important, but only *because* it is the family home of *precious* humans!

Similarly, instead of promoting the truly egalitarian ideal that there should be no racist bigotry *because all humans are equally precious (regardless of skin color/race;*

ethnicity/ nationality/ culture; religion; language; sex/gender; social class; ability or disability/disorder), Neo-Marxists instead, in typical Marxist fashion, pit what they have labelled the "oppressed Black/Non-White" class (or other minority) against what they have labelled the "White privileged" class. In the name of "fighting racism," Neo-Marxists hypocritically judge whole groups of humans negatively merely by the color of their skin! In *prejudiced* and *racist* fashion *imputing guilt* upon someone *merely because of the color of their skin*, as if merely having the same (White) skin color as a slaver of centuries ago somehow makes *anyone* with White skin alive today "culpable" for long-past injustice done by someone long-dead who *happened to have the same skin color.*

As a "White" Ukrainian (Canadian), member of the white-skinned Ukrainian ethnic group which (like the white-skinned Jewish ethnic group) was victim of one of history's biggest genocides murdering many millions (perpetrated by others with white skin, on a different continent than the Americas), this author notes that the only genocide approaching a million murders of humans with black skin, the Rwandan Genocide of the Tutsi ethnic group, was similarly perpetrated by others with black skin (the Hutus), similarly on another continent (Africa). So, whatever dregs of remaining despicable bigotry based on long-past slavery and past civil rights inequities still exist in America, (which the officially Pro-Choice-legal-human-killing abortion "Black Lives Matter" Identity Politics organization, run by self-described Marxists, in Marxist fashion seek to foment new hatred over for Marxist political purposes, burning cars in America as I write this), I note that such continuing racism is not even near the most recent nor the most deadly of bigotries. And this *Equal Human Rights for All Humans* author whose ethnic group suffered a major genocide murdering 7-10 million precious humans resents Marxist "Black Lives Matter" Identity Politics ideologues absurdly trying to make me somehow "responsible" for despicable leftover American racism (and should "apologize" for it) *just because I happen to have white skin.* All while, being officially Pro-Choice, these 2020 "Black Lives Matter" Marxist ideologues practice the deadly legal human-killing abortion bigotry against preborn humans which was started 100 years ago in 1920 by the very same Marxist government which murdered 7-10 million of my "white-skinned" ethnic group in 1932-33.

What could be more *racist* than treating "White" skin as *evil* and insisting that anyone with white skin today "apologize" for someone else's crimes of centuries ago? This makes as little sense as insisting that a Japanese child today "apologize" for the dishonorable Japanese sneak attack on Pearl Harbor in 1941 (where the Japanese dishonorably pretended to be engaged in peaceful diplomatic negotiations with the neutral United States right up until their unprovoked attack which killed thousands). This inane practice of Neo-Marxist Identity Politics ideologues, who are just fomenting resentment and hatred between groups for the typical Marxist purpose of creating the political instability necessary for a Marxist takeover, goes so far as to disdain and disparage anything at all they ignorantly perceive in *racist* terms as "White." Thus, the great literature of Shakespeare, who has been famous for over 400 years precisely because he captures insightful and timeless, *cross-cultural* truths of the human condition (which is why Japanese film directors have been motivated to make movies based on Shakespeare plays), has been ignorantly written off by racist Identity Politics ideologues as the work of "dead White men" and removed from school curricula. What could be more *racist* than literature being judged (and included or removed from school curricula) merely by the *skin color* of the author?

Neo-Marxist Identity Politics ideologues have recently (at time of writing) fomented unrest and riots involving the tearing down of statues even of "White men" who did the most to *fight* racism, such as Abraham Lincoln, who declared war on the seceding Southern American states in order to *end* Black slavery in America; such as Sir Winston Churchill, who successfully fought the Nazi regime in order to end its racial, White Supremacist bigotry. Statues of Catholic Christian Saints (generally famous for loving God and loving all humans made in God's Image) have likewise been recently torn down or defaced. The current (at time of writing) rioting with the message "defund the police" also of course simply serves to facilitate a Marxist takeover (less police to maintain peaceful law and order). All of these actions, like removing the literature and statues of "White men," are merely *typically Marxist* ways of *cutting off a culture from its history,* so that a (totalitarian) Marxist government can more easily be raised in its place. As the Nobel Prize-winning historian Aleksandr Solzhenitsyn, expert in totalitarian Soviet Marxism noted,

> *"To destroy a people, you must first sever their roots."*
> — *Aleksandr Solzhenitsyn*

Professor Jordan Peterson has also noted,

> *"The group identity game ends in blood. It doesn't matter who plays it. Left-wingers play it: Blood. Right-wingers play it: Blood. And lots of it. Not just a little bit. You can't play the Identity Politics game.*
> *Well, so what do you do instead? You live the mythologically heroic life as an individual. That's the right place to work. And that's the message of the West as far as I'm concerned. We figured that out. We figured out that the collective identity was not the pinnacle statement... Not that collective identities have no value. Obviously, family has value; and your organizations have value, all of that. That's not the issue. The issue is, 'what's the paramount value?' What's the metric by which people should be measured? And the answer is: they should be measured as individuals. As if they have a divine soul. They should be measured in that manner."*[9]
> –*Professor Jordan B. Peterson*

Identity Politics ideologues even (in gross ignorance) judge (and reject) Christianity disdainfully as a "White" religion, simply because the Europeans practiced it, even though Christianity began in the Middle East, and within the first generation of Christ's Apostles had spread from India to Britain – Christianity remaining the largest and *most diverse* group of humans on the planet to this day. And still the source of *The Foundational Principles of Human Rights and Democracy.*

---

[9] From Dr. Jordan Peterson | Is Neo-Marxism on the rise?
https://www.youtube.com/watch?v=G7e_BaXU3mA, *accessed August 25, 2020*

Of course "Black lives matter," because *all human lives are equally precious*, according to the Traditional Western (Christian and Pro-Life) *Foundational Principles of Human Rights and Democracy.* But the fundamentally anti-democratic dishonesty of Identity Politics ideologues is revealed by the fact that the official "Black Lives Matter" organization even gets *angry and upset* if one says "all lives matter" in response to their statement "Black lives matter." Putting the certainly true statement that "Black lives matter" in its proper context of democracy-grounding *equal human preciousness* – Black lives certainly matter, *because* all human lives matter, which is *why* humans of all kinds should work together in *mutual respect* and for the Common Good – takes away their ability to dishonestly use the phrase to foment resentment and hatred for divisive and polarizing Marxist purposes. Marxism requires hatred and resentment between groups, and there is so much hatred in the official "Black Lives Matter" movement that in July 2020 a 24-year-old nurse and mother was ambushed, fatally shot in the back for saying "All Lives Matter" to "Black Lives Matter" ideologues.[10]

Note that the "Black Lives Matter" official organization is not just "Neo-Marxist," but actually run by self-described Marxists, who have been specifically inciting people to riot for the typical Marxist purpose of creating enough political instability to assist a Marxist takeover, or at least enough to manipulate political concessions.

In any case, what is very clear is that whatever "good" things today's Pro-Choice, legal human-killing Extremist Left seeks to do, whether "fight racism," "protect the environment," or "make sure children are wanted and loved," they do all these things in a perverted and wrong way which harms or kills more humans and foments resentment and hatred between humans. So . . .

It is clearly true that **There is No Fruit Without Roots. We cannot keep the wonderful fruits of Human Rights and Democratic Freedoms without their Christian and Pro-Life Roots. Regardless of what percentage of a democratic country are practicing Christians,** *lasting* **democracies must minimally maintain a proper, healthy respect for Christianity as the historical root and Source of** *The Foundational Principles of Human Rights and Democracy.* **Government persecution or restriction of Christian belief or practice is a sure sign of ultimately Democracy-ending 'Creeping Totalitarianism.'**

<u>CORE PRINCIPLE OF LASTING DEMOCRACY #9</u>: <u>UNDERSTANDING PROPAGANDA AND CENSORSHIP</u>
Lasting Democracy has a proper understanding of censorship and propaganda and uses intellectual honesty when judging the use of either. No government can avoid the use of propaganda to promote desired ideas and attitudes in the population (like anti-smoking campaigns), and no government can avoid the use of censorship to reduce undesirable ideas and attitudes in the population (child pornography is rightly censored). But *healthy* democracies only propagate objective, genuine truth and only censor objective, genuine

---

[10] https://www.lifesitenews.com/news/24-year-old-mom-ambushed-and-killed-after-saying-all-lives-matter-family?utm_source=must_reads, accessed July 17, 2020.

untruth, *for the purpose* of the genuine *good* of and never for the *harm* of all *equally precious humans.*

Propaganda and Censorship – Every government uses *Propaganda* to promote or "propagate" attitudes in the population considered desirable – whether based on lies/errors for negative societal effect (like Nazi anti-Semitic propaganda which promoted societal hatred for ethnically Jewish humans which made it easier for the Nazi government to murder Jewish humans in the millions) or based on truths for positive effect (like anti-smoking, anti-racist or even youth bicycle safety campaign propaganda which influences the population to adopt attitudes and practices which genuinely help them individually or socially). Every government uses *censorship* to reduce attitudes in the population considered undesirable – whether based on lies/errors for negative societal effect (like Soviet censorship of news to manipulate the population to support the totalitarian Soviet Marxist government which enslaved them) or based on truths for positive effect (like censoring child pornography and anti-Semitic hate literature).

So, the question is not whether or not to use propaganda and censorship (which cannot be avoided) but *how to use them (based on truths not falsehoods/errors) for the maximum benefit to human individuals and human societies.* Just which current Western propaganda should continue because it is based on truths which genuinely benefit humans (like anti-smoking propaganda), and just which current Western propaganda should be ended or altered because it is based on ignorance and errors or false, pseudo-science which are genuinely harming humans and genuinely undermining our whole free and democratic way of life? Just precisely where should the line be drawn between what is not censored and what is censored, what is promoted and what is not promoted, *for the genuine protection of human individuals and for the genuine protection of Human Rights and democratic freedoms generally?*

Both words (*propaganda* and *censorship)* have come to often have negative connotations because of high-profile negative uses like the Nazi *politically extremist* anti-Semitic *propaganda* which promoted or "propagated" hatred of Jewish humans based on false lies against Jewish human dignity, which unscientifically asserted or implied that Jewish humans were somehow "subhuman" or "less human than other humans" in order to justify the Nazis killing Jewish humans in the millions. Similarly dishonest, the Soviet Marxist Communist/Socialists running the Union of Soviet Socialist Republics (USSR) *censored* news, omitting or misreporting facts to *tailor* "public opinion" to be *favorable* to the oppressive totalitarian Soviet regime which effectively enslaved them. The Soviet Marxist censorship went so far as to for over 50 years deny the *Holodomor* Genocide, where the Soviet government similarly killed (this author's fellow) Ukrainian humans in the millions in 1932-33. Until the Soviet regime ended and its secret documents were declassified and the full truth was revealed (though note that the Marxist Communist/Socialist censorship of the *Holodomor* Genocide was not only carried out by the Soviets in the Union of Soviet Socialist Republics. *Western* Soviet sympathizers (Atheists, Marxists, Communists and Socialists) likewise conspired to bury the truth about the *Holodomor* Genocide when British journalists tried to expose it. Also, remember that legal human-killing abortion was *first* legalized by the same *politically extremist* oppressive totalitarian Soviet Marxist Socialists in 1920, who shortly thereafter committed the *Holodomor* Genocide in 1932-33; and remember that legal human-killing abortion was *next* legalized by the same oppressive totalitarian Nazi government which legally killed Jewish humans in the millions, who *first* legalized human-killing abortion in 1934).

But, despite negative and ultimately murderous use of propaganda and censorship by the first two, totalitarian States to legalize abortion, **both propaganda and censorship in themselves are morally neutral** and each can be used in either negative or positive ways for either negative or positive purposes, and as suggested, it is completely impossible not to use them. Anti-smoking campaigns or bicycle helmet safety are classic positive uses of propaganda, specifically promoting or propagating the desired attitude in the general population (often aimed particularly at young people who are vulnerable to becoming addicted to smoking or to having bicycle accidents). In this case the propaganda is positive in both implementation and purpose. The honest facts of the harm of smoking is presented, not dishonest nor misrepresented "facts," and the purpose of the propaganda is for the genuine good health and benefit of those who are influenced by it. Legitimate uses of propaganda should always be intellectually honest and so should always be based on "propagating" true facts, and for the good of those influenced by it and for the good of society at large. Propaganda, which at its best is just a method of spreading genuine *education* of true facts (like that smoking really is scientifically proven to be harmful to one's health), should never be used with bad will nor to make others fear and hate themselves nor hate and harm other precious humans.

Legitimate propaganda will never be based on lies or false science which contradicts well-established principles of real science or history, or else it will ultimately be harmful, even if supposedly done for the "benefit" of people. Such as wrongheadedly trying to make people "feel better" about having a biological disorder by *dishonestly telling them they do not have one, but that their condition is just part of a newly (and unscientifically) "expanded" range of "normal" and "healthy."* This kind of thing, now commonly seen among the severely intellectually dishonest (and among the "ideologically lobotomized" and among the philosophically *Relativist-not-Realist*, who have a very poor grip on Science and a poor grip on Reality itself), is ultimately a subtle *"selective bigotry,"* which is typically promoted *only by (Relativist-not-Realist) Pro-Choice bigots* who consider *disabled* human babies in the womb the *top priority for abortion* and generally promote human-killing euthanasia / "assisted suicide" for born humans they *acknowledge* as having a disorder.

[Note: there is a lengthy rough-draft *digressio* about this subtle "selective bigotry" which is published in the author's book *Pro-Life Equals Pro-Democracy*; referring to a thoughtful "12 Principles of Human Dignity and Human Disorder" published in the author's book *DEMOCRACY 101*]

Unlike the negative and harmful unscientific propaganda which has been promoted by bigoted Pro-Choice politicians, the Pro-Life position and mindset is based upon *established truths of Human Rights History, Logic and Science* (like that preborn humans are humans; and that killing humans is wrong; and that lasting freedom depends on these being legally recognized). The Pro-Choice position and mindset is based on the *denial of scientific facts,* like when they claim preborn humans are not humans (and so do not have Human Rights), and use this denial of scientific fact to justify harming people, killing the most vulnerable human babies, still in the womb, even though these young humans are scientifically verified to be *just like each one of us when we were their age* (so to deny *them Inherent Human Rights* is to logically *deny* our own *Inherent Human Rights*; and more, is to deny all common sense and logical, scientific reason, as shown in *DEMOCRACY 101* and *Pro-Life Equals Pro-Democracy).*

Some Pro-Choice political parties in power are now using negative propaganda to *propagate unscientific ideology* (regarding abortion or otherwise), while at the same time using negative censorship to *censor verifiable scientific facts.* To the unscientific Pro-Choice mentality which denies preborn humans are humans, **Science itself is a crime when it does not support a Pro-Choice political party's various unscientific ideologies** (Pro-Choice and otherwise). In this author's country, there are now a number of laws under which people can be arrested and hauled before a judge just for speaking or expressing on signs *scientific facts* which do not support the Pro-Choice and other ideologies which are being pushed on the populace by the various unscientific statements and claims of officially Pro-Choice political parties, whose human-killing legal abortion stance itself follows well-established totalitarian anti-Democratic precedent. Most in officially Pro-Choice political parties do not even *realize* how inherently totalitarian their legal human-killing abortion stance is – but their extremist unfamiliarity with the Pro-Life *Foundational Principles of Human Rights and Democracy* is precisely what makes them *incompetent* to lead a LASTING democracy.

◆

The reader should be very wary of how an underlying philosophical worldview favoring *Relativism over Realism* – which most Pro-Choicers and Neo-Marxist / "Cancel Culture" ideologues in governments and media (and "Big Tech" and elsewhere) have (see Chapter 3) – affects their use of propaganda. Relativists are primed to use propaganda only in the negative use described above, that aims to propagate their personal, subjective opinion in the general population without honest or intelligent considerations of objective facts or truths of science, history, or anything else. Because Relativists are subjectivists who favor *subjective* opinions and feelings over *objective* facts or truths, which they doubt or deny exist, making everything merely *subjective* and therefore *relative.* Relativists therefore find it easy to say things like "well, that's true for *you*; this (contradictory) thing is true for *me*." They thus blithely violate the Principle (or Law) of Non-Contradiction ("something cannot both be, and not be, at the same time and in the same respect;" "a statement cannot be both true, and false, at the same time, and in the same respect"). Which is the easiest thing in the universe to prove! (try giving an example that breaks it), and is an essential part of the Aristotelian/Scholastic Realism which is foundational to all logic and science. **What makes Relativists/subjectivists so politically dangerous is that they accept no *objective facts* exist to be the "tie-breaker" that says "this person's *subjective opinion* more closely matches objective, scientifically verifiable reality than this other person's, so this person's opinion is right/correct or better because it takes better account of *objective reality*, and this other person's opinion is wrong/incorrect or worse, because it takes less account of objective reality." At first Relativists may seem congenial, because they will not say anyone or anything is wrong. Everybody's opinion is *equal*, and you cannot *hurt anyone's feelings* by telling them they are wrong about anything! But in politics, since Relativists/subjectivists (like most Pro-Choicers and Neo-Marxists and Socialists, whose ideologies are rooted in Relativism not Realism) ultimately admit no objective facts to help determine just what is the** better or best political opinion to put into practical public policy, the only thing they *do* accept to decide public policy is *power*. The only thing that ultimately matters politically to politicians influenced by Relativism instead of (or more than) Realism is the *power* to have their subjective political opinion *enforced* in public policy instead of other subjective political opinions. Even well-established facts of history and weighty scientific evidence are frequently not capable of changing the mind of a Relativist not Realist. So Relativists use whatever tactics are available - whether violence/military might or *manipulation, intimidation and dishonesty* (including the constant "manufactured outrage" typical of the Pro-Choice Left) to (as much as they can manipulate and intimidate others into letting them get away with it) *forcefully impose* upon everyone else their *subjectively preferred* political policy. And, if they can get away with it, they will *silence* or even criminalize the speaking of well-established facts and science that *does not support their subjective political opinions* (which is why this author can be arrested and imprisoned in my country for, where it is most pertinent to do so, speaking well-established science and history, under Pro-Choice laws that specifically silence any Pro-Life speech of any facts at all that in any way do not support, or discourage, the Pro-Choice, legal human-killing position. I can be arrested and jailed in my country for pointing out the historical facts that human-killing abortion was first legalized in Soviet Russia by the same government that later legalized the human-killing genocide of my ethnic group. Speaking those *facts* certainly violate the current law that makes *illegal* anything - even just "staring" at an abortion clinic - that in any way expresses "*disapproval of abortion.*" As I said, to Relativists, only *power* to *enforce* your *subjective opinion* in public policy matters, *not facts* which help determine the (objectively) better or best public policy. So, Relativists who find no problem with legal human-killing by abortion also find *no problem passing laws restricting free speech of opinions different than theirs.* And no objective facts are admitted to dissuade a subjectivist from pursuing their personally preferred political policies. So, Relativists cannot easily be swayed by facts to realize that their political opinion is *wrong*. Which is exactly why (Relativist) Marxists and Socialists have never learned that Socialism is simply *too unrealistic* to ever work in the *Real universe* - no matter how many tens of millions have died under Marxist policies in Socialist States. Thus, Relativist Neo-Marxists today are *still*, as I write this, trying to accomplish a global Marxist "Great Reset!" Since the first ten million killed were of my ethnic group, I will never allow today's unthinking Relativist Neo-Marxists who today want to "Reset" the planet on Marxist principles (using the Coronavirus Pandemic as an excuse) to manipulate and intimidate me into shutting up about just what their underlying philosophy and ideology is, and just where it leads. Like Aleksandr Solzhenitsyn and Jordan Peterson warned the West before me (though I started working on this HUMAN RIGHTS EDUATION FOR LASTING FREE DEMOCRACY when Relativists took doctors' freedom of conscience away, almost two years before Dr. Jordan Peterson became famous for standing up against one of many Relativist assaults on Free Speech in our country. As I write this, a father where I live since last week is in jail precisely for calling his daughter his daughter and using scientifically accurate pronouns about her. Exactly as Professor Peterson predicted would happen under current Canadian laws against Free Speech. Laws against Free Speech passed by Relativists who (as Relativists) have no strong grip on science or facts, who, because they cannot justify their various unscientific ideologies based on science or facts, they instead dishonestly use totalitarian laws and police to silence the speaking of objective facts which disagree with their preferred subjective opinion). Returning to the initial application of this *digressio* to propaganda: To Relativists in media and government, with vacuous *ideology* instead of the solid *Human Rights education* collected in this book series, propaganda just means making posters and ads and videos and so on to try to make the general population agree with and support their ideologies (however unscientific) *without any reference to nor any honest, intelligent analysis of objective facts.* You cannot reasonably expect intellectually dishonest *Relativists not Realists* in government, who have tenuous grasp of science or reality, to propagate accurate science in the general population – regarding abortion, the Coronavirus Pandemic, or anything else (especially if they are Socialists or Neo-Marxist Identity Politics ideologues, excited to misuse the Coronavirus Pandemic to attempt a global Marxist "Great Reset." The first ten million murdered victims of Marxism, from my ethnic group, compel me to warn the world's citizens they must *learn to recognize Relativist and Marxist-influenced propaganda* which is usually unscientific at least in as much as it pretends that established facts and qualified medical and scientific voices against their ideology or global agenda *just do not exist* - since *Relativists not Realists* are not compelled by any intellectual honesty to acknowledge the existence of anything that stands in the way of them *politically enforcing their subjective opinion or implementing their agenda.*

Addendum: Many governments legitimately use propaganda campaigns to warn pregnant mothers of human babies to not drink alcohol nor smoke while pregnant, because it can *harm their human baby.* This is based on *accurate science*, and the message of the propaganda, if heeded, will genuinely benefit the precious human child and mother for the rest of their lives. **If these governments were genuinely concerned for the lives and well-being of human mothers and their babies, however, they should be warning mothers with posters of the genuine dangers to their precious human child that abortion will kill their child (and increase the mothers' chance of various health problems including Cancer, as has been amply proven by very many scientific studies).** This selective use of propaganda reveals a "Jekyll and Hyde" government, which sometimes acts as if all humans are equally precious and should be protected from harm – even in the womb - and sometimes acts as if NOT all humans are equally precious, and some humans can be *killed* when deemed "inconvenient". And passes laws against the free speech of peaceful Pro-Life Human Rights advocates. Why should any humans TRUST such an unstable "Jekyll and Hyde" government, which is so inconsistent about something so basic to governing humans as whether or not *Human Rights are for All Humans?*

CORE PRINCIPLE OF LASTING DEMOCRACY #10: HUMAN LIFE ISSUES ARE NON-PARTISAN –
PRO-CHOICE VS. PRO-LIFE IS NOT "LEFT" VS. "RIGHT" BUT EXTREMIST TOTALITARIAN VS. DEMOCRATIC THINKING (Democratic Thinking Which Both Political "Left" and "Right" Shared at the Formation of Our Western Democracies)

"Pro-Life" and "Pro-Choice" mindsets are distinct ways of thinking about human life that have drastically different ultimate logical political outcomes once mature: The "Pro-Life" mindset that every human life without exception is supremely and equally precious and therefore must be *free* from government coercion to without impediment seek and find this truth about *inherent* human preciousness and *inherent* Human Rights logically leads ultimately towards democratic say or vote for *every* equally precious human. The "Pro-Choice" mindset wherein parents have the "Right to CHOOSE" to raise or KILL their own human children means humans are *not* inherently precious but humans can be killed when deemed inconvenient, as in any totalitarian State, which logically leads ultimately towards totalitarianism (which is why in fact the two oppressive totalitarian States which committed history's two biggest genocides were also the first two nations to legalize abortion - before legalizing genocide. Which is why the totalitarian Soviet Marxist State which first legalized abortion in 1920 and which legalized the genocide murder of millions of this writer's ethnicity in 1932-33 also made it illegal to speak of the legal human-killing; and which is why officially Pro-Choice political parties in this writer's supposed democracy today have passed laws *against* Free Speech of Pro-Life views advocating *Equal Human Rights for All Humans* precisely where it is most pertinent to do so – today's officially Pro-Choice political parties have imitated the totalitarian Soviets both in legalizing human-killing abortion and in suppressing Free Speech against legal human-killing). The Pro-Life mindset saturating a society makes governmental totalitarianism *unthinkable* in a way nothing else can; while the Pro-Choice mindset saturating a society makes governmental totalitarianism *inevitable.*

How could the Pro-Choice denial of the *Inherent Human Right to Live* which grounds Free Democracy, by legalizing human-killing by abortion, following the genocidal Soviet and Nazi precedents of legalizing abortion, possibly make any society more just, free or compassionate? (The Soviets and Nazis were the first to legalize abortion specifically because neither evil regime believed *killing humans is wrong*). Rather, the essentially Pro-Life *Foundational Principles of Human Rights and Democracy* mean that unhappily pregnant women (for sympathetic or unsympathetic reasons) are equally as precious as their human babies. Thus, a "Pro-Life-minded" society that truly supports *Equal Human Rights for All Humans* without exceptions (since exceptions are inherently bigoted); a society that truly supports the *equal human preciousness* that is the very foundation of Free Democracy, a society which is thus drenched in Pro-Life thinking, will both protect preborn humans (just like every one of us at their age) in the womb, *and* find creative ways to assist and support unfortunate women pregnant when they do not wish to be (whether due to rare sympathetic cases like rape, or otherwise) so that these precious human women do not come to feel so desperate or devoid of options that they are tempted to commit abortions which kill their equally precious human children. Abortions which, if legal, follow totalitarian precedents and legally eradicate the *Inherent Human Right to Live* which is foundational to Free Democracy for all humans. But a society that foolishly and unwittingly compromises Free Democracy by following the legal human-killing precedent of the genocidal Soviets and Nazis, the two extremist political parties which were the first to legalize abortion, is naturally in very grave danger of eventually losing all pretense of Free Democracy. As proved (among other things) by the fact that this Human Rights scholar and author (and other peaceful Pro-Life Human Rights advocates) can be arrested and jailed in his country for saying "killing humans is wrong because Human Rights are for all humans;" and real doctors who follow the ancient Hippocratic Medical Tradition that *doctors do not kill* can lose their jobs; under current laws and policies passed by Officially Pro-Choice political parties in power. Because legal human-killing is inherently politically extremist and requires more totalitarian laws (ending Free Democracy) to keep the human-killing legal long-term.

Political "Left" and "Right" used to share the essentially Pro-Life conviction that without exception *killing humans is wrong*. *Extreme Left* Soviet Marxist Communist Socialists and *Extreme Right* Nazi Fascists (but note that "Nazi" is short for "National Socialists" in German) were the first two political parties to legalize human-killing by abortion. **Human Life issues are non-partisan and "Pro-Choice" vs. "Pro-Life" is NOT an issue of political "Left" vs. "Right." *"Pro-Choice" vs. "Pro-Life" is rather an issue of Fundamentally Totalitarian and Extremist Thinking that supports Human-Killing vs. Fundamentally Democratic Thinking that supports Human Protection.***

♦

A few more quotes from the longer Pledge of Allegiance to Democracy first published in DEMOCRACY 101 . . .

. . . **LASTING democracies** have no business legislating human life and death in matters like abortion and euthanasia because only *totalitarian States* think they are *not obligated* to protect all human lives but have the power of life or death over humans (of any age or state of health) . . .

Killing Humans is Wrong. No Exceptions. Killing Attackers in Self-Defence; Police Officers or Prison Officials Killing Dangerous Criminals in the Course of Attempting to Apprehend Them or Administering Death Penalties (Where They Still Exist) to Protect the Public from Them; and Just War Against Bigoted and Dangerous Aggressive States are Not "Exceptions" to the Principle of *Equal Human Preciousness* that Means *Killing Humans is Wrong*; Rather, These are Instances of "the Lesser of Two Evils," Where It May Regrettably be Necessary, in Order to Protect Many Precious Innocent Human Lives from Evil, to Kill Dangerous Criminals or Aggressors (or Soldiers Serving Evil, Aggressive States) . . .

Throughout History Since the 4th Century, in Either Traditional Monarchy or Modern Democracy, Human Safety and Prosperity Depends on Governmental Accountability to the [implicit; underlying] *Foundational Principles of Human Rights and Democracy* . . .

The Democratic Ideal of the People's Democratic Self-Rule Must be Served and Not TREASONOUSLY Usurped by Political Parties in a Truly Democratic Government "of the People; by the People; for the People"; Human Safety and Freedom Depends on Political Parties [and Police] Also Being Held Accountable to the *Foundational Principles of Human Rights and Democracy* . . .

I recognize that Human Rights and Democracy's vital foundations were laid so long ago (in the 4th Century) that simple ignorance of them accounts for much of the current 'Creeping Totalitarianism' (voting citizens and the politicians they vote for literally *do not know* what their Human Rights and Freedoms were built on) and to correct this ultimately democracy-destroying ignorance . . . **I Pledge to Spread Knowledge of Democracy's Historical and Logical Foundations . . . Articulated in the *Foundational Principles of Human Rights and Democracy* (and Core Principles of Lasting Democracy) [the Human Rights History, Science and Logic supporting these principles laid out in Articles 13-45 of *The Pledge of Allegiance***

to Democracy published in DEMOCRACY 101; and introduced in the books *Pro-Life Equals Pro-Democracy, Killing Humans Is Wrong and No Fruit Without Roots*] until there are enough EDUCATED voters to ensure LASTING freedom resting on Democracy's firm ["Pro-Life"] foundations . . .

CONCLUSION: Democracies Which Want to *Last* as Democracies (and Make Totalitarianism *Unthinkable* for the Future) *Must Constitutionally Enshrine The Foundational Principles of Human Rights and Democracy* and Must Ensure These Principles are Taught to Citizens as the Foundations of Western Freedom.

These Principles Include Freedom of Thought/Freedom of Religion, but *Educated* Thought Means Christianity Must at Least Be *Respected* as the *Source* of the Traditional Western, Judeo-Christian and "Pro-Life" *Foundational Principles of Human Rights and Democracy*. Anti-Christian Bigotry Is the Surest Route to Eventual Totalitarian Oppression Without Christianity's Principles Which Mean Without Compromise that Killing Humans Is Wrong Because All Humans Without Exception are Equally Precious and Have Inherent Human Rights Beginning with *The Inherent Human Right to Live.*

Human-Killing Abortion MUST be Re-Criminalized in Any LASTING Democracy as a Necessary Condition of Democracy Lasting; and the Formal Science of Logic Should Be Taught in Public Schools, to Ensure Citizens and Politicians Know How to Think Logically and With Intellectual Honesty and are No Longer Fooled by Ignorant Logical Fallacies Such as Those Which are the *ONLY* Arguments Offered to Support Pro-Choice Abortion Human-Killing .

ANNOUNCING THE FLAG OF DEMOCRACY AND THE GLOBAL SOLIDARITY MOVEMENT

The "Flag of Democracy" reproduced below is a symbol of the new *Global Solidarity Movement* for Traditional Western Values in public policy which is hereby announced in this book

KNIGHTS OF HUMAN RIGHTS,
LADIES OF LASTING DEMOCRACY
Handbook Manifesto of the Educated
Global Solidarity Movement
Against Uneducated Global 'Creeping Totalitarianism' Now *Accelerating*

The Flag of Democracy was designed by William Baptiste, author of the HUMAN RIGHTS EDUCATION FOR LASTING FREE DEMOCRACY book series (*DEMOCRACY 101; Pro-Life Equals Pro-Democracy; Killing Humans Is Wrong; No Fruit Without Roots; THINKING REVOLUTION: THE INTELLECTUAL HONESTY CHALLENGE; Equal Human Rights for All Humans,* and the Handbook Manifesto *KNIGHTS OF HUMAN RIGHTS, LADIES OF LASTING DEMOCRACY*).

The Flag of Democracy is a symbol of the new worldwide grassroots movement of *The Pledge of Allegiance to Democracy* taken and stood up for in *Solidarity* amongst Human-Life-and-Freedom-Lovers worldwide, for the sake of Western Human Rights and Freedoms first weathering the current multi-faceted assaults of 'Creeping Totalitarianism' now *accelerating*, and then lasting for centuries on Free Democracy's solid traditional, historical and logical foundations which are incorporated into Traditional Western Values. The Traditional Western Values and core beliefs undergirding all Western Science, Logic, Technology as well as all Western Human Rights and Democratic Freedoms, including *(Scientific) Realism* instead of *(Skeptical) Relativism* as one's basic underlying philosophical worldview; along with Traditional Western Values introduced into the West in the 4th Century by the Christian Church, such as *equal human preciousness without exception which governments are obligated to protect* (and ultimately serve). Which ended the pre-Christian norms of "Pro-Choice" legal human-killing by abortion and totalitarian government.

◆

141

On the two ribbons in the Peace Dove's mouth the Flag displays the two *Foundational Principles of Human Rights and Democracy* identified and articulated from Human Rights History, Science and Logic in *The Pledge of Allegiance to Democracy*, in the simplified words:

Foundational Principle of Democracy #1: Every human life, without exception, is SUPREMELY and EQUALLY precious.
Foundational Principle of Democracy #2: Every human life must be free from government coercion in matters of belief so they may freely seek and find this beautiful truth foundational to democracy.

The Pledge of Allegiance to Democracy was first published in the author's book *DEMOCRACY 101*, and its Foundational Principles were then again published in his book *Pro-Life Equals Pro-Democracy*, and will be again in the new book manuscripts *Killing Humans Is Wrong* and *No Fruit Without Roots*, all by William Baptiste, non-partisan thinker and Founder of the new non-profit Human Rights Education organization *Human Rights and Freedoms Forever!*

The Flag of Democracy has been developed for Human-Life-and-Freedom-Lovers to literally rally behind as they work to convince their compromised democracies to constitutionally enshrine the traditional principles (like *equal human preciousness* without exception) which will allow Human Rights and Democracy to last for the long term on their historical and logical foundations. The Flag of Democracy can be flown below or beside any national or sub-national (provincial or state) flags as a symbol of a nation's commitment to Lasting Democracy (the Flag of Democracy designed by William Baptiste and beautifully rendered by artist and poet Nicolas Carnogursky is reproduced below). Marching under the flag at Pro-Life rallies and other protests of 'Creeping Totalitarianism' (such as many new laws worldwide restricting free speech, especially of "Pro-Human-Right-to-Live" or "Pro-Life" values) would be very appropriate. Remember, reading *The Pledge of Allegiance to Democracy* first published in DEMOCRACY 101 (its *Foundational Principles of Human Rights and Democracy* and *Core Principles of Lasting Democracy* next published in *Pro-Life Equals Pro-Democracy* and this book) will change your life; spreading the Pledge will change the world (by ending 'Creeping Totalitarianism' so Democracy can last). The Flag of Democracy, bearing *The Foundational Principles of Human Rights and Democracy*, is also the visual symbol of THE THINKING REVOLUTION declared in *Pro-Life Equals Pro-Democracy*.

Note: You can E-mail

DemocracyStore@WilliamBaptisteHumanRightsAndFreedomsForever.com

to pre-order the Flag of Democracy, or to express your interest in being informed when the flag is produced so you may order it. Please include your preference for desk flags, medium or full-size flags or posters or T-Shirts when they are ready, and put "Flag" in the subject line.

Those interested in producing flags (or Flag merchandise like T-shirts with the Flag on it) in cooperation with *Human Rights and Freedoms Forever!,* to be advertised and made available at the online Democracy Store at
https://WilliamBaptisteHumanRightsAndFreedomsForever.com should also email the above address.

CHAPTER 3:
PHILOSOPHY

Getting to the Very Bottom of the Problem to Solve It

[CHAPTER 3 is drawn from the much longer Philosophical "Phootnote" to Chapter 11 in the author's book *PRO-LIFE EQUALS PRO-DEMOCRACY* (Published by Westbow Press January 2021)]

Lasting Human Rights and Democratic Freedoms (and Science Itself) Can Only Be Built Upon a Consistent Underlying Philosophical Worldview of Philosophical *Realism*; All Current Threats to Human Rights and Free Democracy (and to Science Itself) Come from Undue Influence of Philosophical *Relativism*.

Understanding the History of Ideas (Philosophy) Helps One to Understand that Today's Destabilizing Political Polarization Over Several Issues Including the Abortion Debate (The Human Rights for All Humans Debate) is Rooted in a Bifurcation in Western Thought Going Back to the 17th Century – a Bifurcation Fundamentally Separating Radically *Skeptical, Relativistic* (Including Nazi, Marxist, Socialist, *Extremist*) Thinkers from *Realist, Scientific* and Logical Thinkers.
Meaning Everyone Should Self-Reflect and (Consciously) Identify Their (Usually Unconscious) Underlying Philosophical Worldview (at Base Predominantly either *Skeptical and Relativistic* or *Realist and Scientific*) So They Can Make an Intelligent Decision Whether or Not They Want to Keep It in the Light of the Key Facts of Science, Logic, Human Rights History (and the History of Ideas).
CITIZENS AND POLITICIANS HAVING A THOUGHTFUL, CONSCIOUS WORLDVIEW IS PART OF *THE THINKING REVOLUTION* NECESSARY TO ENSURE LASTING FREE DEMOCRACY Based on *Education*, Rather Than Citizen Voters and Elected Politicians (and Unelected Bureaucrats/Civil Servants, Judges and

Journalists and "Big Tech" Billionaires and Personnel) with Thoughtless *Ideology* Tearing Down Democracy's Realistic, Scientific, and Pro-Life Foundations in Ignorance.
(Ideologues Witlessly Destroying Democracy with their Uneducated Pro-Choice Legal-Human-Killing Ideology Witlessly Following 1920 Marxist Soviet Legal Abortion Precedent;
and/or Neo-Marxist Identity Politics with its "Cancel Culture" Censoring ("Cancelling") Those Who Disagree with Them, *even Hard Scientists and Medical Experts* Who Naturally Disagree with the Unscientific Absurdities of *Relativists Not Realists*;
and/or Radically Skeptical Postmodernist Ideology that Denies Objective Facts and Science, Developed by Marxists to Protect Marxism from Facts).

Note that this book has stated from the introduction that the "touchstone democracy test" issue of legal abortion (started in 1920 by *totalitarian Marxists*) is so devoid of factual support that legal abortion is entirely intellectually indefensible in a free democracy and is only supported by the intellectually dishonest (hence *The Intellectual Honesty Challenge* in these pages giving Pro-Choicers the chance to intelligently defend legal abortion in the light of the facts, *if they can* – that is *the challenge*). Abortion is only still legal because the Pro-Choice side has dishonestly ignored the overwhelming facts of Human Rights History, Logic and Science collected in this book, and refused to have a serious, honest Abortion Debate (Human Rights for All Humans Debate). *But, while any intelligent person with a decent grip on Reality will easily concede to the overwhelming undisputed facts of Science, Logic and Human Rights History laid out in this book and in more detail in the author's previous book Pro-Life Equals Pro-Democracy, there is another, deeper layer to the current problem of Pro-Choice, Neo-Marxist Identity Politics "Cancel Culture" ideologues now ruining many Western governments with 'Creeping Totalitarianism': these ideologues have no grip on Reality because of bad philosophy.* Underlying the Marxist precedent of legal abortion; and Neo-Marxist Identity Politics; and the "Cancel Culture" which now readily "cancels," censors and censures even qualified experts and scientists who disagree with them, is *the vacuous Postmodernist philosophy developed by Marxists which is so radically philosophically skeptical* that it *denies the existence* of any *objective* facts that can be known and thus absurdly *rejects even Science and Logic*, giving priority to personal, subjective "feelings" and opinions over facts (as an intellectually dishonest way of defending intellectually indefensible Marxism from facts).

REALISM VERSUS RELATIVISM OVERVIEW:

The Top Facts of the History of Philosophy, Most Pertinent to Understanding 21st Century Polarized Western Politics (Rooted in a 17th Century Bifurcation of Philosophy into Two Major Incompatible Streams). Aristotelian (later Scholastic) Realism Versus Cartesian (later Postmodernist) Skepticism/Relativism: Two Opposed and Incompatible Streams of Western Philosophy Lead Naturally to Today's Bifurcated and Divided Western Politics.

Chapter 3: Philosophy

Are You Fundamentally a Realist Who Believes the Universe We Humans Commonly Perceive We Live in is (Objectively) REAL?

Or Are You Fundamentally a Skeptic Who Denies or Doubts Anything Outside of Your Own Mind is Real (Such that You Can "Create Your Own Reality" and "Create Your Own Morality"); Such That There Is No Objective Reality But Only Subjective Opinions, Such That Between Any Two Humans (If Other Humans than You Even Exist) There is No Objective Truth But Everything is Relative?

Aristotelian Realism Accords with the Common Sense Which Keeps Humans from Dying Stupidly, and Gave the West Science, Logic, and Technology. The Traditional Western Pro-Life Family Values Which Include and Support The Foundational Principles of Human Rights and Democracy Were Built in the Philosophical Framework of Aristotelian Realism, and Can Be Scientifically Verified as Providing the Best, Healthiest Context for New Humans to Be Brought Into the World and Raised to Physically, Psychologically and Emotionally Healthy Human Maturity in Stable, Loving Families Which are the Building Blocks of Politically Stable, Caring Societies.

In Contrast, Cartesian Skepticism Denies or Doubts the Certainty of ANYTHING Except One's Own Mind, and Gave the West:

Solipsism Which Denies One Can Certainly Know Anything Outside One's Own Mind Even Exists;

Atheism Which (Rooted in Skepticism about the Universe Even Existing) Denies Any Intelligent Orderer of the Universe to Account for the Intricate Order of the Universe Which May Not Even Exist;

Relativism Which Denies There Are Any Objective Facts (or Science or Logic), Accepting Only Subjective Feelings and Opinions (Because in the Skeptical Stream of Philosophy, Only Your Own Mind Certainly Exists, So Why Accept Any Opinions Not Your Own? Without any Knowable Objective Facts, Everything is Subjective and Relative);

Moral Relativism (Rooted in Atheist Relativism Which Doubts or Denies Objective Facts of Any Kind) Which Denies Any Moral Absolutes Like *Killing Humans is Wrong* or the *Inherent Human Right to Live* or Any *Human Rights* to Ground Free Democracy (Note the Anti-Realist Philosophical Connection: There Were Not Significant Numbers of Atheists Until After There Were Radical Skeptics Denying Reality Itself Exists; There Were Not Significant Numbers of Moral Relativists Until After There Were Relativists Denying Anything Objectively or Certainly Exists);

Secularism Which (Adopting Atheist Moral Relativism) Claims Traditional Religious Values (Including *The Foundational Principles of Human Rights and Democracy* like *Equal Human Preciousness*, Which Were Introduced into the World by Biblical Judeo-Christianity) "Have No Place in the Public Sphere;"

Absurdism & Nihilism Which Deny Any Objective Facts or Meaning in the Universe;

Existentialism Which Tries to "Assign" Meaning to an Otherwise Uncertain and Meaningless Universe, with Mixed Political Results for Human Safety — Existentialist Nietzsche Influenced the Nazis; a "Successful" Existentialist is Merely One Who Avoids Solipsism and Suicide by Subjectively Assigning Some Kind of Meaning to a Universe Objectively Uncertain at Best, Meaningless and Absurd at Worst – Subjective Meaning Which Can Be Beneficent (When Existentialists Like Kierkegaard Assign Meaning by Embracing Christianity) or

Murderously Totalitarian (Existentialist Marxist Sartre Inspired Marxist Despot Pol Pot and ¼ of Cambodia Died);

Experientialism/Pragmatism Which Like its Root Radical Skepticism Also Prioritizes Subjective Experience Over Any Scientific Notion of Objective Reality — Popularized by Atheist Relativist John Dewey Who Was Extremely Influential in (North) American Education, Effectively Making Atheist Relativist Assumptions Ubiquitous in Western "Education," Thus "Priming" the West for: (Atheist Relativist) Marxism (Communism and Socialism) Which Unrealistically Promises a Seductive "Classless Egalitarian Utopia Where No-one Owns Anything and Everyone is Happy" But Which In Practice Has Always Resulted in Oppressive Totalitarian States Murdering Millions Because Atheist Marxism is Rooted in Radical Skepticism and Relativism and NOT Rooted in *Reality* (Unrealistic Marxism Has Killed More Humans than Anything Else – Both Born and Preborn, the First Marxist State Being the First State to Legalize Abortion, and Shortly Thereafter the Same Marxist State Legalized the Genocide of this Author's Ethnic Group);

Coming Full Circle Back to the Radical Philosophical Skepticism Which Ultimately Yielded Atheist, Relativist Marxism in the First Place, Western Marxists in Western Universities More Recently Developed Radically Skeptical Postmodernist Philosophy to Save Marxism from the Overwhelming *Facts* That Marxism Does Not Work in the Real World (Proved by over 94 Million Killed by Marxist Policies in the 20th Century Alone), By Being So Radically Skeptical That All *Facts*, Science and Logic and Objectivity are Denied (Leaving Nothing "Admissible" to Convince Today's Neo-Marxist Ideologues, Who are Usually Pro-Choice "Identity Politics" and "Cancel Culture" Ideologues, to Replace Their Marxist-Influenced *Ideology* with *Education*);

Nobel Prize-Winning Russian Author and Historian of Marxism Aleksandr Solzhenitsyn Confirmed That Western Education and Media Were Marxist-Influenced and Taking the West Towards the Same Totalitarian Ends as in Marxist Soviet Russia, Just by a More Subtle and Insidious Route (Which Can Be Demonstrated Since the 1930s When *Western* Media Hid the Marxist Soviet *Holodomor* Genocide of this Author's Ukrainian Ethnic Group in Soviet Marxist Socialist Ukraine – Officially Known as the *Ukrainian Soviet Socialist Republic* – *Western* Media Giving the Pulitzer Prize to the Dishonest Marxist New York Times Journalist Who Covered Up the Genocide While Discrediting and Firing the Honest Journalists Who Tried to Reveal the Genocide While it was Happening; and the Western Marxist-Influenced Education and Media Solzhenitsyn Warned the West About Still Protects Marxism from Facts, Which is Why Everyone Knows and Rightly Abhors the Right-Wing Extremist Nazi Atrocities, But Hardly Anyone Knows Nor Rightly Abhors the Left-Wing Extremist Marxist Atrocities Which Killed Far More Precious Humans in More Countries than the Nazis Ever Did – and Marxist Ideology Still Runs Rampant in Today's Western Pro-Choice Left Which Follows the Original Marxist Practice of Legal Abortion, First Legalized in Marxist Russia in 1920);

Marxism's Latest Form, Morphing to Adapt to New Times as Marx Himself Predicted it Would, is Neo-Marxist Identity Politics, Which Just Like Classic Marxism Unrealistically Reinterprets All History and Toxically Bifurcates All Past and Present Societies Into Adversarial "Privileged" and "Oppressed" Classes, Making Mutual Cooperation for the Common Good Based on Equal Human Preciousness Impossible. Marxist (and Neo-Marxist Identity Politics) Thinking by Marx's Design Exaggerates Existing Resentments Over Past (Even

Long Past) Injustices (Like Centuries-old Slavery) and Foments Renewed Hatred Between Those Labelled "Oppressed" and "Privileged" Specifically in Order to Create Enough Political Instability to Create Opportunity for a Marxist Takeover of the Government. Marx Himself Considered Bloody Revolution and Violence the Necessary First Stage of Marxist Implementation, and Encouraged the Violence Typically Used Since in All the Genocidal Vain Attempts to Implement the Unrealistic "Marxist Egalitarian Utopia" (This Typical Marxist Pattern is Currently Demonstrated by the Officially Pro-Choice, Identity Politics Organization Run by Self-Described Marxists, Currently (2020) Encouraging Riots and Burning Cars in the U.S.)

The two streams of Western Philosophy which now (after centuries of building up to this) have more or less logically resulted in today's above political polarization which threatens the continuance of Free Democracy and Human Rights are *Aristotelian Realism* and *Cartesian Skepticism*. Today's political differences are literally rooted in a difference between (philosophically speaking) a fundamentally *realistic* or fundamentally *skeptical and relativistic* underlying view of the universe or philosophical worldview.

Aristotelian Realism is the Fount of the Stream of Western Philosophical Thought Which Begins with the Common Sense by Which All Humans Daily Live Our Lives and Preserve Them from Death, Which has Yielded Science, Logic and Technology

Aristotelian Realism is the fount of the stream of Western philosophical thought which begins with the Common Sense by which all humans daily live our lives and preserve them from death, by assuming as *First Principles* that the universe/reality we perceive with our senses is indeed *REAL* (with real dangers that can hurt us, like fire and cliffs and buses which might hit us if we step into their path, all of such dangers which we daily avoid through *Common Sense*). Aristotelian Realism which accords with and assumes Common Sense has given us:

- all Western Logic and Science, built on the genius polymath Aristotle's *First Principles of Being/Existence* which precisely describe the orderly nature of the *ordered cosmos* of Reality as humans daily experience it and as Science studies it (such as the Law or Principle of Non-Contradiction, "Something cannot both *be* and *not be* at the same time, and in the same respect." Even in our most fevered dreams, we cannot even *imagine* something that violates this principle of *objective reality*).
- Aristotelian Realism grounds the philosophical school of *Scholasticism* (sometimes called *Thomism* after Saint Thomas Aquinas, Scholasticism's pre-eminent practitioner). *Scholasticism* dominated and characterized the *schools*, that is, the *university system* in Europe from 1100-1700 – up to and including and after the Scientific Revolution which established Modern Science and the Modern Scientific Method within the European universities.

- Aristotelian Realism grounds the Scottish School of Common Sense Realism, which was a Common Sense response to the Radical Skepticism of Scotsman David Hume, who was influenced by Cartesian Skepticism and was the first to take it systematically to some of its more absurd and dangerous conclusions which *divorce human minds from Reality*. In intensely practical terms: humans will die or be seriously injured if they do not consistently concede that there is at least *a strong correspondence* to what we humans commonly *perceive as real* (like sunshine; fire; oceans; other humans; the air we breathe; the bus coming our way) and an *objective external reality* independent of our individual humans minds or ideas. Scotsman Thomas Reid, the best representative and founder of the School of Common-Sense Realism, wrote:

---

*"... there are certain principles... which the constitution of our nature leads us to believe, and which we are under a necessity to take for granted in the common concerns of life, without [necessarily] being able to give a reason for them—these are what we call the principles of common sense; and what is manifestly contrary to them, is what we call absurd .
.."*

First Principles in any field of study cannot necessarily be "proven" in a strict sense, nor deduced from other principles, but they can be demonstrated as *necessary* for the field of study to proceed at all. The simple fact is, we humans will die or be seriously harmed (or institutionalized as insane and a danger to self or others) if we do not acknowledge *self-evident aspects of Reality*; if we do not follow Common Sense and treat *commonly experienced reality* as indeed *real*. Common Sense and Science both assume a *high correspondence* between the common human experience of what is real, and the objective reality of Reality. Long before Thomas Reid articulated Common-Sense Realism in response to Modern Philosophy's Cartesian Skepticism as radically articulated by Hume, Aristotle himself noted that those who disagreed with his "First Principles of Being" were still *forced by the ordered nature and structure of reality itself* to act in their *daily* lives *as if he was right*. No matter how fervently anyone denies Aristotelian Realism with their mouths (including today's skeptics and relativists and postmodernists and Marxists and Neo-Marxists — who are all frequently Pro-Choicers), they all live in the same commonly-perceived universe with the rest of us, and they all act *daily* as if Aristotle was right (if they do not, for long enough, they can die very stupidly). Existence itself (Being itself, Reality itself) is structured in such a way (such an ordered, structured way, as *Realism* describes) that you just have to, because Aristotle is *right* in saying things like "something cannot both be and not be at the same time and in the same respect" (and the other of his *First Principles of Being* describing self-evident aspects of Reality which are the starting point for Science). The Principle of Non-Contradiction articulates the ontological/ metaphysical reality grounding Science, which has the result in statements that "a statement cannot be both true and false at the same time, and in the same respect" — which grounds Logic, and gives us a way to speak about *Reality* precisely, logically, scientifically, *realistically*.

CHAPTER 3: PHILOSOPHY

Daniel J. Sullivan describes the close relationship between Common Sense and Science (and philosophical Realism) more precisely in the following quotation from his 1957 book: *An Introduction to Philosophy: Perennial Principles of the Classical Realist Tradition*. He was very aware of modern non-realist (skeptical and relativist) philosophies which compromised both Science and Common Sense, and therefore he concludes, "Any philosophy, therefore, that strays very far from common sense is suspect. If it goes so far as to contradict the basic certitudes of common sense, then it is guilty of denying reality itself, and on this point common sense can pass judgement on it." In this passage he actually uses the term "philosophy" without specifying he means Realist philosophy (as specified in his subtitle) because he wrote *before* such *unrealistic*, anti-scientific, skeptical and relativistic modern philosophies had yet taken over whole Western universities and governments and cultures/societies. Back when "university-educated" was much more likely to mean one actually had a trained mind with more than just Common Sense, but scientific and logical reasoning skills building on Common Sense, as follows:

Common sense refers to the spontaneous activity of the intellect, the way in which it operates of its own native vigor before it has been given any special training. It implies man's native capacity to know the most fundamental aspects of reality, in particular, the existence of things (including my own existence), the first principles of being (the principles of identity, noncontradiction, and excluded middle), and secondary principles (the principles of sufficient reason, causality, etc.)

One of the points that links [Realist] philosophy and common sense is that they both use these principles [articulated clearly by Aristotle, the "Father of Realism," hence starting and grounding all Western Logic, Science, and Technology]. They differ however in the way they use them. Common sense uses them unconsciously, unreflectively, uncritically. They can be obscured or deformed for common sense by faulty education, by cultural prejudices, by deceptive sense imagery. [Realist] Philosophy on the contrary uses these principles critically, consciously, scientifically. It can get at things demonstratively, through their causes. It can therefore defend and communicate its knowledge.

The certainties of common sense, the insights of a reasoning which is implicit rather than explicit, are just as well founded as the certainties of [Realist] philosophy, for the light of common sense is fundamentally the same as that of [Realist] philosophy: the natural light of the intellect. But in common sense this light does not return upon itself by critical reflection, is not perfected by scientific reasoning. [Realist] Philosophy, therefore, as contrasted with common sense is scientific knowledge; knowledge, that is, through causes.

A second point which links [Realist] philosophy and common sense is that they take all reality for their province—common sense blindly, in a kind of instinctive response of the individual to the totality of experience; [Realist] philosophy consciously, in the endeavor to give every aspect of reality its due. This claim of [Realist] philosophy to know the whole of reality does not mean the [Realist] philosopher makes pretense of knowing everything—the human intellect cannot exhaust the mystery of the smallest being in the universe, let alone everything. It remains true, nevertheless, that all things are the subject matter of [Realist] philosophy, in the sense that the [Realist] philosopher [including scientists, since Natural Science is built on Realism — for centuries in the universities what we call Science was called

Natural Philosophy; scientists were called "Natural Philosophers," in the Realist (Aristotelian, Scholastic, Thomist) tradition] takes as his angle of vision or point of view the highest principles, the ultimate causes, of all reality. Along with common sense, then, [Realist] philosophy seeks the comprehensive, all-inclusive view of reality; it is the knowledge of all things.

[Realist] Philosophy is thus close to common sense and at the same time different from it. It differs from common sense because it holds its conclusions scientifically, with a clarity and depth inaccessible to common sense. It is close to common sense because it shares the universality of common sense and a common insight into the fundamental structure of reality. We might even say that [Realist] philosophy grows out of common sense, and that common sense taken in its strict meaning is a kind of foreshadowing, a dim silhouette, of [Realist] philosophy proper [and therefore of science proper]. Any philosophy, therefore, that strays very far from common sense is suspect. If it goes so far as to contradict the basic certitudes of common sense, then it is guilty of denying reality itself, and on this point common sense can pass judgement on it.

Unfortunately, the West would soon after Sullivan's eminently sensible 1957 book, in the 1960s, abandon Traditional Western Values, which were developed in the framework of Realism, as the guide of societal standards and public policy. The West was soon to abandon both Common Sense and (scientific) philosophical Realism (and all objectivity) for radically skeptical (and subjective) philosophical Relativism; the West was soon to abandon the (essentially "Pro-Life," and Judeo-Christian) *Foundational Principles of Human Rights and Democracy* for Atheist Moral Relativism as the new guide for Western society and public policy, in the 1960s Sexual Revolution. The Sexual Revolution which created demand for legal abortion to kill all the unwanted humans naturally produced by immaturely and irresponsibly engaging in Nature's way of generating new precious humans without any intention of doing so. Legal abortion which, the second human-killing abortion was de-criminalized (1969 in the author's country), legally eliminated the *Inherent Human Right to Live* and thus *removed* the solid foundation of all Western rights and freedoms, opening the way for the return of totalitarianism in the West which we are in fact seeing today – for example, this author can be arrested and jailed for peacefully saying "killing humans is wrong because Human Rights are for all humans" anywhere remotely near where humans are being legally killed in violation of their Human Rights; and under several recent laws speaking verifiable science is now a crime when it contradicts the Pro-Choice and other unscientific, relativistic ideologies of Pro-Choice political parties in power. It took this long to start to see the full rotten, anti-scientific and anti-democratic fruit of the Sexual Revolution and the legal abortion it demanded (following the Morally Relativist and genocidal Soviet and Nazi legal abortion precedents) because of centuries of Western good habits of thinking and behaving. Centuries of Western Science built on philosophical Realism and centuries of Western freedom built on *The Foundational Principles of Human Rights and Democracy* were not immediately erased in the West with the Sexual Revolution and legal abortion. But their eventual demise we are now starting to see was made *inevitable* in the present Western Society no longer solidly grounded in Realism nor in *The Foundational Principles of Human Rights and Democracy.*

Chapter 3: Philosophy

Dr. Jordan Peterson, my countryman and the world's informal "Professor of Free Speech," in his June 2020 article "The activists are now stalking the hard scientists,"[11] rang the clarion bell to warn us that the so-called "politically correct" (and intellectually *dishonest* or, to use Solzhenitsyn's word, intellectually *"impaired"*) Relativist, Neo-Marxist Identity Politics "Cancel Culture" mob, which long ago took over the Social Sciences in most Western universities, are now attacking and punishing the "hard" sciences, the Natural Sciences too – evidently wanting everyone to have brains as untrained, dull and "mushy" as theirs which no longer even benefit from the above-described Common Sense which is the natural gift of humans. For in Sullivan's quote above he noted that the natural human apprehension of those *self-evident aspects of reality* articulated clearly by Aristotle as the First Principles of Being "can be obscured or deformed for common sense by faulty education." Which is clearly the case with the (anti-Realist) Relativist, Marxist-influenced education Solzhenitsyn warned us about in many of today's Western universities, which now churn out supposedly "university-educated" graduates with heads filled with *ideology instead of education*, who are so "dumbed down" by faulty education that many (notably our Pro-Choice legal human-killing politicians) have not only never been trained in logical, intellectually honest thinking, but they have even lost access to humanity's natural gift of Common Sense and its ability to implicitly comprehend self-evident aspects of *reality itself!*

The West, after flirting with Atheist Moral Relativism for a long time (since Atheism's first foray into politics, the bloody French Revolution, and its *Reign of Terror*), in the 1960s finally actually *abandoned* Traditional (democracy-grounding) Western Values, turning the West back towards the primitive and brutal pre-Christian times when human sexuality was completely unrestrained, human-killing abortion was legal, and governments were totalitarian (that is, setting the range of what humans may or may not believe; setting the level of persecution or toleration for humans who did not agree with the government; and holding the power of life and death over the governed: government deciding just what rights humans did or did not have, just when and how just which humans could be killed, without any regard for any *Inherent Human Rights* not given by the government). And you could be arrested and imprisoned for peacefully standing up for the lives of humans the government said it was OK to kill, like I can be so arrested today under current laws passed by philosophically and morally Relativist, Pro-Choice politicians and parties (so uneducated in Human Rights History that they witlessly follow the philosophically *Relativist not Realist* totalitarian Soviet Marxist and Nazi Extremists' precedent of legal human-killing by abortion).

The gradual degradation of Western freedom started accelerating with the 1960s Sexual Revolution which turned sex partners from precious *persons* and life-partners to naturally build a human family with, into mere pleasure *objects* to be selfishly used and then thrown away for the next, *objectified* human pleasure object. The precious human children naturally produced by sex were then also thrown away in human-killing abortion instead of being raised to human maturity lovingly within the *human family* naturally created by the sexual union of the sex partners. Note that cross-culturally and throughout all history (before the recent Sexual Revolution) *marriage* was the universal, cross-cultural social norm for sexual relations, for good reasons

[11] https://nationalpost.com/opinion/jordan-peterson-the-activists-are-now-stalking-the-hard-scientists#main-content , accessed July 5, 2020.

rooted in biology itself. Scientifically, biologically speaking, a "successful" sexual encounter is one that produces the next generation of the human species so that the human race continues. Getting pleasure from sexual encounters that do not achieve this vital biological goal is still a legitimate part of marriage which serves biology. Biologically speaking, sex is pleasurable *because* this helps *emotionally bond* the sex partners so they can be loving *mother and father* to any human children naturally produced precisely by their sexual union! Scientifically speaking, sex is pleasurable in order to help form the strong emotional bonds that make a human family (bonds socially confirmed and supported within the wider human community through the universal cross-cultural norm of marriage), *because* the next generation of the human species has by far the *best chance* of growing up safely into a physically, psychologically and emotionally healthy human adulthood within such *stable, loving human families* which are the building blocks of *politically stable, caring human societies.*

Note that Relativist (therefore anti-Realist and anti-scientific) philosopher Karl Marx, in his *Communist Manifesto* and elsewhere, specifically mocked "the traditional family" which is supremely beneficial according to principles of Biological Science. It is thus unsurprising that today's Marxists and Neo-Marxist Identity Politics "Cancel Culture" ideologues who are currently undermining Free Democracy from its very foundations have also abandoned and mocked "the traditional family." "The traditional family" as articulated by traditional Western, Judeo-Christian Pro-Life Family Values which historically helped Western Civilization to grow beyond the brutal, oppressive totalitarianism of the ancient, pre-Christian West, and eventually establish Human Rights and Free Democracy upon Traditional Western Pro-Life Family Values.

It is important to thoughtfully reflect upon human sexuality, in its full emotional and biological power, and to realize that sex which generates human beings is so powerful that any human society's guiding attitude towards sex determines our human destiny as either valuable *persons* to be protected or as *tools* to be used and thrown away. The 2015 Ontario Sexual "Education" curriculum teaches young children in Canada's most populous province *that sex is primarily for recreational pleasure* (this "education" was introduced by the most philosophically *Relativist not Realist* and the most totalitarian-oriented government in Canada's history, which passed the first several totalitarian laws which motivated this author's book series HUMAN RIGHTS EDUCATION FOR LASTING FREE DEMOCRACY). *If sex is primarily for recreational pleasure* then other humans are sex objects or *tools* to be used for our pleasure, the humans produced by sex can be killed by abortion as unwanted tools, and when human tools no longer serve the State/society the State sanctions their killing by euthanasia (and shames them into asking for it in "assisted suicide") as worn-out tools to be thrown away. But, *if sex is primarily for lifelong-committed loving marriages naturally generating new precious humans in stable loving families (the building blocks of stable loving societies)*, then humans are always valuable *persons* who must never be mere tools for others' sexual pleasure nor mere tools serving a greater State/society, but rather the State is always *obligated* to protect and serve precious human *persons*, which is the necessary foundation for the Human Rights and Democratic Freedoms which only ever developed in Western *Christian* Civilization which lived by this traditional Judeo-Christian sexual ethic and *traditional Family Values.*

So ironically, what the "Sexual Revolution" called the "sexual *repression*" of the traditional, Christian sexual ethic is what brought *real freedom* to unrestrictedly sexual but politically oppressive totalitarian Western Society starting in the 4th Century; and what the "Sexual Revolution" called "sexual *freedom*" is what is bringing back the *real repression* of the ultimately totalitarian or 'Creeping Totalitarian' Pro-Choice philosophy which contradicts the *primary human right to live upon which all Human Rights and Democracy depends*. So-called Christian "sexual repression" *directing* sexuality into *mature* committed loving marriage and family life brought *actual freedom* into Western Civilization, and so-called "sexual freedom" for *immature* sexual pleasure-seeking is bringing back *actual repression* with the compromise of Human Rights and Freedoms for the sake of being able to legally kill the unwanted humans produced by sexual pleasure-seeking *and restricting the democratic freedoms of those medical professionals and other Pro-Life Human Rights advocates who would defend human lives because human lives are always precious*. Once again, scientifically speaking (that is, speaking within the framework of the philosophical *Realism* which grounds Science, *Realism* which more explicitly articulates the self-evident aspects of *reality* which are more implicitly apprehended by the human intellect as Common Sense), sex is pleasurable in order to help form the strong emotional bonds that make a human family (bonds socially confirmed and supported within the wider human community through the universal cross-cultural norm of marriage), *because* the next generation of the human species, biologically speaking, has by far the *best chance* of growing up safely into a physically, psychologically and emotionally healthy human adulthood within *stable, loving human families* which are the building blocks of *politically stable, caring human societies*. It is only philosophical *Relativists not Realists*, whose very grip on *reality* itself (and Science itself; and Common Sense itself) is very weak because of their Relativist (and usually Marxist-influenced) *ideology instead of education*, who are inclined to ignore or doubt the science and sound reason and logic which affirms that Traditional Western Pro-Life Family Values best support human biology for the best physical, psychological and emotional human health, individually and in human society.

In conclusion of this introduction to philosophical Realism and its effects on human society, before below considering philosophical Skepticism and Relativism and their effects on human society:

According to both Common Sense and Aristotelian Realism (and the Scholasticism which assumes both, which dominated the universities until well after Modern Science was created in them), I, the author, indeed exist, as a human being with a human body and mind (in fact, with all the attributes of a human *psyche*, Greek for *soul*, classically understood to include *intellect*, *emotions*, and *will*, all studied in the field of *Psychology*). And all other human beings I perceive around me (and all my readers like YOU) do in fact *exist*. We can only learn to read at all, and understand anything we read, and not die stupidly every day, by assuming, as Aristotelian Realism does, that the universe really exists, and runs according to certain ordered, structured First Principles and Scientific Laws.

The Traditional Western Pro-Life Family Values which include and support *The Foundational Principles of Human Rights and Democracy* (as this book demonstrates) were built in the philosophical framework of Aristotelian Realism. Moreover, Traditional Western Pro-Life Family Values can be *scientifically verified* as providing the best, healthiest context for new humans to be brought into the world and raised to physically, psychologically and emotionally *healthy human maturity* in *stable, loving families* which are the building blocks of *politically stable, caring societies.* But you can only get such positive political results for countries with millions of humans by treating the world/universe we humans all commonly perceive around us as *Real.*

The natural world/universe around us (our environment) which we constantly respond to and interact with, and which imposes needs for life like air, water, food, *indeed exists.* Therefore, we cannot dispense with eating, drinking or breathing, or else we will die, no matter how much some skeptic Postmodernist and Neo-Marxist professor might have convinced you that "nothing can be known for certain" or that you can "choose your own truth." Such ignorant Postmodernist and/or Neo-Marxist Skeptics and Relativists themselves *all live by Common Sense Realism or else they die,* which is why we can *safely ignore* skeptic Postmodernist and Neo-Marxist professors and "social-justice-warrior" political activists and their claims. In fact, our safety as individuals and as a society depends upon us ignoring and rejecting Radically Skeptical Cartesian, Postmodernist, Atheist, Relativist, Marxist claims and the "ideologically lobotomized" claims of Neo-Marxist Identity Politics with its "Cancel Culture." Because:

Cartesian Skepticism is the Fount of the Stream of Western Philosophical Thought Known As "Modern Philosophy," Which Has Yielded Every Anti-Scientific, Relativistic and Dangerous Philosophy from Solipsism to Marxism Murdering Millions

Cartesian Skepticism is the fount of the stream of Western philosophical thought known as "Modern Philosophy." It begins with René Descartes, "The Father of Modern Philosophy," and his famous statement "I think, therefore I am" (French: *"Je pense, donc je suis."* Latin: *"Cogito, ergo sum"*). The statement is first mentioned in a 1637 book; the concept reflected upon in detail in his 1641 book *Meditations.* It was only the second of six meditations presented in the book as taking place over one week, and Descartes himself did not remain so radically skeptical as he is in that meditative intellectual exercise. However, our ideas, good or bad, can take on a life of their own without us, and the practical effect upon history of "I think, *therefore* I am" was unfortunately to *remove all Modern Philosophy after him* from being grounded in *Reality*, by prioritizing *thought* over *being/existence.* This "Cartesian Split," splitting Western Philosophy *away* from Aristotelian Realism's former prioritization of *existence* which gives us Science and technology and accords with the Common Sense which daily keeps us alive, has instead given the West:

- *Solipsism* - the philosophical position that (mimicking severe mental illnesses which *divorce the patient from Reality*) denies or seriously doubts that anything or anyone at all exists outside of one's own mind, or can be known to exist for certain.
- *Cartesian Skepticism*, according with Descartes' statement "I think, *therefore* I am" as elaborated in his second of six 1641 *Meditations*, that he could only be absolutely *certain* of the *real* existence of *his own mind* which he knows thinks. Though Descartes himself did not remain so

Skeptical (he was too smart for that), he unwittingly opened up Modern Philosophy after him to the most Radical Skepticism of solipsism and every *radical doubting of Reality* position leading up to it, including:

- *Atheism*, which of course denies or doubts the existence of God the (unseen) Creator and Orderer of the Universe (assumed in Aristotelian Realism as the source of the universal, cosmic *order* which Science studies), when Modern Philosophy following Cartesian Skepticism even denies or doubts the existence of the (seen) physical Universe itself, and denies or doubts the existence of any other minds than one's own! And:

- *Relativism*, which follows from Radical Skepticism and Atheism. Assuming nothing can be known to *objectively* exist for certain, outside of one's own mind, individual *subjects* each *subjectively choose* what they believe exists or does not exist, what is true or not true. Thus, they say unscientific and illogical things like "that's true for *you*, this [contradictory thing] is true for *me*," violating the Law of Non-Contradiction itself, the first and easiest to prove of *The First Principles of Being* which Science and Logic are built upon. Relativists absurdly deny the easiest to prove Universal Law, ultimately because, as radical Skeptics, they deny any *objective external Reality* (such as recorded facts or observed scientific data) which might furnish tie-breaking *evidence* that one human subject's *opinion* of what is true better accords with *objective external Reality* than another's. Since Relativism denies even the objective physical reality which Science studies with academic rigor, all the more so Atheist Relativism results in:

- *Moral Relativism*, Ethical Relativism, and with it the "impaired thinking ability" Solzhenitsyn points out. Impaired thinking ability which allows solid *education* to be easily replaced by vacuous *ideology*. *Ideology* which has unleashed murderous evil upon the Earth on a scale previously unimaginable. As Solzhenitsyn wrote, "Ideology – that is what gives evildoing its long-sought justification and gives the evildoer the necessary steadfastness and determination. That is *the social theory which helps to make his acts seem good instead of bad in his own and others' eyes* . . .Thanks to ideology the twentieth century was fated to experience *evildoing calculated on a scale in the millions*." Many influenced by Relativism try to seem more intelligent and reasonable by claiming they accept scientifically proven realities as *real*, but they consider anything in the moral sphere to be *relative*. Solzhenitsyn would certainly rebuke these in any case (he noted, "those people who have lived in the most terrible conditions, on the frontier between life and death . . . all understand that between good and evil there is an irreconcilable contradiction, that it is not one and the same thing—good or evil—that one cannot build one's life without regard to this distinction. . . "). But moreover, Moral Relativists often have very little understanding of what makes something scientifically proven, and like any Relativist may be prone to simply *claim* things they believe are "scientifically proven." Relativism in general and Moral Relativism in particular are *both* intellectually dishonest and hypocritical. Honestly convinced and consistent Relativists need to be contained in mental health wards for their own safety and that of others; most hypocritically keep alive daily by following Common Sense Realism but still form their political opinions according to incompatible Skeptical Relativism. And no one will scream louder than a Moral Relativist when they think their own rights are being denied (including Moral Relativist Pro-Choice bigots who deny *Equal Human Rights for All Humans* and so are fine with killing preborn humans *in denial of their inherent, equal, inalienable Human Rights*). The huge political danger from Moral Relativists comes from the necessary fact *they can accept no Moral Absolutes* like *killing humans is wrong* nor any *Inherent Human Rights* which governments are obligated to protect; nor can they accept any authority higher than the government to which the government is *accountable* for how it treats the humans it governs. Which is why all the representatives of Atheist, Relativist, Marxist countries on the United Nations' original Human Rights Commission refused to even vote on the UN's magnificent 1948 *Universal Declaration of Human Rights* (and why all Marxist States have committed millions of murders). Atheism, rooted in the Radical Skepticism made possible by Descartes and Modern Philosophy, has given the West:

- *Secularism*, which proceeds from Atheist Relativism, especially Moral Relativism, meaning no moral absolutes *like killing humans is wrong* can be consistently applied or else secularists complain of "religious values in the public sphere" (religious values like *Equal Human Rights for All Humans* and all of *The Foundational Principles of Human Rights and Democracy*, which are specifically Biblical and Judeo-Christian in origin – as is the key insight of the Aristotelian philosophical Realism which grounds all Science, that the universe is an *ordered cosmos* and *not a random, undirected chaos*, which is *why* Nature is susceptible to scientific studies that reveal the underlying *orderliness* of the universe. And which is *why* the Modern Pure Sciences and the Modern Scientific Method only developed in Christian Europe which built itself deliberately on Biblical insights).

- Such Atheist Relativism, rooted in the Radical Skepticism made possible (if unwittingly) by Descartes, and by how Modern Philosophy unfortunately developed after him, has, unfortunately, above all given the West below-described *Marxism* (Communism/ Socialism), Atheism's by far most sophisticated and popular political theory for organizing human societies – utterly rooted in *Skeptical Relativism* and utterly incompatible with *Scientific Realism*, which is why Marxism *never works in the Real World*, but consistently has distinctly the *opposite* of its claimed intended effects of "making the world a better, more equal, place" where "no-one owns anything and everyone is happy" under highly centralized State control of resources (in theory, equitably distributed). But Marxist, Socialist States always consistently devolve into what Solzhenitsyn described as merely "the equality of destitute slaves" (the world's first Marxist State, the Union of Soviet Socialist Republics/USSR organized around Soviet Russia, actually first *legalized human-killing* by abortion, *and then by genocide*!). One of Marxism's many flaws is that because it requires tight State control of resources and so on it cannot tolerate normal free-thinking variety of opinions, nor free speech that criticizes just how the State goes about its tasks and so countless individuals always get imprisoned or executed "for the good of the State." Solzhenitsyn's *The Gulag Archipelago* describes how the ravenous gulag prison system in the world's first Socialist Marxist Relativist State had to be set up almost immediately. But Marxist-influenced ideologues, because they are Relativists who *reject objective facts* in favor of *subjective feelings and opinions*, are rarely *swayed* by these *facts* to abandon Marxism. Marxist-influenced ideologues, because they are Relativists who *reject objective facts* in favor of *subjective feelings and opinions*, are rarely *swayed* by these *facts* to abandon Marxism. Instead, they just brainlessly spread Marxism in newer forms, yielding Marxism's immense current popularity in the West (especially in its newer form of the Neo-Marxist Identity Politics Solzhenitsyn commented on in a 1983 speech, wherein he noted *"Atheist teachers in the West are bringing up a younger generation in a spirit of hatred of their own society . . ."* Solzhenitsyn, the world's foremost expert on Soviet Marxism, living 18 years in the U.S., confirmed that U.S., Western mainstream media and education were Marxist-influenced and were taking the West towards the same ultimately totalitarian ends as Marxism took his beloved Russia – just by a different, more subtle and insidious route. This current, ultimately anti-democratic Atheist Relativist Marxist influence in the West was greatly facilitated by the previous Western popularity of:

(Atheist, Relativist) *Pragmatism/ Experientialism*, which is rooted in Atheist Relativism and like it emphasizes *subjective experience* as having priority over any Realist and Scientific notions of *objective Reality* (which approach, of course, ultimately goes back to Descartes' unwitting introduction of *radical skepticism* into Western Philosophy, which came precisely from Descartes (in his second *Meditation* of six) giving his own *subjective experience* and his personal, subjective ability to *think* about it priority over any notion of *objective existence* independent of his own mind — as in his famous but erroneous statement, "I think, *therefore* I am," which in practical effect *unhinged from Reality* "Modern Philosophy" after Descartes, by doubting any possible *certainty* outside one's own mind and thought. Hence, to a *pragmatist*, only what is (subjectively) *experienced* is "real," and (pragmatically) "truth" is just "whatever works." Because Science works so consistently well, Pragmatism inconsistently tries to incorporate science, using it just "because it works," while *inconsistently denying* Science's actual foundations in philosophical (Aristotelian, Scholastic, Thomist) *Realism* - absurdly denying *why* Science works, which is because Science's underlying worldview and *First Principles* accord with the *objective Reality of the universe* which Science studies as *real, objective* and existing *independently* of our subjective minds and experience. What makes Pragmatism/ Experientialism (sadly) important to the current threats to Free Democracy (and to Scientific thinking, where in the author's country people can now be arrested or hauled in front of a tribunal for speaking verifiable scientific facts which do not support the new-fangled anti-scientific ideologies of Pro-Choice Left governments) is that the primary promoter of this Pragmatist, Relativist philosophical worldview was John Dewey (1859-1952).

Dewey was hugely influential in American education, and well beyond America's borders. Devoutly Atheist (and Relativist), he was one of the signers of the original 1933 Atheist *Humanist Manifesto,* which at the time honestly described Atheist *Secular Humanism* as an *Atheistic religion* intending to replace traditional "theistic" religions (such devout Atheists later realized that they could get a lot more influence in Western society than their tiny numbers deserved, a kind of "Atheist Apartheid," by *pretending* that Atheism was *not* ultimately just another underlying *religious worldview* accepted on *faith not proof* (in the non-existence of any Orderer God who gave the universe its *intricate order* which Science studies only because of its *First Principles* which from the beginning of Science *assumed* such an Orderer); and by *pretending* that traditional theistic religions *"had no place in the public sphere"* — even though nothing could be more asinine, since, as this book demonstrates, Traditional Western (Judeo-Christian) Pro-Life Family Values include and support *The Foundational Principles of Human Rights and Democracy* without which (see Chapter 2) the West *could never have developed* and is *predictably losing* its traditional Human Rights and freedoms – and this author can now be arrested in Canada for peacefully saying "killing humans is wrong because Human Rights are for all humans" under current provincial laws passed in mere *weeks* (in 2017) or *days* (in 2020) by *officially Pro-Choice*, effectively *Neo-Marxist Extremist Left* philosophically *Relativist instead of Realist* political parties in power).

Atheist Relativist Dewey's vast educational influence in the West thus popularized the *myth of opposition* between (Judeo-Christian) Faith and (Scientific) Reason. A vacuous myth *which could only be believed by someone utterly uneducated in the actual, utterly Judeo-Christian and Theistic history of Science* from ancient (Theistic) Aristotle to the (all devoutly Christian) founders of Modern Science and the Modern Scientific Method in the Scientific Revolution which occurred only in the Christian universities of Christian Europe (which had themselves organically grown out of the Medieval Christian "Cathedral Schools" which had started with intense scholarly study of the Bible and then branched out into all other fields of knowledge – **all motivated by the ancient Jewish and Christian** *scholarly emphasis* **on the** *search for objective Truth in all its forms* (which had made Aristotle's famous pupil Alexander the Great put the scholarly Jews in charge of the great ancient Library of Alexandria in Egypt, which Alexander had named after himself). But such *facts* do not matter at all to at bottom Skeptic Atheist, philosophical Relativists who *deny any objective facts* in favor of mere *subjective feelings and opinions* – including experientialists/pragmatists like pre-eminent American "educator" John Dewey.

Thus, entirely *ignorant* of Science's historical and logical foundations and without any real motivation to trade their current *ideology* for actual *education,* Atheist Relativists (like John Dewey was) are simply *ignorant* of the *facts* that Aristotle's *First Principles of Being/Existence* which underlie all Western Science, Logic, and Technology merely expanded the prior essentially *Biblical* insight Aristotle's ancient Socratic School had been previously exposed to, that the Universe is an *"ordered cosmos"* with an intelligent Orderer (and NOT an ultimately *"random, undirected chaos"*). Thus, entirely *ignorant* of Science's historical and logical foundations and without any real motivation to trade their current *ideology* for actual *education,* Atheist Relativists (like America's top "educator" John Dewey was) are simply *ignorant* of the *facts* of the *formation of Modern Science and the Modern Scientific Method* by the devoutly Judeo-Christian *theists* of the 16th and 17th Century Scientific Revolution (like Copernicus, Kepler, Galileo, Sir Francis Bacon and Sir Isaac Newton) working from *key insights* the West originally learned *from the Bible (Jewish Bible/Christian Old Testament),* expanded by ancient (Greek Socratic School) *Theist*

Aristotle into *The First Principles of Being/Existence* such as the Law of Non-Contradiction, which *make all Western Science, Logic, and Technology possible.*

Of course, John Dewey and today's similarly Atheistic, Relativistic "thinkers" (I must use the term only *loosely* because of their manifest *intellectual dishonesty*) are apparently completely *ignorant* of the fact Greek Aristotle was preserved from the so-called "Dark Ages" following the Western, Latin-speaking Roman Empire's 476 AD destruction at the hands of overwhelming barbarian tribes, in the Eastern, Greek-speaking Roman (Byzantine) *Christian* Empire which lasted for another 1000 years, until its 1453 conquest by the Muslim Turkish Ottoman Empire. The Christian Church in Ukraine (this author's faith tradition) was originally evangelized by ancient Greek-speaking Christianity in 988 AD, when all of Ukraine whole-heartedly underwent mass Christian baptisms in rivers – so completely and honestly embracing Christianity that it is impossible to speak of the history of Ukraine since without referencing the Christian Church. Which is why the Relativist Atheist Marxists/ Communists/ Socialists who militarily conquered the briefly independent Ukraine went to such lengths as committing the 1932-33 *Holodomor* ("Murder by Starvation") Genocide against this author's fellow Ukrainian, Eastern Rite Christians (mostly rural farmers. This author's Ukrainian Greek Catholic Church later became the largest underground Church of the 20th Century: it officially *did not exist* under Soviet Communism but emerged 5 million strong when the Socialist Soviet Union dissolved)[12]. The *Holodomor* was after they had killed the Russian Tsar who had ruled both Russia and Ukraine for centuries, and after they in the bloody 1917 "Great October Socialist Revolution" (months after Solzhenitsyn's conception) had firmly established philosophically *Relativist not Realist,* Atheist Marxist Communist Socialists into sole ruling political power for the first time. The Relativist Atheist Marxist Soviets had to murder an estimated 7-10 million of my Ukrainian ethnic group in the *Holodomor* Genocide in order to break the Christian spirit of Ukraine to resist Relativist Atheist Socialists who (just like Neo-Marxist Identity Politics "Cancel Culture" Socialists today) were attempting to rewrite history and culture in Marxist terms of "oppressed class rejecting and overthrowing previous 'privileged/oppressor' class in order to establish Marx's egalitarian utopian vision"). The Atheist Soviet (and later Atheist Chinese, Vietnamese, Cambodian, Korean, etc.) *philosophically Skeptical and Relativistic Marxists*, who explicitly deny the (Aristotelian and Scholastic) philosophical *Realism* which grounds all Scientific enquiry, throughout the 20th Century could not accept the *facts* and tremendous evidence that despite their best attempts to realize the *unrealistic* Marxist utopian vision, Marxism just does not work in the *Real World* – because they were *Relativists not Realists,* who believe in *subjective opinion* over *objective facts* (which Relativists deny, instead accepting contradictory absurdities like "that's true for you; this contradictory thing is true for me"). And because Relativists who think even facts are "relative" are usually Moral Relativists as well, they had no moral problem murdering

---

[12] There were (and are), of course, many more than five million underground Christians in Marxist, Communist, Socialist China – but they belong to hundreds or thousands of the tens of thousands of splintered denominations or sects of Western Rite Christianity since Western Rite Christianity's Protestant Reformation, and thus there are not so many as five million Chinese Christians from any one Christian denomination/sect, which is why this author can confidently refer to Eastern Rite Christianity's Ukrainian Greek Catholic Church as the largest underground Church of the 20th Century, 5 million coming up from the underground when Soviet Marxism in Ukraine ended – plus more than that many in the worldwide Ukrainian diaspora, which includes more Ukrainians in this author's country of Canada than any other country outside Ukraine.

many millions of Ukrainian humans in order to help set up the world's first State run by Relativist Atheist Marxist Socialist "thinkers," the Union of Soviet Socialist Republics (USSR). Other Relativist Atheist Marxists later had no problem killing one quarter of Cambodia's population, and committing countless atrocities in Vietnam, North Korea (etc.) while still trying to implement unrealistic Marxism in the Real World. And the Marxist-influenced today still claim everyone else who has tried to establish a Marxist utopia before just somehow did it wrong when *every single attempt descended into murderous totalitarian oppression*, but they will (somehow) succeed! Marxist (and today's Pro-Choice Neo-Marxist Identity Politics "Cancel Culture") ideologues just keep trying to hammer (and sickle) the "Red Square peg" of Marxism into the "round hole" of *reality*, no matter how many precious humans (born and preborn) are killed in the attempts. It is difficult to convince them to stop trying (and stop hurting humans) because their brains barely function due to the "ideological lobotomy" or "impaired thinking ability" due to Relativism of which Solzhenitsyn spoke. Because as philosophical *Relativists not Realists*, they just do not have any solid grip on *Reality*.

But, thankfully for Western Science and Technology (and freedom!), Eastern, Greek Rite Christians (like this author!) preserved ancient Greek Aristotle, "the Father of Realism," so that after the "Dark Ages" following the barbarian conquest of the Western Roman Empire, Aristotle could be re-introduced into the West in the new (medieval) Western university system, which was the fertile intellectual ground where the introduction of the "Father of Realism" Aristotle *made Science as we know it take off by leaps and bounds*. Ignorant Atheists ("farting with their brains" their insubstantial condescending "Atheistic flatulence" that demeans religious believers as somehow "backwards" and "unscientific") simply know almost nothing of the origins and logical development of Science from ancient through to modern times. The history of Science discussed in this author's book *DEMOCRACY 101* (and citing an eminent scientist who actually knows the history of his field):

... the whole modern university system historically grew out of Christian Europe's medieval cathedral schools, first dedicated to scholarly Bible study which then branched out into all the other fields of knowledge and scholarship. Theology – The Study of God and All Things in Relation to God – was historically "the Queen of the Sciences" and Christian "religious colleges" are still at the core of all the oldest and most established universities today. The University of Paris, also known as the Sorbonne, grew out of the Notre Dame de Paris Cathedral School. The central College of Sorbonne was one of its colleges of Theology. Doctoral degrees were first introduced here.

Note that the Latin word scientia means "knowledge" – at base a science is simply a field of knowledge, which is why we speak of "social sciences" and "human sciences" which include psychology. Theology was known as "the Queen of the Sciences" because it included all other fields, being the formal study of God and all things in relation to God – a broad field without the narrow focus of some fields but yielding a wide berth of knowledge in many fields.

Today, when we say "Science" in English and other languages, we usually mean natural science or the Science of Nature, those sciences or fields of knowledge like Physics, Chemistry, and Biology which study some aspect of Nature. The "Pure" (Natural) Sciences study and

Chapter 3: Philosophy

observe nature purely for its own sake; for whatever can be discovered about nature; the "Applied" (Natural) Sciences apply what has been discovered about nature to useful purpose including the "Industrial" Science of making things which we call technology. For centuries in universities this that we now call Science was called "Natural Philosophy," and the highest level or doctoral degree (doctor is Latin for teacher) in the Natural Sciences (as in other fields) is still called a "Doctor of Philosophy" degree (Ph.D. for short).

Stephen M. Barr (Ph.D. – his is from Princeton University where he was awarded a fellowship "for distinguished research") is a practicing scientist who does research in theoretical particle physics and cosmology, and is Professor of Physics at the University of Delaware; and he is also someone who has actually bothered to learn the history of the Science he makes such distinguished use of and so does not make the grossly ignorant and uneducated statements Atheist scientists frequently do. In his short 2011 book Science and Religion: The Myth of Conflict . . . after noting the two now-discredited late-19th Century (one-century old) books which have been identified as being most responsible for the current popularity and the current form of the Enlightenment-era (two-century old) Myth of the Conflict Between Science and Religion, Professor Barr notes the historical reality:

"The medieval [Christian] universities were the first institutions in human history where science was studied and taught on a continuous basis from generation to generation by a stable community of scholars. Before this, it had always depended on the whims of wealthy and powerful individuals. As the noted historian of Science Prof. Edward Grant put it, the medieval universities "institutionalized" science. Moreover, they produced hundreds of thousands of graduates, who were introduced to scientific questions and from whose ranks scientific talent could emerge. The scientific community and the scientific public created by the medieval universities were the soil in which the seeds of the Scientific Revolution germinated. Most of the great figures of the Scientific Revolution were educated in universities that had been founded in the Middle Ages."

That is to say, most of those most responsible for the modern Scientific Method were trained in Science at universities that grew out of the Christian cathedral schools and which for centuries had been taught by Christian priests and monks who had studied Science as a prerequisite for studying Theology. As the following Articles [in the author's book DEMOCRACY 101] will elaborate, those most responsible for modern Science (and the modern Scientific Method) were devout Christians (both Catholic and Protestant) – and absolutely no Atheists! And far from Christianity being a detriment to scientific enquiry, the Judeo-Christian Biblical Revelation of a Creator God who ordered the Natural Universe actually spurred the European scientific quest to find patterns of order in nature, which is why the Pure Sciences and the modern Scientific Method developed only in Christian Europe and NOT the Far East – the Far Eastern religious traditions had no rational, intelligent orderer God to set up the universe with rationally discernible Laws, so no attempt was made to look for such Laws, even though otherwise they were capable of the detailed observations of nature which Science requires and occasionally made discoveries about nature based on these. Yet developed no systematic Pure Sciences as developed only in Christian Europe! The Far East only had the Applied Sciences like Engineering, wherein human ingenuity applied to very practical problems used whatever was known to build gradually better bridges,

buildings, and weapons. Western technology eventually outdid all others because the vast intricate detail about the natural universe discovered by the Western Pure Sciences "super-charged" what the Applied Sciences – including the Industrial Science of Technology – had to work with. And Christian scientists are operating from the same basic worldview of an ordered cosmos (not random chaos) with an intelligent orderer when they are in labs doing science and when they are worshipping in Church and practicing their beliefs, which cannot be said of religious Atheist scientists and those of other (non-Abrahamic) religions, whose religious faith operates from a different basic worldview than that which they use in a science lab – Atheists having merely borrowed the Scientific Method from the Christians who developed it, and those in countries without an Abrahamic Faith tradition having merely adopted Western Science (as it was fully-formed by the Christian West) without understanding its underlying Judeo-Christian First Principles.
– William Baptiste, DEMOCRACY 101, citing Dr. Stephen M. Barr

---

Atheist Relativists and Pragmatists like Dewey, with their *ideology instead of education*, just do not know nor "get" any of the above. Thus, Pragmatism (Experientialism) and John Dewey's (unfortunately) extremely influential use of it in American education is largely responsible for the "dumbing down" of (North) American education, by replacing the underlying worldview of traditional Scientific Realism from which we get Science, Logic (and ultimately technology) with an unstable and illogical underlying worldview of Atheist Relativism — Pragmatism/ Experientialism actually bringing to the forefront of "education" the "subjective experience over objective reality" by which Descartes foolishly (accidentally) unhinged Western thought from Scientific Realism in the first place. *After the devout Christians of the Scientific Revolution* like like Copernicus, Kepler, Galileo, Sir Francis Bacon and Sir Isaac Newton had done most of their work in founding Modern Science. Of these, only Isaac Newton had not yet already finished his contribution to Modern Science and the Modern Scientific Method when Descartes first published his *Meditations*, the second of six *meditations* which had the unfortunate effect of popularizing the erroneous and anti-Realist, anti-Scientific conclusion, "I think, *therefore* I am." Of course, Newton and all Western Science since *ignored* the Radical perceptual Skepticism unwittingly unleashed into "Modern Philosophy" by Descartes (who did not remain in radical Skepticism himself – he was indeed too smart for that).

This is why absolutely no Atheists were involved at any stage of the development of Science, nor of the Modern Scientific Method: precisely because Atheism is historically and logically rooted in Radical Skepticism and Relativism; precisely because Atheists effectively deny the universe is an ordered cosmos (which implies an intelligent Orderer), and instead assert the opposite, that the universe is ultimately entirely random and undirected by any God — leaving no reason to look for *patterns of order* in Nature as did all the theists (mostly Christians) who *actually developed Science* from ancient to modern times. Theists including Aristotle, the "Father of Realism" and the "Father of Science." The brilliant ancient Greeks of his Socratic School rejected the traditional pagan Pantheon of "gods" on Mount Olympus (Zeus, Apollo, Aphrodite etc.) as *silly superstition*, but *worshipped* the *Absolute Being* (Who necessarily exists; Who *is* existence itself) upon whom all *contingent beings* depend (*contingent*; unnecessary and changeable beings who did not always exist and may go in or out of existence, including planets and humans). Science is specifically the study of (material) *contingent* existence brought into being by and *ordered* intelligently by the Absolute Being, who necessarily exists and cannot not exist.

So, Atheist Relativist "Experientialist/Pragmatist" John Dewey, possibly the most influential "educator" in American history steeped (North) American education in the same Atheistic Relativism (itself steeped in Radical Skepticism) in which oppressive totalitarian States (especially Marxist Socialist States) are. Ultimately anti-scientific Philosophy that makes a mockery and a joke out of today's Western educational system — and which is driving us towards the totalitarian future Aleksandr Solzhenitsyn predicted precisely because of such Atheistic Relativism which destroyed his country too. Atheistic Relativism which is today still producing mush-for-brains anti-scientific Relativists with what Solzhenitsyn called "impaired thinking ability." Such that even the supposedly "university educated" can no longer understand basic science like the fact *preborn humans are humans* and therefore *abortion kills humans* (with massive intellectual dishonesty, Pro-Choice politicians will avoid admitting this simple science if they can get away with it); nor can they even understand a basic, perfectly sound and scientific logical syllogism like *All Humans have Human Rights. Preborn humans are humans. Therefore, preborn humans have Human Rights.* Nor do they even understand basic Biological Science like that in mammalian and other species, males are males, females are females, with real biological differences that are important to the survival of the species. *Objective scientific facts* (like *maleness* and *femaleness* are encoded in the DNA in *every cell* of a mammal's body) mean nothing to philosophical Relativists to whom everything is *subjective opinion* and therefore *personal choice*, however. But this Relativistic lack of intelligent, scientific understanding does not just make Relativists silly people, unfortunately. No, they are also ultimately *dangerous* silly people, because this Relativism is the same underlying bad philosophy that underlies Atheist totalitarian Marxist Communist Socialist ideologues, and thus, like them today's Pro-Choice anti-scientific Relativist politicians have no problem passing laws and policies against Free Speech of verifiable science, wherever science does not support totalitarian ideologies. Totalitarian ideologies including totalitarian "Pro-Choice" legal human-killing abortion ideology, which follows the 1920 totalitarian extremist Left-wing Soviet Marxist and 1934 totalitarian extremist Right-wing Nazi Fascist precedents of legal human-killing abortion. "Pro-Choice" Relativists (and pragmatists) easily kill humans following evil Soviet and Nazi precedents because nothing at all is *evil* when everything is *relative*, and because everything, even human-killing, comes down to personal "choice" for a subjectivist (experientialist/pragmatist) Relativist (including Moral Relativist) and philosophical *Skeptic* who at bottom is not even *certain* anything outside of his or her own mind even exists, after all. But Solzhenitsyn reminds us:

"... those people who have lived in the most terrible conditions, on the frontier between life and death, be it people from the West or from the East, all understand that between good and evil there is an irreconcilable contradiction, that it is not one and the same thing—good or evil—that one cannot build one's life without regard to this distinction. I am surprised that pragmatic philosophy consistently scorns moral considerations; and nowadays in the Western press we read a candid declaration of the principle that moral considerations have nothing to do with politics. I would remind you that in 1939 England thought differently. If moral considerations were not applicable to politics, then it would be incomprehensible why

England went to war with Hitler's Germany. Pragmatically, you could have gotten out of the situation, but England chose the moral course, and experienced and demonstrated to the world perhaps the most brilliant and heroic period in its history."
— Aleksandr Solzhenitsyn

Hence, *before* Moral Relativism and everything that comes with pragmatist/ experientialist skepticism/ relativism and *subjectivism over objectivity* (planted firmly in North American education by pragmatist John Dewey) grew up and took hold of the West by the time of the 1960s Sexual Revolution, Western nations like England *still had the moral compass and fortitude of character* to militarily oppose Adolf Hitler's bigoted *Extremist* Right-wing Nazi Fascist regime which rejected Traditional Western Values including the *equal human preciousness* that undergirds free democracies. Which is why England declared war on Nazi Germany and led the Allied nations in the successful fight for freedom built on Traditional Western Values. But *after* Moral Relativism and everything that comes with the pragmatism now in Western schools took its grip on Western society and culture, the West *freely followed Nazi Extremist precedents* and legalized human-killing abortion (and later legalized human-killing euthanasia). *Before* Moral Relativism rooted in philosophical Skepticism became a feature of Western culture in the Sexual Revolution which formally abandoned democracy-grounding Traditional Western Values, the Free West still had enough gumption to declare war on Nazi Germany to protect humanity from Nazi legal human-killing evil. Including legal abortion and euthanasia for which Nazi doctors were condemned at the Nuremberg War Crimes Trials, because these were recognized as further Extremist Nazi *crimes against humanity* which criminally violated the Human Responsibility to recognize and protect Human Rights in all other humans. But *after* Moral Relativism became a feature of Western culture, the West started *freely, willfully* taking on these evil human-killing practices which the evil Nazis would have *forced* upon the Free West if the Nazi Extremists had won World War II! And the ultimate result of such Moral Relativism is, predictably, the ultimate loss of our Western freedoms to legal human-killing political extremism.

Thus, in 2015, in my country's most populous province doctors had their Freedom of Conscience and Religion – and their freedom to practice the ancient *non-killing* (Hippocratic) Medical Profession – taken away by policies forcing them against their conscience to facilitate human-killing abortion and newly-legalized human-killing euthanasia. At the end of a public monthly meeting organized by local doctors in January 2015, when there was news of this impending policy, the main doctor asked me to address the crowd about the problem after the regular itinerary was finished. I said in my address "this is the line in the sand. If they get away with this policy, religious freedom is on the way out. The attacks will not stop there." Someone from the crowd humorously suggested later that, being winter in Canada, it was actually "the line in the snow." Much later the provincial Superior Court actually admitted that policies and legislation since 2015 requiring Pro-Life (Traditional Hippocratic) doctors to facilitate human-killing abortion and euthanasia against their conscience do in fact violate doctors' Freedom of Religion which is supposed to be guaranteed in the Canadian Charter of Rights and Freedoms. Yet the Court still judged that this suppression of doctors' democratic freedoms of Conscience and Religion was somehow *acceptable* in the case of making doctors provide "healthcare." What Solzhenitsyn called the "impaired thinking ability" of *Relativism* even in otherwise intelligent educated officials (who still lack the HUMAN RIGHTS EDUCATION FOR LASTING FREE DEMOCRACY identified from History, Science, Logic and Philosophy in this book series) means stupid judgements from courts. In what *objective reality* could killing humans be reasonably called "healthcare"? "Healthcare," for those too ideologically lobotomized to know, is supposed to improve the overall health of humans, not to end their health and their lives. For 2500 years the ancient Hippocratic Medical Tradition to "do no harm" meant *doctors do not kill* – and whenever a pregnant woman came into a doctor's office, the doctor as a rule understood he or she had *two patients*. The oldest forms of the Hippocratic Oath specifically prohibited human-killing abortion and euthanasia. But to a Relativist with little grasp on any objective reality, it is easy to merely *label* what is in precise scientifically verifiable fact *human-killing abortion* which typically dismembers, decapitates and disembowels unique humans as "healthcare." How can killing a unique individual human life with absolutely unique human DNA reasonably be called "healthcare" at all, never mind using this dishonestly misdefined "healthcare" as an excuse to trample doctors' normal (and supposedly constitutionally guaranteed) democratic freedoms of conscience and religion? But deep-down philosophical *Relativists not Realists* have no good sense of history, science, or logic, so Relativist-influenced judges all over the world find it really easy to mangle and ignore the democratic constitutions of their particular country by simply (and with intellectual dishonesty) relabelling important terms as something they are not, according to their *ideology not education*; or misinterpreting their nation's (and the United Nations') founding democratic documents without any educated nor intelligent appreciation of the original historical context in which these documents were written – documents which, properly and contextually interpreted, were intended to keep the future of these democracies democratic! But today, fundamentally Relativist and/or Marxist-Socialist-influenced ideologues in positions of authority interpret founding democratic documents however they like, to the detriment of their democracies; and to the detriment of the United Nations; noticeable above all in the ways that today's nations and United Nations shamelessly promote the legal human-killing by abortion first legalized by the oppressive totalitarian Soviets and Nazis *who did not believe killing humans is wrong*; in utter denial of any *inherent, equal, inalienable Human Rights* which ground lasting free democracies.

All the way back in 2015 when doctors' freedom of conscience and religion was taken away (this violation later upheld by a Relativist - therefore incompetent - Superior Court), I then predicted my current reality of the last several months, where I and over 5 million other people have (just like in Marxist totalitarian States!) been banned by the government from holding or attending any public worship service (using the Coronavirus Pandemic as an excuse), *while we are allowed to attend secular activities with hundreds of other people at a time*, in crowded malls, restaurants and fun centers and museums and so on. Back in 2015 I said that the governments passing the kinds of totalitarian laws and policies against Freedom of Religion I first saw in 2015 would take advantage of any later instability, like a war *or a pandemic*, to oppress religious freedom even more. And just recently I was in a provincial Supreme Court observing the proceedings of a constitutional challenge to the bigoted double standard of "Coronavirus Measures" restricting sacred activities much more harshly than secular activities, wherein the Supreme Court's final judgement, like the boneheaded and bigoted judgement against doctors' rights above, again admitted that the government policy clearly did infringe on constitutionally guaranteed freedoms of religion, speech, assembly and association, *but somehow nevertheless were justified.* When such a bigoted double-standard for secular versus sacred activities could never be reasonably justified by the Coronavirus Pandemic, because a virus follows biological not spiritual laws and will not spread any more nor any less based on whether the purpose of a gathering is secular or sacred. So, if the highly Socialist-influenced, officially Pro-Choice legal human-killing governing political party (which makes sure all its provincial and national members *reject* the Pro-Life *Foundational Principles of Human Rights and Democracy* identified from History, Science, Logic and Philosophy in this book series) claims it is *not* bigoted against religion, then it should have "Coronavirus Measures" imposed on religious activities which are commensurate with those imposed on secular activities; if it is bigoted, then it should at least be *honest* about it and simply impose an extra tax on Christians and other religious believers for existing and for worshiping, like they do in countries without traditional Western values like religious freedom. But do not dare to dishonestly claim you are "protecting us from the virus" by allowing us to go to fun centers and restaurants with hundreds of others but not allowing us to gather to worship! Note too, that as expected from *Relativist not Realist ideologues*, all of the "Coronavirus Measures" in any case are developed and upheld in court *while never engaging and just pretending there is no vast movement of medical professionals against Coronavirus alarmism and against lockdowns (which have never been medical procedures) who have associated in various professional groupings including the signatories of the Great Barrington Declaration of over 55,500 and counting medical scientists and other medical professionals who powerfully testify, and are backed up by the publicly available Coronavirus statistics, that oppressive Coronavirus Measures that restrict normal democratic freedoms for the general population are no longer necessary (and only "Focused Protection" for the minority actually vulnerable to the Coronavirus should continue).* If the Marxist "Great Reset" piggy-backing on the Pandemic, which is so well served by unmedical lockdowns – and by people getting used to *not being free* like they used to be – was not a goal of so many Relativist and Marxist and globalist ideologues worldwide, the Pandemic would long be over already. It only continues into 2021 because of *Relativism not Realism* in action – anything ideologues do not like and cannot beat otherwise, they just *pretend it does not exist!* Thus, many tens of thousands of qualified medical and scientific voices against oppressive Coronavirus policies are censored and buried by the mainstream media (now intertwined with "Big Tech") which Solzhenitsyn long ago warned us was Relativist, Marxist influenced and taking the "Free West" eventually to totalitarian ends *like these undemocratic restrictions the world now lives under,* with no end in sight as long as Relativist and Marxist-influenced ideologues control public opinion through mainstream media and "Big Tech." Whose personnel are hereby given THE INTELLECTUAL HONESTY CHALLENGE in Chapter 7 as part of the THINKING REVOLUTION, wherein they are challenged to finally start THINKING honestly and logically – challenged to finally get a HUMAN RIGHTS EDUCATION FOR LAST FREE DEMOCRACY and become part of a FREE and prosperous human society built on *(Scientific) Realism not (Skeptical) Relativism* and built on *Equal Human Rights for All Humans.*

But long before the Coronavirus Pandemic, it was already true that sensible judgements cannot be expected from those influenced by Relativism and Marxism. With philosophical *Relativists not Realists* in government long before the Pandemic, it is not even really surprising that in only three weeks in 2017, where this author and Dr. Jordan Peterson lived, the officially Pro-Choice (and effectively Neo-Marxist *Extremist* Left-wing, totalitarian-oriented) government passed laws meaning peaceful Pro-Life Human Rights advocates can be arrested and jailed for speaking verifiable scientific facts about abortion, or doing any kind of advocacy on behalf of *Equal Human Rights for All Humans.* Other jurisdictions copied this law including another Canadian province controlled by Pro-Choice Relativist politicians which passed a similar totalitarian law *in only 8 days,* March 2-10, 2020. Similarly, a Relativist judge told a father where I live that he will go to jail if he speaks verifiable scientific facts to or about his daughter (including calling her his daughter, even though every cell in her body is scientifically, demonstrably female; his daughter who has already been permanently chemically sterilized against her father's will by newfangled unscientific ideology promoted aggressively by Pro-Choice Neo-Marxist *Relativist* (therefore *anti-Realist*) political parties in power. [Update: In a serendipitous example of how we are all in the flow of *Living History* happening all around us, just as I was about to upload to my publisher this first Emergency Edition/Advance Reader Copy in early 2021, I received news that that father *is now in jail* for calling his daughter his daughter and for using accurate pronouns reflective of scientifically verifiable reality about her. The father with sardonic gratefulness wryly commented that at least "The court was gracious enough to say that they could not police my thoughts." [13] My fellow Canadian intellectual for Free Speech, Professor Jordan Peterson, has been proven *exactly right* for standing up and saying in 2016 that the totalitarian Bill C-16 (since made law) he became famous for opposing would precisely lead to this kind of absurd and totalitarian restrictions on free speech. A father is in jail just for talking about the scientific fact he for the last 14 years has had a daughter, not a son. But Relativist *subjectivists*, having no grip on any *objective reality*, find it very easy to dishonestly *relabel* anything according to their vacuous *ideology* instead of according to any solid *education.* And when Relativist subjectivists are politicians or judges, they have time and again proven only too willing to use *force of law* to *force into silence* anyone who actually believes in Science and Logic and facts and not in their Relativist ideologies which have nothing to do with facts.

In any case, all of the academic and media and "Big Tech" censorship supporting such abject political stupidity;

disallowing academic research projects that would expose facts about government-approved ideological foolishness;

contrary-to-fact *pretending* that there is *not* a vast amount of highly qualified medical science testimony *against* Coronavirus alarmism and lockdowns, in order to use an unnecessarily ongoing and never-ending "Pandemic State of Emergency" to facilitate the Marxist "Great Reset;"

now even making speaking verifiable Science a crime and politically promoting new forms of the anti-scientific, Skeptical, Atheistic, Relativistic Marxism which has killed more humans than anything else in history –

all this is now happening ultimately because in the 17th Century *Cartesian Skepticism* unhinged Western Philosophy from the previously dominant Aristotelian (and Scholastic) *Realism* which gave the West Logic, Science and Technology. So, continuing the above bulleted list of the various things which have come into the West through Cartesian Skepticism:

---

[13] See https://thepostmillennial.com/rob-hoogland-canada-prisoner-of-conscience, accessed March 19, 2021.
https://www.breitbart.com/tech/2021/03/18/canadian-man-jailed-after-misgendering-his-daughter/, accessed March 19, 2021.

- *Marxism,* which, starting from Atheism (Solzhenitsyn confirms that Atheism is no side feature but is integral to Marxism) is by far the most sophisticated and popular of Atheistic political theories. Marxism is so insidiously, seductively popular that there are still, as Solzhenitsyn noted of the 1920s and 1930s (when Marxists were cannibalizing his beloved Russia and committing the *Holodomor* Genocide of this author's ethnic group), "an enormous number of Western intellectuals" of Atheist/ Marxist/ Communist/ Socialist bent, who "refuse to see communism's crimes" or "try to justify them." These include the Marxists who, to save Marxism from being debunked by the *facts* that Marxism in practice always leads to horrendous and genocidally murderous totalitarian States, developed and continue:
- *Postmodernist philosophy,* which denies the reality of even facts and Science, reviving the most radically skeptical conclusions of Cartesian Skepticism which most (including Descartes himself) had refused to live by. The Postmodernism that keeps Marxism alive tends to often go side-by-side with:
- *Neo-Marxist Identity Politics,* which continues Marx's radical and unrealistic reinterpretation of all history and politics as an inherently adversarial (and therefore toxic to *cooperation* for the Common Good) "class struggle" between those labelled "oppressed" and "privileged," intending to create by any means a seductive Marxist-type egalitarian utopia – undaunted by the *facts* that any type of Marxism has always resulted in oppressive totalitarian States due to Marxism's fundamental flaws, because Identity Politics is deeply rooted in the same radically skeptical and vacuous philosophical origins as solipsism, which ultimately *denies or doubts Reality as we all daily experience it even exists.*
- *Neo-Marxist "Cancel Culture,"* which continues classic Marxism's *Skeptical Relativism not Scientific Realism* by wherever possible erasing and silencing ("cancelling" or censoring) voices, *even expert scientific voices,* against their ideological agendas, *just like all Marxist states controlled society by controlling which voices are heard.*
- On the (only somewhat) more positive side, the stream of Western Philosophy emanating from Cartesian Skepticism includes *Existentialism,* which tries to "make the best of" the radical uncertainty dominating Western Philosophy since Descartes, by bravely, courageously facing the (since Descartes) apparently meaningless universe which we cannot even be sure really exists outside of our own minds, taking responsibility for our own actions as we seek to apply some kind of meaning to our human lives. Existentialism nominally accepts the reality of other minds than one's own (but cannot be certain about this). Taking responsibility for our own actions is, of course, very mature and good (and something Marxism never does – Marxism always blames someone else for "oppressing" us, fomenting resentment and hatred which Marxism intends to spill over into bloody revolution to overturn the existing government, so that a Marxist egalitarian utopia can be attempted . . . even though every attempt in history has resulted in millions of murders in oppressive totalitarian States). Unfortunately, because Existentialism assumes the *radical* not *reasonable* doubts inherent in Cartesian Skepticism, and thus, is

ultimately unsure of any *objective* reality, Existentialist individuals *subjectively* and individually apply meaning to life, meaning which can have widely divergent political consequences for other humans (who may or may not even exist, in Modern Philosophy which started with Cartesian Skepticism. A "successful" Existentialist life is one that avoids both solipsism and suicide by assigning meaning to an otherwise meaningless universe and takes responsibility for one's actions while doing so). Kierkegaard, generally recognized as the first Existentialist, gave meaning to his life in the face of the radical doubts ultimately unleashed by Cartesian Skepticism by choosing to take the "leap of faith" required to embrace Christianity. This kind of way around radical skepticism *in faith* works well in practice for one's self and other humans, because Christianity is the source of *The Foundational Principles of Human Rights and Democracy* (Descartes himself had remained devoutly Christian to stay sane). But Atheist (and thus Moral Relativist) Existentialist Nietzsche despised what he called the "slave morality" of Christianity; he despised not only Marxist Socialism but also Democracy (built on Christian principles) for promoting (in different ways) human equality (though in Marxism, humans are equal but not precious, which is why so many get murdered in Marxist States). Nietzsche's way of assigning meaning to the otherwise meaningless and lonely existence left by the radical skepticism inherent in Modern Philosophy since Descartes was to (like a true Atheist Moral Relativist) *create one's own morality*, with a "will to power." Nietzsche's thought, which despised human equality in favor of elitism of the "exceptional" (like himself, of course), ultimately influenced Hitler and Nazism. Brilliant Nietzsche, much more intellectually honest than his fellow German Atheist Marx, perhaps moreso than some Existentialists was *tormented* by the radical skepticism inherent in Modern Philosophy since Descartes, which naturally leads to solipsism or Nihilism. The Merriam Webster Dictionary defines Nihilism as "a viewpoint that traditional values and beliefs are unfounded and that existence is senseless and useless. *Nihilism is a condition in which all ultimate values lose their value.*" Nihilist Nietzsche in his book *The Gay Science* has a character called "the Madman" declare "God is dead! God remains dead! And we have killed Him! How shall we comfort ourselves, we who are the biggest murderers of all?" It seems Atheist Nietzsche could find no comfort for his "Existentialist Angst" and, although he (like a successful Existentialist) avoided solipsism and suicide, he still actually spent the last 11 years of his life in an insane asylum – in a way becoming himself "the Madman" who proclaimed "God is Dead." And sadly, his thought becoming more popular after his death, his biggest effect on history was first:

influencing the Nazis (his influence on the Nazis was specifically mentioned at the Nuremberg War Crimes Trials of the Nazis) and second:

his "God is dead" phrase being popularized in the New York Times in the 1960s, this phrase has since been used axiomatically by Atheists whose (frequently Marxist!) leanings are among the biggest threats to Free Democracy which is built on Christian principles.

Frenchman Jean-Paul Sartre too, like Nietzsche, was an Atheist Existentialist whose personal, "subjective" attempt to bring meaning to an "objectively" meaningless existence without any objective certainty at all (thanks to Cartesian Skepticism) did more to harm humans, because he actually embraced and promoted Marxism, which has killed more humans than anything else in history. Existentialism's emphasis on "taking personal responsibility" in Sartre perhaps softened the typical Marxist approach of never taking personal responsibility but blaming others for your misfortunes, violently overthrowing whatever "privileged" class "oppresses" you in order to initiate a Marxist State. So, Sartre never joined a Marxist, Communist party. But still Sartre (like all the "enormous number" of Western Marxists Solzhenitsyn criticized for this) *hid, made excuses for* and *tried to justify* all the Marxist Soviet Union's atrocities. Sartre even actually attacked later Soviet Leader Khrushchev's refreshing candor in admitting and condemning the worst Soviet Marxist atrocities under former Soviet Marxist Leader Josef Stalin - because telling the truth about Marxism is bad for Marxism (Solzhenitsyn, who exposed Marxism's ideological and practical evil in *The Gulgag Archipelago*, had as a motto "one word of truth outweighs the whole world"). Sartre's French Marxist writings were inspirational for the Khmer Rouge (Communist Party of Kampuchea) under Pol Pot in Cambodia, who first studied in Paris, where his French Marxist professors encouraged his plan to initiate a "Marxist utopia" in Cambodia, which (because Marxism never works) resulted in the deaths of one quarter of Cambodia's population through mass starvation and genocides against Cambodia's ethnic minorities (both recalling the earlier *Holodomor* ["Murder by Starvation"] genocide through enforced starvation against this author's ethnic heritage in the Marxist USSR). Sartre's contemporary and erstwhile friend Albert Camus is also known as an Existentialist, a categorization he himself denied, because instead of trying to subjectively and responsibly assign meaning to one's meaningless existence in a meaningless universe as Existentialists do, Camus instead advocated giving in to or *embracing the absurdity of such existence,* in:

- The philosophy of *Absurdism*, which, deeply rooted in the radical expression of Cartesian Skepticism which has been a powerful undercurrent of Western philosophy since Descartes' 17th Century error, highlights and embraces the supposed absurd incongruity between the human drive to search for meaning in life, and the supposed inability of humans to find any satisfactory meaning in a universe which (since the Cartesian Split) is presumed meaningless, purposeless, irrational and chaotic, or at least unknowable to be otherwise.

But, this author contends, there is no need to so give in to the alleged "absurdity of human life," nor any need to try to wiggle out of the demented solipsism, denying or doubting Reality itself outside one's own mind, which is the logical end of Cartesian Skepticism, whether by the "Cartesian Circle" Descartes himself used, or by Existentialism's brave facing of the meaningless and uncertain universe left by Cartesian Skepticism (with very mixed political results for human safety coming out of Existentialist philosophers). There is no need to "try to make the best of an ultimately uncertain and meaningless existence" as Existentialism does, because such doubts are *radical* not *reasonable* doubts, and there is good *reason* to return to the previous dominant stream in Western Philosophy (which scientists never stopped operating within) which accepts our *common human experience of the universe* (without which you could not even read this book, nor understand it) as *real*. Ancient Aristotelian Realism *ignores Modern Cartesian Skepticism* and all the vast doubts it has brought about in Modern Philosophy since the 17th Century, and just goes on as before Modern Philosophy, *successfully plugging away* at gradually unravelling the secrets of the material universe humans live in through Science; and ingeniously applying what the Pure Sciences discover in the Applied and Industrial Sciences including *Technology*. The fact that Science works at all, and provides us with amazing new technologies previously undreamed of, is a powerful testament to the veracity of the Aristotelian Realism which Cartesian Skepticism denies or unreasonably doubts...

... by happy accident (or Providence) this author shortly before this Emergency Edition's rushed publication to help save Free Democracy from Relativists came across the 1957 book *An Introduction to Philosophy: Perennial Principles of the Classical Realist Tradition* by Daniel. J. Sullivan. Glancing through, it appears to be an excellent text on Realism. Written before the West abandoned Traditional Western Values in the 1960s and replaced *The Foundational Principles of Human Rights and Democracy* (Judeo-Christian in origin) with Atheist Relativism and Moral Relativism, as the West's "guiding principles for public policy" – ultimately resulting in the current 'Creeping Totalitarianism' now accelerating towards the totalitarian end of the Free West which Solzhenitsyn warned the West was coming due to the West's embracing Relativist, Atheist, Marxist principles. Sullivan's text furnishes these thoughts on Descartes' subjectivism which almost four centuries ago unleashed the false thinking now undermining Human Rights and freedoms globally:

[Descartes'] position is called subjectivism because it is based on the consciousness of the thinking subject, making the objects of knowledge a part of the thinking subject himself, his ideas, his feelings and so forth, so that there is no objective, external test of truth. Descartes, when he demanded proof for the existence of the outside world, started a false problem which gave rise in modern philosophy to innumerable errors: a false problem because the question is asked in such a way that no answer is possible... We do not invent, or create the existences which form the field of our knowledge. We <u>discover</u> these existences, and there is no possible way of knowing what has, in fact, been given existence other than to discover it... For the philosopher to ask proof of the actual existence of contingent things, including his own existence, is to betray [to not accept] the evidence of the fundamental intuition of his senses and intellect. It is to ask proof for what does not need proof, for what indeed cannot be proved, since it is prior to proof and implied in all demonstration. "The one reason why we state that we exist and that London is in England is because reality is that way. Being is the lord of the intellect and whenever we make a judgement that we know is true and certain, it is because being is so presented to the intellect that reality determines, forces and constrains us to consent to it. There can be no turning back at this point because in the field of knowledge-content the intellect is the servant, reality the master, and it is reality that dictates to the intellect, not vice-versa."

... We may conclude by affirming that when the subjectivist asks you to prove the existence of the world of bodies, he is refusing to accept the evidence in the only place where it can be found—in the world of bodies itself. In fact, this is the only conceivable place where it can be found, since it is a contingent existence not made by us or brought into existence by our thought. The arbitrary refusal of the subjectivist to accept the evidence in the only place where it can be found precludes beforehand the possibility of any answer, as in the classical example of a man who asks what numbers make up twelve, but precludes you from using twice six, or three times four, or twelve times one. [A classical example from Aristotle's mentor Plato]

Descartes' (temporary for him) radically skeptical subjectivism encapsulated in the error "I think, *therefore* I am" absurdly tried to make his own intellect and comprehension dictate what is real, when in fact (prior, and independent) *reality* dictates to the intellect (through the senses) the *evidence* of reality. What is real is *evident* to us, through our senses, which is why all of us individual human subjects gathered around the same breakfast table see (that is, we *experience* the *evidence* of through our sense of sight) the same orange on the table. The orange by its very existence makes *evident* its reality upon us through our senses. And if you, a subjectivist and relativist around the table, deny the orange is real, deny the *evidence* of the orange's existence the only place it can be found (through your senses), even though you see it just like the rest of us around the table do – no matter how strenuously you philosophically deny the real existence of the orange, the concrete, commonly experienced *reality* of *Reality* means you simply cannot prevent yourself from also experiencing the *evidence* of the orange's real existence through the rest of your senses (hearing, touch, taste and smell) when I whip the orange in your face and you hear me say "silly Skeptic Relativist, deny this!" As this author has stated elsewhere, the *reality* of *Reality* imposes or forces itself upon each of us individual human subjects with *common consistency* through our *common human senses* which we *reasonably* accept as putting us more or less directly in contact with a really existing universe of Reality external to and independent of our minds. A real universe studied as *real* by *really existing* (pure) scientists who are, by accepting this universe's *reality* and closely examining it, able to *discover* ever-new things about Reality they did not invent, but which give other (applied) scientists new and deeper information about the universe they can creatively use to invent new technology . . . all based on Realism not Relativism. All this fruitfulness from accepting the (common, sensory) *evidence* that the universe is real means it is eminently reasonable to accept the universe is real. It is in fact unreasonable – and literally dangerous – to *not* so accept the evidence of external reality the only place it may be found, through our senses. No matter how strenuously you skeptics and relativists deny the existence of the Mack truck sliding out-of-control towards you on its side, you *will* get squashed like a bug if you unreasonably take no steps to avoid it because you doubt its real existence independent of your own mind (a mind physically associated with a brain which may end up spread over the Mack truck's windshield . . .). It is *radical not reasonable* skepticism, and intellectual dishonesty, to keep denying all the sensory evidence of the external reality we individual humans all commonly experience daily and cannot get out of contact with *unless we literally go insane* and so become irrelevant to the external world we deny. No sane person lives like this, nor can skeptics and relativists survive long (outside of a mental institution where competent *realists* look after the safety of deranged *skeptics*). It is ultimately *hypocritical* (and politically dangerous for everyone else) for you to survive every day only by acting according to the evidence that Reality is real from the only place that evidence comes – your senses – but then make your political philosophy and undertake political actions based on radical skepticism and relativism which *radically doubt or deny reality*, like Marxists and all other Moral Relativists do.

Daniel J. Sullivan's book *An Introduction to Philosophy: Perennial Principles of The Classical Realist Tradition* also provides a response to the skeptic, which also in the end urges the skeptic to reasonably abandon his or her philosophical skepticism for the sake of intellectual honesty and consistency, also noting (like Aristotle noted of his critics millennia ago) that it is actually impossible to live consistently as a skeptic. The untrained human default is to live (and not die) according to Common Sense which unconsciously, implicitly grasps the essence of *Reality* articulated scientifically by *Realism* anyway. So one might as well choose to live consciously by the underlying philosophical worldview of *Realism* that can (unlike Skepticism and Relativism) be *realistically* (and fruitfully!) lived:

To demonstrate the error of skepticism to the skeptic is impossible because the skeptic refuses to accept the principles which make demonstration possible... It is not necessary to question the sincerity of the person who calls himself a skeptic but it is legitimate to remind him of the difference between a verbal [claimed] doubt and of what is implied by real doubt. Real doubt paralyzes activity. If you had a <u>real</u> doubt whether or not your food was poisoned you would not eat it. If you had a <u>real</u> doubt of the safety of the elevator you would walk. If you had a <u>real</u> doubt doubt of the destination of your train, you would get out and ask. Of course, if you had a <u>real</u> doubt of everything you would doubt the very existence of the food, of the elevator, of the train. You would also doubt, <u>really</u> doubt, the existence of other people, of your own past, of the immediate future. If a person <u>really</u> doubted all the evidence of his senses and intellect, he would be able only to lift his little finger, as Aristotle puts it. The absolute skeptic is reduced, in short, to the existence of a vegetable.
This is one check, then, that can be made against the absolute skeptic. Does he really act as though he had a real doubt of everything? For if someone asserts a philosophical position as true, it is legitimate to ask whether he acts in accordance with his asserted philosophy.

In this case, this author posits, since it is impossible to live a human life at all as a consistent skeptic or relativist, then *get real!* Those who hold Pro-Choice or Marxist or other Morally Relativist philosophical and political positions have positions which are built upon the erroneous and absurd *radical doubt or denial of reality itself* inherent in philosophical Skepticism and Relativism. Skepticism and Relativism which are *opposed* to the philosophical *Realism* which accords with the innate human gift of Common Sense that daily *keeps us alive* and which puts us daily into *contact with reality*. Skepticism and Relativism which are *opposed* to the philosophical *Realism* which, building on (innate and unconscious) Common Sense and making it scientific, critical, conscious, gives us Science, Logic, and Technology. And gives us a *realistic* philosophical framework within which to fruitfully live our human lives. This book, even in this unedited first "Emergency Edition" form which is published early to combat the speeding freight-train of once 'creeping' totalitarianism *now accelerating fast towards free democracy's destruction in the West,* has already amply demonstrated from Human Rights History just how insidiously dangerous Pro-Choice and Marxist and other philosophically Relativistic positions are, and how necessary to ongoing human safety and freedom are *The Foundational Principles of Human Rights and Democracy*, which are of course built on philosophical *Realism*, thus having a good grip on *Reality* and according with Common Sense!

. . . How does all the above History of Philosophy and above philosophical considerations affect current Western and world politics? Both the *Realistic* and the *Radically Skeptical and Relativistic* streams of Philosophy, which are entirely incompatible with each other, have been concurrently *strongly* influential in Western and world society and culture for centuries now. Meaning most people, influenced by both streams, have unconsciously, gradually, gravitated towards and more or less settled *on one or the other* as their "dominant" underlying worldview concerning their (usually subconscious) assumptions about the big "First Order Questions" of the nature and meaning of the material universe we humans commonly perceive and daily interact with – and humanity's place and purpose (and our own individual place and purpose) within that universe. Ultimately resulting in a *polarized*, bifurcated current Western politics, rooted ultimately in polarized, fundamentally incompatible, underlying fundamental philosophical assumptions about the universe and about humanity. Of course this has a major affect on whether we accept the legal killing of humans, which is the central topic of the author's book *Pro-Life Equals Pro-Democracy* in which this discussion was first printed! So naturally, the political polarization largely falls along the lines that those who are strongly *for* the legal killing of humans by abortion, or who vote for political parties now "officially Pro-Choice" (parties which now often no longer even accept members who are not Pro-Choice; and which "purge" from their ranks "old guard" party members who are still Pro-Life), tend to be primarily (at least unconsciously) *philosophical relativists.* They tend to be primarily (at least unconsciously) *philosophical realists,* those who are Pro-Life (easily accepting the *scientific reality* that preborn humans are humans, without trying to wiggle out of this *reality* like relativists do), or who vote for political parties which – though too often too terrified of Marxist-influenced Mainstream Media to be officially Pro-Life – yet are still "big tent" and freethinking enough to accept into their party Pro-Lifers with their Traditional Western Pro-Life Family Values that Free Democracy is historically and logically built on . . .

Since most people have not consciously been taught nor learned the above *History of Ideas,* most people have not consciously thought through their underlying philosophical options, nor have most people consciously *chosen* a basic philosophical worldview. Thus, most people have just unconsciously *absorbed* various, and not necessarily consistent, *assumptions* about the basic nature of the universe and the nature and meaning of human life, from their environment, and from whatever level and type of education they have had. Which may have been a good education based on established facts of Science and History, including the History of Philosophy so they might make some form of conscious judgement about their philosophical options; or a bad education that imparts *ideology* instead of genuine *education*, as that spread by the Marxists who developed Postmodernist philosophy to protect Marxism from the facts that Marxism never works in practice. The Sullivan quote above notes that faulty education like this, now all too common in Western universities (as Solzhenitsyn warned us), can actually mentally *impair* people from fully accessing the

Common Sense, humanity's innate gift that puts humans in contact with *reality*, which accords with the philosophical Realism which grounds Science, Logic, and Technology.

The current political bifurcation of society which makes it so hard to find common ground is ultimately rooted in the fact that the relative strength or weakness of one's firmly Realistic or Radically Skeptical influences and assumptions will incline each person to gravitate to either the Realistic or the Skeptical/Relativistic as their "general worldview," which will influence their politics. And chances are many people have some inconsistent and incompatible assumptions that they absorbed and live according to in different areas of their lives – including some silly assumptions they would never choose consciously, and for good reason, which is why THE THINKING REVOLUTION proclaimed in this book is so important, so that most people can at last *consciously identify* and live by a *consistent* underlying philosophical worldview – which will greatly help resolve the current political bifurcation and division of society which is ultimately rooted in opposing and incompatible philosophical views of the universe and human life as a whole.

"One world, one mankind cannot exist in the face of ... two scales of values: We shall be torn apart by this disparity of rhythm, this disparity of vibrations."
— Aleksandr Solzhenitsyn

Yes, I am here making a value judgement that a Realistic education is good, and a Skeptical education is bad, but that judgement is made based on my *knowing* the History of Ideas/History of Philosophy, and *knowing* the History of World Politics so I can see how the former has affected the latter. Most Pro-Choice, Neo-Marxist Identity Politics "Cancel Culture" ideologues and "social justice warriors" have neither a broad understanding of Philosophy nor History (nor Science, nor Logic . . .)

In fact, Professor Stephen Hicks, author of *Explaining Postmodernism: Skepticism and Socialism from Rousseau to Foucault*, having studied the origins and current state of Postmodernism, notes that the current (2nd/3rd generation) of Postmodernists is of lower intellectual quality. Naturally, since their skeptical ideology means they have never had the rigorous education the first generation had before they came to their erroneous conclusions.

" Nothing worthy can be built on a neglect of higher meanings and on a relativistic view of concepts and culture as a whole."
"The generation now coming out of Western schools is unable to distinguish good from bad. Even those words are unacceptable. This results in impaired thinking ability."
"... We have arrived at an intellectual chaos."
— Aleksandr Solzhenitsyn

The first generation of Postmodernists, well-educated themselves but becoming skeptical and relativistic, absurdly concluded there is no objective reality – so they do not need to take science, logic, rationality, nor the quest for objectivity seriously. So, their students *start off* not even taking science, logic, rationality, nor the quest for objectivity seriously. So, in Western universities, as Solzhenitsyn warned of the dangers of Relativism, you end up with Ph.D.s who do not even take science, logic, rationality, nor the quest for objectivity seriously. Ph.D.s who have not developed higher order thinking skill-sets themselves, who emphasize *feelings* instead of *thinking*; and *opinions* instead of *facts* (facts which they absurdly think do not exist or cannot be known anyways). Postmodernist philosophy means new professors promote emotionalism and (brainless) political activism instead of thinking (which the professors do not know how to do very well themselves). These next generation professors of less intellectual capacity and less intellectual honesty train the next generation after them for *a progressive devolution of intellectual quality*. We are seeing the result of radically skeptical Postmodernist philosophy over a few generations, and suffering the results in politicians who, because of being exposed to or explicitly trained in Postmodernist philosophy in universities, have, in a more vernacular term, "mush for brains." We are seeing and suffering the political activism of "social justice warriors" and politicians inspired and guided by those with high intellectual dishonesty and/or "mush for brains."

A big danger Professor Stephen Hicks notes is that Postmodernist professors who do not believe in any objective truth, only subjective opinion, are spreading their subjective opinions to their students *instead of training them to think for themselves,* instead of making sure they know the previous generations of thought, analyze them and make their own decisions as free thinkers. So, like Aleksandr Solzhenitsyn noticed and warned the West decades ago but the West did not listen, *the universities are becoming less and less truly educational*, and less and less relevant to real life – except for how relevant to real life it is that supposedly university-educated people (including politicians) now spout ultimately anti-democratic (and anti-scientific) ideologies (including but not limited to legal human-killing Pro-Choice ideology) which endanger both society and now Science and scholarship itself . . .

. . . So, if you claim that the Radically Skeptical stream of Philosophy is superior to or more correct than the Realistic stream of Philosophy, that means that deep down, in your unconsciously assumed philosophical worldview, you really do not know for certain that anything outside of your own mind even exists. That means, if you are correct, you therefore must have "just made up" this author, and your iPhone, or else you were deceived by some "evil demon" (as Descartes postulated) with nothing better to do than *deceive* you into sensing an objective reality with authors and iPhones, when "in fact" nothing outside your mind really exists. So, if you are correct that the Radically Skeptical stream of Philosophy is more accurate than Philosophical Realism which assumes the universe Science studies actually exists, then it ultimately *cannot really matter to you* what happens in World Politics, since to you none of that world/universe external to and independent of your mind actually exists anyway. So, *please get the hell out of politics.* Politics cannot actually matter to you if the world that engages in politics is not actually real, so please, on the chance that the rest of us actually exist, like we think we do, please, please get the hell out of politics. *Real people* have already died in the tens of millions from deep-down radical skeptic anti-scientific Pro-Choicers and Neo-Marxist Identity Politics "Cancel Culture" ideologues like you being politically active and trying to brainlessly make the "Red Square peg" of Marxism fit into the "round hole" of Reality, when it just does not fit. In the *Real World* all humans commonly perceive but which the rest of us (unlike you radical skeptics) assume is *real*, peaceful Human Rights advocates like this author can now be arrested and jailed for saying "killing humans is wrong because Human Rights are for All Humans" under totalitarian laws passed by intellectually dishonest (or "ideologically lobotomized") Pro-Choice legal human-killing Identity Politics ideologues like yourself, with an underlying radically skeptical *lack of grip on reality* and this has to stop. *Real people* will thank you for stopping, and you have plenty of good reason for doing so, as in the further *pensées* below . . .

. . . Skeptics grossly overstate the importance of the *limitations* of our human senses . . . The very limitations of our human senses are accounted for by Aristotelian Realism and the Scientific Method. As we observe discrepancies in our observations, we make new scientific theories to account for the data. We invent new procedures and new scientific instruments for collecting more data, and/or better quality data, all from *TRUSTING* our human senses and our observations of the Natural Universe, in order to come up with an even better scientific theory that better approximates objective reality. Yes, it is an approximation, but yes, we can learn more about it, which is why Science continues and gets more and more detailed and precise – according to Aristotelian Realist Principles not Cartesian Skeptical ones . . . all of the necessary assumptions of Science - and of Common Sense - are all inherited from or rooted in the Realist tradition back through Saint Thomas Aquinas and the Scholastic Tradition, all the way back to Aristotle . . . even the possibility of the occasional need for a new paradigm or theory to account for more, better observational data in the future of scientific enquiry is part of the Pure Sciences and the Modern Scientific Method as developed within the Scholastic (and Thomist) philosophical tradition in the European universities, firmly grounded in Aristotelian Realism . . .

. . . Atheism and Secularism are both ultimately and fundamentally *religious* philosophical positions with clear perspectives on "First Order Questions" (or "religious questions") of the nature of the universe and the meaning of human life – and how public political policy should be guided. Typically, Atheists and Secularists ridiculously claim that traditional theistic and (in the West) Judeo-Christian religious perspectives and values should have "no influence in the public sphere," even though it is Biblical, Judeo-Christian religious principles which include and uphold *The Foundational Principles of Human Rights and Democracy*, and even though the lack of these Judeo-Christian principles in all Atheist (usually Marxist) States has been direct cause of horrendous atrocities, and murders and genocides killing millions of humans. The typical Atheist and Secularist views on the big "First Order" questions, as shown in this author's books, are completely devoid of any significant Human Rights Education; and are based in *ignorance* of rather than any *knowledge* of the Human Rights History, the Science and Logic (and the History of Science and Logic) which helps identify *The Foundational Principles of Human Rights and Democracy* . . . But . . .

. . . The (devout Christian) scientists (Both Catholic, like Galileo, and Protestant, like Newton) who developed the Scientific Method, by doing so made up for the major weakness in Aristotle. Aristotle's articulations of the First Principles of Being or First Principles of Existence remain the solid foundation of all logic and science . . . However, when it came to articulating specific scientific theories to account for observed data, since Aristotle (grounded by Realism) basically started the entire endeavor of Science, he started with no collected scientific data at all, so of course not all of his theories to account for the (extremely limited) data he had access to were correct, we now know. But we know it *because* the scientific *process* Aristotle started makes detailed observations of Nature and theorizes about the data, abandoning older theories when more, newer, better data becomes available and reveals weaknesses in the older theories, requiring newer better theories be formulated to account for more and superior data. Theories which themselves will be modified or abandoned in the future, when more or better data is available. It would be silly to criticize Aristotle for being millennia later proven *wrong* about some of his specific biological theories in ancient times, when, unlike today's scientists, he had *no* collected data nor past thoughtful theorization to ground his initial scientific theories upon. But he gave us Science itself – including Science's ability to observe and correct weaknesses in past theories when new data becomes available. Aristotle's *First Principles of Being/Existence* – and of Science which studies existence – were and are rock-solid. But Aristotle, as effectively the very first Scientist of course did not start off with millennia of already-gathered scientific observations and insight like today's scientists do, "standing on the shoulders of giants" who have gone before them, as Sir Isaac Newton said. Newton who, with all the other (devoutly Christian) founders of Modern Science in the Scientific Revolution, were at last able to identify and overcome the one major weakness of Aristotle. Particularly, Aristotle lacked the later-developed Scientific Method. Aristotle's Science included little or no "experimentation" as we know it today; but only detailed observations of nature and rudimentary deeper investigations of nature like dissecting animals to "look and observe what is inside" as part of Aristotle's beginning the Science of Biology . . .

First Order Questions and Worldview: Why Is There Something Rather Than Nothing? Is Your Worldview Fundamentally Realist (and Scientific) or (Like Marxism's) Radically Skeptical (That Is, Out of Touch with or Denying Reality). Your Politics Follows Suit . . .

What it comes down to is that in attempting to answer deep First Order questions about the nature of existence, such as "where did the universe come from?" and "Why is there something and not nothing?," whether you are Atheist or Christian or anything in between, you are ultimately forced to assume that *something* has simply always existed or by its nature simply *cannot not exist*, whatever that *something* is. If to answer the question "where did the universe come from" you posit that the universe we humans experience our whole lives in was created and/or ordered by some superior being or god or gods (Science Fiction humorist Douglas Adams writes "The Jatravartid People of Viltvodle Six firmly believe that the entire universe was sneezed out of the nose of a being called The Great Green Arkleseizure"). This invites the obvious question, where did that superior being/god or gods/arkleseizure come from? With this kind of answer it is easy to fall into an absurd infinite regression which just begs the question or avoids the issue of the ultimate foundations of existence (the world was created by this which was created by that which was created by . . . *ad infinitum*).

To avoid infinite regression (and to avoid the demented *solipsism* which denies any existence outside of your own mind, in which case you may as well not bother with anything political at all because your mind just made up me and my book and any political parties you could vote for), and to give a serious answer to the question "where did the universe/existence as we know it come from," we in the end have to accept that *something* is pre-existent, *something* has just always existed or cannot not exist.

Just what is that *something*? Only two real options are forthcoming: Either *matter* (the material substance of which the physical universe that daily confronts us is made) is that which has simply always existed and cannot not exist; or *God* is that which has simply always existed and cannot not exist. Pantheism attempts to equate the two, suggesting that ultimately the material universe and everything in it (the planets and stars, any proposed intermediate pantheon of gods, your body and brain, the table you are sitting in, the air you breathe and the food you just ate) is God.

So, (unless he is a lonely solipsist who is only certain his own mind exists), the Atheist must ultimately choose to believe in *matter* as that which has simply always existed and cannot not exist. There is "stuff" or material, matter, which daily confronts our human senses with the physical existence of our planet, our bodies, the air we breathe. The Atheist, who believes in no God superior to or beyond the physical universe, ultimately must accept this *matter* as pre-existent, always just existing. But the Atheist cannot account for (nor predict from Atheist principles and assumptions) the supremely intricate and marvelous *order* of the physical universe, which is why Atheists had nothing whatsoever to do with the founding of Modern Science and the Modern Scientific Method. The Pantheist too, who just calls the material universe God, likewise cannot account for nor predict the wonderfully delicate and intricate order of the material universe, which is an *ordered cosmos* and not a *random chaos*. Which is why Modern Science never developed where Pantheistic (or Atheistic) religious conceptions of the universe of existence hold sway.

But the Christian (or Jew) is informed by the Judeo-Christian Bible that the material universe we humans live our whole lives in was both created and ordered by the pre-existent, intelligent and personal God who "in the beginning" of the created universe of space-time *already existed.* The Bible's first words are "In the beginning, God created the heavens and the earth" [that is, the universe](Genesis 1:1). God's constant and unending, eternal (timeless) existence is just assumed while describing the beginning and ordered fashioning of the material universe of space and time and matter which humans live in (note Modern Physics confirms the Bible's presentation of time itself as part of the created order of the universe, which therefore God's existence is not subject to, but is Eternal or timeless). God later in the Bible reveals Himself as "I AM," and the Bible's Covenant Name for God is derived from the Hebrew for the verb "To Be," by name thus establishing God as "He who exists;" Being itself, the Absolute Being/Existence on whom all other ("contingent") being (including the created universe) depends for its existence - and for its intricate *order*.

The second verse of the Bible (Genesis 1:2) indicates that the created universe was initially "formless," and proceeds to poetically describe (in ways the Bible's non-scientific original readers could understand) God giving *form* and *order* to that initially "formless" or chaotic matter of the created universe. The Christian (or Jew) accepts *God* instead of mere formless matter as *that which has simply always existed and cannot not exist.* In doing so, the Christian (or Jew) both accounts for the universe's order and in fact predicts that the created material universe must be an *ordered cosmos*, not a *random* and undirected *chaos.* Thus, the Christian, the Jew, and those influenced by Biblical Judaism and Christianity are motivated to look for *patterns* of order, the signs of an *ordering intelligence or designer*, when looking at nature. In particular, the Socratic School Greeks who well knew the Jewish Bible/Christian Old Testament because they respected the older Hebrew/Jewish culture's *Wisdom* (Biblical Jewish King Solomon's wisdom was legendary), got from the earlier Judeo-Christian Scriptures their key notion that the universe of Nature is an *ordered cosmos* and NOT a *random chaos* - and for this reason they started looking at nature for discernible patterns of *intelligent order* and found them, becoming the earliest recognized scientists (Aristotle articulating the *First Principles of Being/Existence* which are foundational to all Western Logic and Science).

Aristotle's First Principles of Being describe the fundamental orderliness (not randomness) of the universe. Aristotle noted in his day that people who disagreed with him were forced by the (ordered and structured) nature of *Reality*, forced by the very nature of the universe to behave *as if he was right* anyway. As indeed Atheists and Postmodernists today, if they want to live and not die stupidly, are still forced to behave as if the universe is highly structured and (intelligently) ordered, no matter how much they try to claim the universe and human life is an (ultimately meaningless) product of undirected, random chance. Which is an Atheistic belief which has justified all manner of atrocities, such as the *Holodomor* Genocide perpetrated by the Atheist Soviets upon my Ukrainian ethnic group. If human beings are ultimately just random sacks of bio-chemicals, then it truly does not matter how one random sack of chemicals treats another, and morality is indeed *relative*, as Atheists claim. Moral relativists of course are left with no mentally consistent way of saying that Hitler or Stalin or Mao – influenced by German Atheist philosophers Friedrich Nietzsche or Karl Marx – were absolutely *wrong* to kill many millions of humans as they each attempted to "make the world a better place" according to their own estimation, or "creating their own morality," as Nietzsche advocated, without reference to the (Judeo-Christian) Traditional Western Values which underlie all Human Rights and Democratic Freedoms.

The Judeo-Christian passionate and academic search for Truth in all its forms led to Alexander the Great (who studied under Aristotle) putting the Jews in charge of the great Library at Alexandria in Egypt (one of the great cities Alexander named after himself). Both Alexandria in Egypt and Antioch in Syria would house early great Christian schools of higher learning, and the modern university system itself literally grew out of the medieval Christian cathedral schools. At the Christian universities of Christian Europe (and only there) the modern Pure Sciences and Modern Scientific Method were born - developed by centuries of Christians (Catholic and later Protestant as well) working from a Biblical worldview and Biblical *First Principles* of the universe as an intelligently designed, *ordered cosmos*, not a random and undirected, chaotic universe. In every century from the 11th to the 20th, Catholic Christian priests were among the greatest scientists on the cutting edge of scientific discovery, often founding whole branches of the Natural Sciences. A Catholic Christian priest (the Reverend Monsignor Georges Lemaître) was even the co-founder of the 20th Century Big Bang Theory which still dominates the scientific field of Cosmology. So, next time you hear an Atheist say that Atheism has anything at all to do with Science, or claim that Christian religious faith is somehow against or incompatible with Science, remember that such Atheists are just intellectually dishonest people spouting their gross ignorance and lack of education. So uneducated and dishonest they are also either clueless about, or deceptively hiding, the fact that Atheists like them running governments have consistently created most of the most horrific and oppressive and murderous totalitarian States of all history. Such as Atheist Soviet Russia, which was first to legalize abortion and thereby legally eradicate the *Inherent Human Right to Live* which is essential to Human Rights and freedoms (before legalizing the genocide of an estimated 7-10 million of this author's ethnic group). One quarter of Cambodia died under Atheist Marxist policies, and atrocities abound in every Atheist Marxist State, which typically have legal abortion and do not believe *killing humans is wrong.* You have to *not know a lot* to consciously choose an Atheist and/or a Pro-Choice abortion position. That is why this author, to save Human Rights and Free Democracy for my self (now subject to arrest for saying *killing humans is wrong*), my own children and grandchildren and everyone else's, has developed (and is still developing) this HUMAN RIGHTS EDUCATION FOR LASTING FREE DEMOCRACY, and has proclaimed THE THINKING REVOLUTION in my first professionally published book, *Pro-Life Equals Pro-Democracy* (unedited as it is because I cannot think and write near as fast as today's Pro-Choice, Neo-Marxist Identity Politics "Cancel Culture" politicians can unthinkingly "cancel" Free Speech and dismantle Democracy without a clue what they are doing).

This author is happy to have intelligent discussion with intellectually honest Atheists who may be Atheist simply due to *ignorance* of many of the facts collected in this author's HUMAN RIGHTS EDUCATION FOR LASTING FREE DEMOCRACY book series. More and more knowledgeable and honest Atheists, in response to current accelerating attacks on Freedom of Speech and other traditional democratic freedoms, have been lately admitting that Christianity may be much more important, even more *vitally necessary,* to the survival and preservation of Western Civilization than they realized. Atheist Historian Tom Holland recently wrote the book *Dominion: How the Christian Revolution Remade the World*, precisely demonstrating this.

But unfortunately, a very large number of ignorant and intellectually dishonest Atheists know and care nothing of the real history and real philosophical foundations of Science, as they bluster their condescending "Atheistic Flatulence" that insults and belittles religious believers as they pretend Science, which could never have started from Atheist principles, somehow belongs to them. These, unfortunately the more common kind of Atheists, are so good at "farting with their brains" this insubstantial "Atheistic Flatulence" that they have given birth to equally unpleasant and insubstantial Secularism, which likewise rejects the Christian heritage of the West and replaces it, usually, with Atheist Relativism and/or Moral Relativism, which is ultimately rooted in the Radical Skepticism which tends to separate humans from any solid base in Reality. Secularism has now taken us to the brink of losing our Human Rights and Democratic Freedoms which depend upon Christian principles. Because Secularism rests on the Atheist Moral Relativism which Solzhenitsyn, after living in the (genocidal) first State built on Atheist principles, noted results in "impaired thinking ability." Every later State built on Atheist principles likewise quickly becoming murderous and genocidal...

. . . This author enjoyed, on Professor Stephen Hicks' website, a cartoon in which a child in pajamas comes into his parents' bedroom and says, "Mom, Dad, there's a Moral Relativist under my bed . . ." In the next panel, a close-up of the child's terrified face, exclaiming, *"they're capable of anything . . ."* ("No more reading philosophy before bed for you, young man . . ."). Yet it is no joke. The biggest real *monsters* humanity has ever known were the Atheist Moral Relativists Stalin and Mao, each of them killing more millions of humans than Hitler's Nazis, as in their morally relative way they each did their best "to make the world a better place" by, in the USSR and China, "attempting to implement a Marxist egalitarian utopia" and "establish a Socialist State." Since Relativists "make their own truth," Socialists can easily ignore and deny the facts of Marxist genocides and millions of murders, and so the "enormous number" of Western Atheists, Marxists and Socialists Solzhenitsyn pointed out, who made sure Marxism would not get the deservedly bad reputation Nazism got, have created the current unstable and polarized political situation. Where millions of Atheists and Secularists in America and the rest of the West (who are usually also "Pro-Choice-to-Kill-Humans" ideologues who follow the Marxist precedent of legal abortion) are in ignorance blithely attempting to "make the world a better place" through Neo-Marxist Identity Politics which, bifurcating all societies with Marxist "oppressed" and "privileged/oppressor" labels, is just as inherently divisive and antagonistic as classic Marxism and cannot possibly serve the Common Good of all humanity (which must be based instead on the *Equal Human Preciousness without exception, which governments are obligated to protect*, which is part of *The Foundational Principles of Human Rights and Democracy* identified from History, Science, and Logic in this book). Marxist (and Neo-Marxist) ideology is all rooted firmly in Atheism and Radical Skepticism which denies or radically doubts *Reality* itself, and is no substitute, of course, for the Traditional Western Values and principles which actually undergird all Human Rights and Free Democracy in the West. Yet Atheists and Secularists with their subjective Relativism which is *out of touch with objective Reality* keep trying to reshape the world according to Atheist Marxist principles (or the newer "Identity Politics" variant of them).

Clearly, Solzhenitsyn's work of exposing the ideological and practical evils of Marxism to help end it remains unfinished – and this author's book *Pro-Life Equals Pro-Democracy*, as a kind of "Sequel" to Solzhenitsyn's *The Gulag Archipelago*, following up on what that "enormous number" of Western Marxists Solzhenitsyn warned us about have been up to since, hopes to help to truly finish Solzhenitsyn's important work. Solzhenitsyn's exposé of Marxist evil in the USSR did much to facilitate the Soviet Union's demise in 1991, which only Solzhenitsyn had predicted. But the West failed to heed his warnings about how the Marxists and Marxist-influenced in the West were shaping the West for a totalitarian Marxist future through controlling the "fashionableness" of just what gets reported in Western news and taught in Western schools and universities. Solzhenitsyn's *The Gulag Archipelago*, by exposing Soviet atrocities and how they were rooted in Marxist ideology itself (they were not Stalinist deviations) indeed made it much harder for Western Socialists to openly admire the Marxist Soviet Union as they had previously.

"But there was never any such thing as Stalinism. It was contrived by Khrushchev and his group in order to blame all the characteristic traits and principal defects of Communism on Stalin—it was a very effective move. But in reality Lenin [in faithful interpretation of Marx] had managed to give shape to all the main features before Stalin came to power."
— *Aleksandr Solzhenitsyn*

But Marx himself in his 19th Century *Communist Manifesto* foresaw that Marxism in future would *adjust and change* for new situations. And indeed, just like the (very) deadly virus that Marxism is, Marxism has "mutated" and "morphed" into new forms just as seductively tempting and insidiously deadly but harder to spot, through radically skeptical Postmodernism, developed by Marxists to protect Marxism from facts, and Western Marxism is alive and well today through Neo-Marxist Identity Politics which maintains the whole approach and character of classic Marxism by reinterpreting all of history, just as Marx did, and dividing all societies past and present into groups labelled "oppressed" and "privileged/oppressor." Ultimately in order to create enough resentment and hatred between groups to create the political instability necessary to take over and *impose* Marxist ideals upon everyone. Western Marxism is alive and well today also through Neo-Marxist "Cancel Culture" which maintains the whole approach and character of classic totalitarian Marxism by *controlling society by controlling which voices and which information gets heard.*

Marx himself knew that his Marxist utopian vision was so radical it would need to be *forced* upon people at first. Eliminating personal property and wealth in favor of State control of resources (as Socialists still seek to do) and doing away with the Traditional Family, which Marx mocked as much as some of today's Neo-Marxist Identity Politics ideologues do, as they too try to rewrite what a human family is. Without any reference to the Science of Biology, which concurs that following Traditional Western (Judeo-Christian) Sexual Values of *sex reserved for marriage* (also the universal, cross-cultural norm for sexual relations throughout history) gives the *best chance* that the next generation of human children naturally produced by the lifetime-committed married sex partners will be raised to emotionally and physically healthy human maturity in a *stable, loving human family* which is the building block of a *stable, loving human society.* But the radically skeptical Atheist Relativism inherent in all forms of Marxism has no use for facts or Science . . .

[A Selection of more pensées follow . . .]

. . .

Science Itself, Not "Just" Free Democracy, Is Now Under Threat (in Western Universities Long Compromised by Marxism as Aleksandr Solzhenitsyn – Who Knew the Signs of Marxism Better than Anyone – Repeatedly Warned the West).
Professor Jordan Peterson Rings the Alarm Bell: "The Activists are Now Stalking the Hard Scientists . . . I Have Watched The Universities Of The Western World Devour Themselves In A Myriad Of Fatal Errors Over The Last Two Decades, And Take Little Pleasure In Observing The Inevitable Unfold . . . *Research Prowess Is No Longer as Important as Willingness to Mouth The Appalling Commonplaces Of Political Correctness In The Hallowed Corridors Of Academe . . .* **Wake up, [Scientists]: Your Famous Immunity To Political Concerns Will Not Protect You Against What Is Headed Your Way Fast Over The Next Five Or So Years . . ."[14]**

. . .

---

[14] https://nationalpost.com/opinion/jordan-peterson-the-activists-are-now-stalking-the-hard-scientists#main-content , accessed July 5, 2020.

185

. . . Atheism and Secularism (and the Relativism and Marxism which influences them) are ultimately religious worldviews requiring a "Leap of Faith" - and are a leap not near as reasonable to take as Christianity, since Christians developed Modern Science in the Christian universities of Christian Europe, working logically from a Christian worldview and from First Principles the West learned from the Bible. Christian Pro-Life Principles also undergird all Human Rights and Free Democracy . . .

. . . Have you heard that "all religions are equal"? This is an Atheist dogma. What it really means is that (from the Atheist perspective), all (traditional, theistic) religions are equally *wrong*; equally *irrelevant to modern life.* While their own (non-theistic, a-theistic) answer to the big First Order or "religious" questions is to believe (*in religious faith not proof*) in the non-existence of any intelligent Orderer of the universe or Creator God. Even though this leaves Atheists with no explanation for the fantastically intricate *order* in the material universe, magnificent and intricate *order* which scientists were only motivated to look for in the first place *because of their "First Principles" assumption* (coming to the ancient Greek scientists from the Jewish Bible, Christian Old Testament, and developed into Modern Science and the Modern Scientific Method by devout Christians at the Christian universities of Christian Europe) that the universe is an *intelligently ordered cosmos*, and NOT a fundamentally *random* and undirected *chaos.* In any case, only someone severely uneducated or unintelligent would ever claim "all religions are equal." All religions (including the ultimately religious philosophical position of Atheism, which believes on faith not proof in the non-existence of God) are manifestly NOT equal, above all *not equal* in *compatibility* with the *Foundational Principles of Human Rights and Democracy.* Which come from Christianity, so Christianity is (by far) the religious worldview *most* consistent with Human Rights and Free Democracy (and most consistent with *Science*), while Atheism is the (ultimately religious) worldview that is among the very *least* compatible with either Human Rights, or Free Democracy, or Science. Atheist (usually Marxist) governments have proven time and time again they are among the most oppressive and murderous governments history has ever known, and logically so, since Atheist Moral Relativists can accept no human-loving God of Christianity to set any absolute standards for human behavior, nor absolute moral principles, such as *killing humans is wrong*; *equal human preciousness*; *Human Rights;* or any of the (Christian) *Foundational Principles of Human Rights and Democracy.* Also, no Atheists were involved in the founding of Modern Science because those who believe in no ordering intelligence for the universe have no motivation to search for *patterns of order* . . .

" Nothing worthy can be built on a neglect of higher meanings and on a relativistic view of concepts and culture as a whole."
"The generation now coming out of Western schools is unable to distinguish good from bad. Even those words are unacceptable. This results in impaired thinking ability."
". . . We have arrived at an intellectual chaos."
— Aleksandr Solzhenitsyn

CHAPTER 3: PHILOSOPHY

♦

"Such as it is, the press has become the greatest power within the Western World, more powerful than the legislature, the executive and judiciary. One would like to ask; by whom has it been elected and to whom is it responsible?"
— Aleksandr Solzhenitsyn

Once Solzhenitsyn was out of the oppressive Soviet Union and in the "Free West," living in the U.S. for 18 years, he noticed and pointed out that the West was headed, if more slowly, in the same direction as the Marxist Soviet Union (towards totalitarianism), only by a different route. Solzhenitsyn even noticed and pointed out how the censorship of news and ideas which was essential to totalitarian Soviet Socialism and Communism just found a new, more subtle and insidious expression in the West:

"Without any censorship, in the West fashionable trends of thought and ideas are carefully separated from those which are not fashionable; nothing is forbidden, but what is not fashionable will hardly ever find its way into periodicals or books or be heard in colleges. Legally your researchers are free, but they are conditioned by the fashion of the day."
— Aleksandr Solzhenitsyn

Those intellectually dishonest (or "ideologically lobotomized") Western, Soviet-sympathizing (often Atheist) intellectuals and Marxist ideologues (with "impaired thinking ability" from philosophical "relativism" Solzhenitsyn spoke of) **never left the "Free West."** Instead, still full of *denial* of all the well-established human-killing evil that has consistently come from any attempts to put Relativist Atheist Marxist Socialist ideology into practice on the State level, they became professors at Western universities teaching Westerners (as Solzhenitsyn indicated in 1983) *to hate their own society* (especially through Neo-Marxist Identity Politics) and they have since raised up generations of Western leaders who have for decades been shuffling off the trappings of Traditional Western Values and Western Christian Civilization (including the philosophical *Realism not Relativism* which grounds Science) on which Human Rights and Free Democracy were historically and logically built. Which is why this author's Prime Minister of a supposed democracy openly admires Marxist Communist China, which has no religious freedom and forced abortions; and which is why this author can now be arrested and imprisoned in my country for promoting *Equal Human Rights for All Humans* anywhere near where humans are being legally killed, following the 1920 Marxist Soviet Socialist/Communist precedent of legal human-killing by abortion.

The now "Pro-Choice Left" today have been formed by for decades witlessly imbibing ultimately anti-democratic and anti-human *extremist* Leftist ideology at Western universities, as well as there imbibing anti-scientific Postmodernist philosophy which demently denies any *objective facts* – Postmodernism was developed by Marxists to protect Marxism from the overwhelming *objective facts* that Marxism/ Socialism, which looks very nice on paper, is fundamentally *unrealistic* and does not work at all in practice, but always results in oppressive totalitarian States murdering millions. Thanks to the centuries-old philosophical errors ultimately resulting in today's Pro-Choice Extremist Left also having *very little grip* on *scientific, objective Reality*. Being thus "ideologically lobotomized" and *divorced from Reality* by a bad underlying philosophical worldview perhaps explains why Pro-Choicers often present themselves as so unintelligent – or so wilfully, culpably unintelligent – stupidity by *choice* – that they do not even "get" the science that preborn humans are humans and thus abortion kills humans; nor do they "get" the logic that to deny preborn humans any *Inherent Human Rights* through legal abortion is to deny ourselves any *Inherent Human Rights*, since all of us began our human existence as preborn humans. There is no way to beat the perfectly scientifically sound logical syllogism *All humans have Human Rights; Preborn humans are humans. Therefore, preborn humans have Human Rights.* But neither facts, nor science, nor logic mean anything to unthinking relativistic Pro-Choice bigots with *ideology instead of education.*

The famous journalist Malcolm Muggeridge before his death insightfully commented upon this (consciously or unconsciously) chosen philosophy yielding "imbecility," in the quotation below.

British journalist Muggeridge had himself been such a supporter of Socialism that when young he actually went to live in the Union of Soviet Socialist Republics, excited to live in the world's first Socialist State. Until while there he witnessed the Soviet *Holodomor* Genocide perpetrated in Ukraine first-hand, tried to report on it, and found himself attacked, discredited, and fired by the Western (Socialist-influenced) journalistic establishment, which actually gave the Pulitzer Prize for journalism to his fellow British (Socialist) journalist Walter Duranty, who denied and helped cover up the genocide, even though he privately admitted he knew about the millions of deaths under Soviet policies. Like the former Marxist Socialist and former Soviet Red Army captain, historian Aleksandr Solzhenitsyn (who was exiled to the West for later exposing Soviet terrors in his book *The Gulag Archipelago*), formerly Socialist Malcolm Muggeridge also saw the Marxist, Socialist corruption of Western institutions (and Science itself, according to Marxist-developed anti-scientific Postmodernism) steadily increase, such that before his death in 1990 he predicted:

So the final conclusion [will] surely be that whereas other civilizations have been brought down by attacks of barbarians from without, ours had the unique distinction of training its own destroyers at its own educational institutions, and then providing them with facilities for propagating their destructive ideology far and wide, all at the public expense. Thus did Western Man decide to abolish himself... himself blowing the trumpet that brought the walls of his own city tumbling down, and having convinced himself that he was too numerous, labored with pill and scalpel and syringe to make himself fewer. Until at last, having educated himself into imbecility, and polluted and drugged himself into stupefaction, he keeled over--a weary, battered old brontosaurus – and became extinct.

CHAPTER 3: PHILOSOPHY

– Malcolm Muggeridge[15]

In the "drugged . . . into stupefaction" part the insightful Muggeridge correctly predicted the recent Western trend in many countries (including this author's) to legalize psychoactive drugs like marijuana, long proven to lead to even harder drug use (and there are even new movements to legalize all illegal mind-affecting drugs). Nothing could be more supportive of an eventual totalitarian takeover of the West than dulling the minds of citizens with drugs so they do not notice (or care) how their democratic freedoms are shrinking under Pro-Choice Extremist Left governments. In fact, this trend just makes it more disturbingly obvious how prophetic was Aldous Huxley's 1932 novel *Brave New World* about a dystopian future. While the USSR, the world's first Socialist State, a totalitarian State which had already legalized abortion, thus starting to control human reproduction in 1920, had already started the 1932-33 *Holodomor* Genocide killing millions of this author's ethnic heritage, Huxley published a dystopian novel describing a future totalitarian world government which controlled human reproduction and kept the masses of humans distracted from realizing how *not free* they were by constant movies and entertainment, encouraging unbridled sexuality, and dulling their minds with drugs. Sound familiar? Today's West is getting closer and closer to Huxley's dystopian totalitarian vision of the future!

Journalist Malcolm Muggeridge witnessed the 1932 *Holodomor* Genocide first-hand while Huxley's prophetic book was published, and personally suffered the totalitarian censorship of the news in support of the totalitarian Soviet State not by Soviet, but by *Western* Marxists and Socialists! And, seeing the growth of Marxist thinking subverting the West ever since, before he died he wrote the West was indeed "training its own destroyers at its own educational institutions, and then providing them with facilities for propagating their destructive ideology far and wide, all at the public expense," Westerners thus "educating themselves into imbecility" — which is so easy to see now with the wide proliferation of anti-scientific Postmodernist thinking developed by Marxists like Jacques Derrida in order to protect Marxism from facts.

Having so "educated themselves into imbecility" as Muggeridge noticed; having developed such an "impaired thinking ability" from relativist philosophy as Solzhenitsyn described, today's legal-human-killing Pro-Choice Leftists do not even realize that the only reason they on the Left (including the "Liberal" media) are sometimes tempted to call outspoken people on the Right "far-Right," or even extremist "Nazis" is because their Pro-Life opponents (including U.S. President Trump who ran on a Pro-Life platform which he has consistently been true to) **only** *look* **"extremely" far to the Right of them – from their vantage point firmly planted on the Pro-Choice, legal human-killing following Soviet Marxist precedent,** *Extremist Left.*

---

[15] https://www.goodreads.com/book/show/5622444-vintage-muggeridge, accessed August 25, 2020.

Some Political Insights Following from The Above
Philosophical "Pensées":
Bifurcated, Incompatible Underlying Philosophical Worldviews Lead Ultimately to Today's Polarized Politics Including the Abortion Debate (The Equal Human Rights for All Humans Debate)

The Traditional Western (Judeo-Christian) Pro-Life Family Values Which Include and Support *The Foundational Principles of Human Rights and Democracy* identified from Science, Logic, and Human Rights History in *Pro-Life Equals Pro-Democracy* are Rooted in the Very Same Philosophical Stream of (Aristotelian and Scholastic) Philosophical *Realism* as Is Science, Logic and Technology — *Realism* Which Accepts the *Objective Reality* of the Physical Universe We Humans All Commonly Perceive and Daily Interact With, and Which Science Studies, Producing *Technology* from What Science Learns About *Objective Reality.*

In Contrast, Today's Pro-Choice, Neo-Marxist Identity Politics "Cancel Culture" and Postmodernist-influenced Politicians and Political Parties are All Rooted in the Anti-Scientific Philosophical Stream of (Cartesian and Postmodernist) Philosophical *Radical Skepticism* Which Denies or Radically Doubts There Even Is Any Knowable Objective Reality Outside of Any Individual Subject's Own Mind. An Ultimately *Diseased* And Hypocritical View of *Reality Itself* Which (While Hypocritically Staying Alive by Accepting Reality) in Philosophy and Politics Denies Any *Objective Facts Which Might Guide Their Politics*, Leaving Only *Subjective Feelings and Opinions* and in Some the Deranged Beliefs People Can "Create Their Own Reality" and "Create Their Own Morality" (The Latter as Atheist Relativist Nietzsche promoted, influencing the Nazis; the Nuremberg Trials of the Nazis were essentially the Free West's judgement for *Realism* over *Relativism* as Necessary for Human Safety, Just as *Realism* over *Relativism* is Necessary for Science) — Today's Pro-Choice, Neo-Marxist Identity Politics "Cancel Culture" Politicians are Rooted in this Very Same Anti-Scientific Stream of Radical Philosophical Skepticism Which (in the Really Existing Universe) Has Given the World Mentally Deranged *Solipsism* (Nothing Exists for Sure Outside Your Mind) and *Marxism's Many Tens of Millions of Murders (the First Ten Million of this Author's Ethnic Group)* in Persistent Denial of The *Reality* that *Unrealistic* Marxist Principles *Do Not Work in the Really Existing World.*

(Marxists, of Course, Were the First Group Murderously Deranged and Divorced from Reality Enough to Legalize Human-Killing Abortion, in 1920, Before Legalizing Genocide.)

"Atheist teachers in the West are bringing up a younger generation in a spirit of hatred of their own society ... [they say] why should one refrain from burning hatred, whatever its basis—race, class, or ideology? Such hatred is in fact corroding many hearts today.

This eager fanning of the flames of hatred is becoming the mark of today's free world.
Indeed, the broader the personal freedoms are, the higher the level of prosperity or even of
abundance—the more vehement, paradoxically, does this blind hatred become . . .
This deliberately nurtured hatred then spreads to all that is alive, to life itself . . .
— Aleksandr Solzhenitsyn

But Skeptics and Relativists (the two always go together), no matter how much they deep down doubt or deny any external objective reality exists (making the existence of anything, including moral values like "killing humans is wrong," *subjective*, and thus "relative" to each individual subject), *always find themselves still stuck in the same commonly-experienced world and universe with the rest of us, and with scientists, who accept as REAL our common human experience of the world, which even enables you, the reader, to read this book and understand it.* Regardless of Relativist notions (rooted in Skepticism that the universe we commonly perceive even really exists at all) that you can "make your own Reality" and "make your own Morality," Relativists still, just like all of us who think the world we daily interact with is *Real*, are daily confronted with the same sense data (that the sun rises in the morning and sets in the evening every day, for Relativists as much as for Realists). Skeptic and Realist alike are forced by the nature of Reality and the nature of our physical senses that put us into *contact* with it, to actually live in the Real World as it is, which Science studies to learn more about it, occasionally making discoveries which later enable clever humans to invent new technologies which can indeed transform our world and the precise way we live our lives. But technological transformations of the world only come from rigorously and logically studying its *Reality,* not from denying or doubting it. Every Skeptic and Relativist stays alive daily only by using Common Sense that assumes the world is *real.* The universe is *real,* therefore, fire and traffic and cliffs are dangerous, and we cannot "make our own reality" wherein these are not dangerous, so we must concede to the common human sensual experience of reality just to stay alive. And it is *not reasonable* skepticism, but *radical* Skepticism, even truly *demented* Skepticism, very like a mental illness which makes us incapable of living in the world and requiring medical care to keep us alive, to not trust that our senses do in fact put humans in contact with a REAL universe external to and independent of our own minds, as Science and Common Sense assume. The only way to "make your own reality" is to reject the one that daily confronts your senses and retreat into madness, insanity; and the only way to avoid a stupid death in this case is to let the medical staff (trained in the real Sciences of Medicine and Psychiatry) take care of you, since you can no longer do it yourself. Radical Skepticism and the Relativism flowing from it is not a way to live, it is a way to die.

Political change can happen in the Real World, but healthy political change can only happen if it is rooted in fundamental, philosophical *Realism* which (scientifically, and grounded in Common Sense) takes the universe of Reality as it is and works within its *real* constraints. Sophisticated but *unrealistic* Marxism which has murdered many millions has resulted from politics rooted in the philosophically Skeptical, Atheistic, Relativistic stream of "Modern Philosophy" since Descartes . . .

Descartes unhinged Western Philosophy from its scientific grounding in Aristotelian and Scholastic *Realism* only inadvertently. He was a good Catholic

Christian who did not foresee the damage and genocides which would result. Descartes escaped radical skepticism himself, but, since our bad ideas can take on a life of their own, he still inadvertently introduced radical Cartesian Skepticism into Western Philosophy, the "Cartesian Split" which foolishly prioritized *thought* over *existence* when Descartes erroneously stated, "I think, *therefore* I am." Following in this philosophical stream, Skeptic German Atheist Relativist Nietzsche promoted the Relativist notion that you can "make your own morality" (a "Master Morality"), later influencing and enabling Hitler's Nazis to run Germany and make its laws from a new Moral Code which included legal racist genocide mass murders in support of a German "Master Race." **Philosophically speaking, Nuremberg later was at base a Trial of *Realism* passing official judgment over *Relativism*, because after Nazi Germany the Free World realized the *Real World* could not afford another Nazi Germany, another State run by Morally Relativistic ideology. The Nuremberg War Crimes Trials of the Nazis assumed and helped us clarify that even though all the atrocities of Nazi Germany were technically *legal*, for the future safety of all humanity, which cannot afford another Nazi Germany, any "sovereign country's" laws are still subject to certain minimal principles which even International Law must formally recognize (not create), principles we now call *Human Rights*, which were in fact formally clarified in the new United Nations' *Universal Declaration of Human Rights*, produced in 1948, while the Nuremberg Trials were still going on.** The same year the Nuremberg Trials called legal abortion in Nazi Germany a "crime against humanity" along with all the other many Nazi crimes against humanity which equally denied Equal Human Rights to some humans. **The Nuremberg War Crimes Trials established that for world human safety, the excuses "it was legal in my country" and "I was just following orders," which in most cases mitigate personal responsibility, did not, could not and must not mitigate responsibility for all the horrors in Nazi Germany that the Nazis led but in which the people participated or collaborated (or at least allowed to happen without resisting, even many otherwise good people,** which is why Professor Jordan Peterson reminds us, "the lesson of World War II: You are the Nazi." Solzhenitsyn confirms, "The battleline between good and evil runs through the heart of every man"). The Nuremberg War Crimes Trials established that these minimal political principles for governing humans we now call *Human Rights*, which are not given by any government and *so cannot be legislated away by any government*, of course imply *Human Responsibilities* to recognize those Human Rights in all other humans (and protect them where they are threatened).

Thus, the Nuremberg War Crimes Trials legitimately prosecuted key figures in Nazi Germany who led or greatly facilitated the mass murders, even though such mass murder was "legal" in Nazi Germany, because these people had *criminally neglected* their *Human Responsibilities* to recognize and protect Human Rights in other humans. Hence, not just the Nazi government leadership, but judges, doctors (especially abortionists), businessmen and others in positions of authority who particularly promoted and facilitated the Nazi crimes against humanity were put on trial at Nuremberg. Businessmen who fulfilled Nazi government contracts for customized equipment with no purpose but to kill large numbers of humans quickly, could not claim they were merely "doing business for the government" in building and supplying the Nazis with instruments of mass murder . . .

The Logical Fallacy of *Invalid Appeal to Authority.*

This is About the Only *Logical Fallacy* in a Logic Textbook Which the Pro-Choice Legal Human-Killing Abortion *Extremist Left* Does *Not* Typically Use to Dishonestly "Defend" Legal Abortion Because They Cannot Find Any Authority Stupid Enough to Claim Abortion is Objectively, Scientifically Good for *Any* of the Humans Involved in It . . .

. . . But The Pro-Choice Neo-Marxist Left Use it to Dishonestly "Defend" Many of Their Other Political Positions; And They Use this Intellectually Dishonest Logical Fallacy to Invalidly and Incorrectly Vilify Anyone Who Disagrees with Them As Somehow "Unscientific" Just for Having a Different Opinion than Themselves, on Topics on Which There is Disagreement Even Among Qualified Experts and Scientists and *Therefore a Non-Expert Citing An Expert Who Happens To Agree with Them Does Not Settle the Issue, Since Qualified Experts Themselves Disagree.* The Marxist-Influenced Western Mainstream Media Which Solzhenitsyn Warned the West About Frequently Support Western Pro-Choice, Neo-Marxist Totalitarian-Oriented Governments in Using the Logical Fallacy of *Invalid Appeal to Authority* by Mostly or Exclusively Reporting on Experts Who Happen to Agree with (or Literally Work For) the Marxist-Influenced Government, While Not Reporting on (and Even Deleting from YouTube!) Experts – Even Large Numbers of Experts and Scientists – Who Disagree with Government Policies – *Deliberately and Dishonestly Creating the False Notion* that "Science" Somehow Backs Up the (Relativist, Marxist-Influenced) Government's Policies [Update: including Coronavirus Pandemic policies], When in Fact the Science Concerning the Policy in Question is Not at All Settled . . .

. . . Unscientific, Relativist politicians and bureaucrats thus blithely make decisions affecting the very health of citizens and their precious children which *ignore or pretends solid scientific evidence against their decision does not even exist.*

[Update: This is becoming increasingly obvious in the case of long-continuing oppressive government "Coronavirus" lockdowns which destroy small businesses and make people dependent upon the centralized government (which supports the centralized Marxist "Great Reset"); and increasingly oppressive mask-wearing mandates during the now long-extended Coronavirus Pandemic, while these governments do not even consider and simply *pretend there is no* Great Barrington Declaration, drafted by world-class infectious disease epidemiologists and public health scientists, and, at time of writing signed by 13,796 (and counting) other medical scientists and 41,890 (and counting) doctors and other medical practitioners. The medical scientist signatures are followed up and vetted, so just which universities or medical institutes these medical scientists work for is verified. This is hugely important medical testimony any *healthy* democracy would seriously consider before ever considering current policies that drastically restrict so many normal democratic freedoms and civil liberties – and destroy the world economy *in order to make people desperate enough* to allow the Neo-Marxists to try their Relativist Marxist "Great Reset."]

Unscientific, Relativist politicians and bureaucrats thus blithely make decisions affecting the very health of citizens and their precious children which *ignore or pretends solid scientific evidence against their decision does not even exist.*

Why? *Because to skeptical philosophical Relativists*, like Pro-Choice politicians, all they need to do is *merely make the claim* that their position is superior, and not actually back it up with facts, well-established facts or otherwise, ultimately *because they do not believe in any objective facts*, but only in subjective feelings and opinions (ultimately because deep down, following the (temporary for him) radical Skepticism of Descartes, they cannot really be *certain* anyone else than themselves even *exists*, so why negotiate with or concede to others of differing opinions? Descartes himself escaped the radical consequences of the Radical Skepticism he unleashed in the world, but his bad idea still haunts and threatens Western Civilization) . . .

. . . Such Relativism is why, as this author has observed, really committed Pro-Choice ideologues may pretend to be intelligent and try to back up their position, but without any commitment to reason or logic or science or facts at all. **Genuinely intelligent and intellectually honest people, who are not "ideologically lobotomized," can be convinced by facts, reason, logic to change their position. But once a committed Pro-Choice ideologue realizes, while in argument with a knowledgeable, intelligent person such as this author and Human Rights scholar, that all the facts of Human Rights History, Science and Logic do not support their Pro-Choice position, and that all their typical arguments for legal abortion are *logical fallacies* (as demonstrated in this book), instead of (with intellectual honesty) changing their position to Pro-Life, they suddenly retreat completely into unintelligent Relativism and claim the Abortion Debate (The Equal Human Rights for All Humans Debate) is *just a matter of subjective opinion*, such that their (uneducated and illogical) Pro-Choice opinion is just as valid as my (highly educated and logical) Pro-Life opinion**. "Well, that's true for *you*, this [contradictory position] is true for *me*." Because to Skeptics and Relativists, there is no objective truth, nor objective facts of any kind. But by so easily accepting such *contradiction* in order to save their weaker position from being proven wrong by the stronger, they actually violate and deny Aristotle's *Principle of Non-Contradiction* — which is the easiest thing in the universe to prove, the first of Aristotle's First Principles of Being, and the foundation of all Logic and Science!

But here is where the Pro-Choice (and/or) Neo-Marxist Identity Politics ideology, rooted in Radical Skepticism and the Relativism that follows, gets really politically dangerous. Since to them there are *no objective facts, only subjective feelings and opinions*, and therefore all politics is just a matter of competing subjective opinions; and since no facts are admissible to settle disputes between subjective differences of political opinion, how are disputes settled so public political policy can be made? The only thing Relativists recognize for this purpose is *power*. Those who have more *power*, more *force*, can get their subjective opinion of how things should be run into political practice, over all competing subjective opinions about politics. Without any objective facts from which to judge the most reasonable, the most logical, the most scientifically sound political policy, which will be most beneficial and safe for the most humans, public policies instead get decided only by *which subjective opinion* has the most *power* to *force* itself upon all other human subjects. And ever since Marxism began, if the Marxist-influenced cannot physically, violently, militarily *force* their Marxist ideology upon everyone in a country through the bloody violent revolution Marx expressly recommended, they will try to *EMOTIONALLY MANIPULATE others into making political concessions to their vacuous and unrealistic ideology*, by using the Marxist system and its categories which are explicitly designed to engender *sympathy* in others. Marx unrealistically and over-simplistically reinterpreted of all political history as one kind of "class struggle" or other between those Marxists label "oppressed" and those Marxists label "privileged/oppressor," just so Marxists can then take the side of the "oppressed" underdog against the "privileged" oppressor, generating sympathy for their political cause because they have painted themselves as the "compassionate" "social justice warrior" and righter of wrongs (even very old wrongs they have dishonestly exaggerated into current hatred and division for Marxist ends. There is no reason today's "White" people here in Canada, where American Black slaves went to be free, need to "apologize" for slavery in another country in another century. Yet Neo-Marxists here in Canada have demanded we do a witch-hunt for "systemic racism" in Canada; Canada which Martin Luther King, Jr. himself said was the "heaven" the American Black slaves were singing about in the classic Negro spiritual songs. While the Neo-Marxists tear down statues and absurdly echo the American BLM call to "defund the police" (note BLM is run by *self-described Marxists*) . . . There is no sense to today's Neo-Marxist Identity Politics, and I believe most who follow it have merely been blinded by the false seductive glimmering beauty of the "Marxist egalitarian utopia" which has deceived so many before. But part of them really does like and appreciate living in a Free country. So, I believe that all that is needed is to really challenge the ideologues, as this book does, forcing them to become consistent and *choose* just which path they will follow, and most once so challenged (as with THE INTELLECTUAL HONESTY CHALLENGE in Chapter 7 of this book) will take the philosophically Realist path which supports Human Rights and Freedoms and rejects Relativistic Marxism in all its forms (including Pro-Choice Neo-Marxist Identity Politics) . . .

. . . it is sadly true that some of the more "ideologically lobotomized" with the relativistic "impaired thinking ability" Solzhenitsyn spoke of will continue to hang on to their *ideology instead of education* with its unrealistic delusions . . . And if the Pro-Choice Extremist Left cannot (yet?) physically or militarily force their Marxist-influenced ideals and opinions (and practices like legal abortion) on the rest of us as did the Marxist Communist Socialists under the blood-stained Marxist despots Lenin, Stalin, Mao, Pol Pot and so on, *they resort to shouting down and trying to verbally (if not physically) slander and intimidate those with different opinions than themselves.* Hence, numerous examples like those of: [note: much more detail on these is included in *Pro-Life Equals Pro-Democracy*]

1. Pro-Choice and/or Neo-Marxist Identity Politics "Cancel Culture" ideologues surrounding Dr. Jordan Peterson's McMaster University talk with megaphone and noisily shouting him down so no one could hear him, with loud repeated vulgar insults and intimidating but absurd accusations (since they could not win an argument with someone so intelligent and honest any other way);

2. Marxist Pro-Choicers organized by the "Proletarian Feminist Front" of the "Revolutionary Communist Party" similarly noisily (and with shrill whistles) shouting down the Candlelight Prayer Vigil Service before the Canadian National March for Life, and intimidatingly standing eye-to-eye with the Pro-Lifers on the stage, literally covering up their Pro-Life signs advocating *Equal Human Rights for All Humans* (while city police who work for the Pro-Choice Mayor who facilitated the first of the laws in Canada to make peaceful Pro-Life Human Rights advocacy a crime, in the national capital run by an aggressively Pro-Choice party, just let the Revolutionary Communist Party-organized Pro-Choicers violate the democratic freedom of expression and assembly of Pro-Life Canadians who actually believe in the (Pro-Life)

Foundational Principles of Human Rights and Democracy – not just at the Prayer Vigil, but the next day police just let the Communist-organized Pro-Choicers interfere with and shorten the March for Life itself by blocking the pre-approved March route);

3. Numerous cases of Pro-Choice university students and/or administration suppressing the free expression of Pro-Life views on university campuses, even to the point of violent destruction of Pro-Life displays (while campus security is conveniently absent) and administration threatening expulsion of and revoking the official university club status of Pro-Lifers – again, because there is no way Pro-Choicers can win rational arguments with Pro-Lifers based on facts, science, logic, reason, as abundantly demonstrated in this book; so philosophically radically skeptical and relativist (often Marxist or Neo-Marxist) Pro-Choicers, who deep down have *so little grip on reality* that they do not believe in nor can be swayed by objective facts, just threaten, intimidate, and shout down all rational discussion in order to keep their uneducated subjective opinion for Pro-Choice legal human-killing abortion legal. *Power and force to impose your own subjective opinion on others and on public policy is all that matters when you do not believe in any objective facts because you are a skeptical Relativist.* [Shortly before publication, this author met a group of university students who revealed another unforgivable sin of universities in my country. Not only does their university unconscionably *not allow* any Pro-Life student club which would engage in intelligent discussion and debate about the merits of the West legalizing human-killing abortion first legalized in 1920 by the totalitarian Soviet Relativist Marxists; when I asked, these *university-educated* students had *never even heard of* Aleksandr Solzhenitsyn, nor of his 35-million-copy-selling book *The Gulag Archipelago,* which exposed the facts of the Soviet Marxist Relativist evil and so helped bring down the genocidal Marxist Socialist Soviet Union. The Marxists Solzhenitsyn warned us have infected Western Media and education have been hiding their tracks well . . .

The GOOD NEWS: As the Only-Seemingly-Powerful Totalitarian Marxist Soviet Union Threatening the World with Nuclear War *Fell Suddenly, Quickly, Bloodlessly* Due to Simple Things Like Solzhenitsyn Merely *Speaking the Truth* Against the Web of Lies that Sustained It; and the *Solidarity Movement* of Soviet-Bloc Citizens who, Despite All Marxist Attempts to Expunge Traditional Western Values, Still Held on to and STOOD UP TOGETHER IN SOLIDARITY FOR the Traditional Western (Judeo-Christian) Values Which Include and Support *The Foundational Principles of Human Rights and Democracy* Identified from Science, Logic, History (and the History of Ideas) in This Book; SO WILL FALL SUDDENLY the Only-Seemingly-Powerful Marxist "Shroud of the Dark Side, Confusing Everything," Which Solzhenitsyn Warned the West had Infected Western Media and Universities, Which it has with its: 1-Radically Skeptical, Anti-Realistic and Anti-Scientific and Anti-Factual Postmodernist Philosophy Designed by Marxists to Protect Marxism from the *Facts* Marxism/Socialism Does Not Work in The Real World; and with 2- Neo-Marxist Identity Politics Which Unrealistically and Toxically Divides All Political Past and Present into Needlessly Adversarial and *Specifically Marxist* Categories of "Oppressed" and "Privileged," to *Create* the Current Polarized Political Instability for Marxist Ends Including Cutting Off

Western Civilization from Its Own History and from the Traditional Western Values Which Made it Great and Free; and with 3-Neo-Marxist "Cancel Culture" Which Just Like Classic Marxism Attempts to Control Society through "Cancelling" Opposing Voices - through Censorship Controlling Just Which Voices and Information Gets Heard; and with 4-Pro-Choice(-to-Kill-Humans) Ideology Following the Totalitarian Marxist Soviet 1920 Legal Abortion Precedent, Which Legally Eradicates the *Inherent Human Right to Live*, Leaving No Minimal Foundation for a Free Democracy (and Explaining the Around 100 Million Murders in Marxist Countries the Last Century Since 1920).

Here is the really GOOD NEWS in all of this. Aleksandr Solzhenitsyn with his book *The Gulag Archipelago* exposing Marxism in practice really did send the torpedo to sink the ship of Marxism which destroyed his country first by making it the world's first (philosophically *Relativist not Realist*) Socialist State. Since his book exposed Marxist lies and evil for all to see, and exposed the roots of all that evil in Marxism itself, proving it was what Marxism required to establish itself, and rampant totalitarianism and human-killing evil was not just an aberration or failure of Marx's followers, but a "congenital birth defect" of Marxism itself, conceived upon all the manifestly stupid and unrealistic assumptions of the stream of bad philosophy identified in this present book, the Marxists and Socialists in the West no longer convinced themselves, and no longer tried to convince everyone else, that Marxism was wonderful. What we are facing today is an already wounded form of Neo-Marxism. Those Western Marxists too dishonest to admit that Marxism did not work and abandon it, dishonestly committed the "sleight of hand" Professor Jordan Peterson and Professor Stephen Hicks have called attention to, re-imagining Marxism as Postmodernism, ultimately resulting in Identity Politics which continues Marxist principles, but not so strong and violent a form. A wounded form which (like classic Marxism) only lives by lies and deceit, but no longer having the bloodlust of classic Marxism. Though they still divide all society and all history into classes labelled "oppressed" and "privileged oppressor," today's Neo-Marxists no longer relish the thought of bloody revenge upon their perceived "oppressors" (or are less likely to; prominent Pro-Life Human Rights advocates have sometimes been deluged with death-threats and "doxing" by Pro-Choice Identity Politics ideologues). But it seems the real vengeful bloodlust of classic Marxism has been made too intolerable by the tens of millions of Marxist murders in all the earlier attempts to establish a Marxist State. So, I believe most who today are fooled by Neo-Marxist ideology are just that – fooled. They do live in the West and enjoy its freedom. They no longer, thanks to Solzhenitsyn exposing the truth about the USSR, hold up the Marxist USSR as their Socialist ideal. If they have kept Marx's foolish and unrealistic Socialist ideals, they no longer have Marx's utter disdain for thoughts of establishing a Socialist State without violence. I think many of them really want the world to be a better place; they are not committed, as classic Marxists were, to violence as the way. They are merely not educated enough to yet understand that the Marxist principles and the Marxist utopian vision itself is dangerous (and inherently violent) because of the false, bad philosophical assumptions it is built on. So, they just need to be educated. This book attempts to provide this HUMAN RIGHTS EDUCATION FOR LASTING FREE DEMOCRACY, and finish Solzhenitsyn's work in ending Marxism, by rooting out the Marxist infestation in the West which Solzhenitsyn's book *The Gulag Archipelago* warned us of; by showing how to build a lasting and just Free Democracy with Equal Human Rights for All Humans without all the Marxist Socialist errors intertwined, which make them foolishly speak of "Social Democracy" or "Democratic Socialism," not even realizing that that is essentially what the Marxist USSR and Cambodia thought they were doing. The Soviets sometimes called their system "Soviet Democracy" and Marxist Cambodia even called itself "Democratic Kampuchea" – and murdered one quarter of the population . . .

. . . It is important to realize that the mighty Marxist "evil empire" of the Union of Soviet Socialist Republics (USSR) itself, which first legalized abortion (eradicating in law the *Inherent Human Right to Live*); committed the first of many Marxist genocides (against this author's ethnic group); and threatened the whole world with nuclear extinction with its totalitarian Marxist ideological opposition to human freedom backed by a nuclear arsenal; *fell suddenly*, quickly and bloodlessly, against all expectations, due to simple things like Solzhenitsyn's motto, "one word of Truth outweighs the whole world." Solzhenitsyn simply spoke the Truth in opposition to the system of lies that sustained the Marxist Soviet Union. Simple things like people living under that oppressive totalitarian Soviet Bloc standing up together in *Solidarity* (in Soviet Bloc Poland) for the Traditional Western (Judeo-Christian) Pro-Life Family Values which include and support what this author has identified from Science, Logic, and Human Rights History as *The Foundational Principles of Human Rights and Democracy*. We too can speak the Truth against the lies of Neo-Marxism, and against the Marxist practice of legal human-killing abortion; we too can stand up together in *Solidarity* for the Traditional Western Values Human Rights and Democracy are built on, to become once again the guiding principles for Western public policy . . . They brought down the militarily mighty but philosophically bankrupt Soviet Union by doing this. We only have to bring down the vacuous silliness of Neo-Marxist Pro-Choice bigots . . .

. . . **The Marxist-influenced do not know how to make the world a better place.** Their Marxist, Relativist assumptions sabotage all their attempts. Categorizing all history and all current societies into toxic adversarial groups labelled "oppressed" and "privileged/oppressor" like Marx did just foments and encourages human strife, and can never even possibly make the world a better place. But *Equal Human Rights for All Humans* based on Traditional Western Values like *equal human preciousness* can. Because these are in fact precisely the historical and logical *Foundational Principles of Human Rights and Democracy* . . .

"In actual fact our Russian experience . . . is vitally important for the West, because by some chance of history we have trodden the same path seventy or eighty years before the West. And now it is with a strange sensation that we look at what is happening to you; many social phenomena that happened in Russia before its collapse are being repeated. Our experience of life is of vital importance to the West, but I am not convinced that you are capable of assimilating it without having gone through it to the end yourselves. You know, one could quote here many examples: for one, a certain retreat by the older generation, yielding their intellectual leadership to the younger generation. It is against the natural order of things for those who are youngest, with the least experience of life, to have the greatest influence in directing the life of society. One can say then that this is what forms the spirit of the age, the current of public opinion, when people in authority, well known professors and scientists, are reluctant to enter into an argument even when they hold a different opinion. It is considered

embarrassing to put forward one's counterarguments, lest one become involved. And so there is a certain abdication of responsibility, which is typical here where there is complete freedom....There is now a universal adulation of revolutionaries, the more so the more extreme they are! Similarly, before the revolution, we had in Russia, if not a cult of terror, then a fierce defense of terrorists. People in good positions—intellectuals, professors, liberals—spent a great deal of effort, anger, and indignation in defending terrorists."
– Aleksandr Solzhenitsyn

But there is HOPE! The solid HUMAN RIGHTS EDUCATION in *Pro-Life Equals Pro-Democracy* [and this handbook] thoughtfully unravels about 380 years of bad thinking which brought us to this current critical 'tipping point' where the West can either lose or reinforce its Free Democracy. Yes, it was a tough assignment, thinking through centuries of errors to unravel them in order to make any sense of the flabbergasting present situation starting shortly before 2015 with the first attacks on Pro-Life (2500-year Hippocratic Medical Tradition) doctors' *Freedom of Conscience*, making me ask "why is my supposed free democracy acting more and more like a totalitarian State and barely anyone is noticing it?" (Other than Professor Jordan Peterson, living a few hours' drive away under the same regional and national governments as this author, who almost two years later became famous for calling attention to some of the many Pro-Choice-Left-led government violations of normal democratic freedoms including Free Speech). It took this author six years of deep thinking, deep reflection on a lifetime of reading and learning (including being a professor teaching a university course covering the period in which *The Foundational Principles of Human Rights and Democracy* were laid), *thinking* as much as possible through much injury and illness affecting myself and my family. But now there is Hope! This book (together with the other book manuscripts on this problem produced in the last six years, to be published next) provides a solidly grounded HUMAN RIGHTS EDUCATION FOR LASTING FREE DEMOCRACY. Which should give the flabbergasted non-extremist political parties, for now mostly on the "conservative Right," *the confidence they now lack to challenge the Pro-Choice, legal human-killing Extremist Left* (remember, this non-partisan scholar does not vilify the Left; only *Extremists* Right or Left, like the Extremist Left Soviet Marxists and Extremist Right Nazis, who were the first two political parties to legalize human-killing abortion. This non-partisan author only calls the current totalitarian-oriented, Pro-Choice-to-Kill-Humans Extremist Left to get back to its democratic roots nearer the political Center – as when U.S. Democrat Eleanor Roosevelt of the "Real" Left led the production of the UN's *Universal Declaration of Human Rights*, which cannot be intelligently interpreted any way that allows for legal human-killing abortion, as shown in my books. Free Democracy for the long-term needs both political "progressive Left" and "conservative Right" to be in a healthy balance and *both* grounded in *The Foundational Principles of Human Rights and Democracy*, if either side has since strayed from this commitment (both sides have in different ways and degrees) – a commitment to democratic principles which was implicit when our modern democracies were first formed. This book just makes those *implicit* foundations of Free Democracy more *explicit*, so they may be restored and more easily maintained in future, so that people and parties are not tempted to stray from them again, for the sake of human freedom that *lasts for centuries* on its firm historical and logical *foundations*.

"If you are willing to say that murder and genocide in many cultures over many decades is wrong, then Marxism is wrong."
– Professor Jordan B. Peterson

As this book shows, the world needs *not* a global "Marxist Great Reset," with all the world's Pro-Choice Legal Human-Killing Neo-Marxist Identity Politics "Cancel Culture" Ideologues enthusiastically using the Coronavirus Pandemic as an opportunity to destroy the global economy and then "reset" it according to the Relativist Marxist ideology which in the past has consistently resulted in among the most oppressive and totalitarian governments known to human history. The world rather needs a global *"Democracy Reboot,"* reloading Western Civilization and Free Democracy's solid *foundations* in philosophical *Realism* and *The Foundational Principles of Human Rights and Democracy*!

CHAPTER 4: STRATEGY

[Drawn from the author's first book *DEMOCRACY 101*, in which the following simple strategy was developed from historical considerations at some length]

The WINNING STRATEGY for the 'Culture of Life' (and Philosophical Realism) to WIN the 'Cultural War' with 'The Culture of Death' (and Philosophical Relativism) to Save Humanity Forever from Bigotry and 'Creeping Totalitarianism' Now Accelerating

"Education is the most powerful weapon you can use to change the world"
— Nelson Mandela

"Democracy cannot succeed unless those who express their choice are prepared to choose wisely. The real safeguard of Democracy, therefore, is education."
—U.S. President Franklin Delano Roosevelt

"There is eternal simplicity to a solution once it has been discovered!"
— Aleksandr Solzhenitsyn

EDUCATION IS ALWAYS THE SOLUTION TO IGNORANCE
"READ, LEARN, SPREAD"
The basics of The Winning Strategy for the 'Culture of Life' to WIN the 'Cultural War' with the 'Culture of Death,' to Save Humanity Forever from Bigotry and 'Creeping Totalitarianism' is for individuals TO GET AND SPREAD A SOLID HUMAN RIGHTS EDUCATION (including the most pertinent facts of Human Rights History, Science, Logic and the History of Philosophy in this book, and in the author's other books in the HUMAN RIGHTS EDUCATION FOR LASTING FREE DEMOCRACY book series; facts which overwhelmingly demonstrate that Pro-Life=Pro-Democracy); an education including The Foundational Principles of Human Rights and Democracy and the Core Principles of Lasting Democracy. Sharing this Human Rights Education with friends, family and elected representatives (and wherever possible with leaders and judges and journalists and those in government or "Big Tech") until there are enough Human-Rights-Educated voters and politicians (and judges and honest journalists and "Big Tech" media influencers) to end abortion and save Democracy. Educated voters do not cast uneducated votes for uneducated "Pro-Choice" politicians who do not have the foggiest clue what The Foundational Principles of Human Rights and Democracy are, nor even that they are literally copying extremist political policy and thinking by supporting legal abortion human-killing.
Political change happens in two directions: from the grassroots bubbling up; or from the politicians trickling down. The more individual voters who get this solid education in the Science, Logic, and Human Rights History (and the History of Ideas) which prove Pro-Life=Pro-Democracy, and spread it to other voters and to their own elected representatives and leaders and judges etc., the quicker (from both directions) the West will end abortion and save Democracy from 'Creeping Totalitarianism.'
A Human-Rights-educated populace will no longer tolerate uneducated extremist human-killing Pro-Choice bigotry against fetal-age humans just like every one of us at their age; nor tolerate other 'Creeping Totalitarianism' restricting normal democratic freedoms (of speech; conscience; religion; assembly; etc.) from the Pro-Choice(-to-Kill-Humans) politicians and political parties in their democracy which they want to stay a democracy.
To Ensure LASTING Democracy in their country, educated voters who, like the original Abolitionists, believe in Equal Human Rights for All Humans (the foundation of Democracy), will like the original Abolitionists incessantly pester their governments to abolish the primary legal Human Rights abuse of their day. For the original Abolitionists, this was legal slavery of Black humans, many who died on crowded slave-ships and in unsafe plantations; for Pro-Life "New Abolitionsts" today, this is the legal abortion-killing of preborn humans who have also had their equal Human Rights denied by uneducated and ignorant bigots who know nothing of The Foundational Principles of Human Rights and Democracy and little of Logic, Science, and Human Rights History. Human Rights-Educated "Democracy Pledgers" or "Knights of Human Rights and Ladies of Lasting Democracy" will incessantly petition their politicians to constitutionally enshrine some formulation of The Foundational Principles of Human Rights and Democracy in their country as a necessary requirement for LASTING Democracy.

. . . how much time is needed for this victory [of ending extremist human-killing Pro-Choice 'Creeping Totalitarianism'— and with abortion ending all the current increasing attacks upon religious freedom and other normal democratic freedoms *by restoring* the fundamentally "Pro-Life" *Foundational Principles of Human Rights and Democracy*] in each country could vary widely from country to country, and depends largely on two factors:

1. Whether the good people in the country embrace the Human Rights Education of *DEMOCRACY 101* [and/or other books in the HUMAN RIGHTS EDUCATION FOR LASTING FREE DEMOCRACY series, like *PRO-LIFE EQUALS PRO-DEMOCRACY* and/or *KILLING HUMANS IS WRONG* and/or *NO FRUIT WITHOUT ROOTS*] themselves with enthusiasm and spread it far and wide, which will make it take less time to defeat 'Creeping Totalitarianism;' or whether the good people largely remain like the good Germans in 1930s Germany – "deniers" who deny how bad things are getting or "despairers" who despair that anything can help and so they do not try, both of these *not doing what they can* to help democracy last, and so it does not. Or it takes a lot longer in that country to stop the 'Creeping Totalitarianism' driven by the fundamental Human Rights abuse of legal abortion, maybe *decades* like it took to end the similar fundamental Human Rights abuse of legal slavery.

2. Whether the anti-traditional, "Pro-Choice-to-Kill-Humans" side in a particular country proves on the whole more simply *uneducated* than *evil*, in which case 'Creeping Totalitarianism' could fall surprisingly quickly, like a house of cards (as fell brutal Marxist Communist Socialist totalitarianism in the Union of Soviet Socialist Republics), simply with the introduction and spread of *DEMOCRACY 101's* solid *Human Rights Education* [more briefly introduced in *PRO-LIFE EQUALS PRO-DEMOCRACY* and *KILLING HUMANS IS WRONG* and *NO FRUIT WITHOUT ROOTS*] which will *educate* the mere *ignorance* of Human Rights history, Science, and Logic, which had been behind most Pro-Choicers' acceptance of vacuous and dangerous "Pro-Choice-to-Kill-Humans" philosophy; or whether the "Pro-Choice bigots" prove on the whole more bigoted, selfish, and evil rather than merely ignorant. In the case where more Pro-Choicers are not just ignorant of the facts in this book, but actually selfish/evil, then even in the face of the overwhelming evidence that *Pro-Life=Pro-Democracy,* more evil than just ignorant Pro-Choicers will still not easily give up the selfish convenience or money profits that come from denying equal Human Rights to some humans in human-killing abortions and the big-money abortion industry, because (like the slavers before them) they care more about personal selfish gain than about lasting Human Rights and freedoms for all humanity. This

kind of actually selfish/evil and extremely intellectually dishonest Pro-Choicers will vigorously oppose *DEMOCRACY 101* [and *PRO-LIFE EQUALS PRO-DEMOCRACY* and *KILLING HUMANS IS WRONG* and *NO FRUIT WITHOUT ROOTS*] with everything in their being. If there are enough of these more *bigoted, selfish and evil* than just ignorant Pro-Choicers in a particular country, in that country it could take much longer to defeat 'Creeping Totalitarianism,' and that country might well even lose all pretense of democracy to 'Creeping Totalitarianism' full-grown, *before coming to its senses* and in the end *rebuilding* democracy so it lasts NEXT TIME on its firm traditional, historical, scientific and logical ("Pro-Life") foundations revealed so clearly in *DEMOCRACY 101* [and introduced in the later books of the HUMAN RIGHTS EDUCATION FOR LASTING FREE DEMOCRACY book series like *PRO-LIFE EQUALS PRO-DEMOCRACY* and *KILLING HUMANS IS WRONG* and NO FRUIT WITHOUT ROOTS].

As a key element of the "WINNING STRATEGY," as a *New Abolitionist*/Democracy Pledger [or more poetically, as a "Knight of Human Rights" or a "Lady of LASTING Democracy] **I pledge** to (like the original Abolitionists) incessantly pester my government to *abolish* the bigoted scourge that denies Human Rights to some humans and is thus undermining Democracy by violating *the supreme and EQUAL value of every human life without exception* which Democracy depends on – the bigoted scourge of democracy which for the original Abolitionists was legal slavery and for New Abolitionists is legal abortion. In brief,

I pledge allegiance to Democracy, and to the above *Foundational Principles of Human Rights and Democracy* on which all Human Rights and Democratic Freedoms are historically and logically built and which they need to last.

[end of excerpt from *DEMOCRACY 101* by William Baptiste, Founder of *Human Rights and Freedoms Forever!* and *The Intellectual Honesty Challenge*, Proclaimer of THE THINKING REVOLUTION]

"In actual fact our Russian experience [of totalitarianism] ... is vitally important for the West, because by some chance of history we have trodden the same path seventy or eighty years before the West. And now it is with a strange sensation that we look at what is happening to you; many social phenomena that happened in Russia before its collapse are being repeated. Our experience of life is of vital importance to the West, but I am not convinced that you are capable of assimilating it without having gone through it to the end yourselves ..."
— *Aleksandr Solzhenitsyn*

"To do evil a human being must first of all believe that what he's doing is good..."
"Ideology – that is what gives evildoing its long-sought justification and gives the evildoer the necessary steadfastness and determination. That is the social theory which helps to make his acts seem good instead of bad in his own and others' eyes....
Thanks to ideology the twentieth century was fated to experience evildoing calculated on a scale in the millions."
— Aleksandr Solzhenitsyn

"... those people who have lived in the most terrible conditions, on the frontier between life and death, be it people from the West or from the East, all understand that between good and evil there is an irreconcilable contradiction, that it is not one and the same thing—good or evil—that one cannot build one's life without regard to this distinction. I am surprised that pragmatic philosophy consistently scorns moral considerations; and nowadays in the Western press we read a candid declaration of the principle that moral considerations have nothing to do with politics. I would remind you that in 1939 England thought differently. If moral considerations were not applicable to politics, then it would be incomprehensible why England went to war with Hitler's Germany. Pragmatically, you could have gotten out of the situation, but England chose the moral course, and experienced and demonstrated to the world perhaps the most brilliant and heroic period in its history."
— Aleksandr Solzhenitsyn

"To reject this inhuman Communist ideology is simply to be a human being. Such a rejection is more than a political act. It is a protest of our souls against those who would have us forget the concepts of good and evil."

"Communism is breathing down the neck of all moderate forms of socialism, which are unstable."

"Socialism of any type leads to a total destruction of the human spirit." — Aleksandr Solzhenitsyn

"The clock of communism has stopped striking. But its concrete building has not yet come crashing down. For that reason ... we must try to save ourselves from being crushed by its rubble."
— *Aleksandr Solzhenitsyn*

Bold Conclusion
to Counter Pro-Choice Governments' Recent Bold Passing of Totalitarian Laws to Silence Pro-Life Human Rights Advocacy, Ending Free Speech and Other Democratic Freedoms
[Quick Summary Excerpted from the author's book *Pro-Life Equals Pro-Democracy.* An entire Chapter follows this quick summary of some major points in that book.]

Officially Pro-Choice Politicians and Political Parties (Who Ignorantly Follow the Precedents of the Totalitarian Soviet Marxist-Communist-Socialist and Nazi [Short for "National Socialist" in German] Parties Which Were the First Political Parties to Legalize Abortion), Like the Soviet (Marxist) and Nazi (Fascist) Parties are Now *Extremist* Parties Which Do
Not Even Hold *The Foundational Principles of Human Rights and Democracy*, Which are Pro-Life;
Pro-Choice Politicians and Political Parties (and Influential Pro-Choice Judges and Journalists and Civil Servants and "Big Tech" Personnel) Generally Do Not Even Know or Understand Enough Science Nor Human Rights History Nor Logic Nor Philosophy to Have an Educated or Intelligent Opinion on Human Life Issues;
(Philosophically *Relativist not Realist*) Pro-Choice Politicians and Political Parties (and Relativist, Pro-Choice Judges and Journalists, Civil Servants and "Big Tech") are Too Untrained in Logical Thinking (and/or Too Intellectually Dishonest and/or Too "Ideologically Lobotomized" into Being "Willfully Unintelligent") to Use Anything Other Than the Typical Logical *Fallacies of Distraction* Which Are the ONLY Pro-Choice "Arguments" for Legal Abortion;
Therefore Pro-Choice Politicians and Political Parties are Neither Qualified Nor Competent to Lead a LASTING Democracy,
as Demonstrated by Recent Totalitarian Laws Including Those Restricting Pro-Life Free Speech, Passed by Pro-Choice (therefore *Extremist*, Legal Human-Killing) Political Parties in Power,
Because Ending Democratic Freedoms is the ONLY Way the Pro-Choice Legal Abortion Position Can Ultimately Prevail,
Since the Great Weight of the Most Pertinent Facts of Science, Logic, Philosophy and Human Rights History Support the Pro-Life Position and the Conclusion that PRO-LIFE = PRO-DEMOCRACY (and Pro-Choice = Pro-Totalitarianism).
Democracies Which Want to LAST Must Constitutionally Enshrine Some Form of the Pro-Life *Foundational Principles of Human Rights and Democracy* Herein,
and Currently Pro-Choice (and therefore Extremist 'Creeping Totalitarian') Politicians and Political Parties Must Get a Solid *Human Rights Education* and

CHAPTER 4: STRATEGY

Return to Their Party's Roots in the Pro-Life *Foundational Principles of Human Rights and Democracy* Which Were At Least Implicitly Held by All Founding Parties of Both "Left" and "Right" at the Founding of Our Modern Democracies. (PRO-CHOICE VS. PRO-LIFE IS NOT AN ISSUE OF POLITICAL "LEFT" VS. "RIGHT" BUT AN ISSUE OF FUNDAMENTALLY TOTALITARIAN THINKING THAT SUPPORTS HUMAN-KILLING VS. FUNDAMENTALLY DEMOCRATIC THINKING THAT SUPPORTS HUMAN PROTECTION).
When Judged According to the Objective Standards of Science and Logic - and Undisputed Facts of Human Rights History – The Pro-Choice Position for Legal Abortion is Revealed as Not Even Remotely Intellectually Defensible, and Not Even Remotely Acceptable in a LASTING Democracy, Which Can Only Last on Democracy's Historic Pro-Life Foundations.

2021 Update: There is no end to the intellectual dishonesty and even blatant stupidity that (philosophically *Relativist not Realist*) Pro-Choice political parties and politicians are capable of, already evident long before the Coronavirus Pandemic became every (almost always Pro-Choice) Neo-Marxist/Socialist or other anti-democratic ideologue's dream opportunity to "Reset" the whole world according to their particular *ideology instead of education.* This Ukrainian Canadian Human Rights scholar and author, as a representative of (only) the first ten million genocide victims of Relativistic Marxist Socialist thinking in Soviet Ukraine, will here detail just one example, after mentioning in passing one other, both very current at the precise time of publication of this handbook. Current examples of 'Creeping Totalitarianism' which has been 'creeping' for decades, and *accelerating* since early 2015 when this author first noticed it in his province and country's laws and policies. (Early 2015 being even before this author's countryman and fellow Canadian intellectual for Free Speech Dr. Jordan Peterson in late 2016 became famous for calling attention to *accelerating* totalitarianism by opposing totalitarian-oriented new bills-now-laws against Free Speech even of well-established scientific principles of biology. Totalitarian laws which Dr. Peterson was, of course, *absolutely correct* in predicting would lead precisely to *last week's* results in our country, where a father near this author *is now in jail* just for speaking out loud the easily scientifically verifiable reality that 14 years ago he had a daughter and not a son (a reality scientifically evident in every cell of his daughter's body. But speaking well-established Science that disagrees with their unscientific ideologies rooted in *(Skeptical) Relativism instead of (Scientific) Realism* is called "hate speech" by the supremely intellectually dishonest and "ideologically lobotomized" who suffer from the illogical and unscientific "impaired thinking ability" which the brilliant Aleksandr Solzhenitsyn noted came from their underlying philosophical and moral *Relativism not Realism.* Note that those people who viciously hate Jordan Peterson and accuse him of every kind of bigotry or "hate speech" just for disagreeing with them on scientific grounds only hate him because as *subjectivist Relativists not Realists* they have no solid grasp of Science nor of *objective Reality*; therefore Dr. Jordan Peterson's deep thoughtfulness and rigorous intellectual honesty reveals their abject lack of such qualities).

To help give the reader a sense of being in the constant flow of *Living History* whereby our collective *future Living History* (whether totalitarian or free) is shaped by *what we do or do not do* in the *present moment of Living History* –
having now mentioned in passing *last week's* nearby development of just one of so many current assaults upon Free Speech and other normal democratic freedoms of Speech, Expression, Assembly, Association, Conscience and Religion (attacks on

Free Democracy which were *already* profuse in my country and throughout the West long before the Coronavirus Pandemic became an *additional* excuse for *(Skeptical) Relativist not (Scientific) Realist*, anti-democratic politicians and political parties in power to restrict usual democratic freedoms while ignoring much hard Science) –

this author will now detail the following current totalitarian reality of *this week* (at time of writing) – as merely *just one example* of *already accelerating* (since 2015) Western totalitarianism *accelerating again since 2020* using the Coronavirus Pandemic as a convenient *excuse* to *even further expand totalitarian government over-reach*:

Where I live, just like in an Atheist Marxist Socialist State, *the government is in complete control of if, when and how Christians and other religious believers gather together (this author for usual democratic freedom's sake has communicated with other local freedom-protestors for normal Free Democracy and so met with both Christians and non-Christians at two local Sikh Temples in late February 2021 to discuss the unacceptable current and still-unending so-called "Coronavirus Restrictions" on public worship, which, completely banning all public religious worship but allowing people to gather near each other in the hundreds for secular activities, are very clearly bigoted against religion like any Marxist State is, in this jurisdiction of over 5 million people)*. Remember that anyone who thinks this handbook is unfair in its considerations and conclusions must take THE INTELLECTUAL HONESTY CHALLENGE in Chapter 7 to determine whether or not they have any intellectual honesty or honest, intelligent credibility at all).

People who used to live under totalitarian Marxist Atheist governments (like the many Cold War Soviet Bloc countries) know this pattern of *different standards for religious and non-religious citizens* well. Under Soviet Marxist Communism/Socialism, my own Ukrainian Greek Catholic Church (the largest underground church of the 20th Century) officially *did not exist* under such *philosophically (Skeptical) Relativist not (Scientific) Realist* Atheist Marxism in the Union of Soviet Socialist Republics (USSR). All our church buildings were confiscated and given to the Russian Orthodox Church which was allowed to exist (as a Russian cultural tradition) but only allowed to function *under strict Atheist Soviet supervision*. The philosophically *Relativist-not-Realist* Atheist Soviets, to ensure Church submission to the Atheist Marxist Socialist State government and ideology, even ensured members of the KGB, the oppressive and totalitarian Soviet Secret Police, would (successively) be installed as the Patriarch (head overseer/bishop or chief pastor) of the Russian Orthodox Church, based in Moscow.

And today, where I live now in the once-free West, under so-called "Coronavirus Measures," sacred/religious activities were *always* restricted much more harshly than secular activities, and since November 2020 for months now public religious worship has been entirely banned. The government cancelled all Christmas 2020 celebrations, even my village's local outdoor Christmas tree festival (which was easy to "social distance" at) — while keeping malls, restaurants, museums, "fun centers" and other secular activities open and even crowded (often still crowded at less than maximum capacity - often half-capacity – supposedly out of consideration of the "novel Coronavirus." So why were churches not allowed anywhere near "half-capacity" attendance? Under so-called "Coronavirus Restrictions" secular activities including restaurants smaller than most worship buildings were allowed by the government to have attendance in the hundreds, including restaurants allowed to serve 100-200 people at one time, *while all public religious worship remains entirely banned*). The Supreme Court of this jurisdiction considered the complaint of some Christian churches over this obviously unfair double standard in Coronavirus Measures. This author was present in the Supreme Court for some of the legal deliberations. But still after months of this even-more-than-previously-unequal treatment of religious versus secular activities using the Coronavirus as an *excuse*, in response to many complaints over the obviously bigoted against religion double standard in "Coronavirus Measures," the jurisdiction's Supreme Court in the end ruled (on March 19, 2021, exactly 4 months after the initial November 19, 2020 total ban on public religious worship) that while the restrictions on public religious worship *did indeed violate the religious freedom which is supposedly guaranteed in this country's Charter of Rights and Freedoms* (as well as violating normal constitutional freedoms of speech, assembly and association), somehow this bigoted double standard against religion was still *"justified,"* and the current "Coronavirus" restrictions banning all public religious worship still stand (while this government still allows hundreds at a time, all day every day, to gather in crowded malls and restaurants and museums and so on). Perhaps as a gesture of the highly Atheist Socialist-influenced governing party's "magnanimous mercy" upon the poor Christians of this jurisdiction of over 5 million people, the government shortly before Easter 2021 told churches they had *temporary permission* to hold indoor worship services - *at only 10% of capacity, up to a maximum of 50 people, which is the highest church attendance allowed by the government since the Pandemic began in March 2020*, and *much less than secular activities* like amusement centers and even many restaurants are allowed - *just for four days* of the next weeks, which would cover the usual Easter Weekend services of some ancient Traditional Christian denominations on Holy Thursday (marking Jesus' Last Supper), Good Friday (marking Jesus' Crucifixion), Holy Saturday (keeping vigil while Jesus was buried in His tomb), and Easter Sunday (marking Jesus' Resurrection). But even this temporary "permission to worship" from the government *was taken away just days before Easter 2021,* Christians finding out on the Monday before Good Friday that *the government in fact would NOT allow them to gather in their churches* - not even at 10% capacity up to a maximum of 50 people - after all. As I said, *where I live, just like in an Atheist Marxist State, the government is in complete control of if, when and how Christians and other religious believers gather together.* All this just highlights the fact that this is about *government control* and *not about the Coronavirus.* Because there has never been any sense nor reason to the disparity, the unequal treatment of sacred and secular activities in this government's so-called "Coronavirus Restrictions." If the restrictions on normal civil liberties and democratic freedoms was actually for the Coronavirus, if the severe restrictions on the churches and synagogues and temples since November 19, 2020, *disallowing even just one hour per week usual public worship*, was actually *reasonable* for stopping the spread of the Coronavirus, then there would be no sense at all that so many *secular* activities are (then and now still) allowed to operate with so much less restrictions, such as restaurants allowed to be open all day, every day, accommodating up to 200 people at any one time, during the same time period since last November.

Because fuzzy-brained *Relativists not Realists* know little of and care less for the *Living History* which has brought us logically to the current critical "tipping point" between totalitarianism and democracy; because those with *ideology* instead of *education* care little for the *Living History* proceeding from the Present Moment which will determine our Western *future Living History* as totalitarian or free, it has become commonplace in my country for high courts to make "judgements" (I use the term loosely) like that above that in the end effectively "agree that current policies or laws restrict constitutionally guaranteed religious freedoms, but who cares?" In 2018 a regional Superior Court for 14 million people actually admitted that policies and legislation governing regional doctors since 2015 requiring Pro-Life (that is, Traditional Hippocratic) doctors to facilitate human-killing abortion and euthanasia *against their conscience* do in fact violate doctors' Freedom of Religion which is supposed to be guaranteed in the country's Charter of Rights and Freedoms. Yet the Court still judged that this suppression of doctors' democratic freedoms of Conscience and Religion was somehow acceptable in the case of making them provide "healthcare." This is an extraordinarily uneducated and unintelligent (*and Relativist not Realist*) judgement in favor of Pro-Choice 'Creeping Totalitarianism' against the Pro-Life *Foundational Principles of Human Rights and Democracy.* Not only is this judgement wholly uneducated in Human Rights History which shows that *Pro-Life equals Pro-Democracy;* not only is this judgement ignorant of the fact that the policy not only violates doctors' personal freedoms of conscience and religion, but violates the 2500-year old Hippocratic Medical Tradition itself, that *doctors don't kill* (not only does it violate the integrity of the medial profession itself). This judgement even violates medical science and common sense itself – because how can killing a unique individual human life with absolutely unique human DNA reasonably be called "healthcare" at all, never mind using this misdefined "healthcare" as an excuse to trample doctors' normal democratic freedoms of conscience and religion? This just calls attention to the huge problem that since abortion was de-criminalized, whole generations of doctors have been trained in medical colleges which caved in to political pressure to accept legal abortion, and we now have "doctors" who do not even *know* that doctors are not supposed to kill the humans they treat (abortion and euthanasia had been *explicitly against* the Hippocratic Medical Tradition for 2500 years). ***Real Doctors Don't Kill Patients!***

Doubtless the philosophical *Relativists not Realists* and/or Pro-Choice(-to-Kill-Humans) Neo-Marxist Identity Politics ideologues, and their ("Cancel Culture") mainstream Western media spouting *ideology instead of education* (as Solzhenitsyn warned us) – and all those regular people they have fooled and distracted with technology so that they live in *denial* like the 1930s Germans did – will say that this author's interpretation of the full significance (and danger) of current events (and current political policies and bone judgements of courts supporting them) is all exaggeration. Which criticism is really just an admission of their ignorance, of their lack of any solid Human Rights education. In their blithering ignorance they will deny this Human Rights scholar's conclusions simply because they do not have enough knowledge of Human Rights History, Science, Logic, nor Philosophy to intelligently interpret the full significance in *Living History* of current events, laws and other social conditions. **Ideologues will deny this book's conclusions also because they lack the sobering perspective this author has which comes from being a member of an ethnic group which suffered genocide committed under the same kind of ideologies they foolishly want to "Reset" the whole world with.** But this sometime-professor and logician as an educator believes education is the answer to problems rooted in ignorance, however, and so it is precisely to bring such people up to speed with current (dangerous and precarious) political realities that this HUMAN RIGHTS EDUCATION FOR LASTING FREE DEMOCRACY book series has been written. So that the good people in Western countries can finally start *together in solidarity* effectively shoring up and repairing the long-eroded *Foundational Principles of Human Rights and Democracy.*

Hopefully, most are still intellectually honest and intelligent enough to learn, become inspired by, and (most importantly) spread knowledge of this HUMAN RIGHTS EDUCATION FOR LASTING FREE DEMOCRACY to others until the needed "critical mass" of educated voters required to ensure lasting freedom is reached in each now-compromised democracy. Even if the most intellectually dishonest and "ideologically lobotomized" will still say, "surely things are not that bad," and will try to convince themselves and others to simply dismiss me and my books with the same offhand and unintelligent and intellectually dishonest carelessness with which they casually dismiss Nobel Prize-winning historian Aleksandr Solzhenitsyn himself (and his 35-million-copy-selling book *The Gulag Archipelago* which revealed to the world the oppressive totalitarian reality of the world's first Socialist country). Hopefully the honest will get and effectively spread this key Human Rights Education even if those most intellectually dishonest will still try to dismiss (or censor or cancel) the undisputed facts collected in this book with the same thoughtless dismissal with which they more recently blithely dismiss the over 55,500 (and growing number of) medical scientists and doctors and other medical professionals who have signed the Great Barrington Declaration

(https://gbdeclaration.org/view-signatures or
Signatures - Great Barrington Declaration (gbdeclaration.org).

Hopefully for Free Democracy everywhere there will not be too many uneducable, hopelessly bamboozled and dishonest Cancel Culture Relativists not Realists who frequently pretend Solzhenitsyn and the Great Barrington Declaration simply do not exist because acknowledging their existence, and acknowledging the Declaration's weighty scientific medical testimony against prevailing "Coronavirus" lockdowns (lockdowns having never been a medical term, but only a prison term), would scuttle their chance to dishonestly misuse the Coronavirus Pandemic as an excuse for a global Marxist "Great Reset" – a goal which today's Neo-Marxist/Socialist ideologues are *very willing to cause any amount of unnecessary Pandemic suffering for* (including forever closing your family business and making you dependent upon government support). For *the same reason* the Soviet Marxist Socialists were willing to look away from facts and commit any number of atrocities including the *Holodomor* Genocide of this author's ethnic group also "for the future glory of" somehow achieving the unrealistic "Marxist egalitarian utopia" through *any* means, through any number of assaults on freedom and atrocities, just because Socialists are not grounded in any kind of honest philosophical *Realism* such as grounds Science, Logic, and Technology. Just because *facts* (regarding the Coronavirus or democracy-grounding *Equal Human Rights for All Humans* or anything else) ultimately do not matter to Relativists.

All the Western Relativist Marxist Socialists influencing mainstream media were just as willing to cover up the *Holodomor* Genocide of 7-10 million of my fellow Ukrainians while it was happening as the Soviet Relativist Marxist Socialists were to commit the genocide – all to protect their precious Relativistic, subjectivist Marxist *ideology* which has nothing at all to do with objectively verifiable facts or *Reality*. Solzhenitsyn himself addressed such Western Relativists who are so dishonest with facts that they never realize the danger they are in (and are spreading to others). After penning 1800 pages (unabridged) of his best-selling non-fiction book revealing the horrors built on a web of lies in the world's first country run on Socialist ideology, with this comment to his "ideologically lobotomized" Western Socialist ideologue detractors he wrote:

"All you freedom-loving 'left-wing' thinkers in the West! You left laborites! You progressive American, German and French students! As far as you are concerned, none of this amounts to much. As far as you are concerned, this whole book of mine is a waste of effort. You may suddenly understand it all someday – but only when you yourselves hear, 'hands behind your backs there!' and step ashore on our [Gulag] Archipelago."
— *Aleksandr Solzhenitsyn, The Gulag Archipelago 1918-1956*

♦

"We all want progress. But progress means getting nearer to the place where you want to be. And if you have taken a wrong turn, then to go forward does not get you any nearer. If you are on the wrong road, progress means doing an about-turn and walking back to the right road; in that case the man who turns back soonest is the most progressive man."
– C.S. Lewis

Remember: As this book shows, the world needs not a global "Marxist Great Reset," with all the world's Pro-Choice legal human-killing Neo-Marxist Identity Politics/ Cancel Culture ideologues "cancelling" expert medical testimony against lockdowns while enthusiastically using the Coronavirus Pandemic as an opportunity to destroy the global economy and then "reset" it according to the Relativist Marxist ideology which in the past has consistently resulted in among the most oppressive and totalitarian governments known to human history. The world rather needs a global "Democracy Reboot," reloading Western Civilization and Free Democracy's solid foundations in philosophical Realism and The Foundational Principles of Human Rights and Democracy, revealed from the disciplines of History, Science, Logic and Philosophy in this book series!

CHAPTER 5:
FOUNDATIONS

[Drawn from the author's upcoming book *KILLING HUMANS IS WRONG*]

Honestly Acknowledging the Foundations of Western Civilization's Freedom:
The Common Creed of Christianity Includes and Supports The Foundational Principles of Human Rights and Democracy

(Principles Which Since the 4th Century Became Embedded into Traditional Western Values - The Neglect of Which Leads Naturally to Today's Accelerating Loss of Freedom to Totalitarianism)

Intro for Non-Christians: Today many non-Christians – and even secularized Christians – are highly critical of Traditional Christianity, but usually without even knowing just what it is they criticize – and without having any idea of how vitally necessary Traditional Christianity is to Western Human Rights and freedoms, both to their origin and to their continuation. Whether non-Christians personally agree or disagree with any of the particulars in the brief Common Creed below, after reading these *10 Articles of Common Christian Faith* at least they will know what Christianity *is*, so they will no longer criticize Traditional Christianity from *lack of knowledge* the way ignorant and uneducated bigots do. Hopefully they will become educated enough, even if they remain non-Christian, to at least properly *respect* Christianity for its unique and vast historical and logical contributions to modern Human Rights and Democracy and International Law (and Modern Science). This is minimally necessary for Free Democracy to last long-term on its foundations, which are both (Judeo)Christian and Pro-Life. This Common Creed is meant to let non-Christians (and secularized Christians) know just what Christianity actually *is* (dispelling their misconceptions) and just what it has *done for them*. Traditional Christianity with its enlightened principles has given them their human freedom from servitude to the government, and their Human Rights, both of which are being gradually lost in the West today specifically because governments no longer properly respect Christianity as the source of the *Foundational Principles of Human Rights and Democracy* introduced into the West by Christianity, which are found in the *Common Creed of Christianity* below. (There is no Free Democracy as we know it without Human Rights. And there are no Human Rights as we know them without Christianity. That is just History).

Intro for Secularized Christians: Secularized Christians

usually have kept bits and pieces of Traditional Christianity which they happen to like, but frequently they just parrot the secular culture's prevailing values, which are based on Atheist Moral Relativism and which have rejected Scientific Realism and *The Foundational Principles of Human Rights and Democracy*. Meaning that just like the current secularized culture of non-Christians, secularized Christians are often:

- *Pro-Choice(-to-Kill-Humans)* (thus denying even the *Inherent Human Right to Live* which grounds all Human Rights and all Free Democracy);
- philosophically *(Skeptical) Relativists* instead of *(Scientific) Realists* (not well grounded in Science nor Reality due to their bad underlying philosophical worldview); and
- often Neo-Marxist Identity Politics ideologues. Giving a negative and anti-democratic and anti-Christian, Marxist twist to things which otherwise would be positive, good and Christian, like concern for the environment and concern to avoid racism and other things discussed in Core Principle of Lasting Democracy #8 in CHAPTER 2: PRINCIPLES. According to Traditional Christianity, the environment should indeed be cared for properly as the Family Home which God made for all God's *precious human children*, without exception made lovingly *in God's Image* (making racism impossible for good, seriously practicing Christians). But Neo-Marxist Identity Politics ideologues just like Marx himself instead over-simplistically and unrealistically *reinterpret all history and all politics in toxic, adversarial terms, pitting against each other groups labelled "oppressed" and "privileged/oppressor." Keeping racism alive long after the abolition of slavery and long after the establishment of equal civil rights by villainizing the "White skin" of those whom Neo-Marxists label the "White Privileged."* Bigoted Identity Politics ideologues absurdly even demand that I, a Ukrainian Canadian member of the ethnic group which suffered history's biggest genocide (the *Holodomor*) at the hands of ideologically Marxist/Socialist bigots like them, still today have to "apologize" for the long-ago-ended slavery of Black-skinned humans in another country in another century, *just because I happen to have the same skin color of those who enslaved others in a long-past century. What could be more racist than Neo-Marxist Identity Politics ideologues imputing guilt upon me for something neither I nor my ancestors did, just because of the color of my skin? While their fellow Western Marxists hid the Marxist Holodomor Genocide of my Ukrainian ethnic group so it was not stopped earlier; and they also deny the facts of their own legal human-killing Pro-Choice abortion bigotry which follows the 1920 precedent of the very same Soviet Marxist Socialist government which later legalized the Holodomor Genocide.* But philosophical *Relativists not Realists* have no use for facts. Relativism and Marxism built on it poisons every otherwise good thing Relativists and Marxists/Socialists try to do. In the case of environmentalism, Neo-

Marxist Identity Politics ideologues pit what they label the "oppressed environment/planet" against the "privileged oppressor" humans, even treating humanity like a "disease" of "Planet Earth" to be "cured" (that is, killed) instead of recognizing each member of the human race as having the "inherent," "equal" and "inalienable" Human Rights proclaimed in the 1948 *Universal Declaration of Human Rights* produced shortly after all the many evil Nazi (politically extremist Right) legal human-killing atrocities like legal abortion, legal euthanasia, and legal genocide (following the prior evil Marxist/ Communist/ Socialist - politically extremist Left - legal human-killing atrocities like legal abortion and legal genocide of this author's ethnic group). Just not "getting" the Traditional Christian principle that *killing humans is wrong*, "ideologically lobotomized" Neo-Marxists with what Solzhenitsyn called "impaired thinking ability" due to their philosophical *Relativism* instead of *Realism*, who include many secularized Christians, are similarly (with similar anti-scientific intellectual dishonesty) obsessed with reducing the number of (that is, killing) as many humans as they can get away with, through legal human-killing abortion and legal human-killing euthanasia and other means, just like the murderous Relativist and/or Marxist politically extremist ideologues before them.

The author hopes that, since secularized Christians already claim the name of Christians anyway, they will become motivated to embrace the fullness of that name upon seeing in this book series the beauty of Traditional Christianity, its essentialness to Western Civilization as the ground of Human Rights and Free Democracy (and Science) as we know them – and the eminent (philosophically *Realist not Relativist*) reasonableness of Christianity which they only doubted because they had been deceived by the Relativist Atheist myth of the supposed "opposition" of Christian Faith and Scientific Reason, a myth which is based on a near-total *lack of knowledge* of the actual, highly Judeo-Christian history of Science briefly overviewed in this book series. Otherwise, secularized Christians will remain as useless (and dangerous) to Lasting Free Democracy and Human Rights as are all others (politically "Left" or "Right" but always *Relativist not Realist*) unduly influenced by Relativism, Secularism (which assumes Atheist Moral Relativism), and/or Marxism/ Socialism or Marxism's new form of "Identity Politics" with its censoring "Cancel Culture."

Intro for Christians:

Jesus' only explicit command was this: "A new command I give you: Love one another ... By this all men will know that you are [Christians], if you love one another" (John 13:34-5). Jesus prayed to His Father "that all [Christians] may be one ... so that the world may believe that You have sent me ... May [Christians] be brought to complete unity to let the world know that You sent me and have loved them even as You have loved me." (John 17:21,23)

This author, who has been a university professor teaching the Early Church Fathers, has a scholarly special interest in the Undivided Early Church of the First Millennium, which possessed a marvelous *unity in diversity* based on Common Faith which understood all Christians are *adopted* by God into one Christian *Family*, despite the many differences in worship customs and practices and even theology (different but complementary academic understandings of the Faith) between different Early Eastern and Western Christian "Sister Churches."

Each Sister Church's differences were rooted in the response of different cultures to the Christian *Gospel*. The "Gospel" literally means "Good News" for all humanity, and the Good News of Christianity included the revelation that every human life without exception (regardless of race/ethnicity, social class or status, or gender) is *not cheap*, to serve a greater State, as was normal in the West and worldwide, but that every human life without exception is *equally precious* to God and equally loved by God, who created every human life, "male and female," "in God's Image," as is stated in the very first chapter of the Judeo-Christian Bible, on the Bible's first page (Genesis 1:27). As Christians over the centuries gradually came to better and better understand and practice the Christian Revelation themselves, these different Christian "Sister Churches" of East and West (in the First Millennium united in one "Universal" (in Greek, *katholikos*, or "Catholic" Christian Church) over the centuries gradually transformed the viciously brutal, oppressive and totalitarian ancient pagan Western Civilization (where "popular entertainment" was torture and murder in the Roman arenas) to be ever more and more *humane*, and ever more and more *free*, based on the below *Foundational Principles of Human Rights and Democracy* which are included in the below *Common Creed of Christianity*. Remember that International Law to protect the basic rights of humans wherever they are in the world, regardless of what country they live in, what religion they follow, or type of government they live under, was founded upon the below principles by devout Christians (both Catholic and Protestant): Friar Francisco de Vitoria; Father Francisco Suárez; Alberico Gentili; Hugo Grotius. (Remember that Modern Science too was developed upon principles below by devout Christians (both Catholic and Protestant): Nicolaus Copernicus; Johannes Kepler; Galileo Galilei; Sir Francis Bacon; Sir Isaac Newton - all the principal figures of the Scientific Revolution which established Modern Science and the Modern Scientific Method).

Today "Christians" as a group remain by far *the largest and most diverse group of human beings on the planet*. There are approximately 2.3 billion Christians in the world – at least some from just about every national or racial/ethnic or cultural group or social class or gender, of all abilities and disabilities, simply because Christianity teaches every single human *without exception*, regardless of race, class, gender, disability or biological disorder (including sex/gender and reproductive disorders) are equally made "in the Image of God" and are *equally precious to God*, with *equal Human Rights* not given by any government and not subject to any government legislation, especially the *Inherent Human Right to Live*. These Christian teachings are the historical and logical foundations of all Western Human Rights and freedoms, as demonstrated in this HUMAN RIGHTS EDUCATION FOR LASTING FREE DEMOCRACY book series.

Christians therefore must become *confident champions in the public sphere* of the Human Rights and freedoms which our democracies have been steadily losing (long before the Coronavirus Pandemic allowed anti-democratic ideologues in governments to accelerate government over-reach with the help of the Marxist-influenced media Solzhenitsyn warned us about, now intertwined with "Big Tech"). Human Rights and freedoms as we know them depend historically and logically on many of our commonly held Traditional Christian principles articulated below. So, Christians must not allow themselves to remain *intimidated into silence in the public sphere* just because philosophical *Relativists not Realists*, including subjectivists and Atheists without any solid grip on Science or History or even objective Reality itself (see CHAPTER 3: PHILOSOPHY) falsely claim Christians should have no voice in public policy (even though *The Foundational Principles of Human Rights and Democracy* come from Christianity!). As demonstrated in this book, they only claim that so that they can be unopposed in attempting to shape the world according to their *ideology not education*; most recently so they can "Reset" the world upon (Pro-Choice-to-Kill-Humans) Relativist Atheist Marxist/Socialist principles, the very principles which in the 20th Century alone killed over 94 million precious humans including ten million of my ethnic group (and started the abortion-killing of precious preborn humans, all because such Moral Relativists do not believe that *killing humans is wrong*).

Most Christians today are from the Western Church and the various historical divisions (into tens of thousands of small sects or denominations) of Western Rite Christianity. This author is an Eastern Rite Christian, the Eastern Rite churches (which number in the dozens instead of tens of thousands) unlike the Western having spent much of history as a persecuted minority in non-Christian (including officially Atheist) countries. This author is a member of the largest underground Church of the 20th Century, the Ukrainian Greek Catholic Church, which officially did not exist under Atheist Relativist Soviet Marxism/Communism in the Socialist Soviet Union, which committed the *Holodomor* Genocide killing 7-10 million of my fellow Ukrainians largely *in order to stifle the traditional Christian spirit of Ukraine*, which was not keen on Atheist Socialism being forcefully imposed on it, because Ukraine has been strongly Christian since the 988 AD enthusiastic mass Christian baptisms in rivers. The globalist "Great Reset" piggy-backing on the global Coronavirus Pandemic is ultimately just another attempt to impose the Atheistic, Relativistic principles of Marxist Socialism, this time globally (as Relativist Atheist Marx intended from the beginning, and all good Marxists have aimed for).

This Eastern Rite Christian scholar and author hopes I can shed some "light from the East" that comes from being part of Eastern Christianity which has long suffered persecution for our commonly held Traditional Christian Faith articulated in the *Common Creed of Christianity* below. Where I live for four months now (at time of writing) we have already been banned from holding or attending public worship services using the Coronavirus Pandemic as a very thin excuse, while being allowed to gather in the hundreds at crowded malls and in restaurants and other venues smaller than many worship houses - just as one would expect in an Atheist Marxist/Communist/Socialist State. Around the world with oppressive "Coronavirus Measures" world citizens are *being prepared for what life will be like* if the Relativist and Socialist ideologues succeed in their "Great Reset" along Marxist lines. But the world needs not a Marxist "Great Reset" but a "Democracy Reboot" that "reloads" *The Foundational Principles of Human Rights and Democracy* which Christianity first introduced into the West.

To assist this, the world needs united Christian witness for our Free Democracy-grounding commonly held Christian Faith articulated in the Common Creed below now more than ever before. Because anti-democratic forces which long before the Coronavirus Pandemic were *already* legislating away normal democratic freedoms of speech, expression, assembly, conscience and religion, in my country and around the globe, are now using the Coronavirus Pandemic as a cover to snuff out the normal civil liberties and religious and democratic freedoms of everyone (Anyone who claims they are not must take THE INTELLECTUAL HONESTY CHALLENGE in the next chapter, to test if they even know how to THINK honestly and logically). Just because, like Socialist-sympathizing New York Times Moscow Correspondent Walter Duranty who denied and hid from the Free West the Soviet Socialist *Holodomor* Genocide of my ethnic group, they think "you can't make an omelet without breaking a few eggs" (Duranty coined the phrase meaning the omelet of a Socialist State – the destroyed eggs were millions of my fellow Ukrainians. *Relativists not Realists* are willing to accept any atrocities as long as they support promotion of their *ideology*). For the sake of ongoing Human Rights and freedoms, the world needs educated and united Christian witness like never before. Therefore Christians should always review and acknowledge this below vast Common Christian Faith before we discuss the areas in which we differ, recalling that (this Early Church scholar testifies) most of the many differences between us are of the sort which did *not divide*, but *mutually enriched* the Undivided Early Church of East and West in the First Millennium, in which the various Eastern and Western 'Sister Church' ordained leaders met and prayed *together* in Ecumenical (Worldwide) Councils of the Christian Church to together prayerfully hammer out the precise theological details of much of the below Biblically-based Common Christian Faith, trusting in Jesus' promise that He would send the Holy Spirit to guide Christians "into all the truth" (John 16:13). There are a few substantial differences among the bulk of today's Christians who share the below vast *common Christian beliefs* which we can and should discuss, but only as loving *brothers and sisters*, children of our common Father God who adopted all of us.

Christians can and should *contend together* over our few substantial disagreements while *affirming together*[16] our below-articulated *vast commonly held*

---

[16] This ecumenically and evangelically fruitful language of both "contending together" over disagreements (not pretending they do not exist for the sake of harmony, which is not true ecumenism) and "affirming together" the far greater and far more important areas of common agreement between today's divided Christians (common agreement articulated in the following *Common Creed*), comes from the ecumenical Evangelicals and Catholics Together (ECT) accord of 1994. In 2012, this author had the privilege of dining with one of its original signatories heavily involved in its development, Dr. Richard Land. Dr. Land was the long-time president of the Southern Baptists' Ethics & Religious Liberty Commission (1988-2013) and has since served as president of Southern Evangelical Seminary. Our meals together were during the 7th Annual Springtime of Faith Rome Summit in which I had been invited to participate as "one of the dynamic leaders building the new springtime" – and I was also the first Eastern Rite Christian to attend the Summits, presenting an update on East-West Christian division and reconciliation – while Dr. Land was the Summit's keynote speaker that year. Ever ecumenically-minded and mindful of the importance of a united Christian witness to the increasingly secularized culture (God bless him!), Dr. Land was also one of the original signatories involved in the 2009 Manhattan Declaration (https://www.manhattandeclaration.org). As I recall, he claimed much less direct involvement in this ecumenical Christian outreach and exhortation to the dying secular

Christian Faith. Christians owe it to the whole world to work out our remaining disagreements lovingly and peacefully, while showing a united front in *global solidarity* for *The Foundational Principles of Human Rights and Democracy* which Christians initially introduced into the West, which are now so badly eroded the world is on the verge of losing all pretense of Free Democracy.

---

culture which cannot keep its freedom without at least respecting the Christian foundations of its freedom. Less involved except for his suggesting to New York's Cardinal Timothy Dolan, "well, we're meeting in Manhattan, so why don't we call it the Manhattan Declaration?"

THE 'COMMON CREED' OF CHRISTIANITY:
10 Articles of Common, Traditional Christian Faith Describing The Vast Common Beliefs of (Eastern & Western) Catholic, Eastern Orthodox, and (Western) Conservative/ Evangelical Protestant Christianity (and 'Messianic Judaism') (On the Basis of this Common Christian Faith Christians can most credibly & effectively together guide Western Civilization into not losing its Human Rights and Democratic Freedoms which depend historically & logically on Biblical, Judeo-Christian principles)

While the precise wording or academic theology varies among Christian denominations and schools, in essence most Christians are united in the following tenets of the Core Christian Faith or "Common Creed" of Christianity, which are usually assumed by most Christians or referred to explicitly in some form in most ancient and most modern Christian "Creeds" or "Statements of Faith."

Traditional Christians, whether (Eastern or Western) Catholic, Eastern Orthodox, or (Western) Protestant/Evangelical, believe:

1. **THE ONE GOD, CREATOR AND ORDERER OF THE UNIVERSE, WHO "IS LOVE" (1 JOHN 4:8, 16), MYSTERIOUSLY (BEYOND MERELY HUMAN COMPREHENSION) EXISTS AS A TRINITY OF THREE PERSONS, FATHER, SON, AND HOLY SPIRIT.** (Note that "God is Love" is the ultimate *foundation* of the below *Foundational Principles of Human Rights and Democracy* which Christianity introduced into the West. Note that the universe being created and *ordered* by an intelligent orderer, and *not* ultimately *random* and undirected, is the starting point and *First Principles* of all Western Science. The ancient Greeks acknowledged as the first scientists got this key notion of the universe as an ordered *cosmos (not* random *chaos)* from their exposure to the older Jewish Bible (Christian Old Testament). Modern Science was logically built upon these Biblical *First Principles* by Christians who developed the Pure Sciences and the Modern Scientific Method in the Christian universities of Christian Europe, the world's first stable long-term community of scientific scholars.)

Traditional Christians, whether (Eastern or Western) Catholic, Eastern Orthodox, or (Western) Protestant/Evangelical, believe:

2. GOD CREATED HUMANITY, BOTH "MALE AND FEMALE," EQUALLY "*IN THE IMAGE OF GOD*" (GENESIS 1:27, FROM THE VERY FIRST CHAPTER AND PAGE IN THE BIBLE). (Note this is the origin of the *Equal Human Preciousness* which grounds Human Rights and Democracy.)

Traditional Christians, whether (Eastern or Western) Catholic, Eastern Orthodox, or (Western) Protestant/Evangelical, believe:

3. GOD CREATED HUMANITY "IN GOD'S IMAGE" *INTENDING* TO HAVE A LOVING *FAMILY* RELATIONSHIP WITH HUMANS DESCRIBED IN THE BIBLE AS *ADOPTION* (ROMANS 8:15), SUCH THAT:
    1) *EVERY HUMAN LIFE WITHOUT EXCEPTION* IS SUPREMELY AND *EQUALLY* PRECIOUS TO GOD AND *THEREFORE*
    2) *ALL HUMANS MUST BE FREE FROM ALL GOVERNMENT COERCION IN MATTERS OF BELIEF/THOUGHT/RELIGION/SPEECH IN ORDER THAT THEY MAY FREELY SEEK AND HOPEFULLY HEAR AND FIND THIS WONDERFUL TRUTH ABOUT HUMAN EXISTENCE, THAT HUMANS ARE EQUALLY PRECIOUS TO GOD.* (Note these two "Pro-Life" principles Christianity introduced into the West are *The Foundational Principles of Human Rights and Democracy* which are the implicit underlying historical and logical foundations of all modern Human Rights, International Law, and Democratic Freedoms, which understandably developed only in the traditionally Christian West. Note that *personhood, charity, hospitals* and *universities* were all developed by Christians for the purpose of expressing or serving the vast dignity of humans made "in the Image of God.")

Traditional Christians, whether (Eastern or Western) Catholic, Eastern Orthodox, or (Western) Protestant/Evangelical, believe:

4. HUMANITY LOST ITS ORIGINAL RELATIONSHIP WITH GOD, THE CREATOR WHO *IS* LOVE, THROUGH SIN (ANTI-LOVE), BUT GOD SO LOVED HUMANITY THAT HE MADE RECONCILIATION POSSIBLE THROUGH THE INCARNATION (ENFLESHMENT) OF GOD THE SON IN JESUS CHRIST THROUGH MARY'S VIRGIN BIRTH, MAKING JESUS *FULLY GOD AND FULLY HUMAN*, ABLE TO MAKE ATONEMENT FOR THE SINS OF ALL HUMANITY, WHICH HE DID BY DYING ON THE CROSS AND

RISING FROM THE DEAD SO THAT HUMANITY CAN BE FORGIVEN AND
SAVED (AND FIND HUMAN FULFILLMENT) THROUGH JESUS CHRIST.

Traditional Christians, whether (Eastern or Western) Catholic, Eastern Orthodox, or (Western) Protestant/Evangelical, believe:

5. WE HUMANS ACQUIRE THIS FORGIVENESS FROM SIN AND SALVATION UNTO ETERNAL LIFE THROUGH, DRAWN AND EMPOWERED BY *GOD'S GRACE*, OUR TURNING AWAY FROM SIN (ANTI-LOVE), ACCEPTING WHAT JESUS HAS DONE FOR US AND COMING INTO LOVING, SAVING RELATIONSHIP WITH JESUS (AND HIS FATHER AND HIS HOLY SPIRIT) THROUGH BELIEF AND BAPTISM, AS JESUS TAUGHT (MARK 16:16: "WHOEVER BELIEVES AND IS BAPTIZED WILL BE SAVED"). THOSE WHO "BELIEVE AND ARE BAPTIZED" BECOME SUPERNATURALLY ADOPTED *CHILDREN OF GOD* AND MEMBERS OF THE ONE *BODY OF CHRIST* THE CHURCH (WHICH MAY BE DESCRIBED AS GOD'S ADOPTED *FAMILY*, BOTH ON EARTH AND CONTINUING IN HEAVEN).

Traditional Christians, whether (Eastern or Western) Catholic, Eastern Orthodox, or (Western) Protestant/Evangelical, believe:

6. IN JESUS' LITERAL RESURRECTION FROM THE DEAD AND ASCENSION INTO HEAVEN.

Traditional Christians, whether (Eastern or Western) Catholic, Eastern Orthodox, or (Western) Protestant/Evangelical, believe:

7. IN JESUS' FUTURE RETURN IN GLORY AND JUDGEMENT AND THE BODILY RESURRECTION OF ALL THE DEAD.

Traditional Christians, whether (Eastern or Western) Catholic, Eastern Orthodox, or (Western) Protestant/Evangelical, believe:

8. IN THE TENETS OF TRADITIONAL (JUDEO)CHRISTIAN MORALITY ("YOU SHALL NOT KILL;" NOR STEAL, LIE, COVET, COMMIT ADULTERY ETC.; DESCRIBED MORE THOROUGHLY IN THE 10 COMMANDMENTS AND JESUS' SERMON ON THE MOUNT, AMONG OTHER PASSAGES OF SCRIPTURE) AS HOW TO BE LOVING AND SO HOW TO PLEASE THE GOD WHO *IS* LOVE (THUS DEMONSTRATING PRACTICALLY THAT DESPITE OUR HUMAN WEAKNESSES WE ARE *CHILDREN* OF THE GOD WHO *IS* LOVE, IN A GRADUAL LIFELONG PROCESS OF *GROWTH IN MATURITY IN LOVE* WHICH MAY BE CALLED *SANCTIFICATION* OR *GROWTH IN HOLINESS*; A GROWTH PROCESS WHICH INDIVIDUAL CHRISTIANS ENGAGE IN ACCORDING TO THEIR CAPACITY AND MOTIVATION BUT WITH ACCESS TO GOD'S EMPOWERING GRACE TO ASSIST THEM TO DO BETTER).

Traditional Christians, whether (Eastern or Western) Catholic, Eastern Orthodox, or (Western) Protestant/Evangelical, believe:

9. IN THE LOGICAL AND LOVING LIMITS OF TRADITIONAL BIBLICAL, JUDEO-CHRISTIAN SEXUAL MORALITY WITH ITS *PRO-LIFE FAMILY VALUES* WHICH UNDERGIRD FREE DEMOCRACY AND ALSO BEST SERVE THE SCIENTIFIC, BIOLOGICAL NEEDS OF THE HUMAN SPECIES: SEX SENSIBLY RESERVED FOR LIFETIME LOVING MARRIAGE BETWEEN AN ADULT HUMAN MALE AND FEMALE WHO ARE NATURALLY EMOTIONALLY BONDED BY THEIR SEXUAL UNION TO FORM A STABLE *HUMAN FAMILY* IN WHICH THEY AS MOTHER AND FATHER (A FEMALE AND MALE ROLE MODEL) RAISE THE HUMAN CHILDREN NATURALLY PRODUCED BY THEIR SEXUAL UNION TO EMOTIONALLY AND PHYSICALLY HEALTHY HUMAN MATURITY IN LOVING HUMAN *FAMILIES* WHICH ARE THE BUILDING BLOCKS OF CARING HUMAN *SOCIETIES*. *THIS BIBLICAL SEXUAL MORALITY IS ESSENTIAL TO HUMAN RIGHTS*: HISTORY DEMONSTRATES THAT ONLY IF THE SEXUAL *PROCESS* IS THUS CONSIDERED *PRECIOUS NOT CHEAP* ARE THE *HUMANS* PRODUCED BY THAT PROCESS CONSIDERED *PRECIOUS NOT CHEAP*. (*Preciously made* humans of the Christian West who believe sex is *precious not cheap, and reserved for marriage,* gradually but logically developed Human Rights and Democratic Freedoms appropriate to their *equal human preciousness* which is championed today by the Pro-Life Movement; while cheap humans *cheaply made* by cheap "sex for pleasure" (instead of precious and exalted "sex for marriage") can be legally killed and typically serve a greater, totalitarian State, as in the ancient pre-Christian West which was typified by *unrestricted sexual practices*, *Pro-Choice Legal Abortion* to kill the unwanted humans produced by immaturely and irresponsibly engaging in nature's way of generating new humans without any intention of doing so; and *totalitarian State government* which held the power of life and death over humans who were considered *cheap not precious* just as the sexual process which produces humans was considered *cheap not precious*. Today's Pro-Choice 'Creeping Totalitarianism' undermining Free Democracy is specifically rooted in the return of unrestricted, immature and irresponsible sexual practices since the 1960s Sexual Revolution; which created demand for the return of Legal Abortion to kill the unwanted humans produced by immaturely and irresponsibly engaging in nature's way of generating new humans without any intention of doing so; Legal Abortion legally eradicated the *Inherent Human Right to Live* which is the historical and logical foundation of all the Human Rights and Democratic Freedoms which developed only in the *Christian* West since the 318 AD criminalization of abortion due to Christian influence; thus today, officially Pro-Choice political parties in power, *specifically to support "abortion access" without anyone complaining about humans being killed*, have been passing *anti-*

democratic laws and policies taking away normal democratic freedoms of speech, expression, assembly, conscience and religion of peaceful Pro-Life Human Rights Advocates and of Pro-Life doctors who follow the ancient non-killing Hippocratic Medical Tradition that *doctors do not kill* (it was in response to such Pro-Choice 'Creeping Totalitarianism' now rapidly accelerating in this author's country that this Human Rights Scholar was motivated to develop the new HUMAN RIGHTS EDUCATION FOR LASTING FREE DEMOCRACY from well-established facts of Science, Logic, and Human Rights History). The return of ancient, pre-Christian *unrestricted sexual practices* in the Sexual Revolution brought the return of ancient, pre-Christian *Pro-Choice Legal Abortion*, which is now in the process of bringing the return of ancient, pre-Christian *totalitarian Pro-Choice government.* Legal human-killing abortion throughout history has always gone hand-in-hand with totalitarian government, specifically because if humans do not even have a legally recognized *Inherent Human Right to Live* because they can be legally killed by abortion, there is no compelling reason for such Pro-Choice governments to recognize a right to vote, or to speak freely, or any other rights. It was specifically the oppressive totalitarian Extremist Left (Atheist) Soviet Communist Party ruling the (Atheist) Union of Soviet Socialist Republics which was the first political party in modern times to legalize abortion – followed by the oppressive totalitarian Extremist Right National Socialist German Worker's Party (commonly known as the Nazi Party, under Adolf Hitler from 1921-1945; not Atheists, but the top-level Nazis were occultists following the occultic mythology of the Aryan Master Race which they used to justify legalizing human-killing by abortion, euthanasia, and genocide in the Death Camps). Both the Extremist Left (Marxist) Soviet Communist Party and the Extremist Right (Fascist) Nazi Party despised Democracy and did not believe that *killing humans is wrong.* Of course any legal human-killing such as abortion and euthanasia (the Nazis were the first to legalize both) is *inherently politically extremist* and depends on the rejection of the Pro-Life *Foundational Principles of Human Rights and Democracy* which Christianity introduced into the West).

Traditional Christians, whether (Eastern or Western) Catholic, Eastern Orthodox, or (Western) Protestant/Evangelical, believe:

10. IN THE INSPIRATION AND INERRANCY OF THE HOLY SCRIPTURES (THE BIBLE) WHICH TESTIFY TO ALL THESE THINGS.

(Note it is especially reasonable for Christians to believe this, because all modern Human Rights and Democratic Freedoms, and all modern Science and Technology, are historically and logically built upon enlightened *First Principles* which the West learned from the Judeo-Christian Bible. Modern Science and the Modern Scientific Method were pioneered specifically by Christian religious believers in the Christian universities of Christian Europe, the world's first ongoing stable community of scientific scholars, the premier figures of "the Scientific Revolution" being particularly devout Christians (both Catholic and Protestant) who developed Modern Science and the Modern Scientific Method logically upon Biblical *First Principles* such as the universe being an *ordered cosmos* – with an Intelligent Orderer or Creator God – and *not* an ultimately random, *undirected chaos*. Modern Human Rights and Democratic Freedoms and International Law to protect humans wherever they are also developed only in Western *Christian* Civilization, primarily developed by devout Christian social reformers (both Catholic and Protestant) seeking to have Christian principles like *equal human preciousness governments are obligated to protect* and the *Inherent Human Right to Live* better put into practice in human societies. Christian principles which are rooted in the Bible's testimony that "God is Love" (1 John 4:8) and so "You shall not kill" (Exodus 20:13) because humans, "male and female," are made equally "in the Image of God" (Genesis 1:27).)

Conclusion: These *10 Articles of Common Christian Faith* entering the West with the 1st Century advent of Christianity and embraced by the West starting in the 4th Century gave *individual humans the means to their greatest possible human fulfillment and happiness* in Family Love both on Earth and eternally in Heaven; and gave *human societies the Foundations for Modern Human Rights, Modern International Law, and Modern Democracy* - and even Modern Science, developed in the Christian universities of Christian Europe from Biblical *First Principles* (even Modern Science depends historically and logically on the universe being an *ordered cosmos* with an intelligent *orderer* as in Article 1 above, and *not* a random, undirected *chaos*!). The vast, practical fruitfulness of this *Common Christian Faith* for humans individually and collectively is WHY Christians today are by far *the largest and most diverse group of humans on the planet*, with 2.3 *billion* Christians who come from nearly every other group of humans, Christians found among nearly every national/racial/ethnic/cultural group, social class, gender and ability or disability. The surest path to the destruction of Free Democracy which was historically and logically built upon the above Christian and Pro-Life principles is the current and growing Pro-Choice and anti-Christian bigotry and illogical "Bulverism" that dismisses Christian ideas out-of-hand as "having no place in the public sphere" when in fact Christian Pro-Life Family Values include and support the absolutely essential *Foundational Principles of Human Rights and Democracy* (and when in fact the Modern University

System itself grew out of the Judeo-Christian scholarly pursuit of the Honest Truth in all its forms). Continued lack of respect for Christianity as the *source* of these democratic foundations (while continuing to follow the evil totalitarian Soviet and Nazi precedent of de-criminalized human-killing abortion, which legally eliminates any legally recognized *Inherent, Equal, Inalienable Human Rights) is* the surest way to ultimately end Free Democracy.

[In the author's upcoming book *Killing Humans Is Wrong The* 10 Articles of Common Christian Faith or the "Common Creed of Christianity" are repeated with Historical Notes and gloss which more fully bring out the vast contribution of Traditional Christianity to Modern Human Rights and Freedoms (and Science).]

CHAPTER 6: HUMAN RESPONSIBILITIES COME WITH YOUR HUMAN RIGHTS

A Non-Partisan Appeal to All Voters and to All with Even More Influence (Especially Billionaires, Media Moguls, Journalists and "Big Tech" Who Control News and Information; Especially Politicians, Political Parties, Civil Servants, Judges, Police and Military Who Control or Enforce Laws and Public Policy):

STOP Neglecting or Avoiding Your Human Responsibilities to Recognize and Protect Human Rights in All Other Humans, and START Standing Up Together in *Solidarity* for *Equal Human Rights for All Humans Without Exception*; and

START Standing Against Uneducated 'Creeping Totalitarianism,' *So That Everyone in the World has a Free Future* (including this author's first grandchild soon to be born).

GET AND SPREAD a Solid HUMAN RIGHTS EDUCATION FOR LASTING FREE DEMOCRACY.

STOP Being (or Being Pawns of) Ideologues *Without a Clue* What are *The Foundational Principles of Human Rights and Democracy*, Because They Lack the *Human Rights Education* Culled from the Disciplines of History, Philosophy, Science and Logic in this Book Series.

START Spreading this HUMAN RIGHTS EDUCATION FOR LASTING FREE DEMOCRACY Until Each Country has More *Educated* Voters (and More *Educated* Politicians, Judges, Billionaires, Journalists etc.) than *Uneducated* Voters (and *Uneducated* "Big Tech" Media Moguls, Police, Civil Servants and Political Parties, etc.) Tearing Down Worldwide Human Freedom and Trampling Human Rights *in Their Ignorance.*

Those Who Refuse this Non-Partisan Appeal to Good Sense and to *Education over Ideology* Must Take the Last Chapter's INTELLECTUAL HONESTY CHALLENGE or Else They Just Prove Their Lack of Intelligence or Their Lack of Honesty (for All to See).

This author, thinker, logician and Human Rights scholar's ethnicity represents (only) the first ten million murdered victims of Relativist, Marxist, Socialist thinking in the Ukrainian Soviet Socialist Republic, in the *Holodomor* Genocide committed by Atheist Socialists who took political power for the first time in the Soviet Union, not long after the author's family moved to Canada from Ukraine (which is likely why I am alive). One of the very biggest genocides of history (though genocide of your ethnic group is not a competition), the *Holodomor* was committed by the same Soviet (politically *extremist Left*) government which was also the very first government since the 4th Century *to legalize human-killing by abortion*. Demonstrating that legal human-killing, by abortion or any other means, is of course politically *extremist* no matter which end of the political spectrum one is on ("Left" or "Right"), the next government to legalize abortion was Germany's under the *extremist Right* Nazi Party ("Nazi" is short for "National Socialist" in German, by the way). The Nazis started their *Holocaust* Genocide murdering millions of Jewish humans by opening up Dachau, the first Nazi concentration/death camp, around the time the *Holodomor* Genocide was starting to wind down in Soviet Ukraine. So, the first two governments ever (since the 4th Century) to legalize abortion both also legalized genocide. Both governments were extremist and totalitarian, telling the governed humans what to believe and do, rewarding or punishing citizens based on their complicity with the ruling political party's ideology.[17] Both governments ultimately holding the very lives of citizens in the government's hands because these governments did not believe *killing humans is*

---

[17] The evil, murderous and genocidal Soviets and Nazis in political power rewarded or punished citizens and groups of citizens based on their complicity or non-compliance with the ruling party's ideology. With the Extremist Left Communist (Marxist) or Extremist Right Nazi (Fascist) ruling political party's ideology. Marxist, Communist China (which is currently engaged in yet another Marxist genocide, and is currently stamping out the last vestiges of freedom in the former British colony of Hong Kong) still does the same thing, rewarding or punishing citizens or groups of citizens based on their compliance or non-compliance with the ruling (one-party-system) Marxist, Communist-Socialist, extremist party's ideology, as one of my country's former Ambassadors to China reiterated in an interview in May 2020, expressing his shock that our supposedly democratic country was now doing the same totalitarian things as Communist China. Since 2018 in my country (where the aggressively Pro-Choice-to-Kill-Humans national leader openly admires Communist China which has no religious freedom and forces mandatory abortions against the mother's will), my government has even started denying usual government funding to charitable groups and businesses which (on grounds of conscience and/or religion) will not make an "attestation" stating they believe in and support the ruling political party's aggressively Pro-Choice-to-Kill-Humans by abortion policies. Policies which emulate the genocidal extremist Soviet and Nazi precedents of legal human-killing by abortion – but the ruling party is far too uneducated and incompetent to even know that! They are far to uneducated and incompetent to know that legal abortion in Nazi Germany was sensibly called "a crime against humanity" at the Nuremberg War Crimes Trials precisely because governing politicians just like everyone else have a Human Responsibility that necessarily comes with their Human Rights, a Human Responsibility to recognize and protect Human Rights in all other humans without exception. This Pro-Choice ruling political party which has failed in its Human Responsibilities is so utterly incompetent to govern a lasting democracy that they actually made a policy which in 2018 denied the usual government funding to help hire summer students to over 1000 charities and businesses which usually qualify for this government funding. A slight softening of the policy's wording for an election year in 2019 still left charities and businesses of good conscience unable to qualify for this government funding. This is a very good program both for students and for charities, but under the management of a Pro-Choice-to-Kill-Humans government you cannot get this government funding if you actually believe in the Pro-Life *Foundational Principles of Human Rights and Democracy.*

wrong and so they did not legally recognize any *inherent, equal, inalienable Human Rights* not given by the government and so not within the government's jurisdiction to *legislate them away.*

But modern Human Rights and freedoms began way back in the 4th Century, when the West learned from Christianity that *killing humans is wrong* because *all humans without exception are equally precious*, and, in what is effectively the first-ever legal recognition and protection of Human Rights, the West then *criminalized* human-killing by abortion and infanticide (also outlawing previously culturally-accepted Western brutalities like gladiatorial fights to the death in the Roman arenas), setting in motion the long and gradual but logical and inevitable process towards modern International Law, Modern Democracy, and Human Rights. A long but logical process described in this HUMAN RIGHTS EDUCATION FOR LASTING FREE DEMOCRACY book series.

But, rejecting this Christian, Human Rights and freedoms heritage embedded in Traditional Western Values since the 4th Century, the Atheist, Marxist Socialists in their many Soviet Bloc Socialist countries (and later Asian Atheist Marxist countries) committed mass murder upon both born and preborn humans with ease because as philosophical *Relativists not Realists* they believed in no moral absolutes and so just did not believe that *killing humans is wrong.* Although like-minded Western Atheists, Marxists, Socialists influencing Western mainstream media hid the 1932-33 *Holodomor* Genocide, and as many earlier and later Soviet Socialist atrocities as they could, from common knowledge in the West, so that they could (dishonestly) continue to point to the Soviet Union, the world's first Socialist State, and its Soviet Bloc allies, as models for the West, the similar atrocities and genocides committed by the Nazis before and during World War II could not be hidden when the war ended. So the world was shocked when so many horrors, above all the Nazi *Holocaust* Genocide murdering 6 million Jewish humans, were revealed. And the world was justifiably horrified to discover that every terrible thing that happened in Nazi Germany under its democratically elected Nazi Party government *was legal.*

Thus, the Nuremberg War Crimes Trials of the Nazis after World War II implicitly established the principle that every human, together with and directly related to their Human *Rights* (which were formalized and made explicit in the UN"s *Universal Declaration of Human Rights* shortly after the War), also had Human *Responsibilities* to recognize and protect these Human Rights in all other humans. It is worth repeating (from CHAPTER 3: PHILOSOPHY) that:

Philosophically speaking, Nuremberg later was at base a Trial of Realism passing official judgment over Relativism, because after Nazi Germany the Free World realized the Real World could not afford another Nazi Germany, another State run by Morally Relativistic ideology. The Nuremberg War Crimes Trials of the Nazis assumed and helped us clarify that even though all the atrocities of Nazi Germany were technically legal, for the future safety of all humanity, which cannot afford another Nazi Germany, any "sovereign country's" laws are still subject to certain minimal principles which even International Law must formally recognize (not create), principles we now call Human Rights, which were in fact formally clarified in the new United Nations' Universal Declaration of Human Rights, produced in

1948, while the Nuremberg Trials were still going on. The same year the Nuremberg Trials called legal abortion in Nazi Germany a "crime against humanity" along with all the other many Nazi crimes against humanity which equally denied Equal Human Rights to some humans. The Nuremberg War Crimes Trials established that for world human safety, the excuses "it was legal in my country" and "I was just following orders," which in most cases mitigate personal responsibility, did not, could not and must not mitigate responsibility for all the horrors in Nazi Germany that the Nazis led but in which the people participated or collaborated (or at least allowed to happen without resisting, even many otherwise good people, which is why Professor Jordan Peterson reminds us, "the lesson of World War II: You are the Nazi." Aleksandr Solzhenitsyn confirms, "The battleline between good and evil runs through the heart of every man"). The Nuremberg War Crimes Trials established that these minimal political principles for governing humans we now call Human Rights, which are not given by any government and so cannot be legislated away by any government, of course imply Human Responsibilities to recognize those Human Rights in all other humans (and protect them where they are threatened).

Thus, the Nuremberg War Crimes Trials legitimately prosecuted key figures in Nazi Germany who led or greatly facilitated the mass murders, even though such mass murder was "legal" in Nazi Germany, because these people had criminally neglected their Human Responsibilities to recognize and protect Human Rights in other humans. Hence, not just the Nazi government leadership, but judges, doctors (especially abortionists), businessmen and others in positions of authority who particularly promoted and facilitated the Nazi crimes against humanity were put on trial at Nuremberg. Businessmen who fulfilled Nazi government contracts for customized equipment with no purpose but to kill large numbers of humans quickly, could not claim they were merely "doing business for the government" in building and supplying the Nazis with instruments of mass murder ...

Before World War II, the extremist Right (Fascist) Nazi Party in power in Germany under Adolf Hitler and the extremist Left (Marxist) Communist Party in the (one-party-system) Union of Soviet Socialist Republics (USSR) under Josef Stalin had signed both public and secret treaties which together agreed that both sides would expand their power and carve up Europe, but would leave each other alone. After Hitler later broke the treaty and attacked the Soviet Union in 1941, at the height of Nazi power, Stalin's USSR joined the Allied nations against the juggernaut of Nazi Germany, being (cautiously) accepted by the Allies (at least on the principle that "the enemy of my enemy is my friend" – at least until the mutual enemy is defeated). Because the Soviet Union was allied with the victors of World War II led by Britain and the U.S.A., the USSR had a large say in the restructuring of the world after World War II, and the USSR was given a permanent seat on the United Nations' Security Council when the UN was formed after the war. Unfortunately for human freedom, those countries militarily "liberated" from Nazi occupation by the Soviets at the war's end just became new Soviet "satellite States" of a huge Marxist "Soviet Bloc" formalized later in the 1955 "Warsaw Pact" during the Cold War.

It is important to understand that all the representatives of Atheist, philosophically *Relativist-not-Realist,* Marxist-Communist-Socialist, Soviet Bloc governments who were on the United Nations' original Human Rights Commission refused to even vote on *The Universal Declaration of Human Rights* produced by the United Nations in 1948. *As Atheists and Relativists they could not accept any moral absolutes like any Human Rights the government had to respect;* in fact, as Atheists, they could not accept *anything* higher than the government, to which the government is *accountable for how it treats the humans it governs.* Which is exactly why all Atheist governments in history have been totalitarian and oppressive to human life and freedom. Unfortunately for Western freedom, Western Atheists and Relativists and Marxists/Socialists influencing Western mainstream media had earlier buried the truth that the Soviet Socialists had committed the *Holodomor* Genocide against this author's ethnic group (along with many other atrocities) even before the Nazis had taken power in Germany (after which the Nazis committed the similar-scale massive atrocity of the *Holocaust* Genocide). So since then, Westerners, though most appropriately despise the (Relativist) Nazis for their atrocities and genocides, *have not been wary of* the Relativist, Marxist, Socialist ideologies which motivated and enabled far, far more human deaths (in more countries over more time) than even the despicable Relativist Nazis were responsible for. We in the West have not been wary of the ideologies which motivated and enabled the dishonesty of the Western Marxists and Socialists who in Western media hid or downplayed the facts of Socialist atrocities and genocides like the *Holodomor.* We have not been watching out for the Western Marxists and Socialists who Solzhenitsyn confirmed manipulate Western media towards Marxist, totalitarian ends, Solzhenitsyn while exiled to the West for 18 years recognizing media here in the West growing in the same "social control via information control" characteristics as the Soviet Marxist media he grew up and lived with in Soviet Communist Russia.

"Ideology – that is what gives evildoing its long-sought justification and gives the evildoer the necessary steadfastness and determination. That is the social theory which helps to make his acts seem good instead of bad in his own and others' eyes ... Thanks to ideology the twentieth century was fated to experience evildoing calculated on a scale in the millions."
– Aleksandr Solzhenitsyn

"Without any censorship, in the West fashionable trends of thought and ideas are carefully separated from those which are not fashionable; nothing is forbidden, but what is not fashionable will hardly ever find its way into periodicals or books or be heard in colleges. Legally your researchers are free, but they are conditioned by the fashion of the day."
— Aleksandr Solzhenitsyn

So now many vacuous and dangerous Relativist and/or Marxist ideologies run rampant here in the West, especially insidious in evolving forms like Identity Politics, "Cancel Culture" and (radically skeptical) Postmodernist philosophy developed by Marxists like Jacques Derrida, which (in denial of Science's *Realistic* foundations) denies any objective facts exist (as an easy way for Marxists to ignore and deny the overwhelming *objective facts* – like over 94 million dying in Socialist countries in the 20th Century alone - that *Relativist not Realist* Marxism/Socialism simply does not and cannot ever work in the *Real* World).

We must remember that the Western Relativists, Marxists, Socialists influencing Western mainstream media who *back then successfully covered up the Holodomor Genocide of my ethnic group and successfully silenced and discredited* the honest whistleblowers who tried to tell the truth of the matter *never went anywhere else.* They, and those they trained to be media moguls and journalists after them are *still with us here in the West.* Encouraged by success after success in, as Solzhenitsyn identified, controlling information by controlling just what is "fashionable" and just what is "unfashionable" to even report on in mainstream news media. So, over the decades they have increased exponentially the numbers of those in the West who share or are at least strongly influenced by their vacuous and dangerous – and fundamentally intellectually dishonest – Relativist, Marxist, Socialist, ideologies. Often expressed in newer forms which include Political Correctness, Identity Politics, and Cancel Culture. Solzhenitsyn warned us all this was happening decades ago; he never changed his prediction of these Western Relativists and Marxists taking the West towards a totalitarian future, and he died only as recently as 2008! But the West did not heed Solzhenitsyn's repeated warnings. Largely because the developing Neo-Marxist "Cancel Culture" subtly "cancelled" common knowledge of Solzhenitsyn himself *first*, such that most younger adults (even "university educated") have never even heard of this important Nobel Prize-winning historian of Marxism in the world's first Socialist State; nor ever heard of his book *The Gulag Archipelago* which exposed the web of lies Soviet Marxism depended upon, even though his book sold 35 million copies, was translated into 30 languages, and helped end Soviet Communism and with it the Cold War.

So, we must remember that those same Western Relativists, Marxists, Socialists who never went anywhere else, who *back then* hid the *Holodomor* Genocide and in media pretended it just did not exist (because it is easy for philosophical *Relativists not Realists and subjectivists* to just pretend any *objective facts* against their ideology *just do not exist*) *NOW* similarly hide *important medical testimony against Coronavirus alarmism and lockdowns*, and they just pretend that *many tens of thousands of doctors and medical scientists against Coronavirus alarmism and lockdowns* just do not exist. Just because Relativist ideologues have no commitment to facts and always choose ideology over facts; just because Western Neo-Marxist Socialism/ Identity Politics/ Cancel Culture is just as much built on a web of lies and dishonesty as was Soviet Marxist Socialism; and just because scientifically unjustified Coronavirus alarmism and lockdowns do much to support a Marxist, Socialist "Great Reset" of the world piggybacking on the Coronavirus Pandemic. it dizzies the brain to see just how many groupings of expert medical scientists, doctors and other medical professionals who testify against any need for the current oppressive "Coronavirus Measures" like lockdowns and mask mandates have just been "cancelled" by the Neo-Marxist "Cancel Culture" which (because they are *Relativists not Realists* who deep down do not believe in objective facts anyways) are in the habit of just pretending any objective evidence or expert testimony against their opinions and ideologies *just do not exist.*

Update: Note that the Great Barrington Declaration's 55,500+ (and counting) medical professional (and medical scientist) signatories are just one of the more international and more prominent of many groupings of medical professionals, doctors and medical scientists against unscientific Coronavirus alarmism and unmedical lockdown imprisonment protocols. Shortly before publication this author learned of yet another new group of doctors and medical scientists against lockdowns in my country, the Canadian Health Alliance, and of an excellent new 11-minute doctors' video *Canadian Doctors Speak Out: Top Reasons Not to Be Afraid of Covid.* The video was "cancelled" and erased only 20 minutes after being posted to YouTube! Non-expert "Big Tech" and news media now regularly thus censor, hide and bury expert scientific and medical testimony that does not fit their chosen narrative in support of their chosen ideology which they desire to "reset" the whole world with, using the Pandemic as an excuse and a cover – with no regard for objective facts, and no matter how many people (or their livelihoods) are harmed. But Relativist/ Marxist/ Socialist-influenced ideologues have always considered their (unrealistic) ends justify any means (even genocide – ask my fellow Ukrainians murdered in the millions by Soviet Socialists, while Western Socialists covered it up).

This author and representative of the first ten million murdered victims of Marxism/ Socialism in the Soviet *Holodomor* Genocide, which was covered up by Western Marxist/ Socialist-influenced mainstream media, hereby scolds YouTube and all "Big Tech" companies now intertwined with Western mainstream media, who should be ashamed of themselves for squelching democratic Free Speech/ Free Expression even of medical specialists, all in order to support an ideologically Marxist/ Socialist "Great Reset" of the globe using the Coronavirus Pandemic as an excuse and cover. The blood of millions (94 million victims of Marxism in Socialist countries in the 20th Century alone) calls out for you "Big Tech" companies to rejoin the human race and publicly repent of and end your current support of Marxist-Communist-Socialist ideology, which has caused more human deaths than anything else in history. YouTube should from now on be called "CensorTube," at least until this Big Tech company (YouTube is run by Google) takes THE INTELLECTUAL HONESTY CHALLENGE in Chapter 7 and publicly repents of its intellectually dishonest but enthusiastic support so far of the Marxist "Great Reset" through the censorship of expert medical testimonies (this author first noted YouTube was censoring and deleting expert medical testimonies to the detriment and harm of many in Summer 2020, and they have just gotten worse, for example, deleting the above March 2021 *Canadian Doctors Speak Out: Top Reasons Not to Be Afraid of Covid* video from YouTube in only 20 minutes from when the video was posted to YouTube. For the sake of future freedom for all, readers must remember (and tell your children) how *"Big Tech" (many companies, including Google/YouTube) did not want you to see this and many other expert medical and scientific video testimonies.* Anyone who has lost their family business to Coronavirus lockdowns or lost family members who died because they did not receive proper medical attention for non-Covid-19 illnesses during the Pandemic lockdowns, or who died from overdoses or suicides due to the psychologically damaging effects of lockdowns, *should always remember that "Big Tech" (notably Google/YouTube which has so far proven itself a top totalitarian censor) did not want you to see the tremendous expert medical testimony evidence that such lockdowns are not helpful, are harmful, and should be stopped. "Big Tech" did not want your government officials who make their oppressive lockdown policies according to Big Tech Media's Coronavirus alarmism narrative, to ever see any expert medical testimony and evidence that oppressive lockdowns are unnecessary and do more harm than good.*

But, since Relativists (who deny objective Reality) instead define "reality" as whatever they want it to be, the (Relativist) Marxist-influenced mainstream media, if or when it acknowledges the existence of evidence against their Coronavirus alarmism narrative at all, they simply mis-define even tens of thousands of doctors' expert medical testimony as "misinformation about the Coronavirus." In dishonest attempts of non-expert media and governments to make the average person unwisely dismiss all the expert testimony and evidence that they are being fooled.

And they get away with this gross dishonesty (and gross undemocratic stupidity) as long as they control mainstream media, and as long as today's good Westerners are like the good but timid Germans who allowed themselves to be *intimidated into silence and submission* by Relativist Nazi totalitarianism. And are *not* choosing to be like the good Poles in Soviet Bloc Poland who successfully undermined hardline Relativist Soviet Communist totalitarianism in the Cold War Eastern Bloc Socialist countries *by standing up together in Solidarity for their Traditional Western Values* (which include and support *The Foundational Principles of Human Rights and Democracy*) to become once again the guide of their country's public political policies and laws.

But if the West and the World are now held hostage (literally imprisoned/locked down in their homes) by their timidity and silence in the face of unscientific Coronavirus alarmism perpetrated by the Relativist Neo-Marxist Pro-Choice legal human-killing abortion *Extremist Left* and its Politically Correct, Identity Politics, Neo-Marxist "Cancel Culture" which immediately "cancels" and *censors from the mainstream Internet platforms* all expert medical testimony which does not support their misuse of the Coronavirus Pandemic as an excuse to attempt a global Marxist "Great Reset," much of the blame can be traced to the fact that for many decades before the Coronavirus Pandemic, *Western nations had already given up their democratic soul* and foolishly followed the totalitarian genocidal Extremist Left Soviet and totalitarian genocidal Extremist Right Nazi precedents of legal human-killing by abortion, which has since left the West without the necessary foundations for lasting Free Democracy, which require uncompromising legal government recognition of *equal human preciousness without exception* and *Equal Human Rights for All Humans.* In Western countries, there was a temporary withdrawing from totalitarian evil influence after the Nazi horrors of World War II were first revealed. But only about 20 years after the *Universal Declaration of Human Rights* was made, Western nations for some reason started to willingly take on the legal human-killing by abortion, and later by euthanasia, which the Nazis would have forced upon the Free West if the evil human-killing Nazis had won World War II!

But, in a charitable belief that most who now consider themselves "Pro-Choice" and support legal abortion are simply more *uninformed* than they are evil, unintelligent, intellectually dishonest or "ideologically lobotomized" (that is, "wilfully unintelligent" and "culpably ignorant"), before delivering in the next and last chapter THE INTELLECTUAL HONESTY CHALLENGE, intended mainly for the most ardent (and most intellectually dishonest) Pro-Choice Relativists and Neo-Marxists, I wanted to in this chapter give **a non-partisan appeal to all readers** simply to **fulfil your Human Responsibilities which are the flip side of your Human Rights**, by **recognizing and protecting Human Rights in all other humans than yourself, which of course includes humans not-yet-born but** *just like you* **when you were their age (such that, if they do not have** *an inherent, equal, inalienable Human Right to Live* **because abortion is legal, then logically** *neither do you).* So, as a final review and reminder from the end of CHAPTER 1: FACTS, to help the more honest do the right thing without having to be *challenged* as in the next chapter, here is a potent consideration to help the still-uncertain reader come to the correct stance needed for Free Democracy to last (on solid foundations) for our children and grandchildren:

Pro-Choice Voters and (Even More Influential) Pro-Choice Politicians, Political Parties, Judges, Civil Servants/Government Employees (Who Have Influence Over Public Policies and Laws); as well as Influential Billionaires, Media Moguls, Journalists and "Big Tech" Employees and Companies (Who Have Influence Over News and Media and Thus Control Public Access to Information) NEED TO REALIZE THAT THEIR PRO-CHOICE STANCE MARKS THEM (TO THE HUMAN-RIGHTS EDUCATED AND TO FUTURE HISTORY BOOKS) as Among the Most Bigoted and Least Intellectually Honest People on the Planet Earth Throughout All Human History

As this thoughtful, highly educated and intelligent and intellectually honest book series reveals, self-described "Pro-Choicers" are among the most hypocritical, most bigoted and least intellectually honest people on the planet. The most bigoted, because they copy the genocidal (philosophically *Relativist not Realist*) Marxist/ Socialist ideologue bigots who *first* legalized human-killing abortion in modern times and *then* legalized the human-killing genocide of millions of my ethnic group, *just like all bigots deny Equal Human Rights to some humans.* Today's self-described Pro-Choicers are also the *least intellectually honest people on the planet* because (see Chapters 7-9 of this author's longer book *Pro-Life Equals Pro-Democracy* for many more details than in this handbook) they justify their beloved legal human-killing abortion following totalitarian Marxist precedent *only by absurdly denying the plain Science* that preborn humans are humans (so Abortion kills humans). And also by *using nearly every intellectually dishonest logical fallacy* in a Logic textbook to try to *dishonestly* wiggle out of *admitting* that *killing humans is wrong,* which is a principle they usually pay insincere "lip service" to, of course *applies to the preborn humans of any age they are eager to kill for their own convenience.*

"Pro-Choicers," whatever their level of societal influence (as above – but just being a voter makes them influential) need to realize that their Pro-Choice position logically implies other things about them they probably do not wish others to think of them (which is the result of foolishly associating themselves with a Pro-Choice position/opinion that involves *killing humans* without first thinking it through scientifically and logically):

1. Being Pro-Choice logically means you do not believe that *killing humans is wrong* (so you are like evil and violent criminals and dictators).

2. Being Pro-Choice logically means you do not believe in *Equal Human Rights for All Humans* (so you are like every bigot or slaveowner).

3. Being Pro-Choice logically means you do not believe *in the science of human life nor the science of logic,* since science confirms preborn humans are humans, and logic confirms they therefore must have Human Rights (so you are *like the uneducated and ignorant*).

4. Being Pro-Choice logically *means you do not know how to think scientifically, consistently nor logically nor honestly* (suggesting you may be like *the unintelligent or mentally deficient* – or perhaps simply *dishonest.* Actually, many people who because of developmental disorders are in fact unintelligent or mentally deficient can still *honestly grasp the truths* that *humans are equally precious* and that *all humans have Human Rights*).

So, Pro-Choice voters, politicians, political parties, billionaires, journalists, judges and "Big Tech" companies and employees who are now intertwined with the Mainstream Media which Solzhenitsyn (the Nobel Prize-winning historian of brutally totalitarian Soviet Marxism/Socialism) repeatedly testified (after living 18 years in the U.S.) was Marxist-influenced, NEED to REALIZE:

When you say, "I believe in a woman's right to CHOOSE to have her baby (or terminate her pregnancy)" you are effectively admitting *you do not actually believe in Human Rights* (which are incompatible) and you do not realize you are saying you do not know how to think consistently, honestly, nor logically (or else you would know they are incompatible).

Your Pro-Choice position says a lot of awkward and embarrassing things about you that you did not realize you are advertising whenever you say that you are Pro-Choice. From now on, get used to EDUCATED people calling you on it and embarrassing you if you are ignorant, unintelligent, or evil and bigoted enough to stay Pro-Choice after exposure to the now readily available HUMAN RIGHTS EDUCATION FOR LASTING FREE DEMOCRACY delineated in this book series from mostly undisputed facts of Human Rights History, Science, Logic, and the History of Philosophy (and of Science).

So do not stay dishonest. Do not look for yet another lying way to dishonestly describe your position *for* the legal killing of humans by abortion (following totalitarian Soviet and Nazi precedents of legal abortion). Your severe intellectual dishonesty has been revealed for all intelligent people to see in this book series. *This is your opportunity to leave lying behind* and honestly become a loving member of the human race who recognizes and supports *Equal Human Rights for All Humans without exception,* which is part of the necessary foundation of all lasting free democracies, as abundantly demonstrated in this book series.

For those who will not take advantage of this chapter's exhortation to simply START to fulfil your Human Responsibilities, and simply STOP lying, there remains THE INTELLECTUAL HONESTY CHALLENGE in the last chapter, next . . .

236

...

CHAPTER 7: THE THINKING REVOLUTION AND THE INTELLECTUAL HONESTY CHALLENGE

[Drawn from the author's upcoming book *THINKING REVOLUTION: THE INTELLECTUAL HONESTY CHALLENGE*]

"Writers haven't got any rockets to blast off. We don't even trundle the most insignificant auxiliary vehicle. We haven't got any military might. So what can literature do in the face of the merciless onslaught of open violence?
One word of truth outweighs the whole world."
— *Aleksandr Solzhenitsyn*

"Abortion is the touchstone issue for determining the health and longevity of any democracy, because wherever human-killing abortion is legal, there is no legally recognized Inherent, Equal, Inalienable Human Right to Live, and therefore no basis for lasting Free Democracy."
– William Baptiste (né Boyko, One of Most Common Ukrainian Surnames), Representative of (only) the First Ten Million Murdered Victims of Marxism in the Holodomor Genocide, Committed by the Very First Marxist State, which was the Very First Modern State to Legalize Human-Killing Abortion

---

The Intellectual Honesty Challenge in Brief: Everyone is uneducated in something before they have opportunity to be educated. It is no shame to admit that one simply did not previously have the necessary Human Rights Education to choose an intelligent and intellectually honest position on the Human Rights for All Humans Debate (the Abortion Debate). No Pro-Choice Legal Abortion supporter (politician or voter or journalist or Big Tech Media outlet) ever chose that position *after* knowing the established facts of History, Science and Logic and Philosophy collected in the author's *Pro-Life Equals Pro-Democracy* and summarized in this *handbook Manifesto,* which means every Pro-Choice Abortion supporter holds a position based on *ignorance* and *lack of knowledge,* which lack of *Human Rights Education* will be corrected by this book. This powerful collection of facts demands a thoughtful and intellectually honest response. *The Intellectual Honesty Challenge* posits that there is no such intelligent response which allows for legal abortion to continue. Anyone currently "Pro-Choice" who disagrees is hereby *challenged* to mount an intelligent and intellectually honest response to this book's conclusions based on facts to see if they can intelligently and honestly "justify" remaining Pro-Choice in light of all the facts, or else concede to this book's conclusions and change their position, as intellectual honesty demands, if they cannot.

This means that:
any politician or political party or police or civil servant or judge or court (which control or enforce public policies and laws), and any billionaires, media moguls, journalists and "Big Tech" (which control news and information) –
any of these (or any regular voters) that claim today's democracies can somehow sustain Free Democracy and Human Rights long-term while remaining Pro-Choice(-to-Kill-Humans), in violation of The Foundational Principles of Human Rights and Democracy and the Core Principles of Lasting Democracy identified from Human Rights History, Science, Logic, and the History of Philosophy in this book (and already declared in essence in the United Nations' 1948 Universal Declaration of Human Rights) –
any of these are proven incompetent/unintelligent or dishonest/evil by the powerful collection of undisputed facts in this author's HUMAN RIGHTS EDUCATION FOR LASTING FREE DEMOCRACY book series including this handbook. If they disagree with this statement, they are hereby *challenged* to mount an intelligent and intellectually honest response to this book's conclusions based on facts to see if they can intelligently and honestly explain *just how* they think they know a better way to sustain Human Rights and democratic freedoms long-term than by implementing and maintaining *The Foundational Principles of Human Rights and Democracy* and the *Core Principles of Lasting Democracy* clarified in this book – or else concede to this book's conclusions and change their position from "Pro-Choice" to "Pro-Life," as intellectual honesty demands, if they cannot. For politicians (or judges or "Big Tech" billionaires and media moguls) to remain Pro-Choice and not take *The Intellectual Honesty Challenge* is to fail it; is tantamount to admitting that one has no intelligent nor intellectually honest justification for remaining Pro-Choice; and therefore, tantamount to admitting one is a danger to Human Rights and freedoms everywhere because of uneducated bigotry that does not recognize democracy-grounding *Equal Human Rights for All Humans.*

Note that major political parties being "officially" Pro-Choice and/or "purging" their parties of Pro-Lifers is a very recent trend, and a very totalitarian trend, following the totalitarian example of the politically Extremist Left Soviet (Marxist)

Communist Party and the politically Extremist Right German (Fascist) Nazi Party which were the first two political parties to legalize human-killing by abortion (the Nazi Party being first to also legalize human-killing by euthanasia). So, it should not be too hard for now-Pro-Choice politicians and political parties to abandon this fairly recent trend of being "officially" Pro-Choice and/or "purging" their parties of Pro-Lifers, *for the sake of lasting rights and freedom for every human.* **This book provides a brief window of opportunity for currently Pro-Choice politicians and parties (and the "Big Tech" billionaires and media moguls who control the news/information politicians set policy by) to "save face"** by simply admitting they previously did not have the necessary Human Rights Education to choose an intelligent and intellectually honest position on the Human Rights for All Humans Debate (the Abortion Debate). This book provides a brief window of opportunity for influential leaders of government, tech, media and industry to simply admit they previously did not have the necessary Human Rights Education (including not having the necessary familiarity with the most pertinent facts of History, Philosophy, Science, and Logic) which they needed in order to know that they should avoid Relativism/ Marxism/ Socialism (which first legalized human-killing by abortion – and then by genocide). They have a brief window of opportunity only to admit that they certainly should not support any current ideas about a "Great Reset" of the globe according to the Relativist, Marxist, Socialist thinking which is in fact behind many of History's greatest atrocities (and remember that Relativism is likewise behind all the Nazi Fascist atrocities on the other extreme of the political spectrum from Marxism/Socialism).

All who consider themselves "Pro-Choice" must realize that from now on, the numbers of Human-Rights-educated citizen voters (and clients of "Big Tech") will just grow and grow, and the longer it takes a currently Pro-Choice politician or political party (or "Big Tech" company or mainstream media channel) to abandon their Pro-Choice stance (and to abandon the Relativist/Marxist/Socialist ideologies which led Socialists to be the very first to legalize human-killing by abortion – and then by genocide) – the more incompetent/ unintelligent or dishonest/ evil (rather than simply uninformed) they will prove themselves to be – for all the voters (and clients) to see. Voters can hasten the restoration of *The Foundational Principles of Human Rights and Democracy*, which should be constitutionally enshrined in their country, by learning and sharing this HUMAN RIGHTS EDUCATION FOR LASTING FREE DEMOCRACY with other voters, so they no longer cast uneducated votes for uneducated politicians (and parties) who have *not a clue* what Democracy is built on nor how to maintain it. Voters should share this HUMAN RIGHTS EDUCATION FOR LASTING FREE DEMOCRACY with their elected representative and political leaders and high court judges, so they learn how to be good, Human-Rights-educated leaders of a LASTING democracy secure on Democracy's historic and logical (and "Pro-Life") *foundations. Pro-Life equals Pro-Democracy and Pro-Choice equals Pro-Totalitarianism.* So Pro-Lifers, to most quickly achieve their goal of ending legal human-killing by abortion, must become freedom-fighters. And freedom-fighters, to most quickly achieve their goal of ending unscientific and undemocratic lockdowns which support the Marxist-Socialist "Great Reset" piggybacking on the Coronavirus Pandemic, must become Pro-Lifers and champions of *Equal Human Rights for All Humans.*

"You can resolve to live your life with integrity. Let your credo be this: Let the lie come into the world, let it even triumph. But not through me."
— Aleksandr Solzhenitsyn

"I add this caveat for Pro-Choice politicians and voters: Stop the lie. Before you read this, you already knew that preborn humans are humans. You already knew that abortion kills humans. You already knew that killing humans is wrong. So all you have to do is stop lying."
– William Baptiste (Whose Ethnic Group Suffered World History's Biggest Genocide at the Hands of the World's First Socialist State, Which was the First State to Legalize Abortion)

"The simple step of a courageous individual is not to take part in the lie. One word of truth outweighs the world."
— Aleksandr Solzhenitsyn

"What good fortune for governments that the people do not think."
– Adolf Hitler
(Whose Genocidal Nazi Party Government was the First Government, Other Than the Genocidal Marxist Soviet Communist Party Government, to Legalize Abortion)

"Logic needs to be compulsory in high schools to ensure future voters and future politicians both know how to think clearly, logically and with intellectual honesty, so they can vote and govern intelligently and not be so easily fooled (even by textbook logical fallacies) into destroying the foundations of their own Freedom. When citizen voters and politicians know neither The Foundational Principles of Human Rights and Democracy, nor how to think

clearly, consistently, and logically (nor how to avoid logical fallacies of reasoning), Free Democracy is sure to fail and not last."
- William Baptiste,
Founder, Human Rights and Freedoms Forever!
Founder, The Intellectual Honesty Challenge
Proclaimer of THE THINKING REVOLUTION

THE INTELLECTUAL HONESTY CHALLENGE

"NO LEGACY IS SO RICH AS HONESTY "– William Shakespeare

To expand upon the above *Intellectual Honesty Challenge in Brief*: For certain, to maintain Free Democracy on its historical and logical foundations long-term, the societies of the "Free West" *must* have an intellectually honest, respectful, intelligent, scientific and rigorously logical dialogue, informed by the most pertinent facts of Human Rights History, Biological Science, and the Formal Science of Logic identified in this book, **in order to settle the central dispute of our time, *The Human Rights for All Humans Debate* (otherwise known as *The Abortion Debate*).** Because the Pro-Choice side of the debate has so far refused to have such a debate, keeping abortion legal by refusing to talk about it (and because Pro-Choice legislators in some jurisdictions now are with great intellectual dishonesty taking away Pro-Lifers' Free Speech in order to silence debate), this book finally, actually **starts** this necessary debate with a large "first salvo" of information culled from the disciplines of Science, Logic, History, and Philosophy, which the Pro-Choice side is challenged to respond to intelligently and honestly after reading this HUMAN RIGHTS EDUCATION FOR LASTING FREE DEMOCRACY book series' initial contribution to intelligent *dialogue*. Clearly identifying the key, crux question at the core of the Abortion Debate (the Human Rights for All Humans Debate), this author asks:

Do humans have Human Rights or not? Are Human Rights for *all* humans, or only for *some* humans, such that *some* humans can be legally killed in a democratic State (as humans are commonly killed in oppressive totalitarian States, such as Soviet Russia, the first modern State to legalize the killing of humans by abortion, or Nazi Germany, the first modern state to legalize the killing of humans by both abortion and euthanasia)?

The "Pro-Life" side of The Human Rights for All Humans Debate (The Abortion Debate) believes that Human Rights are for *all* humans without exception ("without distinction of any kind" in the words of the *Universal Declaration of Human Rights*); the "Pro-Choice" side of the Human Rights for All Humans Debate (the Abortion Debate) believes that *not all* humans have equal Human Rights, but that *some* humans can be legally killed by abortion (and/or euthanasia). The "Pro-Choice" side of the debate effectively believes this but they are never intellectually honest about it, and they only ever use what the Science of Logic calls "Fallacies of Distraction," and other textbook logical fallacies, to support legal abortion, in order to *avoid* ever even engaging the key question of the Human Rights of the young humans who (scientifically speaking) are indisputably killed in abortions, which is actually the very crux of the Abortion Debate. To keep abortion legal, the "Pro-Choice" side of the Human Rights for All Humans Debate, the Abortion Debate, have for decades refused to even talk about the crux question of the Abortion Debate but have only *distracted away from it* with great intellectual dishonesty, and usually without any educated knowledge at all of the most pertinent facts of Science, Logic, and Human Rights History laid out in this book.

Since the "Pro-Choice" side has so far refused to even have a proper, intellectually honest Abortion Debate to settle the *Equal Human Rights for All Humans* question at the center of the debate, the author has had to publish *Pro-Life Equals Pro-Democracy* and this book to finally, actually **START** the necessary Abortion Dialogue and Debate properly, by laying out clearly the key facts of History, Science, and Logic which, the author posits, overwhelmingly prove the first book's title, that Pro-Life Equals Pro-Democracy (and Pro-Choice Equals Pro-Totalitarianism).

So, *The Intellectual Honesty Challenge* (for dedicated Pro-Choice "hostile readers") is:

Can you write and send to the author at

HonestyChallenge@WilliamBaptisteHumanRightsAndFreedomsForever.com

an intellectually honest and intelligent defense of your Pro-Choice position that does not use the usual Pro-Choice logical fallacies exposed as such in this book, and does not ignore established facts of Human Rights History, Science, and Logic laid out in this book, as Pro-Choicers have done for decades in order to dishonestly keep abortion legal? Is it even possible to make an intellectually honest defense of the Pro-Choice position for Legal Abortion in the light of the most pertinent facts of Science, Logic, and Human Rights History?

This collection of facts is far too powerful to ignore. Thus, to remain Pro-Choice but not respond to *The Intellectual Honesty Challenge* is to fail it; and is to tacitly admit that you *have no intelligent nor honest justification* for remaining on the "Pro-Choice" side of the Human Rights for All Humans Debate (the Abortion Debate).

♦

"Abortion is not a 3rd option [to parenthood or adoption] because [unlike parenthood or adoption] it dismembers, decapitates, and disembowels a baby."
– Stephanie Gray

"Violence does not and cannot flourish by itself; it is inevitably intertwined with lying."
— *Aleksandr Solzhenitsyn*

"Let us not forget that violence does not live alone and is not capable of living alone: it is necessarily interwoven with falsehood. Between them lies the most intimate, the deepest of natural bonds. Violence finds its only refuge in falsehood, falsehood its only support in violence. Any man who has once acclaimed violence as his method must inexorably choose falsehood as his principle."
— *Aleksandr Solzhenitsyn*

"Violence does not necessarily take people by the throat and strangle them. Usually it demands no more than an ultimate allegiance from its subjects. They are required merely to become accomplices in its lies."
— *Aleksandr Solzhenitsyn*

The author respects an honest attempt to defend your Pro-Choice position against the mountain of evidence that Pro-Life = Pro-Democracy collected in this book, and will be very happy to continue respectful dialogue with you. Intending to be the world's informal "Professor of Human Rights," this author considers no opponent an enemy, but a precious human being who, it is hoped, will become convinced to treat all other humans as precious. **This is our Human Responsibility which comes with our own Human Rights: to recognize "*inherent*," "*equal*," "*inalienable*" Human Rights in all other humans, "without distinction of any kind," in the words of the *Universal Declaration of Human Rights.*** If you are intellectually honest enough to discover the attempt to refute this book forces you to change your position from "Pro-Choice" to "Pro-Life," as, the author posits, intellectual honesty demands, then please also email the results of your attempt to *The Intellectual Honesty Challenge* at the above email address.

For the particularly hostile reader who insists on being an enemy, remember that respectful, rational submissions are preferred as a sign of intellectual honesty (only those whose position is weak feel they need to use outrage and abuse or name-calling to "win" an argument); but, if you feel you cannot defend your position without resorting to feelings and insults (or ridiculous and unsustainable accusations of "hate speech" or irrational "phobias" in anyone who disagrees with you, as

"Intellectophobes" resort to because they cannot win honest and intelligent arguments), by all means go ahead and express yourself as you wish to *The Intellectual Honesty Challenge*. Your response will make clear to all how you fared in *The Intellectual Honesty Challenge*. **The author welcomes all three types of responses of Pro-Choice Legal Abortion supporters to the *Intellectual Honesty Challenge*:**

1. ***Intellectually Honest and Respectful Attempt* to refute the author's conclusions in this book or his other works, which invite more respectful dialogue** which the author will respond to respectfully, intelligently, and honestly (as necessary pointing out the respondents' continued errors in Logic or Science or merely pretending established facts do not exist in order to support their Pro-Choice position); the author will continue a back and forth dialogue as long as the respondent is up to it, since it is important to Lasting Democracy that such intelligent dialogue between the polarized sides happens in Western Society;

2. **Intellectually Honest Attempt to refute this book which ultimately lead to the Pro-Choice respondent conceding that Intellectual Honesty demands the major conclusions of this book (or *Pro-Life Equals Pro-Democracy* or the author's other works in the HUMAN RIGHTS EDUCATION FOR LASTING FREE DEMOCRACY book series) be accepted;**

3. **Intellectually Dishonest and/or Disrespectful Ravings and/or Groundless Intimidating Accusations in Logically Fallacious attempts to intimidate those who disagree with them into silence,** which show the Pro-Choice person making the accusations to be an **"Intellectophobe"** - afraid of intellectually honest, rational, respectful, intelligent, scientific and rigorously logical debate about their Pro-Choice position which they would *lose* on the basis of established facts of History, Science, and Logic.

Samples of all three types of responses to *The Intellectual Honesty Challenge* (and any further back-and-forth responses) will eventually be put into a new book on the state of the Dialogue that needs to happen in Western Society over the central controversy of our time, the Human Rights for All Humans Debate (otherwise known as the Abortion Debate). That this debate actually be carried out intelligently is vitally necessary because no society can remain stable and safe and free when there is such polarised disagreement over something as basic to free society as whether humans have Human Rights (in which case abortion, which kills humans, is wrong) or whether Human Rights are for all humans not just some humans (in which case abortion, which kills humans, is wrong).

"There can be no acceptable future without an honest analysis of the past."
— *Aleksandr Solzhenitsyn*

Abraham Lincoln faced precisely the same kind of societal division over precisely the same question of *Equal Human Rights for All Humans*. Democracy-grounding *Equal Human Rights for All Humans* were then compromised by the legal slavery of

Black humans precisely as *Equal Human Rights for All Humans* are now compromised by the legal killing of preborn humans (just like each of us at that age, meaning to deny preborn humans an *Inherent Human Right to Live* is to deny ourselves any *Inherent Human Right to Live*). In his own day noting this great bifurcation and division among the American people on such a fundamental issue to democracy as whether or not all humans have *Equal Human Rights*, Lincoln famously said:

"A house divided against itself cannot stand. I believe this government cannot endure permanently half-slave and half-free.
[today he might say the American government cannot endure permanently half-Pro-Choice and half- Pro-Life. That is, the American government cannot endure permanently half-Pro-Choice-to-Kill-Humans and half-Pro-Human-Right-to-Live]
I do not expect the Union to be dissolved - I do not expect the house to fall - but I do expect it will cease to be divided. It will become all one thing or all the other."

Lincoln's words in a directly parallel situation to today's situation mean that Free Democracy (based on Traditional Western beliefs about *equal human preciousness)* is so fundamentally incompatible with either legal slavery of humans or legal killing of humans by abortion that neither can last long-term in a healthy democracy.

Part of the *Intellectual Honesty Challenge* is this: Pro-Choice politicians and parties (and voters) *not* responding to the *Intellectual Honesty Challenge* after exposure to the book *Pro-Life Equals Pro-Democracy* (or any of the author's other works which prove from Human Rights History, Science and Logic that *Pro-Life = Pro-Democracy and Pro-Choice = Pro-Totalitarianism*), but continuing to be ardently Pro-Choice, is tantamount to you as a Pro-Choicer *admitting* that you are intellectually dishonest (or unintelligent), if not actually evil, for insisting on maintaining the legal abortion-killing of humans after being exposed to the most pertinent facts of biological Science, sound Logic, and the entirely totalitarian and anti-democratic history of the practice of legal abortion throughout History.

This truly non-partisan Human Rights scholar also notes that continuing to *refuse to oppose* legal human-killing abortion after exposure to this HUMAN RIGHTS EDUCATION FOR LASTING FREE DEMOCRACY will also mark as *spineless unprincipled cowards* those politicians and political parties which are not officially Pro-Choice but who have thus far *allowed legal human-killing abortion following totalitarian Soviet and Nazi precedent to exist unchallenged; and allowed the recent Pro-Choice anti-democratic laws against Freedom of Speech, Expression, Assembly, Conscience and Religion of Pro-Life Human Rights advocates and others to exist unchallenged.* (And far-too-often allowed the unscientific Coronavirus alarmism in support of a Marxist "Great Reset" to continue unchallenged). It is unconscionable that this author can *still* be arrested and imprisoned in his national capital (and the entire region of 14 million inhabitants around it) for saying "killing humans is wrong because Human Rights are for all humans" under Pro-Choice totalitarian laws still in force even though the officially Pro-Choice (therefore politically extremist, legal human-killing) political party that passed the totalitarian law was in the last election reduced to a mere 7 seats in the regional legislature ("the minivan party").

Apparently due to insufficiently educated *ignorance* of Free Democracy's Pro-Life foundations revealed in this book series, even the world's political parties which are not Pro-Choice (and include Pro-Lifers) have thus far been *afraid* to roll back Pro-Choice totalitarian laws which have no place in any *healthy* democracy. *Pro-Life equals Pro-Democracy and Pro-Choice equals Pro-Totalitarianism.* So Pro-Lifers, to most quickly achieve their goal of ending legal human-killing by abortion, must become freedom-fighters. And freedom-fighters, to most quickly achieve their goal of ending unscientific and undemocratic lockdowns which support the Marxist-Socialist " Great Reset" piggybacking on the Coronavirus Pandemic, must become Pro-Lifers and champions of *Equal Human Rights for All Humans.*

ABOUT THE AUTHOR OF THIS HUMAN RIGHTS EDUCATION FOR LASTING FREE DEMOCRACY

(The Man and the Message)

"William Baptiste's work is crucial."
- Dr. Andrew Bennett,
Senior Fellow, Religious Freedom Institute (Washington, DC);
Director, Cardus Religious Freedom Institute (Ottawa);
Canada's first Ambassador of Religious Freedom,
appointed by Prime Minister Stephen Harper

The Voice Speaking with Intellectual Honesty and Clarity to Our Unstable Times (Where Free Democracy Itself is Threatened) How to Build Human Rights and Democratic Freedoms to Last for Centuries on Their Firm Traditional, Historical, Logical and Philosophical Foundations

William Baptiste: Life-Long Learner; Scholar; Logician; Political
Philosopher; Ecumenist; Theologian;
Author of DEMOCRACY 101; Pro-Life Equals Pro-Democracy; KNIGHTS OF
HUMAN RIGHTS, LADIES OF LASTING DEMOCRACY
Founder of Human Rights and Freedoms Forever! and The Intellectual
Honesty Challenge;
Non-Partisan Thinker Calling All the World's Political Parties of Left and
Right to Together Constitutionally Enshrine *Equal Human Preciousness* and
Equal Human Rights for All Humans and Thus Explicitly Restore *The
Foundational Principles of Human Rights and Democracy* If They Have Strayed
from Free Democracy's Implicit Foundations; Proclaimer of THE THINKING
REVOLUTION;

(and Like Everyone Else in One Degree or another, William Baptiste is a
Broken and Flawed Human Being Nevertheless Still Called (by Divine Love) to
Make the Universe a Better and More Loving Place Because He is in It)

Like All Humans, Called to The *Universal Human Responsibility* to
Recognize *Equal Human Rights* in All Other Humans, which is the Foundation
of Free Human Societies and the Antidote to All Bigotry and Totalitarian
Genocide,
Such as That Bigotry Behind the Legal Genocide Which Murdered Millions
of Humans of William's Ethnicity, and the Legal Human-Killing Bigotry Started
by *the Very Same Genocidal Murderers* - Legal Abortion -
which Still Continues to Kill Millions of Humans Today *Under Unwittingly
Totalitarian-Oriented and Bigoted Pro-Choice(-to-Kill-Humans) Governments*
which, Clueless that They Are Following Oppressive Totalitarian Precedent,
Just Like the Genocidal Murderers Who First Legalized Abortion are Now
Passing More and More Totalitarian Laws Against Free Speech in order to
Keep Their Legal Human-Killing Legal, Against the Mountain of Evidence from
Science, Logic, Human Rights History, and the History of Philosophy (Collected
in William's Books) that *Pro-Life = Pro-Democracy and Pro-Choice = Pro-
Totalitarianism.*

William Baptiste as a Human Rights Scholar Can Be Arrested and Jailed in
His Country for Peaceful Human Rights Advocacy and for Speaking Scientific
and Historical Facts Supportive of Democracy-Grounding *Equal Human Rights
for All Humans*. Legal Abortion, Which Follows Totalitarian Legal Human-
Killing Precedent in the First Place, Logically Requires Such Totalitarian Laws
Against Free Speech, and the Ultimate End of Free Democracy, in Order to
Keep Such an Inherently Anti-Human and Totalitarian Practice as Abortion
Legal Long-term.

ABOUT THE AUTHOR

William Baptiste from a highly educated sense of *Living History* speaks boldly and intelligently and articulately for the voiceless and silenced victims of bigotry and its most extreme form, genocide:
William speaks for the millions of silenced victims murdered in the bigoted *Holodomor* Genocide of humans of his own Ukrainian ethnic group; he speaks for the millions of silenced victims murdered in the bigoted *Holocaust* Genocide of humans of the Jewish ethnic group (plus disabled humans), Ukrainian and Jewish humans sharing a scholarly "Ukrainian-Jewish Encounter" as victims of history's two biggest bigoted genocides which occurred about the same time;
and he speaks for the millions of voiceless humans murdered in the Abortion Genocide of preborn humans just like every one of us at their age, which was started precisely by the *very same perpetrators of the world's two biggest genocides against the Ukrainians and Jews*, the (Marxist) Union of Soviet Socialist Republics (USSR) and Germany Under Adolf Hitler's (Fascist) National Socialist German Worker's Party (Nazi Party for short), the Soviet Marxists and Nazi Fascists being the first (extremist, totalitarian) political parties to legalize human-killing by abortion *precisely because these evil totalitarian regimes did not accept Democracy-grounding Equal Human Rights for All Humans nor the Inherent Human Right to Live.*
William Baptiste with fierce intelligence champions the Democratic Free Speech of *Pro-Life Human Rights Advocates* and *Real Doctors who do not kill humans*, Free Speech on behalf of Democracy-grounding *Equal Human Rights for All Humans*, against all the increasingly common totalitarian *Free Speech-ending* and *Democracy-ending* Pro-Choice laws and policies passed by ignorant Pro-CHOICE bigoted politicians worldwide who (like all bigots) CHOOSE just *which* humans they think have equal worth and rights and just *which* humans they think have no Human Rights and can be legally killed – just like the Soviet and Nazi bigots who were the first to legalize human-killing by abortion (and by euthanasia; and by genocide – all because they were evil and did not believe *killing humans is wrong*).

Before his Ph.D. studies at the Sheptytsky Institute and being a professor at Dominican University College (where he replaced Dr. Andrew Bennett, appointed Canada's *Ambassador of Religious Freedom*), William Baptiste got his Master's Degree with Honors at Franciscan University of Steubenville (FUS), where the Philosophy Chair testified in writing to the University President and others of

---

"his tremendous academic talent" and "considerable power of mind;"
noting
"It is very difficult to conquer certain ideas, especially in a discipline that is not one's own, and yet he did that in a seemingly easy and effortless way. He was able to master the ideas and "clothe" them in his own words with nothing lost in the translation. It is an extremely rare kind of student who can make a difficult discipline one's own in the space of a semester."

William Baptiste has since used this genius intelligence and a lifetime of reading (and haunting academic libraries, sometimes sleeping in them to the chagrin of university officials) to thoughtfully discern and lay out clearly from the tangled webs of historical details the "golden threads" woven throughout history that give us all our Human Rights and democratic freedoms. It helped that he was professor of a university course covering the period during which what he has identified as *The Foundational Principles of Human Rights and Democracy* were laid; and covering many of the thinkers who laid them throughout the West.

At FUS, the famous Dr. Scott Hahn wrote William's work was

"outstanding," "excellent," "clear, thoughtful and thorough"

and the Theology Chair Dr. Alan Schreck endorsed William's educational Donum Veritatis - The Gift of Truth Ministries

"as an effective and important means to spread the faith and to promote Christian unity... It really is a 'gift' to the 'Internet Generation.'"

William was invited three times to the ecumenical Springtime of Faith Rome Summits (Catholic and Evangelical Christian leaders meeting with Vatican Officials) for being considered **"one of the dynamic leaders building the New Springtime of Faith."** William was the first Eastern Rite Christian to attend the Summits, as a member of the 20th Century's largest underground Church, which officially did not exist in the totalitarian Marxist Union of Soviet Socialist Republics (USSR) which committed the *Holodomor* Genocide against his ethnic group.

The Director of the Metropolitan Andrey Sheptytsky Institute of Eastern Christian Studies (MASI), the Very Reverend Stephen Wojcichowsky, confirmed that

"Mr. Baptiste is an exceptionally talented [doctoral] student"
and that
"the professors and staff of the Sheptytsky Institute are pleased that William has chosen to pursue this important [ecumenical doctoral] work at our Institute, which shares his ecumenical spirit and prays with him that Christ's disciples may indeed 'be one ... so that the world may believe'" (John 17:21),
adding that
"He has an indomitable determination to use his many gifts to serve God by working towards the reunification of the Church and bringing the Good News of salvation to the world ... William has infectious confidence in the love and power of the Holy Trinity and he manages to exude the joy of the Holy Spirit even when facing challenging difficulties."

Having taught a course in the Formal Science of Logic, as a logician William Baptiste reminds all those who would read his above Christian qualifications and be tempted to simply dismiss his books ***merely on that basis*** (instead of engaging with their powerful facts and logic with intellectual honesty), that to do so is to commit what the Science of Logic calls "the genetic fallacy" combined with "circular reasoning," known as "Bulverism." He writes,

"Intellectually dishonest, bigoted anti-Christian and Pro-Choice "Bulverism" first assumes that Christians and Pro-Lifers are wrong and then "justifies" turning off the brain and not listening to facts and logic presented by Christians and Pro-Lifers merely on the basis of the "wrongness" assumed but not proved (circular reasoning). Intellectually lazy Bulverists say things like "you only believe that because you're a Christian/Pro-Lifer," as if the origin or "genetics" of their opponents' belief justify simply dismissing their position (the genetic fallacy), without any regard to the overwhelming facts of Science, Logic, and Human Rights History (and the History of Philosophy) which support the conclusions that Pro-Life = Pro-Democracy and that Christianity, if it need not be individually embraced, must at least be respected by governments as the origin and source of the underlying Foundational Principles of Human Rights and Democracy, in any country that wants to remain a free democracy and not eventually fall to current 'Creeping Totalitarianism' now undermining Democracy from its very foundations."

William declares:

"No intellectually honest person can deny Western Human Rights and freedoms start with The Foundational Principles of Human Rights and Democracy identified herein (like equal human preciousness and the Inherent Human Right to Live), which Christianity introduced into the West, and only the intellectually dishonest would dismiss these books lightly and without engaging with their undisputed scientific and historical facts and sound logic. But LASTING Democracy, religious freedom, and Human Rights for all requires that in response to current 'Creeping Totalitarianism' these books start a DIALOGUE in Western nations about just how to ensure these highest of Western values last for the long-term."

[2021 Update:] William's initial professionally published contribution to this dialogue, to finally start it properly (and possibly to end it quickly), is *Pro-Life Equals Pro-Democracy*, published by Westbow Press in 2021, as a kind of "sequel" to Aleksandr Solzhenitsyn's *The Gulag Archipelago*. A new book to help finish Solzhenitsyn's brilliant work of exposing and helping end the philosophical errors (and naturally resulting political atrocities) of Marxism (atrocities like the first legal human-killing by abortion and by genocide) – in recognition of the first ten million victims of Marxist ideology in practice, from William's Ukrainian ethnic heritage, in the Marxist Soviet *Holodomor* Genocide (Preceded by the first human victims of legal abortion in the same genocidal Socialist Soviet Union. Followed by many more tens of millions of victims of Marxist ideology killed in the Cold War Marxist Soviet Bloc and in Marxist China, Cambodia, Vietnam, North Korea and so on). Because (as shown in William's books) Marxism is deeply rooted in philosophical *Skepticism* and *Relativism* (instead of the philosophical *Realism* which grounds Science, Logic, Technology, Human Rights and Free Democracy), those influenced by Relativist and Marxist thinking (including Pro-Choicers who follow the Marxist precedent of legal abortion) are prone to not take objective facts seriously nor honestly, but they wriggle out of admitting facts which do not fit their ideology as much as they can (Pro-Choicers typically avoid admitting obvious objective scientific facts like *preborn humans are humans* so *abortion kills humans*), and they build their politics on *ideology* instead of *education*. William explains,

---

Solzhenitsyn wrote,

"To do evil a human being must first of all believe that what he's doing is good..." and wrote "Ideology – that is what gives evildoing its long-sought justification and gives the evildoer the necessary steadfastness and determination. That is the social theory which helps to make his acts seem good instead of bad in his own and others' eyes... Thanks to ideology the twentieth century was fated to experience evildoing calculated on a scale in the millions."

This is why Marxists (and today's Pro-Choice Neo-Marxist Identity Politics " ideologues, with their "Political Correctness" and "Cancel Culture") have never learned from all the tens of millions of human deaths resulting from every single attempt to implement at the State level the seductively beautiful-sounding but unrealistic "Marxist egalitarian utopia where no-one owns anything and everyone is happy." Because what Solzhenitsyn called their "impaired thinking ability" coming from Relativist Marxism means they never learn that Relativistic Marxism just does not work in the Real world. They just keep trying to hammer (and sickle) the "Red Square peg" of Marxism into the "round hole" of Reality, no matter how many tens of millions of humans are killed in the repeated attempts. One quarter of Cambodia's population died under Marxist policies, but such facts make little difference to Relativists like Marxists (and Pro-Choicers) who doubt or deny objective facts and insist that everything is subjective and therefore relative. This subjectivist lack of grip on objective Reality is why Marxists (and today's Pro-Choice Neo-Marxists practicing "Political Correctness," "Identity Politics," and "Cancel Culture") are fundamentally dishonest and end up setting up political policies and systems built on a web of lies, just like the one Solzhenitsyn exposed in the world's first Marxist Socialist State, the totalitarian Soviet Union which was the first State to legalize human-killing by abortion. Relativist Pro-Choicers following their example today cannot even use language honestly and scientifically, calling what scientifically-speaking are undisputedly unique fetal-age human lives mere "uterine contents" (Planned Parenthood's term) or "tissue blobs." Pro-Choicers accuse Pro-Life Human Rights Advocate politicians of being "against a woman's right to choose" because they cannot even speak honestly and scientifically about the fact they as Pro-Choicers believe in the right to CHOOSE to KILL what scientifically-speaking are unique living individual biological human organisms (just like each of us at their age) with absolutely unique human DNA utterly distinct from their parents at every age and stage of their human life-cycles (zygote to senior adult). Science and facts ultimately mean little to those influenced by Relativist and Marxist thinking, which is so dishonest (thanks to its "ideology over education") that the Soviet Marxist Holodomor Genocide killing 7-10 million humans of my ethnic group in 1932-33 was at the time covered up not only in the Socialist Soviet Union but also by Western (philosophically Relativist not Realist) Marxist/Socialist-influenced mainstream media, which actually gave the Pulitzer Prize to the dishonest New York Times journalist who denied the genocide, and discredited and fired the honest whistle-blower journalists who tried to expose the killing while it was happening.

So, we in the West must now realize just how long Western mainstream media has been Marxist-influenced (and Relativist-influenced). Solzhenitsyn, living in the U.S. for 18 years after he was exiled from Marxist Soviet Russia for exposing its evils in The Gulag Archipelago (published 1973), as a Nobel Prize-winning author, historian and the world's foremost authority on Soviet Marxism, confirmed that the same insidious (philosophically Relativist not Realist and therefore anti-scientific) Marxist ideology which he said "cannibalized" his beloved Russia had also infected Western education and mainstream media as well, through "an enormous number of Western intellectuals who felt a kinship and refused to see [Marxist] communism's crimes. When they no longer could do so, they tried to justify them." Solzhenitsyn repeatedly warned the West this Relativist, Marxist influence in education and media was taking the West towards the same totalitarian ends as the Soviet Union, just more slowly and by a different route. Solzhenitsyn lamented,

"In actual fact our Russian experience ... is vitally important for the West, because by some chance of history we have trodden the same path seventy or eighty years before the West. And now it is with a strange sensation that we look at what is happening to you; many social phenomena that happened in Russia before its collapse are being repeated. Our experience of life is of vital importance to the West, but I am not convinced that you are capable of assimilating it without having gone through it to the end yourselves ..."

Seeing Solzhenitsyn's prediction starting to more dramatically come true at the end of 2020, in 2021 William Baptiste quickly followed up Westbow Press's publication of *Pro-Life Equals Pro-Democracy* with the self-published and unedited "Emergency First Edition/ Advance Reader Copy" of his new book

KNIGHTS OF HUMAN RIGHTS, LADIES OF LASTING DEMOCRACY
Handbook Manifesto of the Educated *Global Solidarity Movement* Against
Uneducated Global 'Creeping Totalitarianism' Now *Accelerating*

as a handbook to quickly educate and equip freedom lovers everywhere to effectively stand up *together* in *Global Solidarity* for democracy-grounding (and philosophically *Realist* not *Relativist*) Traditional Western Pro-Life Family Values in public policy. So they can learn to be like the good Poles who stood together in *Solidarity* against the oppressive totalitarian Relativist Marxist ideology which had enslaved Poland, thus undermining hardline Soviet Marxist Communism in the Soviet Bloc and helping to bloodlessly end the totalitarian Soviet Union (and with it end the

Cold War). Instead of being like the good Germans who *lost their democracy to totalitarianism* because they allowed themselves to be intimidated into *silence* and *separation* by their totalitarian-oriented National Socialist (in German, *Nazi* for short) ruling political party which (like too many Western political parties today) did not believe in *Equal Human Rights for All Humans* (hence the genocidal totalitarian, politically extremist-Right Nazi Party was the next political party after the genocidal totalitarian, politically extremist-Left Soviet Marxist Communist Party to legalize human-killing by abortion and by genocide).

Expecting his own first grandchild by end Summer 2021, to save Human Rights and democratic freedoms for everyone's children and grandchildren against all current and future threats to Free Democracy, William Baptiste has clearly articulated Democracy's implicit foundations embedded in Traditional Western Values, making them into explicit *Foundational Principles of Human Rights and Democracy*, plus 10 *Core Principles of Lasting Democracy*, which can be constitutionally enshrined in Western nations to give Human Rights and freedoms a secure foundation for centuries. At this critical 'tipping point' between totalitarianism and democracy in 2021, William declared THE THINKING REVOLUTION for the first time in print in *Pro-Life Equals Pro-Democracy* and in the shorter follow-up book *Knights of Human Rights, Ladies of Lasting Democracy* launches a *Global Solidarity Movement* for these key Traditional Western Values which Democracy was built on to be the continued guide of public policy, a movement which can rally under the Flag of Democracy William designed for the purpose, which states the necessary starting point right on the flag:

Foundational Principle of Democracy #1: Every human life, without exception, is SUPREMELY and EQUALLY precious.

Foundational Principle of Democracy #2: Every human life must be free from government coercion in matters of belief, so they may freely seek and find this beautiful truth foundational to democracy.

Human Rights and Freedoms Forever!

With his health finally on the upswing in 2021, after years of thoughtfully writing the book manuscripts while dealing with serious injury and serious injury complications like severe infection requiring extensive further surgery, plus internal bleeding, anemia and debilitating headaches which took excessive time to diagnose and treat because of hospital lockdowns during the Coronavirus Pandemic, William Baptiste in 2021 is now launching the (still unedited) first books of the HUMAN RIGHTS EDUCATION FOR LASTING FREE DEMOCRACY book series, and finally launching in earnest the educational Non-Profit Organization (NPO) *Human Rights and Freedoms Forever!* he founded to further develop, polish and spread the HUMAN RIGHTS EDUCATION FOR LASTING FREE DEMOCRACY the world now so desperately needs to retain its freedom, which NPO he has been preparing to launch in earnest while convalescing and writing the book manuscripts. Those who want to help support and spread this HUMAN RIGHTS EDUCATION FOR LASTING FREE DEMOCRACY (poetically-speaking, becoming "Knights of Human Rights, Ladies of Lasting Democracy"), can contact *Human Rights and Freedoms Forever!* to order the books, flags and promotional materials, donate, volunteer (become local "Volunteer Democracy Leaders" in your area!), or book William Baptiste as a speaker for your human-life-and-freedom-loving event!

WilliamBaptisteHumanRightsAndFreedomsForever.com

WilliamBaptiste.com

HUMAN RIGHTS EDUCATION for LASTING FREE DEMOCRACY

More Contact Information in Next Section

YOU CAN HELP FREE DEMOCRACY LAST FOREVER! CONTACT, DONATION AND VOLUNTEER SUPPORT INFORMATION

to Assist Human Rights and Freedoms Forever! with the Further Development and Distribution of William Baptiste's HUMAN RIGHTS EDUCATION FOR LASTING FREE DEMOCRACY Book Series (DEMOCRACY 101; PRO-LIFE EQUALS PRO-DEMOCRACY; KILLING HUMANS IS WRONG; NO FRUIT WITHOUT ROOTS; EQUAL HUMAN RIGHTS FOR ALL HUMANS; THINKING REVOLUTION: THE INTELLECTUAL HONESTY CHALLENGE; KNIGHTS OF HUMAN RIGHTS, LADIES OF LASTING DEMOCRACY and Other Print/Audio/Video Works in Support of LASTING Human Rights, Religious Freedom, and Democracy Itself Worldwide . . .

William Baptiste's New Non-Profit Educational Organization *Human Rights and Freedoms Forever!* needs your assistance in further developing and distributing William Baptiste's books and other educational resources; in having them translated, and in making educational audio and video resources based on this content. Plus promotional materials to equip "Knights of Human Rights and Ladies of Lasting Democracy" for the great task of making sure Human Rights, Religious Freedom, and Free Democracy itself survives the current attacks of 'Creeping Totalitarianism' and then thrives for centuries, secure on Democracy's historical and logical foundations in Traditional Western Values.

YOU can participate in this Democracy-preserving task by becoming a Volunteer Democracy Leader in your city or by becoming a Patron of *Human Rights and Freedoms Forever!* by donating at

WilliamBaptisteHumanRightsAndFreedomsForever.com

To become a "Volunteer Democracy Leader" in your city, e-mail
VOLUNTEER@WilliamBaptisteHumanRightsAndFreedomsForever.com

For more donation options than those on the website, e-mail
DONATE@WilliamBaptisteHumanRightsAndFreedomsForever.com

To book William Baptiste as a speaker, e-mail
BOOKINGS@WilliamBaptisteHumanRightsAndFreedomsForever.com

To Pre-Order or to express interest in buying (or making!) Flags of Democracy, posters, bumper stickers, T-shirts or other materials to promote a HUMAN RIGHTS EDUCATION FOR LASTING FREE DEMOCRACY, e-mail
DemocracyStore@WilliamBaptisteHumanRightsAndFreedomsForever.com

Hostile readers who disagree with this book's conclusions can take THE INTELLECTUAL HONESTY CHALLENGE in this book to see if they can make an intelligent case for remaining Pro-Choice – and concede that *Pro-Life = Pro-Democracy* if they cannot: e-mail

HonestyChallenge@WilliamBaptisteHumanRightsAndFreedomsForever.com

For more information, e-mail
INFO@WilliamBaptisteHumanRightsAndFreedomsForever.com
Telephone: 1 (613) 761-0147
P.O. Box 2302, Hope, BC, V0X 1L0, Canada

WilliamBaptisteHumanRightsAndFreedomsForever.com

WilliamBaptiste.com

HUMAN RIGHTS EDUCATION for LASTING FREE DEMOCRACY

Made in the USA
Middletown, DE
15 May 2021